Advancement in Medical and Wellness Tourism, Part A

ENTREPRENEURSHIP AND TECHNOLOGY IN TOURISM AND HOSPITALITY

Series Editor: Anukrati Sharma
Professor, Dept. of Tourism & Hospitality, University of Kota, India; Director, Skill Development Centre, University of Kota, India

The *Entrepreneurship and Technology in Tourism and Hospitality* (ETTH) series explores the dynamic intersection of entrepreneurship and technological advancements within the highly competitive tourism and hospitality sectors. This innovative series delves into a variety of pressing topics, highlighting how the relentless evolution of technology and artificial intelligence shapes entrepreneurial opportunities and drives the creation of new business ventures. Each volume in the series aims to provide valuable insights into the challenges and trends impacting these industries, making it a vital resource for understanding the future of tourism and hospitality.

Catering to a diverse audience, the ETTH series will be of interest to scholars and practitioners from various fields, including Management, Commerce, Tourism, Hospitality, Marketing, and Computer Science. Through a combination of theoretical knowledge, practical applications, and case studies, the series equips readers with essential skills for effective business planning, while fostering a deeper understanding of the technological innovations transforming tourism.

Advancement in Medical and Wellness Tourism, Part A: Entrepreneurship and Technology

EDITED BY

ANUKRATI SHARMA

University of Kota, India

and

SHRUTI ARORA

Modi Institute of Management & Technology, India

emerald
PUBLISHING

United Kingdom – North America – Japan – India – Malaysia – China

Emerald Publishing Limited
Emerald Publishing, Floor 5, Northspring, 21-23 Wellington Street, Leeds LS1 4DL.

First edition 2026

British Library Cataloguing in Publication Data
A catalogue record for this book is available from the British Library

ISBN: 978-1-80592-984-0 (Print)
ISBN: 978-1-80592-983-3 (Online)
ISBN: 978-1-80592-985-7 (Epub)

Printed and bound by CPI Group (UK) Ltd, Croydon, CR0 4YY

Dedicated to every doctor who goes beyond duty, bringing anticipation to hearts and curing to those who travel in search of care.

Contents

About the Editors

Anukrati Sharma is a Professor and Head in the Department of Tourism and Hospitality at the University of Kota, Rajasthan, India. She also serves as the Director of the Skill Development Centre, Director of the Office of International Affairs, and Chairperson of the Women Cell at the University. In addition, she is the Dean (Honorary) of Tourism and Hospitality at Vishwakarma Skills University, Jaipur, and a member of the Board of Management at the University of Kota. Holding a PhD in Tourism Marketing from the University of Rajasthan, she is currently pursuing her DLitt on Sustainable Tourism Development. Her areas of expertise include tourism marketing, skill development, event and sports tourism, and international business. She has authored and edited more than 30 books with leading publishers, such as Emerald, Springer, Routledge, Apple Academic Press, IGI Global, and CABI. A recipient of the UGC Research Award, she is also the Book Series Editor for Emerald, CABI, Apple Academic Press, and Anthem Press. She has presented papers and delivered keynote addresses in several countries, including Sri Lanka, Indonesia, Uzbekistan, Malaysia, and Turkey, contributing extensively to global tourism research and sustainable development.

Shruti Arora is an Associate Professor at the Modi Institute of Management & Technology, Kota, Rajasthan, and an Internal and Co-opted Member of the Committee of Curriculum (COC) in Travel and Tourism Management at the University of Kota. With over 17 years of teaching and research experience, she specializes in marketing management, consumer behavior, tourism, and event management. She earned her PhD from the University of Kota, focusing on the growth and development of the event management sector in Rajasthan. She has authored and co-edited several Scopus-indexed books with reputed publishers such as Emerald, Apple Academic Press, Bentham, and CABI. Her ongoing projects include an edited book with Springer and Routledge. Her research contributions include numerous national and international journal publications and presentations at global conferences in Sri Lanka, Turkey, and the UK. She received the Best Women Researcher Award (2024) from Inspira Research Association and serves as Associate Editor for the *International Journal of Academic Excellence & Research*. Her academic endeavors reflect her passion for advancing sustainable tourism, innovative marketing, and skill-based education, fostering academic excellence and industry relevance among students and professionals alike.

About the Contributors

Ansar Abbas serves as the Associate Professor (Management) and Associate Dean, Faculty of Management Sciences, and Faculty of Social Sciences and Humanities, Hamdard University, Pakistan. With extensive teaching and research experience in business, management, leadership, and organizational behavior, his expertise spans various areas. His research interests include transformational leadership, ethically responsible leadership, climate change, and spirituality, focusing on the intersection between sustainable practices and positive psychology. In addition, he has made a significant contribution to the academic community by reviewing nearly 1,000 scientific papers for reputable journals. In addition, he has published numerous research papers and book chapters, further advancing the field.

Mansoor Ali is Assistant Professor in the Department of English at Kohat University of Science & Technology (KUST), Kohat, Khyber Pakhtunkhwa, Pakistan. He holds a PhD in English, and his research spans motivational factors in English language learning, sociolinguistic issues, and teaching–learning practices in English as a Foreign Language (EFL)/English as a Second Language (ESL) contexts. His studies include investigations of female learners' motivational orientations at KUST, speaking anxiety among Pakistani students, and textbook task analysis from a communicative language teaching perspective.

Amer Hani Al-Kassem is a distinguished Jordanian Scholar specializing in human resources management (HRM). He earned his PhD in Business Administration from Rajasthan University, India, in 2001, after completing his master's degree (1998) and BA in Economics and Political Science in India. He currently serves as Associate Professor at Al-Dhaid University College, Sharjah, UAE. He previously served as Dean of the HRM School at City University College of Ajman (2015–2019) and led the Tourism and Hospitality Department at Prince Sultan College, Saudi Arabia, for 14 years. His career reflects over two decades of excellence in teaching, research, and academic leadership.

Daniel Ameanyeawu is an Adjunct Lecturer at the Accra Institute of Technology, where he teaches human resource (HR)-related courses for the past 4+ years. With an ACIB qualification from the Chartered Institute of Bankers, Ghana, he brings a unique blend of banking and HR expertise to his teaching. He is passionate about harnessing the power of HR to drive economic development and sustainability in Ghana. He believes in leveraging HR strategies to enhance organizational performance, promote inclusive growth, and contribute to national development goals. Through his teaching and interests, he aims to shape the next generation of HR professionals in Ghana.

Tiurida Lily Anita, PhD, is an Associate Professor at Bina Nusantara University with over 20 years of experience in service management and hospitality. She is a Nationally Certified Lecturer (SERDOS), BKD (Faculty Workload) Assessor for the Ministry of Higher Education, Nationally Certified Trainer, Internal Auditor at Bina Nusantara University, and Professional Assessor for Indonesia's Hospitality Certification Body. She holds a doctoral degree in Service Management and a Master's in Hospitality Management from Trisakti University, as well as a diploma in Hotel Administration from STP Bandung. Her work focuses on education, research, and professional development in tourism and hospitality.

Muhammad Jamil Anjum, PhD (Management Sciences), Universiti Teknologi Malaysia, is a Management Scholar whose research focuses on information systems adoption, Enterprise Resource Planning (ERP) implementation, working-capital and corporate finance, entrepreneurial intention, and supply-chain/ management practices. He has authored empirical studies on ERP success and user satisfaction, working-capital management and firm profitability, factors influencing entrepreneurial intention among graduate students, and dividend-policy/stock volatility in Pakistani firms. His work appears in national and international journals and conference proceedings, contributing applied evidence from Pakistan and Malaysia to managerial practice and policy discussions.

Aishwarya Arya, pursuing PhD in Management, accomplished her bachelor's and master's from the Institute of Hotel Management and Catering Technology, Lucknow, in Hospitality Administration thereafter another Master's in Travel and Tourism Management. She started her academic career in the year 2019 from IHM Lucknow, previously worked with Babu Banarsi Das University, Lucknow, as an Assistant Professor. She presented and attended many national and international conferences, seminars, and webinars. Her area of specialization includes room division, hospitality management & sales, and marketing. She has patents published under the Office of the Controller General of Patents, Designs and Trademarks, Department of Industrial Policy and Promotions, Ministry of Commerce and Industry, Government of India. ORCID: https://orcid.org/0009-0000-4236-3983.

Moushumi Banerjee, PhD, has 21 years of experience in teaching and the hospitality industry. She has actively guided students in industrial training and placements at national and international hotel chains. She has contributed to curriculum development and has industry experience as an Executive Housekeeper. She has actively participated in faculty development programs, conferences, and workshops, and has published research papers in peer-reviewed and *Scopus* journals and books. ORCID: https://orcid.org/0000-0002-3767-2949.

Sarita Bhardwaj, a dedicated visual artist and emerging academic, is currently pursuing her PhD in Fine Arts at Lovely Professional University, Punjab. She completed her master's degree in Fine Arts from Apeejay College of Fine Arts, Jalandhar, securing 4th position under Guru Nanak Dev University, Amritsar, in 2021, and earned her undergraduate degree from Ramesh Chandra Kala Devi College, Mathura, affiliated with Dr Bhimrao Ambedkar University, Agra. She also holds diplomas in Art and Craft, Computer Applications, and Computer Accounting. She has participated in national and international exhibitions, art camps, and conferences, and has served as an Assistant Professor at HMV College, Jalandhar. Her research centers on traditional arts and visual culture. ORCID: https://orcid.org/0009-0004-2410-0695.

Nigora Bukharova is Head of International Cooperation at the Tourism Development Research Institute under Uzbekistan's Ministry of Ecology, Environmental Protection, and Climate Change. An accomplished economist, she specializes in tourism education, lifelong learning, and management. Her research spans cultural theory, governance, social inclusion, gender and race narratives, and agritourism. She has authored over 30 publications, with recent work focusing on regional tourism clusters for sustainable growth in Uzbekistan. She contributed to the 2021 Uzbekistan–China project on tourism-led poverty reduction and women's development, advancing innovation and inclusive, competitive tourism development.

Abhay Chamoli is a Senior Scale Assistant Professor at the School of Hospitality Management, IMS Unison University, Dehradun, with a PhD in Hotel Management focusing on consumer behavior toward local cuisines. His research explores food-related personality traits and the impact of local and organic foods on tourist experiences. He has published over 20 research papers in esteemed journals indexed in Scopus, ABDC, and UGC Care, alongside several authored book chapters. He has also secured four patents for innovations in kitchen and bar equipment and actively contributes to international conferences and faculty development programs as a resource person. ORCID: https://orcid.org/0000-0002-9278-6850.

Gopali Dayal, PhD, is an Assistant Professor at Shoolini University specializing in Management, with a focus on human resource (HR) practices, marketing education, and student development. With over six years of experience in teaching, research, training, and academic leadership, she has developed self-learning models and led placement initiatives across India, guiding more than 800 students into employment. Her academic contributions include 20 Scopus-indexed publications, conference presentations, and 3 patents in HR innovation and artificial intelligence-driven job satisfaction systems. She actively engages in curriculum design, research supervision, and industry collaborations to bridge academia and practice.

Saurabh Dixit is a distinguished academician, administrator, and former Army officer, currently serving as Professor and Nodal Officer at the Indian Institute of

Tourism and Travel Management, Gwalior, under the Ministry of Tourism, Government of India. With over three decades of experience in teaching, research, administration, and industry, he specializes in tourism management, smart tourism, information technology, and adventure tourism. A Computer Engineering graduate with postgraduate degrees in Management and Tourism and a PhD in Tourism, he has authored 6 books, published 50+ research papers, developed 27 UGC e-Pathshala modules, and under guided many research scholars.

Ali Faik is a student in the Management Study Program at Universitas Siber Asia, Jakarta, Indonesia. His very interesting research with the concept in the hospitality industry and a master's degree in Hospitality Management with a nuanced focus on the antecedence of consequences relationship quality are both conferred by Trisakti University in Jakarta. His academic interests include hospitality management, service management, brand management, customer behaviour, marketing management, digital marketing, E-commerce, and management information systems in hospitality industry.

Rakotoarisoa Maminirina Fenitra, PhD, is a dedicated Researcher and Educator specializing in human behavior and psychology studies. He holds a PhD in Management Science with professional experience spanning across countries, including Indonesia, Malaysia, Pakistan, and Madagascar. His work is focused on advancing knowledge in pro-environmental behavior, digital transformation, well-being, and positive psychology, particularly exploring their link to sustainability in management, marketing, and tourism. Committed to fostering collaboration, he strives to bridge these areas to better understand how human behavior can contribute to personal and environmental well-being. He is committed to bridging the gap between research and practice by translating academic insights into practical, actionable instruction.

Rakotovao Finaritra Manovosoa, PhD, is Professor of Marketing and the Executive Director at ISCAM Business School, Madagascar. His research focuses on customer satisfaction, loyalty, and perceived value, with particular relevance to services, festivals, and tourism. He has served as a permanent member of the National Board of the Collective of University Professors of Madagascar. In addition to his academic role, he also acts as a Consultant for Madagascar's Ministry of Higher Education and Scientific Research.

Arsheed Ahmad Ganie, PhD, is an Assistant Professor in the School of Social Science and Humanities at NIILM University, Kaithal, Haryana, India. A prolific researcher, he has authored over 20+ papers in prestigious national and international journals and contributed to numerous scholarly book chapters. Beyond his research, he is a dedicated mentor who has successfully guided three PhD scholars to completion. Known for his technical proficiency and exceptional communication skills, he blends academic rigor with a self-motivated drive for continuous growth.

Kushagra Garg is a Doctoral Researcher in Sociology at Banasthali Vidyapith, Rajasthan, specializing in climate resilience, gender equity, and sustainable development. A certified academic leader and government-registered copyright holder, he has completed advanced training in artificial intelligence applications (IIT Delhi), ethics in teaching (IIT Madras), and quantitative analysis (G.B. Pant Institute). He serves as a peer reviewer for Sage and IJRISS with over 350 manuscripts evaluated. His scholarly works include contributions to books such as *Power of Mass Media* (2025) and *Development Communication in the Digital Era* (2025). Actively engaged in international conferences, his research integrates sustainability, gender, and governance frameworks to inform inclusive policy and social innovation.

Piali Haldar, PhD, earned her MBA degree from the Institute of Rural Management Anand and completed her PhD at Birla Institute of Technology, Mesra. Her core areas of specialization include rural marketing, rural development, branding strategy, and consumer behavior. With over 20 years of experience in academia and research, she has published extensively in renowned journals listed in ABDC and Scopus. She has authored one textbook on marketing and edited four academic books. She has presented her research at numerous national and international conferences and has contributed more than 50 papers to reputed journals, edited volumes, and conference proceedings. ORCID: https://orcid.org/0000-0003-4729-6964.

Imran was born on March 3, 1986, in Mingora, Swat, Khyber Pakhtunkhwa, Pakistan. He earned his BA (Honors) in Sociology from the University of Malakand (2004–2008), receiving a gold medal, followed by an MPhil in Sociology from the University of Agriculture, Peshawar, where he secured first position. He completed his PhD in Sociology (Social change and development) from the University of Peshawar in 2020. He previously taught at Kohat University of Science and Technology (2011–2013). Currently, he serves as Assistant Professor and In-Charge of Social and Gender Studies at the University of Swat and is an Higher Education Commission of Pakistan (HEC)-approved PhD supervisor.

Ajay Prakash Jaiswal is Assistant Professor in Applied Arts at the School of Liberal and Creative Arts, Lovely Professional University, Punjab. He earned his PhD, BFA, and MFA in Applied Arts from Banaras Hindu University (BHU), Varanasi. With over 15 years of academic and professional experience, he has taught at the University of Allahabad, Kurukshetra University, and IIT-BHU. His work includes creative teaching, curriculum development, and mentoring in the visual arts. His research examines traditional Indian esthetics and modern advertising under globalization. He has presented papers on folk culture, gender, and visual representation, and contributes professionally as a graphic designer and typographer.

Ankit Kumar is pursuing a PhD in Management from C.S.J.M. University, Kanpur, and has experience in academic as well in hospitality industries. His industry and teaching experience has been very satisfying, and he has continuously upgraded his skills in his respective field. He has a patent published under the Office of the Controller General of Patents, Designs and Trademarks Department of Industrial Policy and Promotions, Ministry of Commerce and Industry, Government of India. He has many papers published in peer-reviewed journals and UGC-listed journals. ORCID: https://orcid.org/0009-0009-5002-4522.

Jeetesh Kumar, PhD, is Head of Research at the Faculty of Social Sciences and Leisure Management, Taylor's University, Malaysia. His scholarly expertise spans economic impact analysis, economic modeling, pro-environmental behavior, sustainable tourism development, and behavioral studies. He has led and contributed to numerous national and international research and consultancy projects, and has published over 100 scholarly works, including peer-reviewed journal articles, and book chapters. He holds key editorial roles, including Associate Editor of the *Asia-Pacific Journal of Innovation in Hospitality and Tourism, Regional Editor for Event Management Journal*, and co-editor of several academic books published by CABI, Emerald, and Springer.

Hande Akyurt Kurnaz received her bachelor's degree from Gazi University, Faculty of Commerce and Tourism Education, Department of Travel Management and Tourism Guidance Teaching. She completed her master's degree in Tourism Management at Muğla Sıtkı Koçman University in 2013 and earned her PhD in Tourism Management from Adnan Menderes University in 2018. She worked as a Research Assistant (2010–2012) and Lecturer (2012–2019) at Muğla Sıtkı Koçman University. She is currently a Professor at Bolu Abant İzzet Baysal University, Faculty of Tourism, Department of Tourism Guidance. Her research focuses on sustainable tourism, gastronomic heritage, rural development, and tourism management.

Suman Lata, PhD, is Assistant Professor (Grade-II) at the Amity Institute of Travel & Tourism, Amity University, Uttar Pradesh, India. She has many publications in reputed journals. She has expertise in research techniques like SPSS, AMOS, PLS-SEM, Meta-analysis, and Content Analysis.

Firdous Ahmad Malik is an accomplished economist and Assistant Professor of Economics at the University of the People. He is currently a Postdoctoral Fellow at Amity University, Dubai. He holds a PhD and MPhil in Economics from Babasaheb Bhimrao Ambedkar University and a Master's in Economics from the University of Kashmir. His expertise spans financial inclusion, microfinance, development economics, and public finance. He has authored 14 books with leading academic publishers, including Springer, Routledge, and IGI Global, and 5 forthcoming titles are scheduled for release with Springer, Palgrave Macmillan, and IGI Global. He has 30+ Scopus-indexed publications.

Dev Kumar Mandal currently serves as an Assistant Professor in the Department of Management at Brainware University, Kolkata. Before this, he worked at ICRA Analytics Ltd and Shriram Finance Ltd. He holds an MBA in Finance and a Bachelor of Commerce degree from Vidyasagar University. Additionally, he has successfully cleared the UGC NET and WB SET examinations in Management. ORCID: https://orcid.org/0009-0005-3740-6885.

Priyakrushna Mohanty is Assistant Professor at the School of Business and Management, Christ University, Bengaluru. He earned his PhD in Tourism Studies from Pondicherry University as a UGC Senior Research Fellow and received the Travel Corporation (India) Gold Medal for academic distinction in his master's program. He also holds a master's degree in Finance and postgraduate diplomas in Rural Development, Research Methodology, and Teaching Skills. With prior experience at IRCTC and as Guest Faculty at Pondicherry University, he has published 50+ papers, presented widely, and has edited 5 books with Routledge, Emerald, Springer Nature, and CABI.

Ali Najeeb is Associate Professor at the Qasim Ibrahim School of Business, Villa College, Maldives. His research interests include higher education leadership, governance and management, sustainability, artificial intelligence, industrial relations, employment law, and labor issues in small island states, migrant workers, and Human Resource Management (HRM)/Employee Relations (ER) in tourism and hospitality industry. He has published several research papers in refereed international journals, shared his experience in local and international panel discussions, and presented his research work in international scholarly conferences. He is a recipient of the Emerald Literati Award for Excellence 2014, the outstanding paper award.

Irfan Nawaz is a Social Welfare Officer at the Federal Ministry of Human Rights, Government of Pakistan. He is an expert in society and technology with respect to social change and its application at different social institutions of society. His area of research interest are child tourism and the role of technology in climate change and its implications for individuals in society. Legal human rights and their violation through technology are the main domain of study in contemporary society.

Nazirullah is a Postgraduate Research student at the Faculty of Applied Social Sciences, Universiti Sultan Zainal Abidin (Malaysia), and CEO of the Centre of Engineering Research Advancement and Technology. He has contributed to national and international projects related to tourism, hospitality, and tourism support. His research interests include tourist destinations, emotional solidarity, sustainability pillars, community values in tourism, violent extremism, honor killing, terrorism, peace and stability strategies, the metaverse and society, and advanced qualitative and quantitative data analysis. He has published on crime–tourism relationships, sociological perspectives, and artificial intelligence for societal improvement and presented at high-impact academic conferences.

Michael Adekunle Oderinde holds a PhD in Human Resource Management. Currently, he is a Lecturer in the Department of Industrial Relations and Human

Resource Management, Lagos State University, Ojo, Nigeria. He enjoys teaching, research, traveling, and solving new challenges. He has published several scholarly writings in both local and international academic journals. He is an Associate Member of Chartered Institute of Personnel Management of Nigeria.

Abraham Israel Ogbaji holds a Bachelor of Science degree in Human Resource Management from Central University, Ghana, and is currently pursuing an MPhil in Human Resource Management at the University of Ghana. He has served as a Teaching Assistant at Central Business School, where he contributes to academic support and research activities. His research interests focus on organizational politics, psychological attachment, and performance management. He is a self-motivated and goal-oriented researcher, dedicated to advancing knowledge in human resource management and organizational behavior.

Lateef Okikiola Olanipekun holds a PhD in Human Resource Management from Lagos State University and a Doctor of Business Administration (Business Management) from Atlanta College of Liberal Arts and Sciences. He is a Senior Lecturer at Accra Institute of Technology Business School, Accra, Ghana, where he teaches human resource-related courses. He is a member of the International Labour and Employment Relations Association. He is also an Associate Member of Chartered Institute of Personnel Management of Nigeria.

Himanshu Pal is a PhD Research Scholar at the Indian Institute of Tourism and Travel Management, Gwalior, under Jawaharlal Nehru University, New Delhi. His doctoral research focuses on Spiritual Tourism and Inbound Tourist Well-being, with a special emphasis on Varanasi. He holds a bachelor's degree in Hospitality & Tourism and a master's degree in Tourism Management from Banaras Hindu University (BHU), along with a Diploma in Yoga from BHU. He has also earned the NCC "C" Certificate and possesses professional experience in the tourism and hospitality sector. His academic interests include spiritual tourism, wellness, yoga, culture, and sustainable development, and he has actively presented his research in academic forums.

Suresh Kumar Velayudhan Pillai, PhD, is Senior Lecturer in Health & Wellness at Taylor's University, Malaysia, who initiated, developed, and taught a new Holistic Approach to Health and Wellness module (integrated form of Ayurveda and Yoga). Since 2015, more than 3,500 students have successfully completed this module. He is a Senior Ayurvedic Physician and Yoga Master who has been providing Ayurveda medical treatments for various illnesses and health and wellness training for general well-being for the last 23 years. In 2020, he was included into the WHO Panel of Yoga Experts. He is also an External Assessor for the Bachelor of Ayurvedic Medical Sciences at Lincoln University College, Malaysia and has conducted Health and Wellness training and workshops for the corporations.

Safia Quadri is currently pursuing her graduation in the Department of Tourism Management at Christ (Deemed to be University), Bangalore. Her research interests focus on the intersection of tourism, artificial intelligence, and emerging technologies. She is particularly interested in how digital innovation is shaping the future of the travel and tourism industry.

Fatma Ahmed Ragab is a Researcher and Faculty member at the Faculty of Commerce, Business Administration Department, Damietta University. She holds a master's degree in Business Administration. Her thesis was distinguished with a recommendation for publication and exchange among Arab and foreign universities. Driven by a passion for making higher education relevant and exciting, her work bridges academic theory with real-world application. Her primary research interests include branding in tourism, corporate social responsibility, and customer interaction with technology. An accomplished speaker and educator, she has presented her research at numerous international forums. ORCID: https://orcid.org/0009-0009-1290-1918.

Neethiahnanthan Ari Ragavan is Executive Dean of the Faculty of Social Sciences and Leisure Management at Taylor's University, Malaysia. With over 28 years of academic expertise, he earned his doctorate degree from the University of Toulouse-Jean Jaures, France. He is deeply engaged in advancing hospitality and tourism education and research across Malaysia and the Southeast Asian region. Currently, he also holds the position of President at the ASEAN Tourism Research Association and contributes actively to numerous international boards. His research interests span areas such as tourism policy, hospitality development and innovation, and higher education systems and models.

Prakash Chandra Rout, PhD, is a tourism and hospitality academic with over a decade of experience across teaching, research, industry, and vocational education. He is currently associated with PSS Central Institute of Vocational Education, Bhopal, and previously served with the Ministry of Education, Ethiopia. His professional engagements include ICIMOD, Kathmandu, and the G.B. Pant National Institute of Himalayan Environment, Gangtok. His work centers on sustainable tourism, ecotourism, market research, and value chain-oriented education. He has led capacity-building initiatives aligned with National Education Policy (NEP) 2020 and National Skills Qualifications Framework (NSQF), strengthening employability and industry–academia linkages.

Shivansu Sachan is pursuing a PhD in Management, a master's holder from Integral University, Lucknow, and a bachelor's from IHM, Lucknow. He has academic and professional accomplishments of six years with renowned organizations and institutes. His teaching career has been very satisfying, and he has continuously upgraded his skills and knowledge by attending many courses and training programs, seminars, and conferences organized by different organizations, and also delivered many lectures in the hospitality sector. He is working as an Assistant Professor at Chhatrapati Shahu Ji Maharaj University Kanpur. ORCID: https://orcid.org/0000-0002-9893-8018.

Rakotoarisoa Maminiaina Heritiana Sedera is a Lecturer and Researcher at the ISCAM Business School, Madagascar. He is a Business of Tomorrow Laboratory member and spearhead of the Entrepreneurship and Innovation Pole at the Business School. In addition, he is Co-founder of ASTA Research Center, an independent research institution in Madagascar. He has published several book chapters and research papers in reputable journals, both international and national.

Atul Kumar Sharma is an Assistant Professor at the Indian Institute of Tourism & Travel Management, Gwalior, India. He is also a UGC-Senior Research Fellow in the Department of Tourism Studies, Pondicherry University. He holds a master's degree in Tourism Management from Banaras Hindu University, India. Previously, he was associated with the Ministry of Tourism as Manager (Government Consultant) for the Central Nodal Agency for Adventure Tourism. With over 13 years of experience as an educator, industry professional, and government consultant, his academic and professional interests include adventure tourism, pilgrimage tourism, smart tourism, and tourism entrepreneurship.

Priya Sharma is an Assistant Professor at Shoolini University Centre of Distance and Online Education, with demonstrated excellence in teaching, research, and academic administration. She holds a PhD in Business Management with specialization in human resource and marketing. She serves as Program Coordinator for the MBA (KPMG) program at Amity (Dubai) and contributes to curriculum development, content creation, learner engagement, and the creation of self-learning materials. Her research focuses on adoption behavior and women empowerment. She is a recipient of the International Grandeur Award (2025) and is recognized for her active engagement in academic forums, workshops, and impactful institutional initiatives.

Surti Sharma is Research Scholar of the University of Kota, Kota (India). The area of her research is sustainability in tourism and hospitality in Rajasthan: a study with reference to Kota. She is a Company Secretary. She holds a postgraduation degree in Business Administration and MCom in Economic and Financial Management, both with distinction. She has completed a faculty development program in Financial Management from IIM-Bangalore. She has qualified for UGC-NET thrice. She has presented research papers at national and international conferences, and her research papers were published in reputable journals and magazines. Also, she has published chapters in international books of Scopus, Springer publications, etc.

Vivek Sharma, PhD, has nearly 15 years of experience and is currently an Assistant Professor at the Government Mahendra Karma Girls College in Dantewada, Chhattisgarh. Alongside earning his Postgraduation in Accountancy and Business Statistics and Doctorate in Economic and Financial Management from the University of Rajasthan, he has undertaken faculty development programs in

Financial Accounting & Analysis from IIM-Bangalore and Financial Accounting from IIT-Bombay. He has cleared the UGC-NET and SET (RPSC).

Ahmad Puad Mat Som, PhD, is a distinguished academic currently serving at Universiti Sultan Zainal Abidin in Terengganu, Malaysia. With a strong expertise in tourism studies, his areas of specialization encompass tourism planning and development, sustainable tourism, community participation, tourism crisis management, and Muslim-friendly tourism. Before this, he held an academic position at Universiti Sains Malaysia and completed a two-year secondment at Al Faisal University, Prince Sultan College for Tourism and Business in Saudi Arabia. He holds a bachelor's degree from Iowa State University, USA, as well as a master's degree from the University of Lincolnshire & Humberside and a doctorate from the University of Strathclyde, UK.

Cheryl Marlitta Stefia is a Practitioner-Lecturer at Universitas Kristen Duta Wacana and a Consultant for NGOs, including ADRA Indonesia. She specializes in Small and Medium Enterprises (SMEs) and entrepreneurship, with a particular focus on endogenous communities and minority groups. Beyond academia, she actively consults for various small businesses, integrating practical insights into her work. Her research focuses on marketing strategy and tourism, for which she has published her research in reputable peer-reviewed journals. She effectively bridges academia and practice, contributing to education, consultancy, and community development.

Amit Tariyal, PhD, is Assistant Professor (Senior Scale) at the School of Hospitality Management, IMS Unison University, Dehradun, Uttarakhand, India. He completed his Management Doctorate in 2022 from IMS Unison University and qualified for UGC NET in Tourism Administration and Management. He has published multiple research papers in ABDC, Scopus, and Web of Science-indexed journals. His research interests include tourism, hospitality, consumer behavior, and service marketing. ORCID: https://orcid.org/0000-0003-3846-9798.

Divya Jyoti Thakur, PhD, is Professor in MMIM, Maharishi Markandeshwar (Deemed to be University), Mullana, Ambala, Haryana, India. She has over 15+ years of academic experience. She is a well-structured academic professional in fostering student learning outcomes through creative and innovative curriculum delivery methods. She has participated in various international and national seminars/conferences/workshops. Under her guidance, three PhD scholars have completed their PhD. She has published 4 edited books and 24 Indian Utility/Design Patents, published 4 International Patent granted along with 40+ research publications in internationally and nationally reputed journals and chapters in books. She has received many awards.

Naresh Thakur is currently serving as an Assistant Professor of Marketing at Gian Jyoti Institute of Management and Technology, Punjab, India. He has a total of 18+ years of experience, out of these he has 14 years of industry experience and 4 years of academic experience. He is driving thought-provoking class debates to promote student engagement and learning. He also provides the mock interview sessions to tackle the placement interviews. Also, he has good research publications in reputed national/international journals, patents, and book chapters. He is a fabulous communicator. He has strong industry connections. He is good at making relationships in industry and academia. He has received many national awards.

Ophelia Delali Dogbe Zungbey is a Senior Lecturer in the Department of Human Resource Management at Central University. She holds a Master of Philosophy degree in Organisation and Human Resource Management from the University of Ghana, Legon, and a Bachelor of Education degree in Business Management from the University of Education, Winneba. She also has a Master of Arts degree in Human Resource Development (HRD) from the University of Cape Coast. Currently, she is a PhD candidate at the Ghana Institute of Management and Public Administration. She is a full member of the Chartered Institute of HR Practitioners, Ghana and the African Academy of Management.

Preface

Wellness tourism today is much more than a travel trend – it's a journey of healing, discovery, and conscious living. This first volume of *Advancement in Medical and Wellness Tourism, Part A: Entrepreneurship and Technology* brings together voices from across the world to explore how health, nature, innovation, and human connection come together to define this growing field. The chapters in this volume paint a rich picture of how wellness tourism is evolving – from ancient traditions and natural therapies to digital wellness platforms and sustainable travel practices. Together, they show how the pursuit of well-being has become both personal and global linking individuals, communities, and destinations through shared values of care, balance, and sustainability.

Readers will find a wide range of perspectives here, insightful analyses of wellness and spa tourism in India, studies on eco-wellness models in Ghana, the influence of technology on guest well-being, the role of marketing and consumer psychology in shaping wellness tourism, and the power of women entrepreneurs shaping this sector. Other contributions delve into the impact of esthetics on happiness, and the growing role of sustainability in shaping responsible tourism experiences. Each chapter, in its own way, reflects the same spirit: that wellness is not just about health, but about harmony with oneself, with others, and with the environment.

We are deeply grateful to all the authors from Africa, Egypt, Nigeria, Ghana, India, Malaysia, Indonesia, Pakistan, Turkey, Uzbekistan, and the Maldives for their selfless contributions, and to the supporters who helped make this volume possible. Their combined efforts have turned this collection into a meaningful dialogue on how wellness tourism can inspire more mindful, inclusive, and sustainable futures. We hope that this book serves as both a resource and an inspiration for students, scholars, entrepreneurs, travelers, and everyone who believes in the power of travel to heal, connect, and transform lives.

Dr Anukrati Sharma
Dr Shruti Arora

Chapter 1

Travel for Health and Wellness: The Diverse Types and Forms of Nature-based Health Tourism

Rakotoarisoa Maminirina Fenitra[a], *Rakotoarisoa Maminiaina Heritiana Sedera*[b], *Rakotovao Finaritra Manovosoa*[b], *Cheryl Marlitta Stefia*[c] *and Ansar Abbas*[d]

[a]*Faculty of Management, Universiti Teknologi Malaysia, Johor Bahru, Malaysia*
[b]*Business of Tomorrow Lab, ISCAM Business School, Antananarivo, Madagascar*
[c]*Faculty of Economics and Business, Universitas Kristen Duta Wacana, Yogyakarta, Indonesia*
[d]*Department of Management, Hamdard University Islamabad, Islamabad, Pakistan*

Abstract

Nature-based tourism (NBT) has grown significantly in recent decades, driven by interest in healthy lifestyles, authenticity, and novel experiences. Nature-based health tourism, in particular, offers wellness benefits while promoting environmental sustainability. Despite its rising popularity, there remains a need to better understand its various forms. This chapter explores the different types of NBT, the activities associated with each, and the motivations behind tourist visits. Drawing on literature and case studies, it identifies key components, visitor purposes, and destination features. The chapter also offers practical insights for researchers, practitioners, and policymakers in supporting sustainable and health-oriented tourism development.

Keywords: Nature-based tourism; health; tourism; well-being; wellness; medical; traditional healing

Advancement in Medical and Wellness Tourism, Part A: Entrepreneurship and Technology, 1–15

Published under exclusive licence by Emerald Publishing Limited
doi:10.1108/978-1-80592-983-320261002

1. Introduction

Tourism plays a vital role in enhancing well-being, particularly through nature-based tourism (NBT), which promotes mental health by encouraging interaction with natural environments (Buckley, 2020). The COVID-19 pandemic further accelerated interest in NBT, with a surge in demand for nature experiences (Derks et al., 2020; Venter et al., 2020). This trend has evolved into nature-based health tourism, which integrates medical, wellness, and spa elements to support emotional, physical, and spiritual well-being (Asan et al., 2024; Baig et al., 2024; Figueiredo et al., 2024). Research shows that such interventions enhance cognitive function, brain activity, and blood pressure regulation (Jimenez et al., 2021). Evidence also confirms that nature-based experiences contribute significantly to physical, emotional, and psychological health, reinforcing their value in wellness strategies (Brymer et al., 2010; Peña-Casillas et al., 2024).

This chapter explores the diverse forms of nature-based health tourism, focusing on how different destinations offer unique activities that support tourist well-being. It categorizes key types of nature-based health tourism to highlight the attractions and experiences that set them apart. Through a critical review of literature and case studies, the chapter builds a theoretical foundation for understanding this emerging field. It examines the growing connection between tourism and health, emphasizing the role of natural environments in enhancing physical, mental, and emotional well-being. The chapter also discusses tourist motivations, the rise of health-conscious travel, and broader cultural and environmental trends driving this shift. Ultimately, it presents nature-based health tourism as a pathway to sustainable tourism development and holistic community well-being.

This chapter categorizes key forms of nature-based health tourism, including wellness tourism (e.g., yoga and spa retreats), traditional health tourism (THT) (cultural healing and natural remedies), and medical tourism (treatment paired with restorative natural settings). It highlights how destinations integrate natural environments with health-focused experiences, shaped by social and cultural contexts. The chapter emphasizes the balance between environmental preservation and meaningful travel, benefiting both visitors and local communities. By consolidating academic perspectives, it clarifies core concepts, refines theoretical frameworks, and identifies future research directions. It also offers practical insights for tourism managers, policymakers, and public health officials to implement sustainable, health-oriented strategies.

This chapter offers a structured exploration of nature-based health tourism. It begins with a literature review that defines key concepts and outlines the links between nature, health, and tourism, followed by an overview of wellness, traditional health, and medical tourism. The methodology section details the systematic review process used to develop a comprehensive understanding of the topic. The discussion explores each tourism type in depth, considering both academic and practical implications. The chapter concludes by highlighting the sector's growing significance, proposing future research directions, and emphasizing the role of sustainable tourism in promoting well-being and conserving natural resources. Through this balanced approach, the chapter supports responsible growth that benefits travelers, communities, and the environment.

2. Literature Review

2.1. Nature, Health, and Tourism

Pessot et al. (2021) define natural resources broadly, including landscapes like mountains, lakes, and forests, as well as by-products such as food, medicine, and cultural heritage. The World Tourism Organization (WTO) views health tourism as using natural assets – like mineral waters and climate – for health services (Hall, 2011). Smith and Puczkó (2015) define it as travel to promote, maintain, or restore physical, mental, and social well-being. Despite varying definitions, health tourism generally involves travel to improve overall wellness. Research shows that nature exposure boosts mood, cognitive function, and reduces stress (Mayer et al., 2009). For example, Wells (2000) found that it significantly aids cognitive development in urban children, while Wells and Evans (2003) reported lower psychological distress in rural children with greater access to nature.

Nature plays a key role in reducing psychological distress, aligning with Ulrich's (1983) Psycho-evolutionary Theory, which suggests nature supports emotional and physiological recovery. Natural environments have been shown to promote calmness, enhance attention, and improve life satisfaction more than urban settings (Kaplan, 1993, 1995; Kamitsis & Francis, 2013). A strong connection to nature is linked to reduced stress, improved mood, and better mental health (Moreno-González et al., 2020). Buckley (2020) found that NBT not only attracts mentally healthy individuals but also enhances well-being, encouraging destinations to promote nature as a health asset (Fenitra, Abbas, et al., 2022). Nature exposure also boosts immune function (Oachiai et al., 2015), improves cognitive performance (Berman et al., 2012), and lowers stress indicators such as cortisol and heart rate (Park et al., 2010). Furthermore, it enhances spiritual well-being, fostering mindfulness and resilience, particularly in those with declining health.

2.2. Nature, Health, and Ecotourism

Ecotourism emerged in the 1980s as a sustainable development strategy that conserves natural resources through tourism revenue. It has since become one of the fastest-growing sectors in tourism, with ecotourists increasing three times faster than conventional tourists and projected to represent 5% of the global vacation market by 2024 (Das & Chatterjee, 2015). This growth reflects rising demand for environmentally responsible travel (Fenitra et al., 2021; Fenitra, Premananto, et al., 2022; Sharpley, 2006). Ecotourism promotes travel to natural areas that support conservation, community well-being, and environmental education (Stronza et al., 2022). When managed effectively, it can protect biodiversity, enhance landscapes, reduce poverty, and improve local livelihoods. However, poorly managed ecotourism may harm wildlife by disrupting behavior and increasing predation risks (Fletcher & Neves, 2012). Still, it remains a valuable conservation tool when carefully implemented.

Health issues are also a growing concern in tourism. Despite preparation, 89.4% of travelers report experiencing health problems, such as diarrhea, which can become serious if untreated (Musa et al., 2004). As a result, healthcare availability and safety are critical to visitor satisfaction and destination choice (Tiwari & Nguyen, 2024). The World Health Organization (1946) defines health as complete physical, mental, and social well-being not just the absence of disease, and notes that health depends on conditions such as peace, housing, education, and a stable ecosystem (McKenzie, 2024). By the late 20th century, public health shifted to focus on creating healthy environments, emphasizing the need to protect nature from human harm as much as protecting people from environmental risks (Brymer & Lacaze, 2013).

2.3. Nature-based Health Tourism

The health benefits of NBT are well-documented. Meyer-Arendt (2004) identified settings such as parks, spas, coastal areas, and retreats as key environments for such tourism. Heintzman (2010) found that visitors often seek spiritual experiences like awe, solitude, and tranquility in nature, which enhances mental and emotional well-being. Nature-based health tourism has grown in popularity among those seeking emotional, physical, and spiritual healing (Asan et al., 2024; Baig et al., 2024; Figueiredo et al., 2024). It includes medical, wellness, and spa tourism. According to Zhong et al. (202), medical tourism involves travel for treatment based on healthcare quality and cost; wellness tourism focuses on maintaining health; and spa tourism offers relaxation and therapeutic services. Fig. 1.1 presents a conceptual model of nature-based health tourism as a triangle centered on health encompassing mental, physical, and emotional well-being. The three subtypes wellness, traditional health, and medical tourism work together to form a comprehensive, nature-integrated health tourism experience.

2.3.1. Nature, Health, and Tourism

In today's fast-paced world, many people seek to enhance their well-being through natural and holistic approaches. Increasingly, they turn to nature, wellness tourism, and healthier lifestyles to balance physical, mental, and emotional health amid modern stresses. Wellness tourism, a rapidly growing segment of nature-based health tourism, offers immediate benefits and has gained further attention due to the COVID-19 pandemic's impact on mental and physical health (Zhong et al., 2023). Moreover, nature provides not only fresh air, exercise, and nourishing food but also a sanctuary for mental and emotional well-being (Parashar & Agarwal, 2024). Research confirms that NBT creates a structured framework to enhance wellness experiences (Clissold et al., 2022). Contemporary work–life balance trends drive people to invest time and resources into recovery,

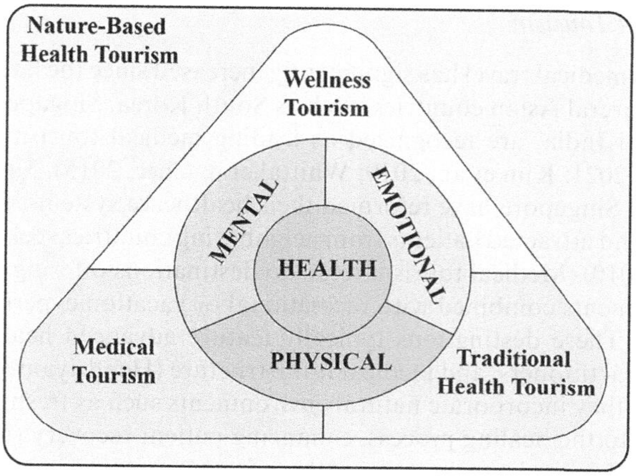

Fig. 1.1. The Concept of Nature-based Health Tourism. *Source*: Created by authors.

health improvement, and illness prevention, making such activities valuable for overall well-being. Further, accessible year-round, NBT destinations offer a variety of wellness activities from hiking and meditation to affordable spa retreats to support visitor health (Pande, 2024). Sometimes these wellness experiences are part of a broader tourism package; other times, they are the primary focus, reflecting growing demand for travel centered on relaxation, rejuvenation, and personal wellness.

2.3.2. Traditional Health Tourism

Over the past few decades, wellness tourism has grown rapidly, with more travelers seeking health-focused services during their trips (Smith & Puczkó, 2014; Smith et al., 2020). This demand has led to the rise of THT, which combines culturally rooted healing practices with travel experiences (Smith & Jenner, 2000). Examples include Ayurveda in India and Traditional Chinese Medicine in China (Gautam & Bhatta, 2020; He, 2015). THT is one of the oldest forms of health tourism, where visitors travel to experience indigenous medical treatments and traditional healing, often alongside leisure activities, blending health and tourism (Speier, 2011). It is considered a subset of nature-based health tourism, utilizing natural resources to enhance physical, mental, and spiritual well-being (Dryglas & Smith, 2024). Tourists benefit from new treatment experiences and the natural environment while escaping daily stress. For instance, health tourism is vital to Thailand's economy. A recent review identified seven key factors shaping its wellness tourism: destination environment, policies, infrastructure, cultural and man-made resources, wellness strategies, innovation, and marketing efforts (Phutong et al., 2021). Together, these elements make Thailand a popular wellness destination offering relaxation and cultural richness in a natural setting.

2.3.3. Medical Tourism

International medical travel has significantly increased since the late 1990s (Connell, 2013). Several Asian countries, such as South Korea, Singapore, Malaysia, Thailand, and India, are recognized as leading medical tourism destinations (Cham et al., 2021; Kim et al., 2019; Whittaker & Chee, 2015). Since the 1980s, Malaysia and Singapore have reformed their healthcare systems, improved service quality, and attracted patients from neighboring countries seeking advanced care (Leng, 2010). Medical tourism refers to destinations offering cost-effective medical treatments combined with recreational or vacation experiences (Nagar et al., 2022). These destinations typically feature advanced healthcare facilities, skilled practitioners, and medical infrastructure (Hendriyanto et al., 2024). Additionally, they incorporate natural environments such as fresh air and green landscapes into the healing process, enhancing patient recovery (McCartney & Wang, 2024). Medical tourism generally falls into two categories: treatment-focused medical tourism (surgeries and medical care) and health and beauty tourism (dental care, cosmetic, and aesthetic procedures) (Sun et al., 2022) (see Table 1.1).

2.4. The Different Types of Nature-based Health Tourism

Nature-based health tourism destinations attract both international and domestic travelers. Culturally and naturally rich countries such as India, China, Singapore, Cuba, Malaysia, and Thailand are well-known for their medical tourism offerings (Hall, 2011). Table 1.1 outlines the main types of nature-based health tourism, highlighting their distinct features and providing examples from empirical studies conducted in various countries.

- *Wellness tourism* focuses on activities that help travelers improve, restore, or maintain their emotional, mental, and physical health (Kim et al., 2019). These benefits often arise through interaction with natural environments and wellness services offered at the destination, such as yoga, meditation retreats, and spa treatments, which enhance cognitive function and emotional well-being (Gkinton et al., 2022). The goal is to support long-term health while providing meaningful and enriching travel experiences.
- *THT* shares similarities with wellness tourism but emphasizes healing through ancient and culturally rooted practices. Treatments often take place in traditional settings – such as temples – or involve rituals and therapies using herbal medicine and natural ingredients (Pollock & Williams, 2000). Tourists are increasingly drawn to these experiences for their authenticity and perceived therapeutic benefits. In many Asian countries, traditional medicine is valued for its effectiveness and natural approach to healing. These treatments are typically administered by skilled local or indigenous practitioners. Overall, THT promotes relaxation and recovery through time-honored, holistic methods.

Table 1.1. Types and Differences: Nature-based Health Tourism.

Type	Destination	Purpose	Activities	Case Study
Wellness tourism	Mindfulness program	Health/ wellness improving tourism	Yoga, meditation, nature therapy, SPA treatments, spiritual retreats	Indonesia (Bali), India, Nepal, Sri Lanka (Dahanayake et al., 2024), Thailand (Praprom & Laipaporn, 2023)
	SPA retreats	Health/ well-being improving tourism	SPA, wellness, natural settings	China (Wangzhou et al., 2023) Spain (Medina-Muñoz & Medina-Muñoz, 2012)
Traditional health tourism	Herbal medicine	Medical tourism	Traditional healing	China, Mauritius
	Cultural practices	Medical tourism	Rituals, cultural ceremonies, spiritual or religious ceremonies	
Medical tourism	Medical tourism	Medical tourism	Medical treatment, post-treatment	India (Romão et al., 2022), Thailand, Malaysia, and Singapore (Hall, 2011). EU Countries (Ulusoy & Tosun, 2020), Thailand, Korea
	Health and beauty tourism	Surgery and beauty treatments		

Source: By authors.

- *Medical tourism* is a subset of nature-based health tourism, but it is primarily outcome-driven rather than experience-focused. It involves travel for medical treatments such as surgeries, critical care, or aesthetic procedures (Tsekouropoulos et al., 2023). These destinations attract international patients due to their high-quality healthcare services and post-treatment care. Some also integrate natural environments into the healing process, enhancing patient recovery. For example, Almodawer et al. (2024) found that Malaysia's medical tourism appeal lies in both its medical quality and supportive natural settings. As Majeed et al. (2017) note, medical tourism often blends allopathic and natural therapies, offering a comprehensive approach to health and healing.

Table 1.1 summarizes types of nature-based health tourism: wellness tourism (yoga, meditation, and spa) popular in Asia; THT (herbal medicine, rituals); and medical tourism (affordable, quality healthcare including surgery). It details destinations, purposes, activities, and case studies.

3. Method

This chapter offers a comprehensive review of existing literature to advance understanding of nature-based health tourism. Peer-reviewed articles from reputable journals indexed in Scopus and Web of Science were systematically analyzed to ensure data quality and relevance (Wickrama et al., 2023). This method supports the development of coherent, evidence-based arguments and conceptual frameworks. It also helps track trends and developments in this emerging field, contributing both to academic discourse and practical application. Ultimately, the review aims to provide readers with a solid foundation and deeper insight into nature-based health tourism (Chigbu et al., 2023).

4. Discussion

This section presents a narrative that explores the concept, foundational knowledge, and types of nature-based health tourism. It aims to clarify key ideas, provide a solid understanding of the topic, and highlight how these insights can inform both theoretical frameworks and practical applications in nature-based health tourism.

4.1. The Concept

The growing demand for nature-based health tourism highlights the need for a solid conceptual foundation and a deeper understanding of its sustainability, environmental impact, and balance between well-being and ecosystem preservation. This chapter provides an overview of nature-based health tourism, exploring its definition, key types, and core characteristics. Nature-based health tourism refers to travel experiences in natural settings where health benefits mental, physical, or emotional are the primary outcomes. As the tourism industry heavily relies on natural resources such as water, landscapes, and forests (Pessot et al., 2021; Ruban, 2021), the quality and conservation of these resources are critical. Destinations offering activities like hiking, spa therapies, meditation, and wellness retreats must ensure that these environments are preserved to enhance both visitor experience and long-term sustainability (Qiu et al., 2023).

Tourists are increasingly motivated by the desire for physical and mental rejuvenation. Engaging in immersive nature experiences fosters inner peace, reduces stress, and supports overall well-being. By integrating well-maintained natural environments with health-focused tourism, nature-based health tourism not only meets visitor expectations but also contributes to sustainable development and the protection of natural ecosystems.

As discussed in this chapter, nature-based health tourism involves activities centered on natural resources that promote health and well-being. Social interaction is a key element, as meaningful connections between visitors, local communities, and service providers significantly enhance the overall experience (Gkinton et al., 2022). These interactions can lead to memorable moments and increase visitor satisfaction. The bond between humans and nature plays a vital role in improving mental and emotional well-being (Figueiredo et al., 2024; Lee et al., 2020). Therefore, destination managers must understand how to balance tourism experiences with environmental preservation and community involvement. Carefully designing these interactions ensures that tourism remains sustainable while maintaining the quality of the natural environment and supporting local well-being.

4.2. Fundamental Knowledge

Numerous empirical studies have sought to clarify and expand the understanding of nature-based health tourism, offering various definitions and discussing its challenges, trends, and key drivers. For example, Nagar et al. (2022) define health tourism as travel undertaken to seek medical care, while this chapter defines *nature-based health tourism* as travel that uses natural resources to promote health and well-being. These experiences aim to foster a strong connection between individuals and nature, often through activities like spa treatments, spiritual retreats, yoga, mud bathing, and sunbathing, which positively impact mental and physical health (Smith & Puczkó, 2008; Voigt et al., 2011). As tourists engage in these experiences, they also develop a deeper appreciation for the environment and the importance of preserving it. Scholars argue that nature-based health tourism is driven by situational, behavioral, and psychological factors especially growing concerns about health and the environment (Pessot et al., 2021). As people increasingly prioritize healthy lifestyles, tourism has become a way to recharge, escape daily routines, and support well-being (Aytaş et al., 2024). In many places, travel now serves both as a reward and a health-enhancing activity (Lama & Martín, 2021). Furthermore, rising interest in environmental sustainability has accelerated demand for nature-based health tourism. This form of travel not only supports personal well-being but also promotes environmental conservation, helping balance tourism growth with ecosystem protection.

4.3. Type of Nature-based Health Tourism

Nature-based health tourism is a broad and multifaceted field that emphasizes the relationship between humans and natural environments to promote well-being (Cooper & Buckley, 2022; Pessot et al., 2021; Zhou et al., 2024). To meet the diverse needs of its market, this form of tourism is divided into three main subtypes, each defined by specific goals and activities. *Wellness tourism* focuses on improving health through activities such as mindfulness, meditation, spa treatments, and other holistic practices aimed at enhancing well-being (Gkinton et al., 2022).

THT centers around culturally rooted healing practices, rituals, and events, often involving indigenous methods and herbal remedies (Iwu et al., 2019). *Medical tourism* combines professional medical treatments ranging from surgeries to cosmetic procedures with the therapeutic effects of natural environments, such as sun, mud, hydrotherapy, or forest settings (Wang et al., 2019). While each subtype varies in purpose, they all share the goal of leveraging natural resources to support health and well-being. Success in this sector relies on ensuring high-quality natural environments and meaningful interactions between tourists, the destination, and its local communities. These elements not only enhance visitor satisfaction but also contribute to the sustainability and competitiveness of nature-based health tourism destinations.

4.4. Implications of Nature-based Health Tourism

This chapter contributes to the growing literature on nature-based health tourism by offering a clear definition and conceptual foundation. It provides readers with a solid understanding of the core principles and various types of this tourism, helping distinguish its subcategories. In response to increasing scholarly interest, the chapter synthesizes existing research to present a comprehensive overview of the field and proposes directions for future studies. Beyond its theoretical contributions, the chapter offers valuable practical insights. Tourism destination managers can use this knowledge to design and market nature-based health tourism experiences aligned with specific visitor needs and environmental assets. The guidance provided here can help destinations develop unique value propositions, enhance visitor satisfaction, and remain competitive. Moreover, policymakers and public health or environmental authorities can benefit from this material when shaping tourism policies. Understanding the key components and requirements of each type of nature-based health tourism will support effective planning, natural resource conservation, and cultural preservation efforts, which are essential elements that sustain this industry. In sum, this chapter serves both as a conceptual guide and a practical tool for researchers, tourism professionals, and policymakers, enabling them to develop strategies that balance tourism growth with environmental sustainability and community well-being.

5. Conclusion

The growing demand for tourism and overuse of natural resources pose significant challenges to sustainability in the sector (Han et al., 2025; Neophytou et al., 2025). As a result, promoting sustainable tourism practices has become essential for long-term development. Nature-based health tourism stands out for its dual benefits, enhancing visitor well-being and preserving the environment. Today's travelers increasingly seek experiences that improve their physical and mental health while minimizing their environmental impact. Nature-based health tourism aligns with these goals by offering meaningful, health-focused activities in natural settings that support both personal and ecological well-being. To meet these evolving expectations, tourism destinations must adopt eco-friendly practices and design activities that promote health and sustainability. Doing so ensures lasting value for visitors, protects natural resources, and secures the future of the industry for generations to come.

References

Almodawer, Y., Alam, S. S., Sinniah, S., & Ali, M. H. (2024). Health tourism in Malaysia: Understanding the drivers of satisfaction and revisit intention. *Tourism Recreation Research*, 1–22. https://doi.org/10.1080/02508281.2024.2379686

Asan, K., Alrawadieh, Z., & Altinay, L. (2024). Connectedness to nature and life satisfaction of seniors: The mediating effects of tourist experience and tourist well-being. *Current Issues in Tourism*, *27*(9), 1496–1512.

Aytaş, G., Ergen, F. D., & Aytekin, E. (2024). Wellness tourism after the pandemic. In C. Tanrisever, H. Pamukçu, & A. Sharma (Eds.), *Future tourism trends Volume 1 (Building the future of tourism)* (pp. 285–298). Emerald Publishing Limited. https://doi.org/10.1108/978-1-83753-244-520241019

Baig, S., Ali, A., & Khan, S. U. (2024). Exploring the interplay of tourism impacts, quality of life, and community engagement in developing sustainable nature-based tourism in Pakistan. *GeoJournal*, *89*(1), 38.

Berman, M. G., Kross, E., Krpan, K. M., Askren, M. K., Burson, A., Deldin, P. J., Kaplan, S., Sherdell, L., Gotlib, I. H., & Jonides, J. (2012, November 1). Interacting with nature improves cognition and affect for individuals with depression. *Journal of Affective Disorders*. https://doi.org/10.1016/j.jad.2012.03.012

Brymer, E., Cuddihy, T., & Sharma-Brymer, V. (2010). The role of nature-based experiences in the development and maintenance of wellness. *Asia-Pacific Journal of Health, Sport and Physical Education*, *1*(2), 21–27. https://doi.org/10.1080/18377122.2010.9730328

Brymer, E., & Lacaze, A.-M. (2013). The benefits of ecotourism for visitor wellness. In R. Ballantyne & J. Packer (Éds.), *International handbook on ecotourism* (1st ed., pp. 217–229). Edward Elgar Publishing. https://doi.org/10.4337/9780857939975.00024

Buckley, R. (2020). Nature tourism and mental health: Parks, happiness, and causation. *Journal of Sustainable Tourism*, 1–16. https://doi.org/10.1080/09669582.2020.17

Cham, T. H., Lim, Y. M., Sia, B. C., Cheah, J. H., & Ting, H. (2021). Medical tourism destination image and its relationship with the intention to revisit: A study of Chinese medical tourists in Malaysia. *Journal of China Tourism Research*, *17*(2), 163–191.

Chigbu, U. E., Atiku, S. O., & Du Plessis, C. C. (2023). The science of literature reviews: Searching, identifying, selecting, and synthesising. *Publications*, *11*(1), 2. https://doi.org/10.3390/publications11010002

Clissold, R., Westoby, R., McNamara, K. E., & Fleming, C. (2022). Wellbeing outcomes of nature tourism: Mt Barney Lodge. *Annals of Leisure Research*, *3*(2), 100077. https://doi.org/10.1016/j.annale.2022.100077

Connell, J. (2013). Contemporary medical tourism: Conceptualisation, culture and commodification. *Tourism Management*, *34*, 1–13.

Cooper, M. A., & Buckley, R. (2022). Tourist mental health drives destination choice, marketing, and matching. *Journal of Travel Research*, *61*(4), 786–799.

Dahanayake, S., Wanninayake, B., & Ranasinghe, R. (2024). Demographics shaping memorable wellness tourism experiences: A comparative analysis. *Tourism and Hospitality Research*. https://doi.org/10.1177/14673584241306368

Das, M., & Chatterjee, B. (2015). Ecotourism: A panacea or a predicament? *Tourism Management Perspectives*, *14*, 3–16. https://doi.org/10.1016/j.tmp.2015.01.002

Derks, J., Giessen, L., & Winkel, G. (2020). COVID-19-induced visitor boom reveals the importance of forests as critical infrastructure. *Forest Policy and Economics*, *118*, 102253.

Dryglas, D., & Smith, M. K. (2024). A critical analysis of how central European spas create health tourism experiencescapes. *Tourism Planning & Development, 21*(5), 570–593.

Fenitra, R. M., Abbas, A., Ekowati, D., & Suhairidi, F. (2022). Strategic intent and strategic leadership: A review perspective for post-COVID-19 tourism and hospitality industry recovery. In P. Mohanty, A. Sharma, J. Kennell, & A. Hassan (Eds.), *The Emerald handbook of destination recovery in tourism and hospitality* (pp. 23–44). Emerald Publishing. https://doi.org/10.1108/978-1-80262-073-320221003

Fenitra, R. M., Premananto, G. C., Sedera, R. M. H., Abbas, A., & Laila, N. (2022). Environmentally responsible behavior and knowledge-belief-norm in the tourism context: The moderating role of types of destinations. *International Journal of Geoheritage and Parks, 10*(2), 273–288. https://doi.org/10.1016/j.ijgeop.2022.05.001

Fenitra, R. M., Tanti, H., Premananto, G. C., Indrianawati, U., & Hartini, S. (2021). Extended theory of planned behavior to explain environmentally responsible behavior in the context of nature-based tourism. *Geojournal of Tourism and Geosites, 39*, 1507–1516. https://doi.org/10.30892/gtg.394spl22-795

Figueiredo, N., Abrantes, J. L., & Costa, S. (2024). Mapping the sustainable development in health tourism: A systematic literature review. *Sustainability, 16*(5), 1901. https://doi.org/10.3390/su16051901

Fletcher, R., & Neves, K. (2012). Contradictions in tourism: The promise and pitfalls of ecotourism as a manifold capitalist fix. *Environment and Society, 3*(1), 60–77.

Gautam, P., & Bhatta, K. (2020). Medical tourism in India: Possibilities and problems of alternative medical treatment. *International Journal of Health Management and Tourism, 5*(3), 181–207.

Gkinton, E., Telonis, G., Halkiopoulos, C., & Boutsinas, B. (2022, September). Quality of life and health tourism: A conceptual roadmap of enhancing cognition and well-being. In *International conference of the international association of cultural and digital tourism* (pp. 651–666). Springer International Publishing.

Hall, C. M. (2011). Health and medical tourism: A kill or cure for global public health? *Tourism Review, 66*(1/2), 4–15.

Han, C., Zhang, H., & Zhang, Y. (2025). Balancing growth and preservation: Strategic pathways for sustainable rural tourism in China's environmental landscape. *Sustainability, 17*(1), 246.

He, K. (2015). Traditional Chinese and Thai medicine in a comparative perspective. *Complementary Therapies in Medicine, 23*(6), 821–826.

Heintzman, P. (2010). Nature-based recreation and spirituality: A complex relationship. *Leisure Sciences, 32*(1), 72–89. https://doi.org/10.1080/01490400903430897

Hendriyanto, D., Kusnadi, I. H., Rahmawati, H. U., Akbar, M., & Nurani, A. S. (2024). Analysis of the influence of facilities availability, human resources and promotion on the improvement of medical tourism in Indonesia. *Innovative: Journal of Social Science Research, 4*(3), 4941–4949.

Iwu, C. G., Choto, P., & Tengeh, R. K. (2019). Sustainability issues of health tourism non-profit-organizations. *African Journal of Hospitality, Tourism and Leisure, 8*(5), 1–15.

Jimenez, M. P., DeVille, N. V., Elliott, E. G., Schiff, J. E., Wilt, G. E., Hart, J. E., & James, P. (2021, April 30). Associations between nature exposure and health: A review of the evidence. *International Journal of Environmental Research and Public Health, 18*(9), 4790. https://doi.org/10.3390/ijerph18094790

Kamitsis, I., & Francis, A. J. P. (2013). Spirituality mediates the relationship between engagement with nature and psychological wellbeing. *Journal of Environmental Psychology, 36*, 136–143. https://doi.org/10.1016/j.jenvp.2013.07.013

Kaplan, S. (1993). The role of natural environment aesthetics in the restorative experience. In P. H. Gobster (Ed.), *Managing urban and high-use recreation settings* (General Technical Report NC-163, pp. 46–49). Forest Service, USDA.

Kaplan, S. (1995). The restorative benefits of nature: Toward an integrative framework. *Journal of Environmental Psychology*, *15*(3), 169–182. https://doi.org/10.1016/0272-4944(95)90001-2

Kim, S., Arcodia, C., & Kim, I. (2019). Critical success factors of medical tourism: The case of South Korea. *International Journal of Environmental Research and Public Health*, *16*(24), 4964.

Lama, A. V., & Martín, M. G. (2021). Decoding escape rooms from a tourism perspective: A global scale analysis. *Moravian Geographical Reports*, *29*(1), 2–14.

Lee, T. J., Han, J.-S., & Ko, T.-G. (2020). Health-oriented tourists and sustainable domestic tourism. *Sustainability*, *12*(12), 4988. https://doi.org/10.3390/su12124988

Leng, C. H. (2010). Medical tourism and the state in Malaysia and Singapore. *Global Social Policy*, *10*(3), 336–357. https://doi.org/10.1177/1468018110379978

Majeed, S., Lu, C., & Javed, T. (2017). The journey from an allopathic to natural treatment approach: A scoping review of medical tourism and health systems. *European Journal of Integrative Medicine*, *16*, 22–32.

Mayer, F. S., Frantz, C. M., Bruehlman-Senecal, E., & Dolliver, K. (2009). Why is nature beneficial?: The role of connectedness to nature. *Environment and Behavior*, *41*(5), 607–643. https://doi.org/10.1177/0013916508319745

McCartney, G., & Wang, C. F. (2024). Medical tourism and medical tourists: Providing a sustainable course to integrating health treatments with tourism. *Journal of Travel Medicine*, *31*(5), taae034.

McKenzie, K. J. (2024). *The pursuit of happiness: Freedom and well-being in positive psychology*. https://aura.antioch.edu/etds/1010

Medina-Muñoz, D. R., & Medina-Muñoz, R. D. (2012). Critical issues in health and wellness tourism: An exploratory study of visitors to wellness centres on Gran Canaria. *Current Issues in Tourism*, *16*(5), 415–435. https://doi.org/10.1080/13683500.2012.748719

Meyer-Arendt, K. (2004). Tourism and the natural environment. In A. A. Lew, C. M. Hall, & A. M. Williams (Eds.), *A companion to tourism* (pp. 423–437). Blackwell Publishing Ltd. https://doi.org/10.1002/9780470752272.ch34

Moreno-González, A. A., León, C. J., & Fernández-Hernández, C. (2020). Health destination image: The influence of public health management and well-being conditions. *Journal of Destination Marketing & Management*, *16*, 100430.

Musa, G., Hall, C. M., & Higham, J. E. S. (2004). Tourism sustainability and health impacts in high altitude adventure, cultural and ecotourism destinations: A case study of Nepal's Sagarmatha National Park. *Journal of Sustainable Tourism*, *12*(4), 306–331. https://doi.org/10.1080/09669580408667240

Nagar, R., Singh, Y., Gobinath, R., & Manoharan, G. (2022, May). Aspects of medical tourism in India: A review. *AIP Conference Proceedings*, *2418*(1), 020030. https://doi.org/10.1063/5.0093282

Neophytou, R., Liasidou, S., Pipyros, K., & Christofi, A. (2025). Artificial intelligence driven adaptive learning methods in sustainable tourism education. *Worldwide Hospitality and Tourism Themes*, *17*(1), 120–131. https://doi.org/10.1108/WHATT-12-2024-0308.

Ochiai, H., Ikei, H., Song, C., Kobayashi, M., Miura, T., Kagawa, T., Li, Q., Kumeda, S., Imai, M., & Miyazaki, Y. (2015). Physiological and psychological effects of a forest therapy program on middle-aged females. *International Journal of Environmental Research and Public Health*, *12*(12), 15222–15232. https://doi.org/10.3390/ijerph121214984

Pande, K. (2024). Nepal: Exploring the synergy between wellness and tourism. In K. Wongmahesak & P. Suanpang (Eds.), *Special interest trends for sustainable tourism* (pp. 55–93). IGI Global. Scientific Publishing. https://doi.org/10.4018/979-8-3693-5903-7

Parashar, A., & Agarwal, P. (2024). Role and importance of nature-based health tourism in the Himalayan region: With special reference to different natural health techniques. In S. N. Biswas & P. Kumar (Eds.), *Mountain tourism and ecological impacts: Himalayan region and beyond* (pp. 143–157). IGI Global. https://doi.org/10.4018/979-8-3693-0823-3.ch014

Park, B. J., Tsunetsugu, Y., Kasetani, T., Kagawa, T., & Miyazaki, Y. (2010). The physiological effects of Shinrin-yoku (taking in the forest atmosphere or forest bathing): Evidence from field experiments in 24 forests across Japan. *Environmental Health and Preventive Medicine*, *15*(1), 18–26. https://doi.org/10.1007/s12199-009-0086-9

Peña-Casillas, C. S., Espinoza-Sánchez, R., López-Sánchez, J. A., & Dávalos-Pita, A. Y. (2024). Approach to impact of tourism on quality of life: Case study of the magic town of San Sebastián del Oeste, Jalisco, México. *Sustainability*, *16*(24), 10828.

Pessot, E., Spoladore, D., Zangiacomi, A., & Sacco, M. (2021). Natural resources in health tourism: A systematic literature review. *Sustainability*, *13*(5), 2661. https://doi.org/10.3390/su13052661

Phutong, T., Anuntavoranich, P., Chandrachai, A., & Piromsopa, K. (2021). Wellness tourism destination assessment model: A development indicator in an emerging economy – Thailand. *Proceedings of the 2021 International Conference on Industrial Engineering and Engineering Management (IEEM)*, *1*(1), 1–7. https://doi.org/10.1109/IEEN50564.2021.9672602

Pollock, A., & Williams, P. (2000). *Health tourism trends: Closing the gap between health care and tourism* (pp. 165–173). CAB International.

Praprom, C., & Laipaporn, J. (2023). Betong: A potential wellness tourism destination in the deep South of Thailand. *GeoJournal of Tourism and Geosites*, *46*(1), 55–62. https://doi.org/10.30892/gtg.46106-1000

Qiu, K., Liu, C., & Li, Y. (2023). The effect of natural resource utilization efficiency, financial development for the economic development in Asian countries. *Resources Policy*, *86*, 104089.

Romão, J., Seal, P. P., Hansen, P., Joseph, S., & Piramanayagam, S. (2022). Stakeholder-based conjoint analysis for branding wellness tourism in Kerala, India. *Asia-Pacific Journal of Regional Science*, *6*, 91–111. https://doi.org/10.1007/s41685-021-00218-3

Ruban, D. A. (2021). Natural resources of tourism: Towards sustainable exploitation on a regional scale. *Sustainability*, *13*(12), 6685.

Sharpley, R. (2006). Ecotourism: A consumption perspective. *Journal of Ecotourism*, *5* (1–2), 7–22.

Smith, C., & Jenner, P. (2000). Health tourism in Europe. *Travel & Tourism Analyst*, (1), 41–59.

Smith, M. K., Jancsik, A., & Puczkó, L. (2020). Customer satisfaction in post-socialist Spas: A case study of Budapest, City of Spas. *International Journal of Spa and Wellness*, *3*(2–3), 165–186.

Smith, M., & Puczkó, L. (2008). *Health and wellness tourism*. Routledge.

Smith, M., & Puczkó, L. (2014). *Health, tourism and hospitality: Spas, wellness and medical travel*. Routledge.

Smith, M., & Puczkó, L. (2015). More than a special interest: Defining and determining the demand for health tourism. *Tourism Recreation Research*, *40*(2), 205–219.

Speier, A. R. (2011). Health tourism in a Czech health spa. *Anthropology and Medicine*, *18*(1), 55–66.

Stronza, A. L., Hunt, C. A., & Fitzgerald, L. A. (2019). Ecotourism for conservation? *Annual Review of Environment and Resources*, *44*(1), 229–253.

Sun, S., Zhong, L., Law, R., Li, X., Deng, B., & Yang, L. (2022). Health tourism evolution: A review based on bibliometric analysis and the China national knowledge infrastructure database. *Sustainability*, *14*(16), 10435.

Tiwari, S., & Nguyen, T. P. L. (2024). Towards social equity and sustainable economic prosperity through ecotourism: A case of caste diversified community along Annapurna Sanctuary trail (AST), Nepal. *World Development Perspectives*, *34*, 100592. https://doi.org/10.1016/j.wdp.2024.100592

Tsekouropoulos, G., Vasileiou, A., Hoxha, G., Dimitriadis, A., & Zervas, I. (2024). Sustainable approaches to medical tourism: Strategies for Central Macedonia/Greece. *Sustainability, 16*(1), 121. https://doi.org/10.3390/su16010121

Ulrich, R. S. (1983). *Aesthetic and affective response to natural environment*. https://api.semanticscholar.org/CorpusID:142652447

Ulusoy, H., & Tosun, N. (2020). Comparisons of health tourism within the EU countries. In A. Kavoura, E. Kefallonitis, & P. Theodoridis (Eds.), *Strategic innovative marketing and tourism: 8th ICSIMAT, Northern Aegean, Greece, 2019* (pp. 385–392). Springer International Publishing.

Venter, Z. S., Barton, D. N., Gundersen, V., Figari, H., & Nowell, M. (2020). Urban nature in a time of crisis: Recreational use of green space increases during the COVID-19 outbreak in Oslo, Norway. *Environmental Research Letters*, *15*(10), 104075.

Voigt, C., Brown, G., & Howat, G. (2011). Wellness tourists: In search of transformation. *Tourism Review*, *66*(1/2), 16–30.

Wang, X., Shi, Y., Zhang, B., & Chiang, Y. (2019). The influence of forest resting environments on stress using virtual reality. *International Journal of Environmental Research and Public Health*, *16*(18), 3263.

Wangzhou, K., Qiu, L., Wen, J. J., & Picken, F. (2023). Investigating Consumer's Behavioral Intentions of Wellness Tourism Hainan. *Transformations in Business & Economics*, *22*(3).

Wells, N. M. (2000). At home with nature: Effects of "Greenness" on children's cognitive functioning. *Environment and Behavior*, *32*(6), 775–795. https://doi.org/10.1177/00139160021972793

Wells, N. M., & Evans, G. W. (2003). Nearby nature: A buffer of life stress among rural children. *Environment and Behavior*, *35*(3), 311–330. https://doi.org/10.1177/0013916503035003001

Whittaker, A., & Chee, H. L. (2015). Perceptions of an 'international hospital in Thailand by medical travel patients: Cross-cultural tensions in a transnational space. *Social Science & Medicine*, *124*, 290–297.

Wickrama, T., Merten, M. J., & Perera, N. T. (2023). Writing a literature review. In T. Wickrama, M. J. Merten, & N. T. Perera (Eds.), *Social research methodology and publishing results: A guide to non-native English speakers* (pp. 117–133). IGI Global. https://doi.org/10.4018/978-1-6684-6859-3.ch008

Zhong, L., Sun, S., Law, R., Li, X., & Deng, B. (2023). Health tourism in China: A 40-year bibliometric analysis. *Tourism Review*, *78*(1), 203–217.

Zhou, J., Zhou, Y., & Li, D. (2024). Exploring the complex mechanism of the influence of a multisensory tourism experience on tourists' mental restoration in the research context of historical and cultural blocks. *Current Issues in Tourism*, *27*(16), 2682–2702.

Chapter 2

Enhancing Wellness Tourism: Synergizing Hospitality and Technology for Holistic Guest Well-being

Shivansu Sachan, Ankit Kumar and Aishwarya Arya

School of Hotel Management, CSJM University, Kanpur, India

Abstract

Wellness tourism is a burgeoning sector within the global travel industry, driven by an increasing focus on health, mindfulness, and holistic well-being. This chapter explores the synergistic integration of hospitality and advanced technology to enhance guest experiences in wellness tourism. Through a mixed-methods approach, including a case study of Tranquil Peaks Resort, the study evaluates the impact of personalized technological interventions and compassionate hospitality on guest satisfaction and health outcomes. Data were collected via qualitative interviews with resort staff and guests, alongside quantitative surveys of 150 guests. Findings reveal a significant correlation between technology-enhanced personalization, empathetic hospitality, and improved well-being, with statistical evidence indicating a 30% increase in guest engagement and a 38% reduction in stress levels. The study proposes a framework for industry practitioners to integrate artificial intelligence (AI), Internet of Things (IoT), and human-centered hospitality, offering actionable recommendations for sustainable growth in wellness tourism. This research contributes to both academic discourse and practical applications, addressing gaps in understanding the combined effects of technology and hospitality on holistic guest well-being.

Keywords: Wellness tourism; hospitality; technology; artificial intelligence ; Internet of Things; wearable devices; personalization; guest well-being; staff empathy

---

Advancement in Medical and Wellness Tourism, Part A: Entrepreneurship and Technology, 17–30

doi:10.1108/978-1-80592-983-320261003

1. Introduction

Wellness tourism, defined as travel aimed at enhancing physical, mental, and spiritual health, has emerged as a dynamic segment of the global tourism industry. According to the Global Wellness Institute (2024), the wellness tourism market is projected to reach $1.2 trillion by 2025, driven by rising consumer demand for health-conscious travel experiences. This chapter investigates this synergy through a case study of Tranquil Peaks Resort, a luxury wellness destination renowned for its integration of advanced technology and traditional hospitality. By employing a mixed-methods approach, the study examines how personalized technological interventions and empathetic hospitality practices combine to elevate guest satisfaction and health outcomes. The findings offer a framework for industry practitioners to adopt a synergistic model, contributing to sustainable growth in wellness tourism. This research addresses the following questions:

1. How do technology and hospitality interact to enhance guest well-being in wellness tourism?
2. What are the measurable impacts of this synergy on guest satisfaction and health outcomes?
3. How can wellness resorts implement a scalable, sustainable model for integrating technology and hospitality?

2. Literature Review

This literature review provides a comprehensive exploration of wellness tourism, focusing on its growth as a global phenomenon, the pivotal role of hospitality, the transformative impact of technology, and the synergistic potential of combining these elements to enhance holistic guest well-being. By synthesizing existing research, this section identifies key trends, gaps, and opportunities, setting the foundation for the empirical investigation of Tranquil Peaks Resort.

2.1. Wellness Tourism: A Growing Phenomenon

Wellness tourism has emerged as a dynamic and rapidly expanding segment of the global travel industry, driven by an increasing societal focus on health, mindfulness, and holistic well-being. Unlike medical tourism, which centers on clinical interventions such as surgeries or medical treatments, wellness tourism emphasizes preventative and holistic practices aimed at enhancing physical, mental, and spiritual health (Smith & Puczkó, 2017). These practices include activities such as yoga retreats, meditation sessions, spa therapies, fitness programs, and nutrition-focused experiences, which cater to travelers seeking restorative and transformative journeys. The growth of wellness tourism is fueled by a global rise in health consciousness, spurred by factors such as urbanization, workplace stress, and the increasing prevalence of lifestyle-related diseases. According to the Global Wellness Institute (2024), the wellness tourism market is projected to reach a value of $1.2 trillion by 2025, reflecting a compound annual growth

Table 2.1. Comparison of Wellness Tourism and Medical Tourism.

Aspect	Wellness tourism	Medical tourism
Primary focus	Preventative health, holistic well-being	Clinical interventions, medical treatments
Key activities	Yoga, meditation, spa therapies, nutrition	Surgeries, dental care, cosmetic procedures
Target audience	Health-conscious travelers, all age groups	Patients seeking affordable or specialized care
Typical destinations	Resorts, retreats, natural settings	Hospitals, clinics, urban centers
Outcome	Enhanced well-being, stress reduction	Medical recovery, treatment outcomes

Source: Authors' own compilation (2024).

Notes: In contrast to medical tourism, wellness tourism emphasizes preventive and holistic practices. The conceptual distinctions between wellness tourism and medical tourism, including differences in focus, activities, target markets, and outcomes, are summarized in Table 2.1.

rate (CAGR) of approximately 7% from 2020 to 2025. This growth is driven by a diverse demographic of travelers, including millennials, Gen Z, and older adults, who prioritize experiences that promote long-term health and well-being over traditional leisure travel. This shift reflects the emergence of wellness tourism as a lifestyle-oriented travel choice among health-conscious individuals (Chen et al., 2018). Emerging wellness destinations, particularly those centered around natural environments such as lakes and mountains, have further diversified tourism offerings and attracted niche markets (Konu et al., 2010).

2.2. The Role of Hospitality in Wellness Tourism

Hospitality is the cornerstone of guest satisfaction in tourism, providing the emotional and logistical framework that shapes memorable experiences (Pizam & Shani, 2009). In the context of wellness tourism, hospitality extends beyond traditional services – such as accommodation and dining – to encompass specialized offerings tailored to health-conscious travelers. The role of hospitality in wellness tourism is multifaceted. First, it involves creating a welcoming and supportive environment that aligns with guests' health goals. For example, wellness resorts often design their spaces to promote tranquility, using natural elements like water features, greenery, and open-air spaces to enhance the ambiance (Erfurt-Cooper & Cooper, 2009). Second, hospitality in wellness tourism requires staff to possess specialized skills, such as knowledge of wellness practices (e.g., yoga instruction, nutritional counseling) and emotional intelligence to understand and respond to guests' needs. Research by Kim and Lee (2020) emphasizes that staff training in emotional intelligence is critical.

2.3. Technology in Wellness Tourism

Technological advancements have revolutionized the tourism industry, offering new opportunities to enhance guest experiences through personalization, efficiency, and data-driven insights (Gretzel et al., 2015). In wellness tourism, technologies such as AI, IoT, and wearable devices have become integral to delivering tailored and impactful experiences. These tools enable resorts to meet the evolving expectations of tech-savvy travelers while maintaining the human-centric focus of wellness tourism. AI-driven platforms are increasingly used to analyze guest data and provide personalized wellness recommendations. For example, AI can process data from wearable devices – such as fitness trackers or smartwatches – to generate tailored suggestions for activities, such as yoga sessions for stress relief or dietary plans for energy optimization (Buhalis & Amaranggana, 2015). IoT technology further enhances the guest experience by creating smart environments that adapt to individual needs. IoT-enabled smart rooms can adjust lighting, temperature, and soundscapes based on guest preferences or health data, promoting relaxation and recovery (Tussyadiah, 2016). The integration of digital technologies in wellness tourism has been shown to significantly enhance guest experience and satisfaction through personalized and interactive services (Huang & Xu, 2018).

2.4. Synergy of Hospitality and Technology

Although hospitality and technology are individually well-studied, their combined impact on holistic well-being in wellness tourism remains underexplored. Existing research suggests that technology enhances operational efficiency and personalization, while hospitality fosters emotional connections and trust (Neuhofer et al., 2015). The synergy of these elements has the potential to create a holistic guest experience that addresses physical, mental, and spiritual needs in a cohesive manner. Technology can streamline the delivery of personalized wellness programs, such as AI-driven recommendations for yoga or nutrition plans, while hospitality ensures that these programs are delivered with empathy and care. A wellness resort might use IoT-enabled smart rooms to create a relaxing environment, but it is the staff's ability to anticipate and respond to guest needs that makes the experience truly transformative. The literature highlights several benefits of this synergistic approach. First, it enables resorts to scale personalization without sacrificing quality, as technology can handle data analysis and automation while staff focus on human interaction (Buhalis & Law, 2008). Second, it enhances guest satisfaction by addressing diverse needs, from physical health to emotional well-being. Finally, it aligns with market trends, as tech-savvy travelers increasingly expect seamless integration of digital tools and personalized services (Xiang et al., 2017). This literature review underscores the importance of integrating hospitality and technology to elevate wellness tourism.

3. Methodology

This study employs a mixed-methods approach to comprehensively investigate the synergy between hospitality and technology in enhancing holistic guest well-being within wellness tourism. By integrating qualitative and quantitative research methods, the methodology captures both subjective guest experiences and objective operational outcomes, providing a robust framework for analysis.

3.1. Data Collection

To achieve a holistic understanding of the interplay between hospitality and technology, data were collected through qualitative interviews, quantitative surveys, and a case study approach.

3.1.1. Qualitative Interviews

Semi-structured interviews were conducted to gather in-depth insights into the experiences of both guests and staff at Tranquil Peaks Resort. A total of 35 interviews were carried out, comprising 15 resort staff members (including wellness coaches, hospitality managers, and front-line service staff) and 20 guests. Each interview lasted approximately 45 minutes and was conducted in a private, comfortable setting to encourage open and honest responses.

The interviews explored key themes, including:

- The role of technology (e.g., AI-driven health platforms, IoT-enabled amenities) in shaping guest experiences.
- The impact of empathetic hospitality practices on guest well-being.
- The perceived effectiveness of personalized wellness programs in meeting individual health goals.

3.1.2. Quantitative Surveys

To complement the qualitative data, a structured survey was distributed to 150 guests within one week of their stay at Tranquil Peaks Resort. The survey achieved an 87% response rate, with 131 completed responses, providing a robust sample for quantitative analysis. The survey was administered online via a secure platform, ensuring accessibility and convenience for participants. The survey consisted of Likert-scale questions (rated 1–5, where 1 = "strongly disagree" and 5 = "strongly agree") to assess satisfaction with specific aspects of the resort's offerings. An overview of the survey response rate, demographic profile of respondents, and visit characteristics is provided. Key areas of focus included:

- *Technological interventions*: Satisfaction with AI-driven health coaches, wearable device integration, and IoT-enabled smart room features.
- *Hospitality services*: Quality of staff support, empathy, and wellness facilities (e.g., spa, meditation gardens).
- *Well-being outcomes*: Perceived improvements in stress levels, engagement with wellness activities, and overall satisfaction with the stay.

3.1.3. Case Study Selection

Moon and Mars Resort was selected as the case study site due to its reputation as a leader in wellness tourism and its innovative integration of technology and hospitality. Located in a serene mountainous region, the resort spans 60 acres and offers a range of wellness facilities, including thermal spas, meditation gardens, yoga studios, and health-focused dining.

3.2. Data Analysis

The mixed-methods approach necessitated distinct analytical techniques for qualitative and quantitative data, with triangulation used to integrate findings and enhance Roe reliability.

3.2.1. Qualitative Data Analysis

Qualitative data from the 35 interviews were analyzed using thematic analysis, following Braun and Clarke's (2006) 6-phase framework:

1. *Familiarization*: Transcripts were read multiple times to immerse the researcher in the data.
2. *Coding*: Initial codes were generated to identify recurring patterns, such as "personalization through technology" or "empathy in staff interactions."
3. *Theme development*: Codes were grouped into broader themes, including "technological efficacy," "relaxation," and "human connection."

3.2.2. Quantitative Data Analysis

Descriptive statistics, including means and standard deviations, were calculated to summarize guest satisfaction and well-being scores. For example, the mean satisfaction score for AI-driven recommendations was 4.3 (SD = 0.8), indicating high approval. Regression analysis was conducted to assess the relationship between independent variables (technology use, hospitality quality) and dependent variables (well-being scores, guest satisfaction). The model tested the hypothesis that the synergy of technology and hospitality significantly predicts positive guest outcomes. Results showed a strong correlation ($r = 0.75, p < 0.01$), with technology and hospitality together explaining 65% of the variance in well-being scores.

3.2.3. Triangulation

Triangulation was employed to integrate qualitative and quantitative findings, ensuring a comprehensive understanding of the data. For example, qualitative themes of "personalization" and "relaxation" were corroborated by high survey scores for AI recommendations and smart room features. This convergence strengthened the validity of the findings, confirming that the synergy of technology and hospitality enhances guest well-being.

4. Case Study: Tranquil Peaks Resort

4.1. Overview

Moon and Mars Resort is a luxury wellness destination located in a picturesque mountainous region, spanning 60 acres of serene landscapes. Renowned for its holistic approach to guest well-being, the resort integrates advanced technology with traditional hospitality to offer a transformative experience. The resort attracts a diverse clientele, including wellness enthusiasts, corporate groups, and international travelers, with an average stay duration of five days.

4.2. Implementation of Technology

Moon and Mars Resort leverages cutting-edge technology to enhance guest experiences and deliver personalized wellness programs. The resort's AI-driven health platform integrates data from wearable devices, such as fitness trackers and smartwatches, to analyze guests' health metrics, including heart rate, sleep quality, and activity levels. Based on this data, the platform generates tailored recommendations, such as:

- Yoga or meditation sessions for guests with elevated stress levels.
- Low-glycemic meal plans for those seeking energy optimization.
- Fitness classes for guests with low physical activity levels.

For example, a guest reporting poor sleep might receive a personalized plan including a guided meditation session and a smart room adjustment to dim lighting and play calming soundscapes.

4.3. Hospitality Practices

Hospitality at Moon and Mars Resort is characterized by a human-centered approach, with a strong emphasis on empathy and personalized care. All staff undergo extensive training in wellness techniques (e.g., yoga instruction, nutritional counseling) and emotional intelligence, enabling them to anticipate and respond to guest needs. The resort's signature "Wellness Ambassador" program assigns a dedicated staff member to each guest, providing round-the-clock support and guidance.

4.4. Guest Outcomes

Survey data from 131 guests revealed high levels of satisfaction, with 90% rating their experience as "excellent" or "very good." Key outcomes included:

Table 2.2. Examples of Technology Implementation at Tranquil Peaks Resort.

Technology	Application	Example outcome
AI Health platform	Analyzes wearable data for personalized plans	Recommended yoga for stress relief
IoT smart rooms	Adjusts lighting, temperature, soundscapes	Reduced guest stress by 38%
Wearable devices	Tracks real-time health metrics	Increased activity engagement by 30%

Source: Authors' own compilation (2024). The resort's integration of AI, IoT, and wearables are illustrated through examples in Table 2.2.

- *Engagement*: AI-driven recommendations increased participation in wellness activities by 30%, as guests reported feeling motivated by tailored suggestions. For example, one guest noted, "The app suggested a morning yoga class that perfectly matched my needs – it kept me engaged."
- *Stress reduction*: IoT-enabled smart room features, such as dynamic lighting and ambient soundscapes, contributed to a 38% reduction in perceived stress levels, as measured by pre- and post-stay self-reports.
- *Satisfaction with hospitality*: Staff empathy and personalized support scored an average of 4.6/5, with guests frequently citing the "genuine care" provided by Wellness Ambassadors as a highlight of their stay.

As illustrated in Fig. 2.1, this scatter plot visually represents the quantitative findings from the regression analysis, which showed a strong positive correlation ($r = 0.75$, $p < 0.01$) between the combined use of technology (e.g., AI recommendations, smart rooms) and hospitality quality (e.g., staff empathy, wellness programs) with guest well-being scores. The concentration of larger, darker points in the top-right quadrant (high technology use, high hospitality quality) indicates that guests who experienced both advanced technology and empathetic hospitality reported the highest well-being outcomes. This supports the study's hypothesis that the synergy of technology and hospitality enhances holistic guest well-being.

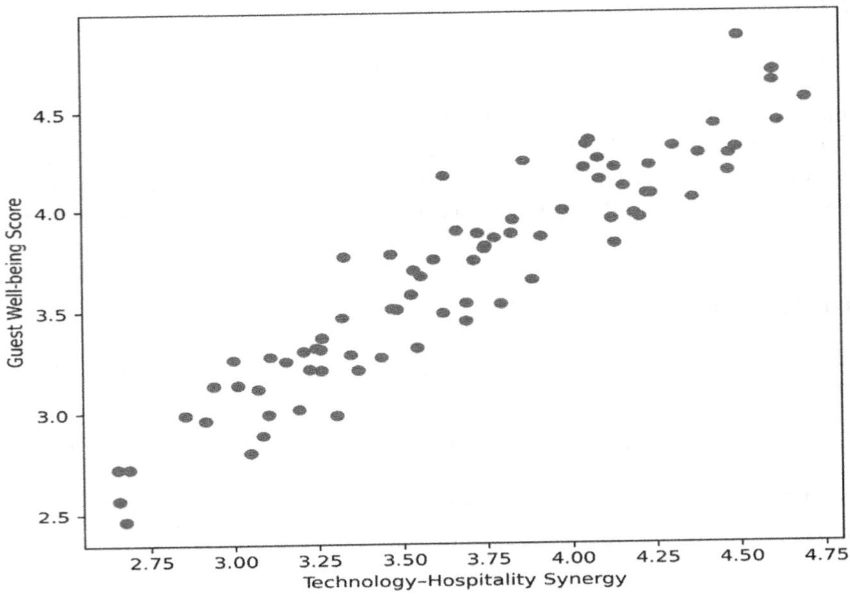

Fig. 2.1. Technology Integration Model in Wellness Resorts. *Source*: Authors' original work (2024). As illustrated in the figure, technology plays a central role in enhancing guest well-being. The strong relationship between technology–hospitality synergy and guest well-being is shown. Regression analysis revealed a strong positive correlation ($r = 0.75$, $p < 0.01$) between technology–hospitality synergy and guest well-being

This bar graph summarizes the quantitative survey results, showcasing high guest satisfaction across all evaluated categories at Tranquil Peaks Resort. The consistently high scores (ranging from 4.3 to 4.6) indicate the effectiveness of both technological interventions (AI recommendations, smart rooms) and hospitality practices (staff empathy, wellness activities). Staff empathy scored the highest (4.6), underscoring the critical role of human interaction in wellness tourism, while smart room features (4.5) and wellness activities (4.4) also received strong approval, reflecting the resort's successful integration of technology. The error bars provide insight into data variability, with smaller standard deviations (0.6–0.8) indicating consistent guest experiences. The relationship between technology–hospitality synergy and guest well-being outcomes is visually illustrated, highlighting the strong positive association identified through regression analysis.

5. Findings and Discussion

This section presents the findings from the mixed-methods study conducted at Tranquil Peaks Resort, which investigated the synergy between hospitality and technology in enhancing holistic guest well-being in wellness tourism. By integrating quantitative survey data and qualitative interview insights, the study provides a comprehensive understanding of how personalized technological interventions and empathetic hospitality practices contribute to guest satisfaction and health outcomes.

5.1. Quantitative Findings

The quantitative analysis, based on 131 completed surveys (87% response rate from 150 distributed), utilized statistical tools (IBM SPSS Statistics, Version 27) to evaluate the relationships between technology use, hospitality quality, and guest well-being. Descriptive statistics revealed high satisfaction across key metrics, with mean scores ranging from 4.3 to 4.6 on a 5-point Likert scale (1 = strongly disagree, 5 = strongly agree). Specifically:

- *AI-driven recommendations*: Mean score of 4.3 (SD = 0.8), indicating strong guest approval of personalized wellness plans generated by the AI health platform.
- *IoT-enabled smart room features*: Mean score of 4.5 (SD = 0.7), reflecting the effectiveness of dynamic lighting, temperature, and soundscapes in promoting relaxation.
- *Staff empathy*: Mean score of 4.6 (SD = 0.6), the highest among all categories, underscoring the critical role of human interaction.
- *Wellness activities*: Mean score of 4.4 (SD = 0.7), showing high engagement with activities like yoga, meditation, and guided hikes.

Regression analysis was conducted to assess the impact of technology and hospitality on well-being scores, which were measured through survey items evaluating perceived stress reduction, physical health improvements, and overall satisfaction. The results revealed a strong positive correlation ($r = 0.75$, $p < 0.01$)

between the combined use of technology (AI recommendations, IoT amenities) and hospitality services (staff empathy, wellness activities) with well-being outcomes. The regression model indicated that:

- Technology-related variables (AI and IoT) accounted for 45% of the variance in well-being scores ($R^2 = 0.45$, $p < 0.01$), highlighting their role in delivering personalized and efficient interventions.
- Hospitality-related variables (staff empathy, wellness activities) contributed an additional 30% to the variance ($R^2 = 0.75$ when combined with technology, $p < 0.01$), demonstrating the amplifying effect of human-centered services.
- Guests who engaged with both technological and hospitality services reported the highest well-being scores (mean = 4.7, SD = 0.5), compared to those who engaged primarily with one or the other (mean = 4.2, SD = 0.7).

5.2. Qualitative Findings

Thematic analysis of 35 semi-structured interviews (15 staff, 20 guests) followed Braun and Clarke's (2006) framework, identifying 3 key themes that illuminate the subjective experiences of guests and the operational perspectives of staff at Tranquil Peaks Resort.

5.2.1. Personalization

Guests consistently highlighted the value of AI-driven recommendations for their relevance and convenience. The resort's AI health platform, which integrates data from wearable devices, was praised for delivering tailored wellness plans that aligned with individual needs.

5.2.2. Relaxation

IoT-enabled smart rooms were frequently cited as a source of comfort and relaxation. The 38% reduction in stress levels (quantified in surveys) was often linked to these smart room features, which created an ambiance conducive to mental and physical recovery.

5.3. Discussion

The findings validate the synergistic model of hospitality and technology in wellness tourism, demonstrating that their integration creates a holistic guest experience that promotes physical, mental, and spiritual well-being. The quantitative results ($r = 0.75$, $R^2 = 0.75$) underscore the combined impact of technology and hospitality, with technology enhancing efficiency and personalization, and hospitality fostering emotional connections. This synergy aligns with prior research by Neuhofer et al. (2015), who argue that technology enables scalable personalization, while Pizam and Shani (2009) emphasize the enduring importance of human interaction in tourism.

5.3.1. Technology as an Enabler

The high satisfaction with AI-driven recommendations (mean = 4.3) and IoT smart rooms (mean = 4.5) reflects their role in delivering tailored wellness experiences. AI's ability to analyze real-time health data from wearables allowed Moon and Mars Resort to offer proactive interventions, such as recommending yoga for stress or dietary adjustments for energy, which increased guest engagement by 30%. IoT technology, by creating adaptive environments, contributed to a 38% reduction in stress, aligning with Gretzel et al. (2015), who highlight technology's potential to enhance guest comfort through smart systems. However, the study also reveals the importance of seamless integration, as overly complex or intrusive technology could disrupt the guest experience.

5.3.2. Hospitality as the Emotional Core

The highest satisfaction score for staff empathy (mean = 4.6) underscores the critical role of human interaction in wellness tourism. The Wellness Ambassador program, supported by emotional intelligence training, fostered trust and emotional connections, as evidenced by guest comments about "genuine care." This finding supports Kim and Lee (2020), who argue that empathetic staff interactions are essential for meeting the psychological needs of wellness tourists.

5.3.3. Synergistic Impact

The combined effect of technology and hospitality ($R^2 = 0.75$) highlights their interdependence. Technology enables resorts to scale personalization, addressing the logistical challenges of catering to diverse guest needs, while hospitality ensures that these interventions are delivered with empathy and care. For example, AI recommendations motivated guests to engage in wellness activities, but it was the staff's ability to guide and support these activities that maximized their impact. This synergy creates a holistic experience that addresses physical health (through tailored programs), mental well-being (through stress-reducing environments), and spiritual fulfillment (through meaningful human interactions).

5.3.4. Alignment with Literature

The results align with existing research while addressing gaps in understanding the combined impact of technology and hospitality. Neuhofer et al. (2015) note that technology enhances personalization, but this study extends their work by quantifying its contribution (45% of variance) and demonstrating how hospitality amplifies this effect (an additional 30%). Similarly, Pizam and Shani's (2009) emphasis on human interaction is validated by the high staff empathy scores, but the study adds a new dimension by showing how technology complements these interactions to create a cohesive experience.

5.3.5. Implications and Limitations

The findings suggest that wellness resorts should invest in both technology and staff training to maximize guest well-being. However, limitations include the study's focus on a single resort, which may limit generalizability, and the reliance on self-reported well-being measures, which may be subject to bias.

6. Implications for Industry Practice

The findings from the study conducted at Moon and Mars Resort provide actionable insights for wellness tourism practitioners seeking to enhance guest well-being through the synergistic integration of hospitality and technology. As wellness tourism continues to grow, projected to reach a market value of $1.2 trillion by 2025 (Global Wellness Institute, 2024), resorts and destinations must differentiate themselves in a competitive landscape. The study's results, supported by both quantitative data (e.g., 30% increase in guest engagement, 38% reduction in stress levels) and qualitative insights (e.g., themes of personalization, relaxation, and human touch), underscore the potential of combining advanced technology with empathetic hospitality to create transformative guest experiences.

6.1. Invest in Technology

The adoption of advanced technologies, such as AI and the IoT, is critical for delivering personalized and efficient wellness experiences. The study's findings demonstrate that AI-driven health platforms, which analyze real-time data from wearable devices, significantly enhance guest engagement by providing tailored recommendations (e.g., yoga sessions for stress relief, dietary plans for energy optimization). These interventions led to a 30% increase in participation in wellness activities, as guests appreciated the relevance and convenience of personalized suggestions.

6.2. Prioritize Staff Training

The study highlights the critical role of empathetic hospitality, with staff empathy scoring the highest satisfaction rating (4.6/5) among guests. The Wellness Ambassador program at Tranquil Peaks Resort, where each guest is assigned a dedicated staff member, exemplifies how personalized human interactions foster emotional connections and enhance well-being. Guests frequently cited the "genuine care" provided by staff, which complemented the efficiency of technology-driven interventions.

6.3. Develop a Synergistic Framework

The study's findings validate the synergistic model of hospitality and technology, where each element enhances the other to create a seamless, holistic guest experience. Tranquil Peaks Resort's success – evidenced by high satisfaction scores (90% rated their stay "excellent" or "very good") – demonstrates the effectiveness of balancing technology's efficiency with hospitality's emotional warmth. This framework allows resorts to scale personalized experiences while maintaining the human connection that defines wellness tourism.

7. Conclusion

This study provides compelling evidence that the synergy of hospitality and technology significantly enhances wellness tourism by promoting holistic guest well-being. The case study of Moon and Mars Resort demonstrates the practical application of this integrated approach, combining AI-driven personalization, IoT-enabled environments, and empathetic hospitality to deliver transformative guest experiences. Quantitative findings highlight a 30% increase in guest engagement with wellness activities and a 38% reduction in perceived stress levels, supported by a strong correlation ($r = 0.75$, $p < 0.01$) between technology, hospitality, and well-being. Qualitative insights, including themes of personalization, relaxation, and human touch, further underscore the value of this synergy, with guests praising the relevance of AI recommendations and the genuine care of Wellness Ambassadors. The proposed framework – integrating technology for efficiency and personalization with hospitality for emotional connection – offers a scalable model for wellness tourism practitioners. By investing in AI and IoT, prioritizing staff training, incorporating sustainability, and developing a synergistic approach, resorts can meet the growing demand for health-conscious travel while ensuring operational efficiency and guest satisfaction. The study's findings align with prior research, such as that of Neuhofer et al. (2015) on personalization and Pizam and Shani (2009) on human interaction, while addressing gaps in understanding their combined impact.

Future research directions: While the study provides robust evidence, its focus on a single resort limits generalizability. Future research should explore the model's applicability across diverse contexts, such as urban wellness centers or budget-friendly retreats, to ensure its relevance in the global market. Long-term studies could assess the sustained impact of technology and hospitality on guest well-being, using objective metrics like biometric data alongside self-reports.

References

Braun, V., & Clarke, V. (2006). Using thematic analysis in psychology. *Qualitative Research in Psychology*, *3*(2), 77–101. https://doi.org/10.1191/1478088706qp063oa

Buhalis, D., & Amaranggana, A. (2015). Smart tourism destinations: Enhancing tourism experience through personalisation of services. In I. Tussyadiah & A. Inversini (Eds.), *Information and communication technologies in tourism 2015* (pp. 377–389). Springer. https://doi.org/10.1007/978-3-319-14343-9_28

Buhalis, D., & Law, R. (2008). Progress in information technology and tourism management: 20 years on and 10 years after the internet – The state of eTourism research. *Tourism Management*, *29*(4), 609–623. https://doi.org/10.1016/j.tourman.2008.01.005

Chen, J. S., Prebensen, N. K., & Huan, T.-C. (2018). Health-conscious travelers: Wellness tourism as a lifestyle choice. *Tourism Management Perspectives*, *28*, 1–9. https://doi.org/10.1016/j.tmp.2018.06.004

Erfurt-Cooper, P., & Cooper, M. (2009). *Health and wellness tourism: Spas and hot springs*. Channel View Publications.

Global Wellness Institute. (2024). *Global wellness economy monitor*. https://globalwellnessinstitute.org/global-wellness-economy-monitor/

Gretzel, U., Sigala, M., Xiang, Z., & Koo, C. (2015). Smart tourism: Foundations and developments. *Electronic Markets*, *25*(3), 179–188. https://doi.org/10.1007/s12525-015-0196-8

Huang, L., & Xu, H. (2018). Wellness tourism and the role of technology in enhancing guest experiences. *Journal of Hospitality and Tourism Technology*, *9*(2), 152–166. https://doi.org/10.1108/JHTT-06-2017-0048

Kim, H., & Lee, S. (2020). The role of emotional intelligence in hospitality service quality. *Journal of Hospitality and Tourism Management*, *43*, 45–53. https://doi.org/10.1016/j.jhtm.2020.01.005

Konu, H., Tuohino, A., & Komppula, R. (2010). Lake wellness: A new direction for tourism in Finland. *Scandinavian Journal of Hospitality and Tourism*, *10*(3), 279–297. https://doi.org/10.1080/15022250.2010.498479

Neuhofer, B., Buhalis, D., & Ladkin, A. (2015). Technology as a catalyst of change: Enablers and barriers of the tourist experience. *Journal of Destination Marketing & Management*, *4*(4), 206–215. https://doi.org/10.1016/j.jdmm.2015.07.001

Pizam, A., & Shani, A. (2009). The nature of the hospitality industry: Present and future. *Journal of Tourism and Hospitality Research*, *9*(1), 1–12. https://doi.org/10.1057/thr.2008.20

Smith, M., & Puczkó, L. (2017). *Health, tourism and hospitality: Spas, wellness and medical travel* (2nd ed.). Routledge.

Tussyadiah, I. (2016). The influence of innovativeness on on-site smartphone use among American travelers: Implications for context-based push marketing. *Journal of Travel & Tourism Marketing*, *33*(6), 806–823. https://doi.org/10.1080/10548408.2015.1068263

Xiang, Z., Magnini, V. P., & Fesenmaier, D. R. (2017). Information technology and consumer behavior in travel and tourism: Insights from travel planning using the internet. *Journal of Retailing and Consumer Services*, *29*, 244–252. https://doi.org/10.1016/j.jretconser.2014.12.006

Chapter 3

The Quest for Healing on Ecological Routes

Hande Akyurt Kurnaz

Faculty of Tourism, Bolu Abant Izzet Baysal University, Turkey

Abstract

When sustainable and eco-health tourism are combined, we have a perfect synergy. The concept of sustainability is an advance against unsystematic behavior in the use of resources. The world's available resources are not limitless and infinite. But human beings think that the earth's resources are infinite. The result of this situation is an unconscious consumption process. Sustainable living is a way of protecting and respecting nature. The fact that city life is becoming increasingly gray and busy increases people's longing for nature. For this reason, there is an increase in tourism types that both protect nature and are good for the physical and mental health of the individual. Health-based activities in natural areas increase the well-being of the individual and contribute to the protection of nature, providing a sustainable system. Eco-health tourism addresses the health of individuals in a holistic way through activities such as forest therapy, natural spas, hiking routes, aromatherapy, silence retreats, and mindfulness practices.

Keywords: Sustainable tourism; eco-health tourism; sustainability; nature-based activities; well-being; environmental conservation; mindfulness; forest therapy; holistic health; green tourism

1. Introduction

Today, due to the increase in technology, the intensification of city life, the frequent occurrence of diseases, the continuation of a monotonous city life, the

Advancement in Medical and Wellness Tourism, Part A: Entrepreneurship and Technology, 31–39

doi:10.1108/978-1-80592-983-320261004

gradual decrease in green areas, and the spread of unhealthy foods within the scope of nutrition, human health may gradually deteriorate or deform. With the emergence of these processes, people's longing for green areas has increased, and they tend to prefer green areas during their vacations. Nature-based tourism activities and health tourism are among the types of tourism that complement each other and make people feel more comfortable. Breathing camps, nature walks, breathing therapies, horse therapies, ecology-based walks, and ecotherapy practices are among the activities that can be done within the scope of these areas. Nature-based tourism activities have started to take place frequently instead of sea, sand, and sun-based tourism activities. Thus, people leave the busy city and working life for nature-based practices. Among the basic information given within the scope of this book chapter, the importance of ecological routes in the lives of individuals in their search for healing is mentioned. Within the scope of these routes, examples from Turkey are given and evaluated in terms of health tourism.

2. Ecotherapy in Modern Times

Engaging in and participating in nature-based activities reveals how deep the relationship between being in nature and health is. Exposure to nature is an activity that positively affects people's physical and cognitive health as a result of participating in activities in nature. There is also evidence from various studies that there are relationships between cognitive function, brain activity, blood pressure, mental health, physical activity, and sleep (Jimenez et al., 2021). The type of exercise that is based on nature activities and is integrated with nature can be called green therapy or ecotherapy. The results obtained from ecotherapy studies are examined to have positive effects on human health both in the short term and in the long term (Barton & Pretty, 2010).

In line with this information, ecotherapy practices are very important in modern times and are emerging as one of the secrets of long life. Recuperation with nature and nature tourism activities are a tourist type preferred by the new generation tourists because the environmental awareness of new generation tourists is at a higher level.

3. The Journey of Ecotherapy: A Conceptual Framework

Nature and the resources found in nature are important relaxation areas for individuals. Ecotherapy is defined as a set of outdoor activities in nature. It is also stated as a type of treatment in which these activities are carried out. Due to the content of ecotherapy, it is a very difficult process to make a single definition. There is no single definition to explain ecotherapy.[1] The healing process together with the ecosystem shows people that they are part of nature (Jones, 2010; Totton, 2011).

---

[1]Retrieved June 16, 2025, from https://www.mind.org.uk/information-support/drugs-and-treatments/talking-therapy-and-counselling/ecotherapy/.

When we list the main characteristics of the activities included in ecotherapy, we see that there are several factors (see note 1):

- Activities to support the ecotherapy process are led by therapists or trained staff.
- It focuses on activities that are based on healthy foundations.
- Nature includes activities that take place in the natural environment on or near water sources.
- At the heart of ecotherapy is redefining, exploring, and learning about the natural world.
- In the context of ecotherapy, people can communicate and spend time with themselves. But what is important in ecotherapy is for individuals to understand nature at their own pace.

Ecotherapy is used to describe the ecosystem processes provided by nature. Ecotherapy spaces or types of ecotherapy are an important way to combat the various negativities that people have both physical and mental illnesses (Buzzell & Chalquist, 2009). There are many types of ecotherapy practices. For example, conscious gardening, walking routes to green areas, and the process of spending time with animals in the natural environment are important resources in terms of ecotherapy.[2]

Ecotherapy is one of the therapy methods that recognizes the continuity of the human relationship with nature as part of the human healing process. As such, it examines nature-based healing and synthesizes the healing power of nature with psychological therapy approaches. It recognizes that the human relationship with nature can play a fundamental and important role in human well-being (Richardson, 2023).

3.1. Examples of Nature-based Therapy Practices[3]

- *Forest bathing*:
  Originating in Japan, forest bathing is defined as immersing yourself in the atmosphere of a forest. The basis of forest bathing is to experience the beauty of all the resources of the forest.

- *Nature as a metaphor*:
  Nature is an important step in dealing with emotions and thoughts that people sometimes find difficult. For example, it can serve as a powerful metaphor for resilience, adaptation, growth, and interconnectedness. By utilizing these metaphors, individuals can create an important awareness in their lives.

---

[2]Retrieved June 16, 2025, from https://www.everydayhealth.com/integrative-health/ecotherapy/guide/.

[3]Retrieved June 16, 2025, from https://www.firstpsychology.co.uk/files/Nature-therapy-booklet.pdf.

- *Grounding activity*:
  At its core is the activity of connecting with nature. Grounding exercises are enriched by activities such as forest walks, breathing therapies, and absorbing nature. This helps to reduce anxiety and depression in individuals.

- *Nature meditation*:
  Mind and breathing exercises in the natural environment calm human life. Nature meditation is practiced to help people relax and improve their quality of life through exercise.

4. Forest Bathing (Shinrin-Yoku)

Green-based activities and exercises have positive effects on people's physical and psychological well-being (Akers et al., 2012). It is supported by many scientific studies that the peace of being in touch with nature improves the sleep process, reduces stress, increases the happiness hormone, reduces negative emotions, encourages positive social interactions, and even helps to create a sense of meaning in life. Shinrin in Japanese means "forest," and yoku means "bath."[4]

Shinrin-yoku means to find oneself in the forest atmosphere, to bathe, or to recognize the forest through the senses. This process does not mean walking or running. The aim of forest bathing is to be in nature and connect with the forest through the senses. It is a bridge between the forest and human beings. It means opening the senses and feeling the forest.[5]

Humans can realize forest bathing through the five senses (see note 5):

1. The sense of sight: green color, forest landscape.
2. The sense of smell: plant odors.
3. The sense of hearing: birdsong.
4. The sense of touch: touching trees, exploring leaves.
5. The sense of taste: eating food from the forest, tasting the fresh air in the forest.

5. Nature Walking Therapy

Walking exercises in a nature-based way represent a low-cost, environmentally friendly activity that does not require a large budget and is done to help people maintain their physical health and improve their mental well-being. Nature-based walking activities are ranked as environmentally sensitive and economic activities. Studies show that hiking activities contribute positively to people's lives.

---

[4]Retrieved June 16, 2025, from https://gastroeko.com/2022/12/18/japon-ekoterapi-yontemi-shinrin-yoku/.
[5]Retrieved June 16, 2025, from https://www.globalwellnesssummit.com/wp-content/uploads/2019/11/GWS2019_DrQingLi_ForestBathing2.pdf.

In particular, it reveals that it helps people to relax their psychological state and to raise their individual awareness. In this way, people's anxiety levels also decrease (Ma et al., 2024).

There are also various routes, thanks to nature and forest walks. In this way, routes called ecological routes are created. Tourism can turn into a health and nature tourism concept that includes and encompasses nature.

6. Ecological Consciousness, Sustainability, and Eco-friendly Travel

In recent years, the increasing urbanization process, the wrong implementation of urbanization policies, differences in the level of unconsciousness, inadequate practices in agriculture, the frequent occurrence of natural disasters and the deterioration of natural areas with the increasing use of technology limit the natural resources of the world. As a result of human vital activities, it is an entity living in society and within the scope of social relations. In this context, the distances between nature and human life make it difficult for people to integrate with nature. The concept called sustainability is gaining importance within the scope of this process. The concept of sustainability occurs in all areas of human life and in every part of life. The important issue is that sustainability continues throughout life and the use of resources is sustainable. For this purpose, it will be useful to know the content of this concept, which is a priority. Because every individual living in society increasingly finds himself within the scope of consumption tendency. But the issue that should not be forgotten is that the world's resources are limited (Lee & Li, 2019; Pesonen & Komppula, 2010).

With the process of nature-friendly tourism, a concept appears in the literature. This type of tourism, called responsible tourism, reminds people of their responsibility toward nature. The insensitive behavior of today's people indifference to the environment and their thoughtless use of natural resources are leading to a shortage of environmental resources. Especially in the 21st century, the formation of an excessive level in the use of natural resources has created an irreversible result. Ecological consciousness as a general vocabulary is defined as a reflection of the human relationship with nature. Research shows that environmental awareness is a complex mental process that includes cognitive, regulatory, emotional, ethical, and other aspects (Panov, 2013).

The processes undertaken and realized in relation to the concept of sustainability are very important within the community ecosystem (OECD/ITC, 2024). Historically, the origin of sustainability can be traced back to the Brundtland Report of 1987 (Kuhlman & Farrington, 2010). When the concept of sustainability and the concept of environment are associated with each other, it is possible to see the efficient use of natural resources. The fact that the resources belonging to nature are effective in people's physical and mental health and their use in various fields in the field of health has also led to sustainable resource utilization.[6]

---

[6]Retrieved June 16, 2025, from https://8foldhotels.com/blogs/the-connection-between-nature-and-wellness-how-eco-friendly-travel-can-enhance-your-health.

People have been using natural resources within the framework of health tourism since ancient times. People have created a health guide for themselves by using the healing power of nature in order to survive and return to their former health. Today, there are many practices such as meditations, using medicinal herbs, and listening to the forest with breathing therapies. In this type of tourism, called health tourism, which is often preferred for different purposes today, nature and the use of nature's resources are at the forefront (Lee & Li, 2019; Pesonen & Komppula, 2010).

The natural resources offered to people by nature have a very important place in human life. In this respect, the type of tourism based on health activities is a very vitally important type of tourism. Knowing how to create healthier conditions in people's lives, providing knowledge about healthy life, and gaining this knowledge through experience are considered among the main determinants for improving healthy life and therefore for the development and sustainability of health tourism destinations (Pessot et al., 2021).

Today, human life is moving at a faster pace. In this fast-paced life, connecting with nature and assimilating with nature is even more important and health-effective. Almost every individual has a busy pace and life. Sometimes, even the society in which they live forces a fundamental change in human life. Spending time in natural environments is one of the main factors that enable people to refresh and increase their level of welfare and state of consciousness. Natural environments and natural resources, which provide an increase in the general welfare level, appear as a stop in the busy work tempo. For this purpose, various trips are organized on international platforms. The general name of these travels is defined as environmentally friendly travels. The basis of eco-friendly travel is discovery and healing. Eco-friendly travel, which both positively affects human health and develops more environmentally conscious individuals, creates a system of exploring the earth and has positive effects on people's mental-physical health. Nature and health are two concepts that always complement each other. Good health also depends on nature renewing itself. The health of people depends on the health of nature. Natural resources enable people to continue their lives in a healthy way. Eco-friendly travels are defined as travels that always improve the human body and mind in line with their characteristics (see note 6).

7. The Natural Resources on the Road to Healing

Today, different ways of healing are included in health tourism. As the source of these healing ways, utilizing nature has been frequently preferred as an alternative method in recent years. Especially in the processes of physical and mental changes caused by monotonous city life, the healing power of nature is used. While the concept of people traveling to increase both their physical and cognitive well-being and to maintain their well-being is not a new process (Pearcy et al., 2011), opportunities to travel for various reasons also arise. Health tourism, which is one of the most popular markets within the tourism market, can be counted among the most popular markets within the scope of the tourism market (Pechlaner & Fischer, 2006).

People can benefit from many natural-based resources in their search for healing. Among these resources, Thermal water ✓, Healing mud ✓, Mineral water resources ✓, and Salty water ✓ can be counted. Natural resources are central to human well-being and life. It is impossible to imagine human life without clean air to breathe, plants and medicinal herbs to eat, and clean water to drink. The major consequence of the unconscious and excessive use of natural resources is defined as damage to the health of ecosystems and the well-being of people. Because every unconscious behavior in nature directly and indirectly affects human life.[7]

Natural resources that are valuable in the search for healing:

- Forests.
- Aromatherapy oils and plants.
- Apitherapy.
- Animal-based therapies.
- Hydrotherapy.
- Walking paths.
- Edible plants.
- Salt and fresh water sources.
- Breathing spaces.
- It is possible to list it as meditation that comes from nature.

8. Conclusion

Factors such as the fast pace of modern life, concretized cities, digitalization, and social isolation have negative effects on the psychological and physical health of individuals. In this context, the need to reconnect with nature is felt more and more every day, and ecotherapy practices, which emerged in line with this need, attract attention as an alternative and complementary healing method (OECD/ITC, 2024).

Ecotherapy is a form of therapy that aims to support the mental, emotional, and physical health of individuals by interacting with nature. This type of therapy not only improves individual mental health but also increases environmental awareness and contributes to a more sustainable relationship with nature. Ecotherapy, which can be practiced in different forms such as forest walks, gardening, meditation in nature, interaction with animals, and outdoor therapies, shows that stress levels decrease and symptoms of depression and anxiety are alleviated as people come into contact with nature (see notes 6 and 7).

Research shows that regular contact with nature reduces cortisol levels, strengthens the immune system, and increases overall life satisfaction. From this perspective, ecotherapy plays a supportive role not only for psychological well-being but also for physical health. Especially for individuals exposed to the

---

[7]Retrieved June 16, 2025, from https://www.iisd.org/articles/deep-dive/sustainable-use-natural-resources-governance-challenge.

negative effects of urban life, ecotherapy is an important tool that provides access to the healing power of nature (OECD/ITC, 2024).

One of the most powerful aspects of ecotherapy is that the individual is seen not only as a "patient" but as a part of nature. This perspective allows the individual to feel themselves as a more holistic being and strengthens their ties with their environment. In addition, individuals' increased interest in nature leads to environmental protection behaviors and promotes ecological awareness. In this respect, ecotherapy supports not only individual health but also social and environmental well-being (Pessot et al., 2021; see note 7).

In conclusion, ecotherapy responds to the important psychosocial needs of our age in terms of offering an alternative to traditional therapy methods and deepening the relationship with nature. Especially today, when individuals are moving away from nature and stress sources are increasing, ecotherapy functions as a healing bridge in the individual–society–nature triangle. Therefore, giving more space to ecotherapy in both individual and social health policies, making arrangements to facilitate access to nature in urban planning, and informing health professionals about ecotherapeutic methods will be important steps for a healthy society (see notes 6 and 7).

References

Akers, A., Barton, J., Cossey, R., Gainsford, P., Griffin, M., & Micklewright, D. (2012). Visual color perception in green exercise: Positive effects of mood on perceived exertion. *Environmental Science and Technology*, *46*(16), 8661–8666.

Barton, J., & Pretty, J. (2010). What is the best dose of nature and green exercise for improving mental health? A multi-study analysis. *Environmental Science & Technology*, *44*(10), 3947–3955.

Buzzell, L., & Chalquist, C. (2009). *Ecotherapy: Healing with nature in mind*. Sierra Club Books.

Jimenez, M. P., DeVille, N. V., Elliott, E. G., Schiff, J. E., Wilt, G. E., Hart, J. E., & James, P. (2021). Associations between nature exposure and health: A review of the evidence. *International Journal of Environmental Research and Public Health*, *18*, 1–19.

Jones, P. (2010). Roosters, hawks and dawgs: Toward an inclusive, embodied eco/feminist psychology. *Feminine Psychology*, *20*, 365–380.

Kuhlman, T., & Farrington, J. (2010). What is sustainability? *Sustainability*, *2*, 3436–3448.

Lee, C. W., & Li, C. (2019). The process of constructing a health tourism destination index. *International Journal of Environmental Research and Public Health*, *16*, 4579.

Ma, J., Lin, P., & Williams, J. (2024). Effectiveness of nature-based walking interventions in improving mental health in adults: A systematic review. *Current Psychology*, *43*, 9521–9539.

OECD/ITC. (2024). *Understanding sustainability initiatives: A typology framework*. OECD Publishing.

Panov, V. I. (2013). Ecological thinking, consciousness, responsibility. V Congress of Russian Psychological Society. *Procedia – Social and Behavioral Sciences*, *86*(2013), 379–383.

Pearcy, H. D., Gorodina, D., & Lester, J. (2011, October 10–12). *Using the resource-based view to explore the Jamaican Health Tourism Sector as a service: A preliminary examination* [Conference proceedings]. 2011 Las Vegas International Academic Conference Proceedings (pp. 837–846). Caesars Palace, Las Vegas.

Pechlaner, H., & Fischer, E. (2006). Alpine wellness: A resource-based view. *Tourism Recreation Research, 31*(1), 67–77.

Pesonen, J., & Komppula, R. (2010). Rural wellbeing tourism: Motivations and expectations. *Journal of Hospitality & Tourism Management, 17*, 150–157.

Pessot, E., Spoladore, D., Zangiacomi, A., & Sacco, M. (2021). Natural resources in health tourism: A systematic literature review. *Sustainability, 13*(5), 2661.

Richardson, M. (2023). *Reconnection: Fixing our broken relationship with nature*. Pelagic Publishing Ltd.

Totton, N. (2011). *Wild therapy: Undomesticating inner and outer worlds*. PCCS Books.

Chapter 4

Myopia in Wellness Tourism

Fatma Ahmed Ragab

Business Administration Department, Faculty of Commerce, Damietta University, Egypt

Abstract

According to the World Health Organization (WHO), people with disabilities (PwDs) represent 16% of the global population, which means that 1 in 6 people has at least 1 type of disability. Despite the continuous growth of this segment, professionals and researchers have a myopia in considering them in industry or academia, especially in niche markets (e.g., wellness tourism). Disabilities not only deprive people from enjoying travel experiences but also deter their families from taking a break from their daily stressful life. Wellness tourism aims to offer relaxing, recreational, and spiritual experiences. When PwDs decide to travel for medical or wellness purposes, they struggle to get enough information about the adaptability of wellness destinations; hence, their relaxing trip turns into a disturbing one. This chapter aims to address the ignored issues in wellness tourism. The chapter consists of five parts. The first part clarifies the distinction among health, medical, and wellness tourism for PwDs. The second part discusses the myopia issue in wellness tourism. The third part studies the diverse barriers that PwDs face before, during, and after traveling. The fourth part delves deeper into the psychological and behavioral consequences of wellness tourism for PwDs. The fifth part proposes recommendations for stakeholders in this field.

Keywords: Disability; tourist with disability (TwD); medical tourism; wellness tourism; inclusive tourism; wellness travel; wellness destination

Advancement in Medical and Wellness Tourism, Part A: Entrepreneurship and Technology, 41–52

doi:10.1108/978-1-80592-983-320261005

1. Introduction

Daily life is overwhelmed with routines, pressures, and challenges, which necessitates the creation of new genres of tourism dedicated to meet consumers' needs for relief (Zečević & Demir, 2022). For some, travel is required for work duties, health care, or personal obligations. Others view travel as an indicator of luxurious life associated with vacations and honeymoons. In both perspectives, tourism creates opportunities to receive treatment, escape stressor, or enhance well-being (Coppola et al., 2012). As a result, tourism provides its seekers with numerous functions.

Given the interconnectedness and interdependence of health and tourism in many aspects, researchers have recently focused on the therapeutic aspects of tourism (Zheng et al., 2025). As disposable income and convenient transportation increased, individuals could afford to travel (Hu et al., 2023), as a result, the need for a new type of tourism emerged, which is wellness tourism. Consequently, researchers' interests in this new branch also increased (Zečević & Demir, 2022).

People with disabilities (PwDs) should not be excluded from experiencing the benefits of traveling, especially if they intend to combine treatment and entertainment on the same trip to a country offering cheaper treatment costs (Rapti et al., 2024). Therefore, PwDs with high incomes are seizing the opportunity to travel abroad to receive the latest treatment methods. In this context, previous studies acknowledge the purchasing power of this segment. They also called their spending the purple pound (Rapti et al., 2024). In literature, families with at least one person with disability have been called families with disabilities (Michopoulou & Hilton, 2021). This is a very misleading term, and we will address the shortsightedness of marketing in dealing with these families in part three of this chapter.

PwDs do not enjoy the same quality of life as their non-disabled peers and they face numerous access barriers (Özcan et al., 2021). These accessibility issues are factors that have been addressed by most countries worldwide. Accessible barriers determine the travel destinations chosen by travelers with disabilities (Rapti et al., 2024). The World Health Organization has developed "accessible tourism guidelines" to ensure that travelers with disabilities enjoy tourism in the future. Hence, removing barriers to achieve accessible tourism empowers disabled people, leading to increased participation, improved health, and enhanced life. Furthermore, tourism not only benefits tourists with disabilities but also reaps economic benefits to the host country (Michopoulou & Hilton, 2021).

1.1. Health Tourism

Health tourism first emerged in ancient ages when individuals traveled in search of relaxation at hot springs or religious shrines (Smith & Puczkó, 2014). With the beginning of the third millennium, people needed solutions for enhancing mental and physical states (Roman et al., 2023). As a result, societies have become increasingly interested in health tourism as a healthy lifestyle.

Health tourism is the big umbrella that includes medical, healing, and wellness tourism. Health tourism promotes physical and mental fitness, efficiency, creativity, and decision-making ability (Roman et al., 2023). It offers different physical, social, and mental practices through the other two types of medical and recreational tourism (Zheng et al., 2025). The essence of health tourism is obtaining curative, preventive, cosmetic wellness, and medical procedures by tourists seeking a tourism experience that combines treatment and entertainment in destinations that are less expensive than their home countries (Molina et al., 2023).

1.2. Medical Tourism

In early civilizations such as India, China, Mesopotamia, and Egypt, health tourism or medical tourism was presented as the people pilgrimage to holy temples to take medicinal baths and hot springs (Molina et al., 2023). In this context, medical and health tourism were used interchangeably in scientific research, but there is a significant development in recent literature to differentiate between them. Medical tourism is defined as a subfield of public health that may be directly or indirectly related to it when medical services are consumed abroad intentionally or accidentally (Rapti et al., 2024). In its early stages, medical and health tourism were a part of the tourism offerings available at spas. At that time, tourists did not prioritize touristic activities, but rather, tourism spending was directed toward treating illness (Zečević & Demir, 2022). Therefore, medical tourists aim to obtain treatment (whether medical or cosmetic) from abroad at the lowest cost (Molina et al., 2023).

The demand for the medical tourism market is high but there is not enough supply to cover it (Rapti et al., 2024). Medical tourism primarily targets individuals diagnosed with chronic illnesses, disabilities, or severe psychological conditions (Zheng et al., 2025), for whom medical tourism is essential to lead a normal life.

Although the medical model lacks a comprehensive view of disability as presented by the social model, it provides a minimum threshold for managers to understand the rights of PwDs (Kim & Lehto, 2013). Consequently, they can customize tourism services and products according to their needs.

Therapeutic programs in tourist destinations may provide opportunities for children with disabilities to learn new recreational skills tailored to their abilities and interests. For example, summer camps attract families to engage their children in therapeutic activities such as animal-assisted therapy (horseback riding and swimming with dolphins), hydrotherapy, and recreational activities such as water playing, crafts making, and competitive and non-competitive sports participating (Kim & Lehto, 2013).

Medical tourism faces two critical issues. First, Service quality profoundly impacts health tourism. International health care must set standards for service providers and medical tourism companies, such as focusing on safety and professionalism (Kulkarni et al., 2025). Second, the legal frameworks emphasize international standards for cosmetic surgery, heart surgery, dental treatment, fertility treatments, organ transplantation, and stem cell transplantation (Cohen, 2014; Foley et al., 2019; Kulkarni et al., 2025).

1.3. Healing Tourism

Healing tourism, a subset of health tourism, has three characteristics. First, it addresses the excessive physical and psychological stresses individuals face in their daily lives, in order to replenish their energy and return to their normal routines with refreshed minds (Kim et al., 2020). Second, it provides transformative benefits such as treatment, intervention, relaxation, resilience, prevention, and surveillance (Zheng et al., 2025). Therefore, it is an opportunity to calm and comfort the mind (Ma et al., 2021). Third, it does not solve the rooted problems of travelers, and therefore this type of tourism is renewable and repetitive (Kim et al., 2020).

Based on the previous characteristics, Zheng et al. (2025) argue that healing tourism is a holistic concept and suggest that it is an independent tourism product. They also set more two basic characteristics for it: first, wellness tourism is often collective, and second, it focuses on relaxation and preventive care. Based on this, Ma et al. (2021) acknowledged that wellness tourism is a product that enhances happiness and the demand for it varies according to customers' segments and preferences. It is worth noting that wellness tourism is a spectrum with two opposite ends: illness and wellness. Travelers who suffer from health problems tend to seek medical tourism, while travelers who suffer from life stressors demand wellness tourism (Zheng et al., 2025). Fig. 4.1 illustrates this continuum.

1.4. Wellness Tourism

The literature acknowledges the ambiguity in interpreting wellness tourism, and there is still no clear and unified definition. Its boundaries overlap with both medical tourism and wellness tourism (Polat & Koseoglu, 2023; Zečević & Demir, 2022). However, it is generally considered an independent sector that promotes

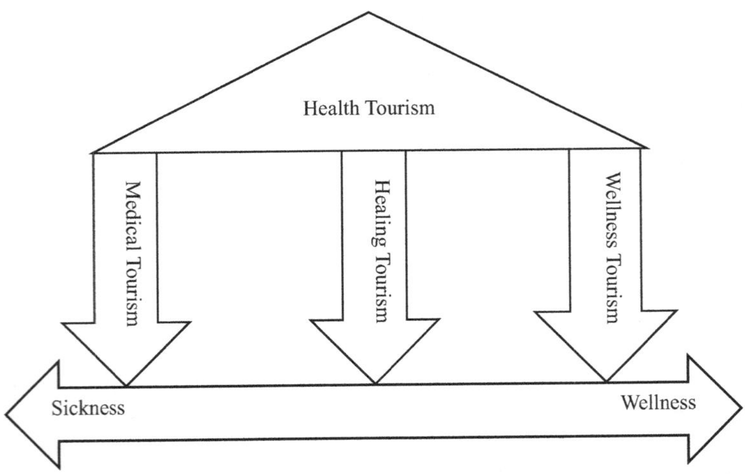

Fig. 4.1. Healing Continuum. *Source*: Configured based on Zheng et al.'s (2025) work.

the holistic well-being of tourists seeking to improve their overall health, rather than as patients seeking treatment (Zhang & Hacikara, 2023).

The history of wellness tourism is rooted in health tourism. It emerged in Europe in 1989 and has spread since the early 1990s, particularly in German-speaking countries. What accelerated the emergence of this type of tourism was the cessation of insurance companies' funding of spas, forcing these facilities to design customized packages to attract guests to pay for these services (Zečević & Demir, 2022).

Wellness tourism has developed different frameworks through the concept of healing, a concept defined by Peng et al. (2025) as a process through which tourists actively deal with physical, psychological, and social traumas by participating in multidimensional activities. These activities facilitate the transformation of stress into positive emotions. Healing is achieved through nature and culture, as natural landscapes alleviate stress and anxiety, while cultural experiences enrich belongingness, identity, and spiritual well-being (Gesler, 1993; Peng et al., 2025). To achieve this goal, wellness tourism must be accessible to all individuals, including those with disabilities (Si et al., 2024).

Wellness tourism is characterized by a diversity of services, and numerous studies have attempted to categorize it based on its services. For example, Lincoln and Guba (1985) classified it as a system of 10 elements: spa, relaxation, thermal, mineral and marine waters, organic products and supplements for nutrition, gyms and sports centers, skin care services, preventive medicine, and lastly, complementary and alternative medicine. Then, Dini and Pencarelli (2022) classified it into similar 10 systems: hot springs, spas, medical tourism, care of the body and mind, enogastronomy, sports, nature and environment, culture, spirituality, and events. This diversity underscores the industry's holistic approach to enhance physical, mental, and spiritual healing (Moriuchi et al., 2024; Polat & Koseoglu, 2023). In conclusion, wellness tourism is a complex, multifaceted sector, offering multiple sets of tourism products. To illustrate these differences, Fig. 4.2 presents some of

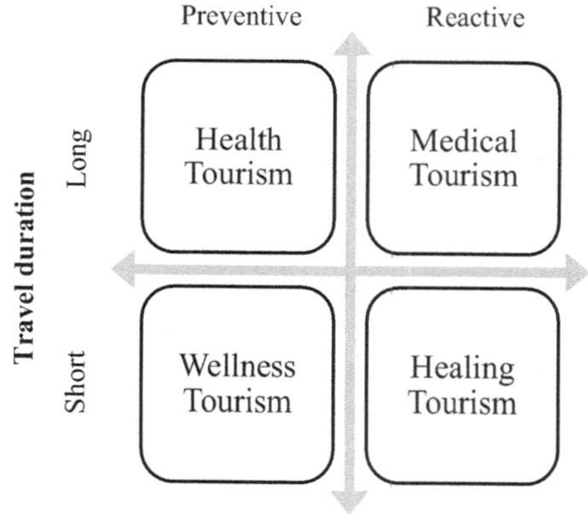

Fig. 4.2. Health, Medical, Healing, Wellness Tourism Matrix. *Source*: Author's own work based on the literature review.

the distinctions among the four aforementioned types according to the period of the travel duration and goal.

2. Myopia in Wellness Tourism

The concept of marketing myopia has evolved since its first introduction by Levitt (1960). Initially, he defined it as companies' focus on products rather than customer needs, leading to a failure to develop products that are suitable for customers not companies. Ten decades later, Day (1999) criticized this approach which focused on targeting markets and customers to gain a competitive advantage. This approach also led to the emergence of another type of marketing myopia which is the excessive focus on the customer and the ignorance of other stakeholders, which harms both stakeholders and customers in the long run (Smith et al., 2010).

Up to date, the tourism sector, whether medical, health, healing, or wellness, suffers from all aspects of myopia. The industry focuses on tourist offers that suit all customers. As a result, they ignored the various needs of all disability types. In summary, there are neither tourism offers designed for PwDs, nor for their stakeholders (e.g., their families). Marketing myopia related to tourists with disabilities is evident in both the academic and professional community, as will be discussed in the following paragraphs.

Over the past decades, research has ignored this demographic, considering it as an undesirable segment because it requires high investment and harms the idealized image of a holiday environment where individuals escape the stresses of life and avoid exposure to unpleasant situations, such as interacting with individuals with physical or sensory limitations (Kastenholz et al., 2015). This approach has been criticized for overemphasizing disability as the individual's responsibility to adapt, rather than the physical and social environment that causes the disability.

This shortsightedness is most evident in the focus of tourism on medical tourism for this segment (Hu et al., 2023). This highlights two debates in the social sciences and tourism marketing. The first debate considers the PwDs as patients who advocate for their rights to receive treatment and access to therapeutic services. On the other hand, marketing research shows PwDs as tourists seeking travel enjoyment through overcoming the obstacles and challenges they face (Polat & Koseoglu, 2023). This divergent view ignores the comprehensive goals of travelers with disabilities who seek various types of tourism, including medical, health, healing, and wellness (Hu et al., 2023; Moriuchi et al., 2024).

Likewise, tourism professionals failed to design accessible, social, and economic offers for them. Ensuring equal opportunities for tourists with disabilities and able-bodied tourists is not an obligation of the sector that must be upheld (Özcan et al., 2021). Therefore, inclusive practices are essential to achieve this justice. Accessible wellness tourism transforms the lives of individuals with disabilities from mere spectators to active participants in this sector (Rubio-Escuderos et al., 2024). Families with a member with a disability demonstrate a desire for available wellness activities such as spas and yoga, and they also prefer outdoor experiences integrated into nature, tailored to their children's physical and mental abilities (Kim & Lehto, 2013).

The participation of PwDs in setting industry standards is essential to overcoming myopia. Their counseling is essential from the beginning of service design. For instance, accommodation preferences – which varies based on the nature and severity of disability – can be deciding factors when selecting tourism packages (Nigg et al., 2024; Rapti et al., 2024). Therefore, the sector's awareness of its contributions is essential to achieve the goal of accessible and wellness tourism (Nigg et al., 2024). Ultimately, meeting the demands of this segment, including elderly tourists, represents a golden opportunity for the wellness tourism sector to align profit with equity and social inclusion (Aytaş et al., 2024; Michopoulou & Hilton, 2021).

3. Barriers in Wellness Tourism for PwDs

This section addresses the barriers faced by tourists with disabilities during travel. These barriers are common to all types of tourism (Rubio-Escuderos et al., 2024).

3.1. The Pre-departure Phase (Planning and Decision-making)

This is the most difficult stage of planning, as the planning process is inherently time-consuming, coupled with a lack of accurate information, particularly regarding accessibility. Furthermore, the company's claims regarding accessibility can be misleading. Therefore, this stage is considered stressful even before the trip begins (Devile & Moura, 2021; Rubio-Escuderos et al., 2024).

3.2. The Travel Phase (Transportation, Accommodation, and Attractions)

This stage reveals the precision of the planning process where the number of operational barriers and the extent to which the tourist can overcome them become clear. Although this is the confrontation phase, the tourist is forced to handle the challenging situations. This stage entails three main points:

- *Transportation*:
  Transportation depends primarily on the infrastructure of both home country and host country. Reliance on internal facilities at stopovers also presents risks and pain points, such as inadequate bathrooms, damage of wheelchairs during storage, and inappropriate treatment by staff (Devile & Moura, 2021; Michopoulou & Hilton, 2021; Rubio-Escuderos et al., 2024).

- *Accommodation*:
  Despite the availability of accessible design standards, their implementation is still not fully implemented. Furthermore, accommodation may lack elevators and may not be equipped with facilities like adequate bathroom door widths, appropriate bed height, or accessible dining areas. Communication with staff also becomes problematic at this stage (Devile & Moura, 2021; Rubio-Escuderos et al., 2024).

- *Tourist attractions and activities*:
  Tourist attractions and activities restrict tourists' enjoyment due to the rugged mountainous regions. Some cultural tourist sites are often designed in a way that does not allow for subsequent modifications, although some cultural tourist sites have already attempted to overcome these obstacles. Furthermore, the lack of rest areas in some of these locations creates stress for tourists (Devile & Moura, 2021; Michopoulou & Hilton, 2021).

3.3. Post-travel Phase (Recollection and Feedback)

The cumulative effect of these barriers – stressful planning, negative encounters, and stressful experiences – is likely to have psychological effects that impact trip recall. Negative experiences leave tourists with bitter memories and are likely to lead to negative reviews. Furthermore, the repeated failure of service providers to deliver on their promises reduces trust, discourages future travel and undermines the well-being (Rubio-Escuderos et al., 2024).

4. Consequences of Inclusion/Exclusion of PwDs in Wellness Tourism

The greatest benefit of tourism is reducing social exclusion by allowing PwDs to participate in the pleasures of travel (Özcan et al., 2021). Second, wellness tourism reduces stress and enhances well-being as PwDs also experience stressors, exacerbated by their isolation and confinement for years (Moura et al., 2018). Third, wellness tourism improves psychological and social dimensions through both coping beliefs and coping strategies. Coping beliefs enable individuals with disabilities to cope with travel fears, adapt to the environment, form friendships, and improve their overall self-esteem. Furthermore, coping strategies enable individuals with disabilities to engage in activities and enjoy the company of other tourists, ultimately improving their quality of life (Si et al., 2024).

On the other hand, the most significant negative aspects of travel barriers are reduced quality of life and low self-confidence. Rubio-Escuderos et al. (2024) found that overprotective families made PwDs dependent, which negatively decreases their self-independence, increases their frustration, and destroys their self-confidence.

5. Recommendations for Stakeholders

The previous sections addressed the marketing myopia, industry myopia, barriers, and consequences of PwDs travel. To address these aspects, a comprehensive model must be proposed to ensure the inclusion of all stakeholders. This section presents some recommendations for formulating this model.

5.1. Government and Policymakers

Governments are the primary authority for implementing and monitoring policies and regulations. They impose accessibility standards in tourist areas and are primarily responsible for inspecting these areas to ensure compliance with these standards and impose necessary improvements (Özcan et al., 2021). Therefore, government should facilitate public–private sector collaboration and activate inclusive tourism initiatives, particularly those led by disability advocacy organizations, which are the safest and most reliable way to provide an accessible travel experience for PwDs (Rubio-Escuderos et al., 2024).

In addition to policies enforcement, infrastructure standards must address the broader social and economic inequalities that underline exclusion. This includes the rights of PwDs during their whole lives in education, healthcare, and employment. If PwDs were considered in basic domains, they were considered in recreational ones (Özcan et al., 2021). Furthermore, governments should focus on local development, identify areas most suitable for wellness tourism, and promote these efforts to maximize economic and promotional benefits for their countries (Aytaş et al., 2024). Ultimately, the role of governments is to create an integrated ecosystem in which accessibility is the norm, not an option.

5.2. Researchers and Academia

The academic community should address the profound conceptual and theoretical gaps in previous studies and adopt interdisciplinary approaches. There is an urgent need to shift the focus from the demand side to the supply side. Specifically, researchers should critically analyze the experience of tourists with disabilities throughout their entire journey, from simply being exposed to the advertisement to completing the trip and returning home (Michopoulou & Hilton, 2021; Polat & Koseoglu, 2023). A central recommendation in interdisciplinary research is that the science of urban architecture, socio-spatial studies, and occupational therapy should integrate to develop comprehensive models that take into account the various psychological, social, cognitive, and systemic burdens of disability (Chrysikou, 2025; Coppola et al., 2012). Research should also explore underrepresented areas of application such as spiritual motivations for travel, post-COVID tourist preferences, and virtual tourism as an alternative to traditional tourism (Aytaş et al., 2024; Kwon, 2022; Zhang & Hacikara, 2023).

5.3. Recommendations for the Tourism Sector

The most important recommendations for the sector are three points:

- *Access to information*:
  The ambiguity of information about accessibility is the biggest problem for tourists. Therefore, it is imperative to provide accurate, clear, reliable, and easily accessible information. For example, technology can be leveraged to provide the latest details about accessibility (such as door widths, step heights, and elevator availability) and publish and update them continuously on all social media platforms and the official website. This can be enhanced with videos and explanatory clips, serving as a virtual experience 24/7 (Aytaş et al., 2024; Michopoulou & Hilton, 2021).

- *Education and training of employees*:
  Training and awareness are a fundamental turning point in this industry, which is primarily based on human interaction between service providers and tourists with disabilities. Therefore, employees must be educated about the benefits of inclusive accessibility in their organizations and provided with a reference guide to provide them with accurate information. This should be evidenced by the development of appropriate language and respectful terms for communication with all guests with disabilities (Michopoulou & Hilton, 2021).

- *Inclusive design and physical adaptations*:
  Decision makers are advised, before beginning the design of future health resorts, to consult with all stakeholders, including PwDs, taking into account all possible obstacles in the customer journey and providing specialized equipment and infrastructure to address any future problems. For existing buildings, simple and economical modifications to entrances and exits, or portable and adjustable elevators, can be offered (Michopoulou & Hilton, 2021).

References

Aytaş, G., Ergen, F. D., & Aytekin, E. (2024). Wellness tourism after the pandemic. In M. Kozak & N. Kozak (Eds.), *Future tourism trends volume 1: Tourism in the changing world* (pp. 285–298). Emerald Publishing Limited. https://doi.org/10.1108/978-1-83753-244-520241019

Chrysikou, E. (2025). Therapeutic architecture and tourism: Exploring potential cross-disciplinary synergies: A Horizon 2050 paper. *Tourism Review*, *80*(1), 151–164. https://doi.org/10.1108/TR-01-2024-0002

Cohen, I. G. (2014). *Patients with passports: Medical tourism, law and ethics*. Oxford University Press.

Coppola, S., Sakornsatian, S., Thongkuay, S., & Trevittaya, P. (2012). Innovative practice in accessible and inclusive tourism. *World Federation of Occupational Therapists Bulletin*, *66*(1), 43–46. https://doi.org/10.1179/otb.2012.66.1.016

Day, G. S. (1999). *The market driven organization: Understanding, attracting, and keeping valuable customers*. Free Press.

Devile, E. L., & Moura, A. A. (2021). Travel by people with physical disabilities: Constraints and influences in the decision-making process. In I. M. Miranda, Z. Breda, & C. Costa (Eds.), *ICT tools and applications for accessible tourism* (pp. 55–73). IGI Global. https://doi.org/10.4018/978-1-7998-6428-8.ch003

Dini, M., & Pencarelli, T. (2022). Wellness tourism and the components of its offer system: A holistic perspective. *Tourism Review*, *77*(2), 394–412. https://doi.org/10.1108/TR-08-2020-0373

Foley, B. M., Haglin, J. M., Tanzer, J. R., & Eltorai, A. E. (2019). Patient care without borders: A systematic review of medical and surgical tourism. *Journal of Travel Medicine*, *26*(6), taz049. https://doi.org/10.1093/jtm/taz049

Gesler, W. M. (1993). Therapeutic landscapes: Theory and a case study of Epidauros, Greece. *Environment and Planning D: Society and Space*, *11*(2), 171–189. https://doi.org/10.1068/D110171

Hu, F., Wen, J., Zheng, D., & Wang, W. (2023). Travel medicine in hospitality: An interdisciplinary perspective. *International Journal of Contemporary Hospitality Management*, *35*(9), 3134–3153. https://doi.org/10.1108/IJCHM-05-2022-0574

Kastenholz, E., Eusébio, C., & Figueiredo, E. (2015). Contributions of tourism to social inclusion of persons with disability. *Disability and Society*, *30*(8), 1259–1281. https://doi.org/10.1080/09687599.2015.1075868

Kim, S., & Lehto, X. Y. (2013). Travel by families with children possessing disabilities: Motives and activities. *Tourism Management*, *37*, 13–24. https://doi.org/10.1016/j.tourman.2012.12.011

Kim, S.-E., Um, S.-H., & Lee, T. (2020). Healing effects from the on-site experiences of tourists. *International Journal of Tourism Research*, *22*(2), 192–201. https://doi.org/10.1002/jtr.2328

Kulkarni, D. G., Kulkarni, G. R., Saurabh, P., & Shome, S. (2025). Health tourism in the era of COVID-19: A bibliometric analysis. *International Journal of Pharmaceutical and Healthcare Marketing*, *19*(3), 591–617. https://doi.org/10.1108/IJPHM-03-2024-0022

Kwon, H. J. (2022). A new trend of tourism in the Post-COVID-19 era: Big data analysis of online tours in Korea. *Social Sciences*, *11*(12), 574. https://doi.org/10.3390/socsci11120574

Lincoln, Y. S., & Guba, E.G. (1985). *Naturalistic inquiry*. Sage.

Ma, S., Zhao, X., Gong, Y., & Wengel, Y. (2021). Proposing "healing tourism" as a post-COVID-19 tourism product. *Anatolia*, *32*(1), 136–139. https://doi.org/10.1080/13032917.2020.1808490

Michopoulou, E., & Hilton, S. (2021). Accessibility to spa experiences. In I. M. Miranda, Z. Breda, & C. Costa (Eds.), *ICT tools and applications for accessible tourism* (pp. 146–168). IGI Global. https://doi.org/10.4018/978-1-7998-6428-8.ch007

Molina, T. M., Morales, C. F., Mujíca, A. G. G., Vásquez, G. B. B., & Quesada, A. C. (2023). Strategies in medical and wellness tourism for economic development in Ecuador and Cuba post COVID. In A. G. G. Mujíca & J. C. G. Sánchez (Eds.), *Smart innovation, systems and technologies* (Vol. 345, pp. 69–79). Springer. https://doi.org/10.1007/978-981-99-0337-5_6

Moriuchi, E., Agrusa, J., & Lema, J. (2024). Strategies for health and wellness tourism development: Thai massage. *International Journal of Tourism Research*, *26*(1), e2622. https://doi.org/10.1002/jtr.2622

Moura, A. F. A., Kastenholz, E., & Pereira, A. M. S. (2018). Accessible tourism and its benefits for coping with stress. *Journal of Policy Research in Tourism, Leisure and Events*, *10*(3), 241–264. https://doi.org/10.1080/19407963.2017.1409750

Nigg, J. J., Plaikner, A., Peters, M., & Haid, M. (2024). Leisure constraints towards accessible tourism: Self-characteristics of people with disability along tourism value chains. *Current Issues in Tourism*, *28*, 3031–3045. https://doi.org/10.1080/13683500.2024.2394965

Özcan, E., Topcu, Z. G., & Arasli, H. (2021). Determinants of travel participation and experiences of wheelchair users traveling to the Bodrum region: A qualitative study. *International Journal of Environmental Research and Public Health*, *18*(5), 2218. https://doi.org/10.3390/ijerph18052218

Peng, C., Zou, Y. G., & Jin, D. (2025). Wellness tourism healing: A systematic review unveiling how cultural symbolic experiences influence health recovery. *Tourism Review*. https://doi.org/10.1108/TR-10-2024-0918

Polat, E., & Koseoglu, M. A. (2023). Wellness tourism scholarship: A research agenda. *Journal of Hospitality and Tourism Insights*, *6*(5), 1860–1889. https://doi.org/10.1108/JHTI-05-2022-0186

Rapti, M., Sepetis, A., & Pierrakos, G. (2024). Medical tourism with emphasis on tourism for people with disabilities in Greece. In M. P. Papadopoulou & E. S. Kakarouka (Eds.), *Springer proceedings in business and economics* (pp. 513–521). Springer. https://doi.org/10.1007/978-3-031-51038-0_56

Roman, M., Roman, M., & Wojcieszak-Zbierska, M. (2023). Health tourism—subject of scientific research: A literature review and cluster analysis. *International Journal of Environmental Research and Public Health*, *20*(1), 480. https://doi.org/10.3390/ijerph20010480

Rubio-Escuderos, L., García-Andreu, H., Michopoulou, E., & Buhalis, D. (2024). Perspectives on experiences of tourists with disabilities: Implications for their daily lives and for the tourist industry. *Tourism Recreation Research*, *49*(1), 48–62. https://doi.org/10.1080/02508281.2021.1981071

Si, Y., Chen, M., Zhang, M., & Xiao, H. (2024). Therapeutic landscapes and tourists' perceived quality of life. *Journal of Destination Marketing & Management*, *33*, 100918. https://doi.org/10.1016/j.jdmm.2024.100918

Smith, M., & Puczkó, L. (2014). *Health, tourism and hospitality: Spas, wellness and medical travel* (2nd ed.). Routledge. https://doi.org/10.4324/9780203083772

Smith, N. C., Drumwright, M. E., & Gentile, M. C. (2010). The new marketing myopia. *Journal of Public Policy & Marketing*, *29*(1), 4–11.

Zečević, M., & Demir, M. (2022). Most prominent topics in wellness tourism research: Topic modelling analysis. In M. B. Demir & G. M. Rančić (Eds.), *Contemporary issues in tourism* (pp. 119–131). University of Maribor Press. https://doi.org/10.18690/um.ft.6.2022.6

Zhang, T., & Hacikara, A. (2023). Virtual tourism and consumer wellbeing: A critical review, practices, and new perspectives. In S. K. Dixit (Ed.), *Handbook of tourism and quality-of-life research* (pp. 545–557). Springer. https://doi.org/10.1007/978-3-031-31513-8_37

Zheng, D., Huang, C., Zhao, Q., & Liu, Y. (2025). Healing tourism: An interdisciplinary review of progress, methods and healthy ageing implications. *Asia Pacific Journal of Marketing and Logistics*, *38*(1), 101–125. https://doi.org/10.1108/APJML-10-2024-1538

Chapter 5

Calm's Canvas: Changing Wellness Travel in India Supported by Artistic Technologies

Sarita Bhardwaj and Ajay Prakash Jaiswal

School of Liberal and Creative Arts (Fine Arts), Lovely Professional University, Punjab, India

Abstract

The developing linkages of wellness tourism, modern technology, and Indian creative traditions are investigated in this chapter. It shows that how modern gadgets are redefining these old practices like dance, ragas, and folk arts by usage of new technological means like virtual reality (VR), augmented reality (AR), and artificial intelligence (AI), thus creating more thrilling and customized therapy experiences in India. With wellness tourism growing across India, its cultural heritage offers explosive possibilities to combine the esthetics of the ancient world with contemporary technological advances. As much as immersive technologies have allowed guests to connect with art by creating a sense of being part of it beyond the wall, with VR experiences, leading to a more connected relationship with classical musical concerts, AI provides people with custom and individual range soundscapes based on their emotional and bodily state. Motion capture allows for even more dimensions and helps participants participate actively in therapeutic dancing lessons. Another aspect that is explored in this chapter is the use of these technologies by rural health retreats to come up with inclusive and financially sustainable models that facilitate local artists, in addition to maintaining the old knowledge system. It highlights the need to have cultural familiarity and connectivity to society in building moral and environmentally sustainable health initiatives. The chapter finally finds a moment when technology and art will work together to provide changing wellness vacations advancing mental health, spiritual growth, and cultural

Advancement in Medical and Wellness Tourism, Part A: Entrepreneurship and Technology, 53–65

doi:10.1108/978-1-80592-983-320261006

appreciation. It puts India at the highest in producing tech-integrated, heritage-based wellness travel.

Keywords: Indian arts; digital well-being; immersive arts; cultural healing; artificial intelligence; rural activation; wellness tourism

1. Introduction

The popularity of wellness tourism is of historical significance when it comes to the change of world travel behavior, as people wish to not only care about their physical health, but also their emotional, mental, and spiritual health as well. Over the past years, this change has extended way beyond the old ideas of vacationing that just idled on leisure and sightseeing. Today, travelers do not hesitate to get involved in experiences that will enhance their inner peace, self-discovery, and long-term personal development. The Global Wellness Institute (2023) reveals that the market of wellness tourism exceeds a trillion dollars and is growing at a faster pace, particularly in Asia-Pacific countries. The changing trends in the travel industry coupled with an increase in the capacity to observe mental health, stress levels, health prevention, and promotion have transformed wellness tourism forever.

India has an exceptionally high profile in this fast-expanding market. India, unlike the majority of destinations, when it comes to holistic healing, does not revolve around spa treatments, massages, or detox diets, but instead, boasts a rich and varied history of treatment methodologies. The ancient life practices of the country based on Ayurveda, yoga, classical music, dance, and complex folk art offer a rich reservoir of approaches that treat the human being as a complete person body, mind and spirit. The traditions are not only techniques of therapy but also a part of the cultural and spiritual fabric of the Indian society. These traditions focus on the importance of balance and harmony and a deeper existence with nature and the self, which makes India a very appealing place to visit as opposed to merely being a way to relax superficially.

Moreover, the influence of the COVID-19 pandemic has become a driver, and the world is paying increased attention to health and wellness. This global trauma of the world has created a greater understanding that mental strength, emotional IQ, and internal balance are fundamental. Because of lockdowns, people were inclined to dive introspectively and address their states of mind and emotional habits, so there was a surge of interest in treatment strategies and approaches that promote emotional recovery and spiritual development. In this regard, the artistic traditions of India, including the therapeutic dancing, mindful music, and meditative painting, would provide an unmatched platform of artistic self-expression and psychological healing.

The only thing about India that is different is that it has a possibility of combining these long-ago artistic and spiritual traditions with modern technological advances. How wellness experiences are designed and delivered is disrupting due to the introduction of new technologies, VR, AR, and AI. Under the guise of VR and AR, the traveler will be able to learn temple dance rituals using a digital prowling, acquaint themselves with the complicated yoga asanas with the help of a holographic supervisor, or study ancient art forms equally interactively anywhere in the world. AI also makes such journeys more personal, which is based on biometric data analysis; it suggests which ragas will help a person heal their emotions, or proposes what type of dancing is the most appropriate regarding the individual's energy levels and mood.

This fusion of the old and new technology is turning wellness tourism into an active rather than a passive form of consumption model, as well as a participatory and highly personified experience. The nature of the visitor has now changed to co-creators of healing experiences; they interact differently with the Indian cultural heritage having in-depth and life-changing experiences. Moreover, the innovations provide a window to democratizing access to traditional Indian arts and enable even individuals who do not have an opportunity to travel physically to the location to enjoy valuable and engaging cultural practices concerning their wellness.

The present chapter will thus explore the manner in which the intersection of the ancient artistic practices of India and the innovative digital technology are transforming wellness tourism. It discusses how immersive and emotionally charged experiences can be developed so that they suit the changing interests of a contemporary traveler. This chapter uses global tendencies and the examples of illustrative cases and current studies to point out the exceptional possibility of India becoming a pioneer in the field of holistic, art-containing wellness tourism. It also presents a critical look at the ethical, socio-economic, and cultural ramifications of such a fusion, especially in the light of how this can make local communities more powerful without losing the authenticity of the traditionally held principles. By so doing, it gives a detailed blueprint of how India can establish itself as a leading player in the next evolution of wellness tourism.

2. Literature Reviews

The development of the phenomenon of wellness tourism as a considerably important worldwide trend stimulated the emergence of scholars' interest in its interactions with traditional cultural spheres, the practices of traditional healing, and the travel experience. According to Voigt and Pforr (2014), the transition between traditional leisure tourism and wellness tourism is associated with the need of travelers to get real, transformative, and whole-body experiences of tourism. The change marks a worldwide reconsideration of the value of intangible cultural heritage in the form of rituals, performing arts, and city-bound practices.

As Cohen and Cohen (2012) point out, these cultural and spiritual aspects are key factors in distinguishing the realm of wellness tourism from the generic medical or spa-related tourism. India is a land with a rich spiritual culture founded on yoga and Ayurveda, in addition to a different artistic heritage, which has always been perceived as a good resource for wellness-related tourism. Academic interest has, however, been purely targeted on yoga and Ayurveda, with very little research on the importance of performing and visual arts in wellness schemes.

Art therapy, which is largely researched across the West, has evinced satisfactory findings concerning psychological health, trauma, and emotional management (Malchiodi, 2013). Its use in tourism situations is relatively understudied; however, it is becoming influential, possibly as travelers are seeking experience learning and self-expression opportunities. As indicated by recent research, practicing the culture of art by taking part in painting, pottery, and textile works enhances mindfulness, social connection, and neuroplasticity as elements of well-being (Stuckey & Nobel, 2010).

Regarding music therapy, neuroscientific data prove that music can regulate emotions, deactivate the stress hormones, and improve cognitive functioning (Koelsch, 2015). The Indian classical music, with the system of raga especially created to achieve a particular state of emotions, has a very specific therapeutic potential. Nevertheless, its incorporation in wellness tourism schemes is relatively low, and further empirical research is mandatory to estimate its impacts on the various tourist groups.

A recent research gap has been the use of immersive technologies in the tourism sphere of cultural heritage. According to Tussayadiah et al. (2018), VR and AR may lead to more authentic and involving experiences because they can improve the cultural authenticity and establish an emotional connection between people. Respectively, Jung et al. (2016) remark that immersive technologies may facilitate learning and communication, particularly, in tourism related to art and heritage. Their incorporation into the wellness programs presents the chance to develop hybrid experiences through the combination of tradition and innovation.

The role of technology in wellness and cultural tourism in the Indian context remains primitive. Even so, innovative initiatives are beginning to appear, in which the VR modules can provide a temple visit, the AI software will create an individualized audio experience that uses biometric data, and the AR guide can teach the newcomer the art of dance or art (Patel & Singh, 2022). On the one hand, they show good prospects, but at the same time, the cultural authenticity, ethical use of data, and technological accessibility need much attention.

The community-based tourism systems have gained attention as a system that is capable of empowering the marginalized communities, sustaining cultural heritage, and ensuring sustainable development (Goodwin & Santilli, 2009; Scheyvens, 1999). At the same time, the situation in India is such that the rural artisan community may lack demand or may have market access issues. By incorporating wellness tourism with their art, they get the opportunity to empower themselves economically and revive their cultures. Nonetheless, there are also dangers that literature cautions would hurt community well-being as well as visitor experiences, including cultural commodification and a lack of equitable distribution of benefits (George et al., 2009).

Moreover, research about cultural appropriation related to ethics has also been at the focus when deliberating about art and wellness interactions. When these sacred practices and cultural symbols are used commercially to make profits without approval and participation of the community to whom they belong, the sacred becomes vulgar and loses its spiritual perspective, as well as the community itself (Zhang & Hitchcock, 2017). These problems need participatory processes in which local needs and fair partnerships are emphasized.

Although current literature on art therapy, wellness tourism, immersive technology, and community-based tourism is abundant, there is a severe lack of interdisciplinary research that would combine these fields, especially in the Indian context. Particularly, there is a lack of systematic research on how safe healing and renewal in traditional arts methods, advanced technologies, and wellness tourism could combine to accomplish mental and emotional recovery, community empowerment, and cultural sustainability.

This chapter also helps to fill these gaps, which helps to contribute to an emergent scholarship on culturally situated, technology-improved wellness tourism. Not only does it introduce a framework of artistic heritage and digital innovation combination, but it also emphasizes the concept of ethics, inclusivity, and care toward the environment. The strategy is on par with the other trends on the global stage of values promotion that supports responsible travel, collaborative value creation, and transformative tourist experiences that foster increased connections to the host, the local people, and the tourism destination.

3. Objectives

To understand how the Indian traditional art forms can be integrated with wellness tourism practice, their therapeutic and spiritual aspects.

In order to examine how VR, AR, and AI play a modern role in personalizing and increasing the level of art-based wellness in India.

To determine the socio-economic, cultural, and ethical effects of art-technology convergence in wellness tourism, as well as to recommend ways of sustainable and inclusive growth.

4. Methodology

The chapter has taken a qualitative and interpretive research approach to explain the relations between art, wellness, and technology in India, on the basis of secondary information within the scholarly writings, industry reports, and policy documents. The case studies of healthy retreats, rural craftwork, and technology innovations have a real-life setting. Comparative examples of similar practices in the rest of the world such as forest baths in Japan, Buddhist retreats in Thailand, and healing dances in Bali can be used to bring to light the distinctive place of India. The style is also based on cultural sensitivity and being ethically tolerant of the customs and art forms. The future study can consider the primary data analysis by interviewing artisans, wellness practitioners, and tourists as well to learn more about it.

5. Wellness Tourism and Art in India

The traditions of Indian art are rooted in the deep spiritual and emotional wellbeing and regarded as the divine practice of self-cognition and the universal harmony (Bhat, 2015). Although Indian wellness tourism was long renowned as limited to yoga and Ayurveda, it is increasingly discovered that India has a lot to offer in terms of healing through its artistic culture. Contemporary travelers are willing to take part in any activity that can heal their body, mind, and soul, and this leads to dance and music being added to the wellness retreats together with the indigenous arts.

Ananda in the Himalayas, Soukya in Bangalore, and Vana in Dehradun have luxury retreats with classical dance, music therapy, and visual arts integrated into total programs. As a vivid example, Ananda provides Bharatanatyam or Kathak practices that make people relate to the spiritual fiction, and Soukya implements the use in terms of raga-based music therapy and art classes with developing mandalas to speak about mindfulness.

In addition to luxury retreats, there are community-based programs that implement art as well, e.g., drum circles that cause social integration and painting sessions like Madhubani, Sanjhi, or Gond art that allow meditation attention. These experiences take the natural elements, promote sustainability, and cultural respect.

Partnerships in wellness attract travelers interested in roots and real experience of a destination. When acting as an active participant in the traditional arts, tourists become the subject of the history of Indian culture, thus they obtain significant emotional and spiritual transformation. The trend is connected with the global trends to conscious and meaningful tourism (Smith, 2017) as well as highlighted community aspect of the related incoming (local artists) and outgoing (the exchange of knowledge). Therefore, wellness tourism under art adds to the experiences of visitors and makes the culture sustainable and provides India with an opportunity to stand out in the arena of global wellness tourism.

6. Digital Technologies and Its Place

6.1. Engaged Artistic Wellness

The technological developments of VR, AR, and mixed reality (MR) have transformed the relationship audiences have with art all over the world, and now India is using those technologies to reinvent its long artistic heritage within the wellness tourist market. These tools make it possible to have more than a passive view of things, but instead find themselves in a new place where they can interact with art in a very sensory, personal way.

With the concept of wellness tourism, VR modules will be able to take visitors to vividly recreated temple settings or even spiritual fairs. Put on a VR headset, and one imagines one is suddenly in the midst of a sacred Bharatanatyam performance in the ancient temple in Tamil Nadu, with every nuance of movements and gestures magnified and commented on in real-time. Tourists have an opportunity to observe these dances and sometimes even engage in them as a virtual participant and learn about the spiritual value and healing potential. In the same sense, AR solutions superimpose traditional dance or painting methods onto real-life skills, so individuals can train and master proper movements and patterns virtually.

Motion capture technology is an additional tool to make these experiences even better as it gives participants immediate feedback concerning their movements. In dance therapy workshops, we can have an example: guests follow the body alignment, posture, and fluidity in wearing motion capture suits. These movements are reflected in digital avatars, and they allow them to be corrected and perfected. Together with physical exercise and computer interaction, this is a holistic approach that enhances man–machine interaction beyond scale, and leads to embodied self-awareness, one of the central aims of healing.

Additionally, AR-based art courses help even amateurs to practice such traditional arts as Kolam, Kalamkari, Sanjhi, or Pattachitra. Progressive visual overlays are used to help the user in comprehending complex patterns, symbolism, and beats of the brush strokes. Such experiences of immersive learning cause a meditative flow state that creates less anxiety and a growth in mindfulness. Wellness resorts such as Vana and high-tech urban wellness facilities have already started deploying such innovations and have already established standards that future art-integrated wellness experiences can strive to meet.

Regardless of the promise, however, there are challenges. The installation costs are very high, special equipment is necessary, and the technological literacy, both of facilitators and rural artisans, is a serious challenge. To resolve these problems, it is essential to provide an investment in infrastructure, the training, and policies of inclusion, to guarantee equal provisions and inclusions.

6.2. AI and Music Therapy

The emotional and therapeutic effect of Indian classical music, and particularly the raga system, has been known to be deep over the centuries. All the ragas are connected to the time of day, seasons, and emotional states, and are thought to work on human physiology and psychology. AI is changing this field and bringing new opportunities to hyper-personally experience healing.

Recent AI algorithms evaluate the heart rate variability, skin conductance, and breath pattern to determine the current emotional and physiological condition of a person. Using such real-time data, AI platforms are able to advise on particular ragas based on the needs of the individual. As an example, a stressed person may be advised to listen to Raga Darbari Kanada in order to feel calmer, whereas a grieving person may be referred to Raga Bhairavi to achieve emotional release (Sharma, 2016).

Such personalization is further increased by wearable devices, called biometric bracelets or smart headbands, that continuously measure physical signs and manipulate the music in real time. This self-reinforcing loop makes a very rich and interactive therapeutic environment. Other resorts also implemented AI personally created-playlists in combination with guided meditation and breathwork, so that a strategic wellness journey available to guests is seamless and highly individualized.

In addition to being passively listened to, AI is also enabling interactive listening to music. Using AI-powered virtual musical instruments, the guests are welcome to test different classical rhythms and melodies and experience self-expression to enhance their creativity during the healing process. These innovations also make classical music therapy accessible to ordinary people, without the need to be musically inclined in order to develop the ability to create music.

6.3. Visual Arts Therapy and Technology

Visual art therapy is a method of using expression through creativity to liberate the emotions or to experience a personal revelation and even psychological recovery. Indian folk and tribal arts (Madhubani, Sanjhi, Warli, Gond, Pattachitra, and Chittara) are traditional arts of India being practiced as forms of storytelling, spirituality, and communion since time immemorial. By incorporating these practices in wellness tourism, the visitors will be able to experience their healing power and also be able to do so while learning about various cultural aspects of India.

During health retreats, the visitors attend supervised classes, where they design customized paintings using nature-derived pigments, which include plants and minerals. After some time, the simplicity of the idea of working on geometric shapes or detailed images creates a state of mediation that allows people to relax and introspect. After participating in mythological stories and nature-related themes, participants can connect to universal symbols and unconscious depths.

These experiences are improved with their technological infiltration. AR uses overlay instructional animations that are guided onto canvases or digital devices to simplify complicated techniques for beginners. VR studio simulations have recreated the artisan-type setting so that visitors can effectively visit the distant villages and see master artists at work even when they cannot afford to travel physically to those areas.

Such programs not only help to recover individuals but also turn into centers of cultural strength and financial power. They are opening up new venues where rural artists can exchange their expertise all over the world and create sustainable employment as well. Wellness travelers, in their turn, also take behind a deepened sense of Indian cultural heritage, which results in enhancing cross-cultural understanding and sensitivity.

7. Sonic Sanctuaries – Music, Technology, and Mental Wellness

The sacred space of sound has been constantly present throughout the spirit and health traditions of India. Whether it is the primordial chant of the vibration of the universe itself, the so-called absolute or one God (Om), the rhythm of the recital of Vedic mantra, and the sonorous tones of the classical ragas, it is the belief that sound is a means between the space and the metaphysical. Historically, the combination of these sonic elements has been applied to quiet the mind, harmonize energies, and sink the practitioner into more advanced states of meditation.

Sound therapy, which in the context of wellness tourism has developed into high-tech, technology-enhanced experiences, now has its origin in simple soothing chants or instrument sessions. Binaural beats, which are auditory illusions due to the playing of slightly different frequencies in the two ears, are being used now with traditional Indian drones, played on strings such as the tanpura and shruti box. Such binaural beats can promote the alignment of brainwaves, meaning that these experiences can result in a relaxed state, creativity, concentration, or even being in a state of deep sleep (Sharma & Desai, 2020).

An increased number of wellness centers in India like Kerala and Goa invest in 3D sound domes, spatial audio systems to simulate the acoustics of ancient temples and nature. When these domes are erected, they produce entirely immersive sessions where sounds are funneled in every direction, such that it resembles the noise of temple chants or the soothing sounds of rivers during a Ganga aarti. This multi-sensory experience engulfs the visitors and makes them want to express their emotions and find their own spiritual depth.

Furthermore, neuro-acoustic stimulation is why current developments are being studied and tested in pilot wellness programs. This method employs the use of sound frequencies that are used to stimulate certain areas of the brain so as to heal specific psychological traumas like anxiety, post-traumatic stress disorder (PTSD), and depression. These technologies together with the time-tested principles of raga therapy in India offer a formidable weapon in mental health.

Indian artists are also playing a role in this movement, by using traditional ragas with the new techno music to create new soundscapes with the thrust of traditional spirituality that younger Indians can connect with as well. Musicians such as Karsh Kale or bands that are exploring fusion genres belong to this new wave, and they attract global tourists with an interest in cultural authenticity and new forms.

The possible way for the future is such adaptive soundscapes where the mode of sound is changed over time with the help of AI algorithms, depending on emotional and physiological feedback of the listener. Envisage a meditation with all the elements, the raga, background drones, and binaural beats, developing in real-time using real-time biometric data received by wearable sensors on each individual guest, allowing an individualized sonic heaven tailored to each individual.

8. Rural Roots, Digital Wings

The villages of India are a gold-mine of living traditions in arts, which may be based either on daily rites and the round of the year. Contrary to commodified forms of art in the galleries, these aboriginal activities are the symbols of the collective knowledge, spiritual metaphors and environmental awareness. Building of woven goods, pottery, mural painting, and folk songs are not only crafts, but rather meditative and community building exercises that promote emotional stability and social conciliations.

It is on this prospect that wellness tourism is slowly being taken out of the urban retreat spas and tourist resorts into rural areas. Experiences such as Gramya Wellness Trails in Odisha, Craft & Calm in Kutch, and other homestay programs in Himachal Pradesh and Rajasthan are all about immersing in the simplicity, creating an authentic experience, and being at one with the self and surroundings.

The tourists are allowed to live with the artisan families, be taught the forms of art, participate in organic farming, ritual, and folk storytelling by a campfire. The engagement in those activities is therapeutic in nature, similar to slow living, and it helps the visitor to get back in touch with the rhythms of nature, in many cases, forgotten in city life.

One factor that is distinct about these initiatives is that women artisans are empowered. Women in most villages become the guardians of art in that they transmit skills through the ages. When these women are used as teachers and facilitators in wellness tourism, livelihoods are not only sustainable, but women become self-confident and community leaders.

Technological integration is like a point of compromise between tradition and modernity. With digital storytelling platforms, VR village tours, and online workshops, the rural artists are able to present their talents to the world audience. Virtual markets enable these craftsmen to offer handcrafted products for wellness, such as herbal soaps, organic fabrics, and folk art to the customers without involving any pay-cutting middlemen, directly at reasonable prices.

These models of wellness in the countryside are made even stronger by environmental sustainability. The usage of natural pigments, recycled materials, and environmentally friendly ways of construction is consistent with the current trends in tourism toward responsible and regenerative tourism around the globe. These programs propose a holistic concept of health, not only curative, but also highly moral in terms of promoting farm-to-table cuisine, local herbal medicine, and the usual health traditions.

Nevertheless, the effective advancement necessitates capacity-building and training programs that would provide the artisans with marketing and digital skills. Such transitions have been aided by the nongovernmental organizations (NGOs) as Dastkar, Tisser India, and Ekatra, who have enabled a new channel of inclusive growth and cultural sustainability.

9. Issues and Moral Concerns

Although the mix of traditional arts and modern technologies has futuristic potential, it also entails intricate puzzles and ethical dilemmas, which have to be dealt with carefully.

Cultural appropriation and misrepresentation: The difference between cultural appreciation and appropriation is thin. Sacred art forms without bargaining with their origins may be contrived, and sacred art may sail a wrong impression to the locals. To assure the authenticity and a mutual respect, it is important that the wellness programs include the local artists as partners and cultural experts.

Technological inequality and digital exclusion: Technology literacy can be a limiting factor for rural artists to take part in digital projects. In the absence of proper training and infrastructure, the chances of urban-based models taking control of wellness tourism are high as it may be at the cost of the very communities that these programs are meant to empower.

Data privacy and consent: It would be necessary to obtain biometric data in order to provide an AI and human curated custom experience of wellness. Transparency in data practice, informed consent, and the best practices in cybersecurity are necessary to safeguard the privacy and win the trust of guests.

Fair and economic sustainability: The fair remuneration or the wage parity and the equitable profit-sharing systems of the artisans are crucial. The essence of wellness tourism can be compromised by rapacious intermediaries or over-commercialization, and the ultimate survival of the traditional practices.

Environmental effects: Mass tourism projects, despite being wellness-oriented, may produce unintended environmental impacts, including depletion of resources, creation of waste, and disturbance of habitat. There is a need to put emphasis on low-impact infrastructure and regenerative behavior when it comes to the preservation of natural ecosystems.

India can adhere to the moral standards of its wellness tourism business and experience inclusive growth by paying attention to such issues on the policy framework level, the community cooperation aspect, and ongoing communication with the stakeholders.

10. Future Trends and Suggestions

Wellness tourism in India is likely to be much more individualized, engrossing, and combined with technology and ancient knowledge. The future is dynamic and exciting, as several emerging trends denote.

Hyper-personalized wellness journeys: Wearables and AI will make it possible to create very hyper-personalized wellness programs when it comes to retreats. The guests can have initial biometric evaluations, which will provide them with an individualized schedule, such as using particular ragas during morning meditations, custom dance moves to balance energy, and personal art actions depending on their emotional state.

Multi-sensory healing environments: The next generation wellness environment will be multi-sensory in nature with a combination of visuals, sounds, and even smell. As an example, an AR experience of a meditation dome may be based on walls projecting a traditional mandala, a rhythmic to raga-based soundtrack, and fragrances imitating temple practice. These set-ups are geared toward enhancing further meditative conditions and thus emotional recollections and comprehensive healing.

Virtual art mentorship and global collaboration: AI will make traditional Indian arts more democratic with the help of virtual mentors and holographic guides. A visitor in Europe may be taught Warli painting by a local artist in Maharashtra through completely paying attention to the virtual world. These models promote international exchange of culture and the generation of new revenue among the rural localities.

Sustainability of environment and regenerative tourism model: It will be imperative to focus on environmental sustainability. Incorporating organic agriculture, generating renewable energy, raiding round kitchens and zero-waste kitchens, and sustainability in facilities, resorts, and wellness centers will become a part of the process. The travelers will resort to more value-aligned experiences that are in accordance with their environmental responsibility.

Policy and capacity building initiatives: To encourage such evolution, to maintain a favorable environment, governments in alliance with tourism boards should provide favorable policies. Digital support investment, the artisan development initiatives, as well as the art-based wellness practitioners certification levels are all-essential.

The benefits of innovation by engaging artists, technologists, psychologists, tourism operators, and policymakers in a common front will not be at the expense of cultural integrity and social equity. Adoption of these futuristic strategies will enable India to become a global player in the area of holistic, art-combined wellness tourism.

11. Conclusion

India is poised on the cusp of a revolutionary chapter of wellness tourism, with all its ancient art and science traditions and contemporary technology innovations working together to form uniquely and deeply immersive and healing experiences. The involvement of classical dance, traditional music, folk art, and native practices in the frameworks of wellness not only improves the visitor experience but also enriches India with its rich culture through preservation and regeneration.

Using immersive technologies, such as VR and AR, and implementing AI to create individual healing programs, India will be able to accommodate the changing demands of international tourists who are after more profound emotional and spiritual experiences. Concurrently, rural artisans must be empowered, green sustainability must be encouraged, and ethical concerns must be upheld so that these innovations can not only help but also not inflict and bring out people in a form of exploitation.

Amidst the global trend of embracing wellness as a means to living a whole-of-life, India can be an example to be followed – wellness experiences in India must not only be luxurious but highly experiential, culturally authentic. Future wellness tourism in India has the chance to adopt a worldwide pattern: a healing place that enriches the soul and rejoices the gift of ages of artistic tradition.

References

Bhat, S. (2015). *Indian art and its spiritual relevance in the modern world*. Rupa Publications.

Cohen, E., & Cohen, S. A. (2012). Current sociological theories and issues in tourism. *Annals of Tourism Research*, *39*(4), 2177–2202. https://doi.org/10.1016/j.annals.2012.07.009

George, E. W., Mair, H., & Reid, D. G. (2009). *Rural tourism development: Localism and cultural change*. Channel View Publications.

Global Wellness Institute. (2023). *Global wellness economy monitor 2023*. https://globalwellnessinstitute.org/

Gupta, N., & Rajan, V. (2021). Therapeutic potentials of Indian folk art: Case studies on Madhubani and Warli painting. *Indian Journal of Art Therapy*, *6*(2), 34–49.

Jung, T. H., Tom Dieck, M. C., Lee, H., & Chung, N. (2016). Effects of virtual reality and augmented reality on visitor experiences in museum. *Information & Management*, *53*(4), 504–516. https://doi.org/10.1016/j.im.2015.12.005

Kapoor, V., & Sharma, A. (2020). Digital wellness: The role of technology in modern healing practices. *Indian Journal of Tourism & Wellness*, *18*(4), 89–104.

Kumar, R. (2018). Revitalizing rural arts through technology: A case study of wellness tourism in India. *International Journal of Rural Tourism*, *14*(2), 115–129.

Mehta, A., & Rao, D. (2019). AI and music therapy in wellness tourism: A study of personalized raga playlists. *Journal of Cultural Tourism*, *10*(3), 204–218.

Mitra, S., & Patel, V. (2018). Motion capture and virtual dance therapies: A new frontier in wellness tourism. *Indian Journal of Arts and Technology*, *12*(1), 45–60.

Patel, R., & Singh, M. (2022). Augmented reality and immersive experiences in cultural wellness tourism. *Journal of Emerging Tourism Technologies*, *7*(1), 51–67.

Sharma, P. (2016). Raga and emotion: The therapeutic use of classical music in wellness. *Indian Journal of Music Therapy*, *22*(2), 67–81.

Sharma, S., & Desai, R. (2020). Healing through sound: The integration of binaural beats in wellness tourism. *Journal of Holistic Health*, *9*(1), 101–115.

Singh, R., & Jain, K. (2023). Wearable technology and AI in personalized wellness programs: Opportunities and challenges. *Journal of Health and Technology Integration*, *4*(2), 88–102.

Smith, A. (2017). Exploring wellness tourism in India: History and contemporary practices. *Wellness Journal of South Asia*, *11*(4), 204–215.

Stuckey, H. L., & Nobel, J. (2010). The connection between art, healing, and public health: A review of current literature. *American Journal of Public Health*, *100*(2), 254–263. https://doi.org/10.2105/AJPH.2008.156497

Zhang, H. Q., & Hitchcock, M. (2017). Cultural tourism and tourism cultures: Theoretical perspectives. *Tourism Culture & Communication*, *17*(1), 1–8. https://doi.org/10.3727/109830417X14902194279257

Chapter 6

Marketing and Consumer Behavior: Jakarta Healthy with Health Mobile Application

Ali Faik[a] *and Tiurida Lily Anita*[b]

[a]*Online Management Study Program, Universitas Siber Asia, Jakarta, Indonesia*
[b]*Hotel Management Department, Faculty of Digital Communication and Hotel & Tourism, Bina Nusantara University, Jakarta, Indonesia*

Abstract

In the evolving landscape of medical tourism, mobile technology plays a pivotal role in reshaping consumer interaction and healthcare engagement. This study develops an empirical framework that examines behavioral dynamics behind continued mobile health application usage within the medical tourism context. Using a structural equation model with Smart-PLS, the research integrates technological readiness, perceived ease of use (PEOU), and perceived value (PV) as exogenous variables, customer satisfaction (CS) as a mediator, and continuance intention to use (CITU) as the outcome. Findings show that technological readiness and PV significantly influence CS and continuance intention, while PEOU has no significant impact. CS plays a mediating role between exogenous variables and continuance intention. These insights provide guidance for medical tourism businesses and application developers to enhance consumer satisfaction and loyalty through health applications.

Keywords: Medical tourism; mobile health application; technological readiness; perceived ease of use; perceived value; consumer satisfaction; continuance intention to use

Advancement in Medical and Wellness Tourism, Part A: Entrepreneurship and Technology, 67–81

doi:10.1108/978-1-80592-983-320261007

1. Introduction

Technology plays a critical role in modern business transactions by offering efficiency and flexibility. However, not all users are comfortable adopting new technologies (Latif & Widyatama, 2021). The rapid advancement of the internet and communication technologies has created opportunities for service providers to innovate and deliver value (Chen et al., 2021; Shin & Dai, 2022). These innovations have transformed service delivery methods and reshaped consumer lifestyles (Yang et al., 2021).

With this development, all individuals or companies can easily access the internet without limits and distances by utilizing the resources they have. Technology will evolve rapidly in this century. However, technology will also run effectively if used in the right and correct use (Shin & Dai, 2022). With these conditions, service providers from all industries will compete to innovate in technology development for the benefit of users and companies.

The innovations carried out include digital transformation of the service system. Where it's interpreted as a change in work methods with the help of technology, so that work results can be effective and efficient (Kinanthi & Sicily, 2024). These innovations will make customers feel that the technology used is easy to understand and operationalize (Mei Min et al., 2022). It's helping and making it easier for customers to get services. The consequences caused include changes in a person's lifestyle and the opening of business opportunities (Yang et al., 2021).

In the business world, companies must be able to develop business strategies to winner the competition (Rachman et al., 2024). With this competition, companies develop technology so they don't fall behind and lose. The development of technology in this day and age is caused by changes in the world related to economic, social, and cultural (Sibarani & Siregar, 2023). So, encourage the community to always follow these developments and align with interconnected needs (Bangun & Rezeki, 2025).

Mobile applications have emerged as essential innovations across industries, including healthcare (Pradipta & Sukarsa, 2022). Both government and private providers now offer mobile health applications to monitor health effectively and improve public awareness (Godwin et al., 2024; Wulur et al., 2020). While adoption of mobile apps has been widely studied in banking, e-commerce, and food delivery services (Elvina & Rahmani, 2023; Japarianto & Anggono, 2020; Wangsadinata et al., 2021), there is limited research on mobile health applications within medical tourism. This study addresses that gap by analyzing how technological readiness, PEOU, and PV affect CS and continuance intention.

Studies that explain the implementation of technological and communication developments in health mobile applications have not been widely done. The study was widely applied to research in the field of banking applications, such as mobile banking applications (Elvina & Rahmani, 2023), the field of general e-commerce Tokopedia (Japarianto & Anggono, 2020; Prajogo, 2021), and food and beverage delivery services, such as Shopee food (Wangsadinata et al., 2021).

In this study, technological readiness, PEOU, and PV in the use of health mobile applications are exogenous variables, while CS is the mediating variable, and cCITU is the outcome. This study aims to find out whether technological readiness, PEOU, and PV affect CS and whether this has an impact on CITU.

2. Literature Review

2.1. Technological Readiness

Technological readiness reflects an individual's willingness to adopt new technologies, influenced by optimism, innovativeness, discomfort, and insecurity (Bagaskara, 2024; Godwin et al., 2024). To learn this technology, readiness from various aspects is needed. Psychological aspects and consumer behavior will greatly influence the use of this technology (Bagaskara, 2024). Technology readiness (TR) is defined as an attitude to be able to accept or reject the presence of a new technology (Marthin & Hadiprawoto, 2022). With the presence of new technology, it's hoped that the advancement of information and technology will be more sophisticated.

In another definition, TR is defined as the mediation between the user of the technology and the technology they use. TR is also referred to as a person's mental readiness to accept innovation in technology (Bagaskara, 2024). This mentality can have positive or negative effects. The goal is to refer to the achievement of acceptance and use of new technologies in human life that are in harmony with work and readiness for the acceptance of these technologies (Chen et al., 2021). Humans will tend to learn about this technology so that life at work can run more easily and comfortably. In the world of work, TR will be harmonized by adopting new technologies in the workplace (Afiana et al., 2024).

Optimism and innovativeness are the drivers for the adoption of new technologies, while discomfort and insecurity are activities that can hinder the adoption of these new technologies (Godwin et al., 2024). Positive readiness supports technology adoption and sustained use (Ismail & Wahid, 2020). In this study, the indicators used in TR are in the dimensions of optimism, innovativeness, discomfort, and insecurity (Afiana et al., 2024).

H1. TR has a significant effect on CS in the use of health mobile applications.

H5. TR has a significant effect on CITU in the use of health mobile applications.

H8. TR indirectly affects CITU through CS in the use of health mobile application.

2.2. Perceived Ease of Use

PEOU refers to the belief that technology is easy to learn and operate (Davis, 1989). Ease of use can drive satisfaction and loyalty (Aziz et al., 2020; Humbani & Wiese, 2019). PEOU is the basic thing that customers receive for the acceptance of technology and the experience gained while using the technology

(Ruangkanjanases & Hariguna, 2025). This can happen if a person believes that the use of technology will make it easier to carry out all their activities.

Technology is increasingly developing, so these developments are awaited by the wider community. The development of technology with a simpler display design for use is an element of PEOU, so that it can be accepted by the wider community and doesn't interfere with productivity (Olivia & Marchyta, 2022).

The customer believes in the use of technology so that he can behave in himself toward the use of the technology based on the feelings felt in the use of the technology, so that it is easy to learn, that is the PEOU, which is part of the system that is formed (Davis, 1989; Duy Phuong et al., 2020). There are three indicators in the measurement of PEOU, including ease of use, ease of learning, and ease of understanding interaction (Ruangkanjanases & Hariguna, 2025).

By feeling happy and happy in the easy use of technology, customers will use it continuously to make their lives easier. So that all the work will be completed properly. PEOU affects CITU (Aziz et al., 2020). With this convenience, a sense of satisfaction and happiness will arise, which causes consumer satisfaction. PEOU affects CS (Humbani & Wiese, 2019).

H2. PEOU has a significant effect on CS in the use of health mobile applications.

H6. PEOU has a significant effect on CITU in the use of health mobile applications.

H9. PEOU indirectly affects CITU through CS in the use of health mobile applications.

2.3. Perceived Value

PV is a part of marketing, where customers get value from what the manufacturer provides, and can be a benchmark for the success of a company (Pratama Hafidz & Huriyahnuryi, 2023). With the value received, more and more can reflect the company's success in managing and selling its products and services. This value is a comparison between the benefits received and the costs incurred by consumers (Soelasih et al., 2024). And this assessment is a PV (Kinanthi & Sicily, 2024).

On this day, value is an important element in creating CS and how to maintain it (Yum & Kim, 2024). With competitive advantages, it can compete with other companies. PV can affect customer happiness (Kinanthi & Sicily, 2024), where the happiness will be reflected in their attitude of accepting/rejecting the product or service. The implementation of PV is the value that consumers feel from their interactions and experiences (Haqqo & Isharina, 2024).

Described as something that is created jointly between producers and consumers, which leads to the value created by each perception (Haqqo & Isharina, 2024). The assessment will have many aspects, either before, during, or after its use, which will ultimately create value. The use of PV is important for business continuity because it's considered the key to success in the company (Vaniara & Pramono, 2022).

With good value for customers, it will definitely create CS. PV affects CS (Kinanthi & Sicily, 2024). And with the value created together by consumers, it is hoped that consumers can continue to always use the product or service. PV affects CITU (Haqqo & Isharina, 2024). In this study, the indicators used in PV include good value for money, reasonable, worthwhile, and give good indicators (Haqqo & Isharina, 2024).

H3. PV has a significant effect on CS in the use of health mobile applications.

H7. PV has a significant effect on CITU in the use of the Traveloka mobile application.

H10. PV indirectly affects CITU through CS in the use of health mobile applications.

2.4. Customer Satisfaction

CS is built on cognitive constructs and emotional constructs (Amoroso et al., 2023). When customers consume products or services for their first experience, satisfaction is determined by the experience they receive (Windiarti & Suwandi, 2022), considering the characteristics and features that fulfill their needs.

Customers will feel satisfied if all their expectations are achieved from the product/service (Wilson et al., 2021). Dissatisfaction will arise if the customer is not satisfied, and dissatisfaction is due to various factors and will cause complaints from customers (Sibarani & Siregar, 2023).

The comparison between what is expected and what is received is CS. Satisfaction arises when performance meets expectations, influencing loyalty and continuance intention (Iqbal et al., 2018; Li & Huang, 2019). If the focus is only on high CS, then customers will easily change their minds if there is something better (Wulandari et al., 2024).

CS can have a positive effect on the services they receive, where CS is a goal for the service company to achieve customer loyalty. CS affects CITU (Li & Huang, 2019). Basically, CS is the success of a business that plays a role in winning in competition (Collins et al., 2021). There are four indicators to measure CS, including evaluation, desire to buy back, recommend, and overall satisfaction (Collins et al., 2021).

H4. CS has a significant effect on CITU in the use of health mobile applications.

2.5. Continuance Intention to Use

CITU is the relationship between the customer's intention and real action based on logic and facts (Hesti Candra Sari, 2022). Continuance intention is the likelihood that customers will continue using a technology, reflecting commitment and loyalty (Tan et al., 2023). It is influenced by satisfaction and PV.

Commitment and loyalty are the process of CITU (Li & Huang, 2019), so that the process can be sustainable. Basically, CITU aims to make customers have a continuous intention to always use.

Customers feel emotionally and cognitively confident in using the product/service and always strive to intend to continue to use a technology (Humbani & Wiese, 2019). CS affects CITU (Kurniawan et al., 2024). There are three indicators in measuring CITU, including: will use, without thinking twice, and will persist in choosing (Soelasih et al., 2024).

Based on the literature review, the research model is as follows (see Fig. 6.1):

3. Research Methodology

The approach in this study is quantitative research. The population in this study is users of health mobile applications. The questionnaire has been tested for distribution before it is distributed to respondents (Humbani & Wiese, 2019). The results of the questionnaire were then analyzed using the partial least square (PLS)-structural equation model (SEM) method to assess the validity and reliability of each indicator in the variable and calculate statistical *T* and *P* values to answer the hypothesis proposed in this study (Wilson et al., 2021). The tool used in this study is SmartPLS version 3.2.9. The sampling technique used in this study is purposive sampling. The purposive sampling technique is part of the non-probability sampling technique. Sampling itself is part of the population to be analyzed. The minimum sample determination for the SEM used in this study is based on the theory by Hair et al., where the number of samples used is 5–10× the number of indicators (Bangun & Rezeki, 2025). Based on this theory, the number of samples for this study is 160 respondents from health mobile application users.

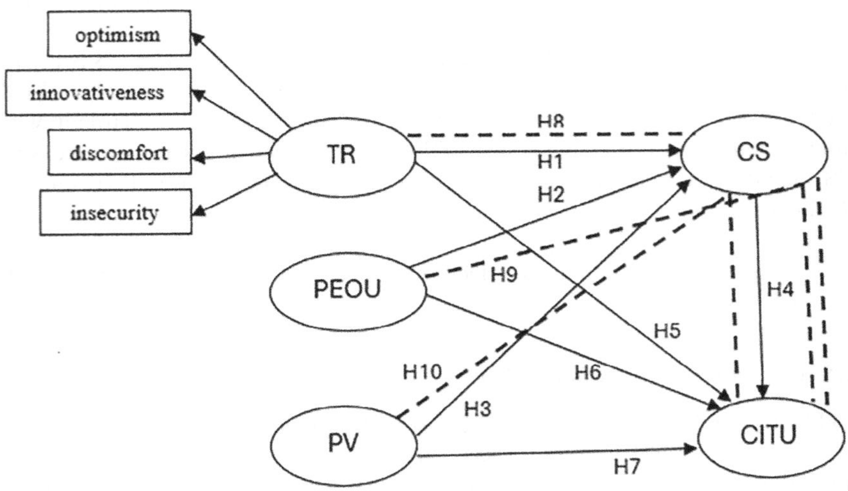

Fig. 6.1. Research Model. *Source*: Data processed by researchers, 2025.

4. Result and Discussion

Demographically, the data obtained from the questionnaire are as follows:

Table 6.1. Demographic Respondent.

Gender	Count	Percentage (%)
Male	89	55.62
Female	71	44.38
Age (Years)	**Count**	**Percentage (%)**
15–20	12	7.5
21–30	46	28.8
31–40	71	44.4
41–50	23	4.9
>50	8	14.4
Education	**Count**	**Percentage (%)**
SMA/SMK	61	38.1
Diploma	22	13.8
Sarjana	49	30.6
Pasca Sarjana	22	13.8
Doctoral	6	3.7
Profession	**Count**	**Percentage (%)**
Private employee	60	37.5
PNS/BUMN/BUMD	18	11.3
Entrepreneurial	44	27.5
Other	38	23.7
Health mobile application used frequency/month	**Count**	**Percentage (%)**
1×	32	20
2×	60	37.5
3×	48	30
>3×	1	12.5
Health mobile application use	**Count**	**Percentage (%)**
Mobile JKN	46	28.7
JAKSEHAT	62	38.7
Halo doc	24	15
Satu Sehat	8	7.6
Other	16	10

Source: Primary data, 2025.

The results in Table 6.1 consisted of 89 male respondents (55.62%) and 71 female (44.38%) respondents, the majority of respondents aged 31–40 years is 71 respondents (44.4%), high-school education is 61 respondent (38.1%), working as private employees is 60 respondent (37.5%), frequency of using health mobile applications as much as 2 times a month is 60 respondent (37.5) and mobile health is often used by JAKSEHAT is 62 respondent (38.7%).

4.1. Measurement Model Evaluation

4.1.1. Structural Model Evaluation

The purpose of testing the outer model is to test whether the data are valid and reliable. To test validity, it consists of a convergent validity test and a discriminant validity test. Meanwhile, testing reliability consists of a composite reliability test and a Cronbach's alpha test.

4.1.2. Convergent Validity Test

To test the validity of the convergent by looking at the factor loading value >0.7 and the average variance extracted (AVE) value >0.5 (Chandrawati & Vidyanata, 2022). The result of convergent validity shows a factor loading value >0.7 and an AVE value >0.5.

4.1.3. Discriminant Validity Test

To test the validity discriminant by means of a cross-loading value of more than 0.7 in 1 variable (Chandrawati & Vidyanata, 2022) and the Fornell–Larker criterion, i.e., with the squared root value of AVE >0.7 or the correlation value of the construct of the variable itself exceeds the correlation of the other variables (Duy Phuong et al., 2020). The results show related cross-loading, where the cross-loading value of all indicators in the construction itself has a greater value than the loading factor indicator in other constructions. This concludes that all unrelated constructions are unrelated and meet the criteria of discriminant validity, and the result is tested using the Fornell–Larker criterion, as shown in Table 6.2.

The test results in Table 6.2 related to the Fornell–Larcker analysis showed that the square root of each construct's AVE was greater than its correlations with other constructs. Taken together, these results confirm that the measurement model demonstrates adequate validity.

4.1.4. Composite Reliability Test and Cronbach Alpha Test

The Cronbach's alpha value is declared reliable if the Cronbach's alpha value >0.7. Meanwhile, the reliability for the composite reliability value is >0.7 (Haryanti,

Table 6.2. Fornell–Larker Criterion.

	CITU	CS	PEOU	PV	TR
CITU	0.850				
CS	0.547	0.847			
PEOU	0.602	0.641	0.902		
PV	0.233	0.497	0.357	0.872	
TR	0.634	0.693	0.930	0.370	0.921

Source: Primary data, 2025.

2020). The following is a table of reliability tests in Table 6.3 show that the Cronbach's alpha value >0.7 and the composite reliability value is >0.7.

Based on the validity and reliability test, all instruments used in this study were declared valid and reliable.

The purpose of testing the inner model is to connect between variables in the study (Chandrawati & Vidyanata, 2022). The measurement components tested in the assessment of the structural model (inner model) are the determination coefficient (R-square) and path coefficient test, predictive relevance (Q-square) model fit (normed fit index – NFI), as well as the results of hypothesis testing.

4.1.5. Determination Coefficient (R-square)

The R-square value for each endogenous (bound) latent variable is the predictive strength of the structural model. Meanwhile, the change in the value of R-square can be used to explain the influence of certain exogenous (free) latent variables on endogenous latent variables. The following is the R-square table in this study. R-square results indicated that 43% of the variation in CITU and 54.7% of the variation in CS were explained by the model.

4.1.6. Path Coefficient Test

Path coefficients show a level of significance in hypothesis testing (Chandrawati & Vidyanata, 2022). The range of values in the path coefficients is in the range

Table 6.3. Reliability Test.

	Cronbach Alpha	Composite Reliability	Result
CITU	0.808	0.886	Reliable
CS	0.870	0.910	Reliable
PEOU	0.885	0.929	Reliable
PV	0.896	0.927	Reliable
TR	0.989	0.990	Reliable

Source: Primary data, 2025.

of −1 to 1, with the note that the values of the range of 0 to 1 are considered to have a positive direction, while the values of the range of −1 to 0 are considered to have a negative direction.

From the results in Table 6.4, it is concluded that all values of path coefficients are positive, except the path coefficient in the PV on CITU is −0.071, which indicates that the influence is negative. The value of path coefficients in the PEOU on CS was −0.048, which indicates that the influence is negative. Path coefficient results revealed:

- TR significantly affects CS and CITU.
- PV significantly affects CS but negatively impacts CITU.
- PEOU significantly affects CITU but negatively impacts CS.
- CS significantly affects CITU.

4.1.7. Predictive Relevance (Q-square)

In this test, the amount of predictive relevance (Q-square) in the structural model serves to measure how well the observation value has been accumulated by the model along with its estimated parameters. If the value of $Q^2 > 0$, it proves that the reconstructed values have predictive relevance, and if the value of $Q^2 < 0$, it also proves that the reconstructed values do not have predictive relevance. The results show that the predictive relevance (*Q*-square) values in the CITU and CS variables are 0.288 and 0.367, which states that the Q^2 value >0 proves that the values have been reconstructed so that they have predictive relevance.

4.1.8. Model Fit (NFI)

One measure of fit in the SEM literature is the NFI, which is to calculate the Chi^2 value of the proposed model and compares it with a meaningful benchmark. This fit model is the standard value required for fitting the research structural model. The NFI value is between 0 and 1. If the approach is 1, the better the level of compatibility of the research structural model. The results show concluded that the NFI value is 0.620 in the saturated model and 0.620 in the estimated model,

Table 6.4. Path Coefficient.

	CITU	CS	PEOU	PV	TR
CITU					
CS	0.240				
PEOU	0.103	−0.048			
PV	−0.071	0.279			
TR	0.399	0.634			

Source: Primary data, 2025.

which indicates that it is approaching to 1 and is interpreted as a better level of structural model fit in this study.

4.1.9. Hypothesis Test

The hypothesis test in this study was carried out using the SEM PLS method through a bootstrapping process with the help of the SmartPLS 3.2.9 program. The relationship between latent constructs can be statistically inferred based on the value of *T* statistics >1.96 or *P*-value <5% is hypothesis accepted, while the magnitude of influence between latent constructs is based on the value of the path coefficient. The results are shown in Table 6.5.

The results in Table 6.5 indicate that *H1*, *H3*, *H4*, *H5*, *H8*, and *H10* are all accepted with a *P*-value <5%, and *H2*, *H6*, *H7*, and *H9* are all rejected with a *P*-value >5%.

5. Conclusion

This study demonstrates that technological readiness and PV significantly influence CS and CITU health mobile applications, while PEOU does not. CS mediates the effects of readiness and value on continuance intention. These findings extend technology acceptance model (TAM) and TR theory to the medical tourism context. CS is a customer's assessment of a product or service he receives and is always compared to what he gets with what he expects. Satisfied if fulfilled, not satisfied if not fulfilled. The level of satisfaction will be translated into CITU because it will be influenced by the CS formed.

This condition will be formed from the customer because they receive benefits in the use of the health mobile application. The customer is satisfied, then CITU

Table 6.5. Hypothesis Test.

	***T* Statistics (|O/STDEV|)**	***P* Values**	**Result**
CS → CITU	2.530	0.012	*H4* Accepted
PEOU → CITU	0.534	0.593	*H6* Rejected
PEOU → CS	0.326	0.744	*H2* Rejected
PV → CITU	0.940	0.348	*H7* Rejected
PV → CS	4.679	0.000	*H3* Accepted
TR → CITU	1.986	0.048	*H5* Accepted
TR → CS	4.394	0.000	*H1* Accepted
PEOU → CS → CITU	0.285	0.776	*H9* Rejected
PV → CS → CITU	2.205	0.028	*H10* Accepted
TR → CS → CITU	2.032	0.043	*H8* Accepted

Source: Primary data, 2025.

will occur, but if the customer is not satisfied, then CITU will not necessarily occur. The achievement of PV is also felt by many customers. The value created will bring benefits to himself and others. Performance improvement is one of the consequences of the value obtained and utilized. The use of technological readiness will bring CS. The PV is a concept that can show how to influence individual behavior for CITU.

To increase the PEOU health mobile application, it is necessary to have guidelines/procedures for using the application so that it is easy to understand. With this convenience, it can make customers to carry out CITU. For app developers and medical tourism providers, the findings emphasize enhancing PV (e.g., cost-effectiveness, usefulness) and ensuring readiness to adopt new features. Ease of use alone may not guarantee long-term adoption.

Finally, to increase the CS of health mobile application users, there needs to be a good breakthrough/innovation so that the application can be used by all ages and all groups, so that it is not limited by space and time. There are variables that are not observed in this study that cause CS and CITU, so that the next study can consider other factors that can affect CS and CITU and their implementation in daily life. The implication of the results of this research on universities is the importance of considering that CS can be maximized to achieve the success of events in marketing and consumer behavior.

6. Data Accessibility and Author Contributions

The data supporting this chapter are openly available and can be accessed through https://doi.org/10.5281/zenodo.20020559. Ali Faik and Tiurida Lily Anita contributed to the conceptualization, development, and preparation of this chapter. Ali Faik contributed to the data collection, data analysis, interpretation of findings, and drafting of the manuscript. Tiurida Lily Anita contributed to the conceptual framework, supervision, critical review, editing, and refinement of the manuscript. Both authors reviewed and approved the final version of the chapter.

References

Afiana, F. N., Rifai, Z., & Frilisia, W. A. (2024). Integrasi technology readiness dan technology acceptance model Terhadap Kesiapan Pengguna Enterprise Resource Planning (ERP) pada Industri Pengolahan Kelapa Organik. *Jurnal Sistem Informasi Bisnis*, *14*(2), 100–110. https://doi.org/10.21456/vol14iss2pp100-110

Amoroso, D., Lim, R., Lei, J., & Saxena, A. (2023). A study of satisfaction and loyalty for continuance intention of mobile wallet in India. *International Journal of E-Adoption*, *15*(1), 1–18. https://doi.org/10.4018/ijea.319313

Aziz, F., Md Rami, A., Razali, F., & Mahadi, N. (2020). The influence of leadership style towards technology acceptance in organization. *International Journal of Advanced Science and Technology*, *29*(7 Special Issue), 218–225.

Bagaskara, M. (2024). The effect of AI on smart customer experience with moderation of technology readiness. *Journal of Social Studies Arts and Humanities (JSSAH)*, *4*(1), 014–021. https://doi.org/10.33751/jssah.v4i1.9954

Bangun, L., & Rezeki, S. (2025). The influence of customer satisfaction and brand trust on customer retention of Telkomsel prepaid card products. *Jurnal Manajemen Bisnis Eka Prasetya Penelitian Ilmu Manajemen, 11*(1), 179–190. https://doi.org/10.47663/jmbep.v11i1.560

Chandrawati, A. A., & Vidyanata, D. (2022). Pengaruh perceived quality dan perceived value of cost terhadap Loyalitas Pelanggan melalui Kepuasan Pelanggan pada Fresh. Co. *Jembatan: Jurnal Ilmiah Manajemen, 19*(1), 49–68. https://doi.org/10.29259/jmbt.v19i1.17758

Chen, S. C., Li, S. H., Liu, S. C., Yen, D. C., & Ruangkanjanases, A. (2021). Assessing determinants of continuance intention towards personal cloud services: Extending UTAUT2 with technology readiness. *Symmetry, 13*(3). https://doi.org/10.3390/sym13030467

Collins, S. P., Storrow, A., Liu, D., Jenkins, C. A., Miller, K. F., Kampe, C., & Butler, J. (2021). Examining whether a self-care program reduces healthcare use and improves health among patients with acute heart failure. *The Guided HF Study, 6*(3), 167–186.

Davis, F. D. (1989). Perceived usefulness, perceived ease of use, and user acceptance of information technology. *MIS Quarterly: Management Information Systems, 13*(3), 319–339. https://doi.org/10.2307/249008

Duy Phuong, N. N., Luan, L. T., Van Dong, V., & Le Nhat Khanh, N. (2020). Examining customers' continuance intentions towards e-wallet usage: The emergence of mobile payment acceptance in Vietnam. *Journal of Asian Finance, Economics and Business, 7*(9), 505–516. https://doi.org/10.13106/JAFEB.2020.VOL7.NO9.505

Elvina, A., & Rahmani, N. A. (2023). Pengaruh perceived usefulness, perceived easy of use, perceived risk, dan perceived compatibility Terhadap Proses Keputusan Nasabah Menggunakan mobile banking Bank Syariah Indonesia. *Jurnal Ilmiah Ekonomi Islam, 9*(2), 2799–2805. http://dx.doi.org/10.29040/jiei.v9i2.8792

Godwin, G., Any, B., Delhi, A., Sunarya, P. A., & Nicola, G. (2024). Pengaruh technology readiness dan satisfaction Terhadap Penerimaan Penggunaan Safe Entry Station. *Technomedia Journal, 8*(3 Februari), 148–167. https://doi.org/10.33050/tmj.v8i3.2179

Haqqo, C. I., & Isharina, I. K. (2024). Influence of content quality and personalization on continuous intention to subscribe Netflix through the mediation of perceived value. *Journal of Business and Management Review, 5*(5), 407–425. https://doi.org/10.47153/jbmr.v5i5.888

Haryanti, S. (2020). Pengaruh Google Classroom melalui Youtube dan Powerpoint terhadap Hasil Belajar Statistika Mahasiswa Tingkat 1 ARO Kartika Indera Persada dengan Pendekatan Partial Least Square (PLS). *Prosiding Seminar Nasional Dan Diskusi Panel Pendidikan Matematika Universitas Indraprasta PGRI Jakarta* (pp. 89–96).

Hesti Candra Sari. (2022). The impact of perceived risk, perceived benefit, and trust on customer intention to use Tokopedia Apps. *Jurnal Bisnis Strategi, 31*(2), 145–159.

Humbani, M., & Wiese, M. (2019). An integrated framework for the adoption and continuance intention to use mobile payment apps. *International Journal of Bank Marketing, 37*(2), 646–664. https://doi.org/10.1108/IJBM-03-2018-0072

Iqbal, M. S., Hassan, M. U., & Habibah, U. (2018). The mediating role of customer satisfaction Impact of self-service technology (SST) service quality on customer loyalty and behavioral intention: The mediating role of customer satisfaction. *Cogent Business & Management, 50*(1). https://doi.org/10.1080/23311975.2018.1423770

Ismail, A. K., & Wahid, A. N. (2020). A review on technology readiness concept to explain consumer's online purchase. *International Journal of Industrial Management (IJIM), 6*(2000), 49–57.

Japarianto, E., & Anggono, Y. D. (2020). Analisa Pengaruh perceived ease of use Terhadap intention to buy Dengan perceived usefulness Sebagai Variabel Intervening Pada Aplikasi E-commerce Tokopedia. *Jurnal Strategi Pemasaran, 7*(1), 1–9.

Kinanthi, G. E., & Sisilia, K. (2024). Pengaruh customer expectations dan perceived value Terhadap customer satisfaction Pada user Aplikasi Dinotis. *JMBI UNSRAT (Jurnal Ilmiah Manajemen Bisnis Dan Inovasi Universitas Sam Ratulangi)*, *11*(1), 853–870. https://doi.org/10.35794/jmbi.v11i1.55094

Kurniawan, A. C., Rachmawati, N. L., Ayu, M. M., Ong, A. K. S., & Redi, A. A. N. P. (2024). Determinants of satisfaction and continuance intention towards online food delivery service users in Indonesia post the COVID-19 pandemic. *Heliyon*, *10*(1), e23298. https://doi.org/10.1016/j.heliyon.2023.e23298

Latif, D. V., & Widyatama, U. (2021, December). The effect of gender in the implementation of self ordering machine in a fast food restaurant. *Turkish Journal of Computer and Mathematics Education (TURCOMAT)*, *12*(11), 1292–1396.

Li, M., & Huang, S. (2019). Understanding customers' continuance intentions toward in-lobby self-service technologies. *Frontiers in Psychology*, *10*(February), 1–12. https://doi.org/10.3389/fpsyg.2019.00332

Marthin, D. C., & Hadiprawoto, T. R. (2022). The effect of omnichannel perceived value and integration toward customer satisfaction: Technology readiness as moderator. *Proceedings of the International Conference on Family Business and Entrepreneurship*, *3*(1). http://e-journal.president.ac.id/presunivojs/index.php/ICFBE/article/view/3768

Mei Min, Jian Ai, Chun Kent, S. et al. (2022). *FACTORS AFFECTING GENERATION Z'S INTENTION TO USE SELF-SERVICE TECHNOLOGY (SST) Mei Min, Chow; 2 Jian Ai, Yeow & 3 Chun Kent, See. 12*(1), 81–96. https://www.e-journal.uum.edu.my/index.php/jbma/article/download/14722/3301

Olivia, M., & Marchyta, N. K. (2022). The influence of perceived ease of use and perceived usefulness on E-wallet continuance intention: Intervening role of customer satisfaction. *Jurnal Teknik Industri*, *24*(1), 13–22. https://doi.org/10.9744/jti.24.1

Pradipta, O. A., & Sukarsa, I. (2022). Pengembangan UI Aplikasi Mobile Konsultasi Karir Menggunakan Metode Lean UX. *Jurnal Ilmiah Teknologi Dan Komputer*, *3*(1), 1–11. https://ojs.unud.ac.id/index.php/jitter/article/download/84782/43682

Prajogo, U. (2021). Pengaruh perceived ease of use dan perceived usefulness terhadap Penggunaan Teknologi Marketplace dengan Attitude sebagai Variabel Intervening. *Jurnal Teknologi Dan Manajemen Informatika*, *7*(1), 62–68. https://doi.org/10.26905/jtmi.v7i1.5942

Pratama Hafidz, G., & Huriyahnuryi, K. (2023). The effect of perceived value on customer satisfaction and customer loyalty in the fast-food industry in Indonesia. *International Journal of Social Science, Education, Communication and Economics (SINOMICS JOURNAL)*, *2*(1), 41–62. https://doi.org/10.54443/sj.v2i1.113

Rachman, A., Fatimah, F., & Tyas, W. M. (2024). Analysis of the influence of brand image, price and service quality on customer loyalty through customer satisfaction as an intervening variable. *Jurnal Comparative: Ekonomi Dan Bisnis*, *6*(2), 209. https://doi.org/10.31000/combis.v6i2.11295

Ruangkanjanases, A., & Hariguna, T. (2025). Examining user satisfaction and continuous usage intention of digital financial advisory platforms. *HighTech and Innovation Journal*, *6*(1), 216–235. https://doi.org/10.28991/HIJ-2025-06-01-015

Shin, H., & Dai, B. (2022). The efficacy of customer's voluntary use of self-service technology (SST): A dual-study approach. *Journal of Strategic Marketing*, *30*(8), 723–745. https://doi.org/10.1080/0965254X.2020.1841269

Sibarani, Y., & Siregar, O. M. (2023). The influence of customer complaint behavior and brand image on the repurchase intention of J&T express services (study on expedition service users in Medan City). *Jurnal Akuntansi, Manajemen Dan Ilmu Ekonomi (JASMIEN)*, *04*(01), 53–60. https://journal.cattleyadf.org/index.php/Jasmien/index

Soelasih, Y., Sumani, S., & David Wetik, J. (2024). Determinants of customer intentions to continue using full-service airlines in Indonesia. *Cogent Business and Management*, *11*(1). https://doi.org/10.1080/23311975.2024.2428780

Tan, M. L., Vinnell, L. J., Valentin, A. P. M., Prasanna, R., & Becker, J. S. (2023). The public's perception of an earthquake early warning system: A study on factors influencing continuance intention. *International Journal of Disaster Risk Reduction*, *97*(September), 104032. https://doi.org/10.1016/j.ijdrr.2023.104032

Vaniara, F. V., & Pramono, R. (2022). The effect of perceived value, customer satisfaction and trust on customer loyalty at The DM clinic in East Jakarta. *Business and Accounting Research (IJEBAR) Peer Reviewed-International Journal*, *6*(3), 1–11. https://jurnal.stie-aas.ac.id/index.php/IJEBAR

Wangsadinata, R., Geraldine, C. N., & Aprillia, A. (2021). Pengaruh technology acceptance model (TAM), perceived enjoyment, Dan Perceived Risk Terhadap Behavioral Intention. *Jurnal Manajemen Perhotelah JMP*, *7*(2), 104–114. https://doi.org/10.9744/jmhot.7.2.104

Wilson, N., Alvita, M., & Wibisono, J. (2021). The effect of perceived ease of use and perceived. *Jurnal Muara Ilmu Ekonomi dan Bisnis*, *5*(1), 145–159.

Windiarti, S., & Suwandi. (2022). The effect of service quality and trust on customer satisfaction at Bca Kcp Jakarta 26. *International Journal of Economics*, *6*(4), 1852–1865. https://jurnal.stie-aas.ac.id/index.php/IJEBAR/article/view/7052%0Ahttps://jurnal.stie-aas.ac.id/index.php/IJEBAR/article/download/7052/2961

Wulandari, A. A., Akbar, A., & Lina, R. (2024). The effect of price and service quality on consumer satisfaction. *Advances: Jurnal Ekonomi & Bisnis*, *2*(6), 351–361. https://doi.org/10.60079/ajeb.v2i6.302

Wulur, L. M., Militina, T., & Achmad, G. N. (2020). Effect of service quality and brand trust on customer satisfaction and customer Loyalty Pertamina Hospital Balikpapan. *International Journal of Economics, Business and Accounting Research (IJEBAR)*, *4*(01), 72–83. https://doi.org/10.29040/ijebar.v4i01.908

Yang, K., Choi, J. G., & Chung, J. (2021). Extending the technology acceptance model (TAM) to explore customer's behavioral intention to use self-service technologies (SSTS) in Chinese budget hotels. *Global Business and Finance Review*, *26*(1), 79–94. https://doi.org/10.17549/gbfr.2021.26.1.79

Yum, K., & Kim, J. (2024). The influence of perceived value, customer satisfaction, and trust on loyalty in entertainment platforms. *Applied Sciences (Switzerland)*, *14*(13). https://doi.org/10.3390/app14135763

Chapter 7

How Perceived Value Influences Millennial Wellness Travel Decisions: Insights from Uttarakhand Region

Amit Tariyal and Abhay Chamoli

Senior Scale, School of Hospitality Management, IMS Unison, University, Dehradun, Uttarakhand, India

Abstract

This study investigates how three dimensions of perceived value: price, quality, and accessibility, shape millennial travelers' preference for wellness destinations in Uttarakhand, India. Using a judgmental sampling approach, responses from 260 participants were analyzed through structural equation modeling (SEM) in SPSS 26 to examine the relationships between observed and latent constructs. The findings reveal that all three dimensions significantly influence millennials' intention to visit wellness destinations, with quality emerging as the most critical factor, followed by price and accessibility. These results highlight the need for tourism stakeholders in Uttarakhand to prioritize authentic, high-quality wellness experiences while simultaneously improving accessibility infrastructure rather than focusing primarily on price competitiveness. The study further emphasizes the importance of standardized wellness certifications and stronger connectivity through public–private collaborations to position Uttarakhand as a high-end wellness destination. By offering empirical insights into value perceptions, the research contributes to wellness tourism literature and provides practical guidance for destination managers.

Keywords: Wellness destination; millennials; quality value; price value; accessibility value; Uttarakhand

Advancement in Medical and Wellness Tourism, Part A: Entrepreneurship and Technology, 83–95

doi:10.1108/978-1-80592-983-320261008

1. Introduction

The 2019 global pandemic was the watershed moment in public awareness of personal well-being and health. While people struggled with the physical and psychological impact of the crisis, there was greater awareness of the holistic practice of health and preventive medicine (Arcese et al., 2024). This momentum produced a swift boost in the popularity of wellness tourism – a type of tourism centered on the pursuit of physical, mental, and spiritual well-being through experiential experience (Backman et al., 2021). Wellness tourism, as the Global Wellness Institute (2025) defines it, is travel linked to the maintenance and enhancement of one's individual well-being. It involves yoga retreats, meditation, spa treatments, nature, and traditional healing. Since 2022, the global wellness tourism industry has been growing exponentially, doubling in value to $637 billion (Gough, 2024), evidence of a general cultural movement toward healthy living and experiential travel.

India, with its culture of holistic healing systems such as Ayurveda, yoga, and naturopathy, is a front-runner in this new industry. The Indian wellness tourism industry is worth $19.43 billion and is growing at a compound annual growth rate of 6.45% (TIMESOFINDIA.COM, 2024). Among the numerous states that add to this growth, Uttarakhand is one of the top wellness destinations. Uttarakhand, situated between the Himalayas, boasts a rich mix of spiritual heritage, natural beauty, and traditional healing (Uttarakhand Tourism, 2025). The state is renowned for its yoga ashrams in Rishikesh, Ayurvedic retreats in Haridwar, and nature-based retreats in Kumaon and Garhwal (Uttarakhand Tourism, 2025). These sites have made Uttarakhand a wellness destination for national and international tourists. From an economic viewpoint, the wellness tourism industry in Uttarakhand is a top sector, contributing 4.59% to direct employment and 8.27% when indirect employment is included (Bhatt & Rawat, 2024).

Despite its growing prominence, Uttarakhand's appeal as a wellness tourism destination remains underexplored in academic literature, particularly in terms of traveler motivations and decision-making processes (Tariyal, Singh, et al., 2023). While existing studies on tourism consumer behavior have primarily focused on demographic trends and general travel preferences (López-Sanz et al., 2021; Panas et al., 2022), there is a noticeable gap in understanding the psychological and value-based drivers that influence destination choices. This gap is especially pronounced among younger travelers, whose preferences and behaviors differ significantly from previous generations.

Millennials of ages between 1980 and 2000 have emerged as a focal population in tourism research (Hotchkiss, 2022; Kurz et al., 2019). Comprising approximately 23% of the global population – some 1.8 billion people – millennials are characterized by high education, internet literacy, and experience-seeking holidays. Millennials in India constitute the majority of the population, with nearly 440 million, 33% of whom live in urban areas (Sengupta, 2023; Tariyal, Bisht, et al., 2023). Surprisingly, nearly 40% of India's urban populations are millennials, and they contribute about 71% of household income (Ahluwalia, 2018), emphasizing how much economic influence and purchasing power they have.

Millennials' travel history is one of distinctive value-orientation and transformative experience orientation. As history's first digital natives, they mindfully seek wellness travel that is personal development, genuine, and sustainable (Deloitte, 2024). Their enthusiasm for wellness tourism is not for amusement only but is highly rooted in self-care, mental well-being, and lifestyle alignment. But millennials are also marked by a paradox in developing nations like India: they desire authentic, traditional healing experiences even as they request modern, sustainable wellness products. This paradox presents a unique challenge and opportunity for wellness destinations like Uttarakhand, which must balance traditional practices and modern expectations.

Although important, millennials' contradictory choices and how they influence their travel decisions are not yet well studied. Particularly in well-integrated wellness tourism places like Uttarakhand, where there are both traditional ways of living and modern tourism facilities, the knowledge of such motivations is important both academically and practically. This study attempts to bridge this gap by investigating the value and psychological determinants of motivation factors of millennial tourists' intentions to travel to wellness places in Uttarakhand.

In addition to examining motivational dimensions, the study also examines the role of perceived value dimensions – that is, price value (PV), quality value (QV), and accessibility value (AV) – on travel intentions. These dimensions are empirically established as good predictors in the tourism literature (Carvache-Franco et al., 2021), but their adoption in wellness tourism, particularly for millennials, is limited. Through the inclusion of these dimensions in the analysis, the study aims to gain a thorough understanding of the motivating dimensions of wellness tourism among young Indian travelers. Lastly, the findings aim to add to destination marketing practices, service delivery, and sustainable development of wellness tourism in Uttarakhand.

2. Literature Review and Hypotheses Development

2.1. Perceived Value

Perceived value is an important marketing construct that reflects consumers' judgment of the value of a product or service in terms of benefits, as opposed to costs, in comparison to other products or services (Kotler & Armstrong, 2021). Unlike objective price-based metrics, perceived value is subjective, formed by personal choice, expectations, and situational variables (Zeithaml, 1988). In contrast to monetary costs, this assessment includes emotional, social, and functional values that impact buying (Zeithaml, 1988). Being a multi-dimensional construct, perceived value is vulnerable to situational factors and can be defined differently in consumption situations (Zeithaml, 1988). In tourism studies, writers highlight perceived value's multi-dimensionality (El-Adly, 2019; Rasoolimanesh et al., 2016), quantified through three main dimensions: (1) QV (e.g., service quality, authenticity), (2) PV (monetary and extramonetary prices), and (3) AV (ease of booking, convenience of location).

Because perceived value is a multi-dimensional construct, it is context-dependent and can take different forms in different consumption contexts (Zeithaml, 1988). In tourism research, scholars emphasize its multi-dimensional nature (El-Adly, 2019; Rasoolimanesh et al., 2016), operationalized through three core dimensions: (1) QV (e.g., service excellence, authenticity), (2) PV (monetary/non-monetary costs), and (3) AV (ease of booking, location convenience).

2.1.1. Quality Value

The concept of QV refers to the perceived usefulness and effectiveness that consumers associate with the functional attributes of goods, services, and amenities (Sheth et al., 1991). In tourism, this includes elements such as infrastructure reliability, cleanliness, food safety, and the authenticity of cultural products like souvenirs (Jiang & Hong, 2021; Wang et al., 2024). Although both price and quality are elements of functional value, they exert different and, in many cases, opposite influences on the perception of consumers. Sweeney and Soutar (2001) argue that while quality would enhance perceived value, price would reduce it, especially in cases where customers perceive a dissonance between cost and service provision.

High-quality facilities that meet or exceed visitor expectations contribute significantly to positive impressions and overall satisfaction (Yu et al., 2023). Arevin (2024) further emphasizes that facility quality often outweighs pricing in influencing destination choice, positioning quality as a key competitive differentiator in tourism markets. Moreover, Qiu et al. (2024) suggest that in contemporary consumer landscapes, QV is essential for fostering long-term success and customer loyalty. However, its influence is not uniform across all contexts. For instance, while quality strongly predicts satisfaction, Jiang and Hong (2021) found that it does not significantly impact destination attachment, indicating that quality alone may not cultivate emotional bonds or repeat visitation. Drawing from this nuanced understanding, the present study proposes the following:

> *H1.* The QV of a wellness destination positively influences millennials' visit intention.

2.1.2. Price Value

PV is a widely recognized determinant of consumer behavior, particularly in the tourism sector, where financial considerations often shape destination choices (Jeaheng et al., 2023; Woo & Kim, 2019). Economic value in tourism encompasses both tangible costs and perceived monetary utility, reflecting a significant trade-off between pricing fairness, service quality, and the experiential benefits received (Kim & Park, 2017). Travelers are increasingly discerning, and competitive, transparent pricing structures have emerged as critical factors influencing destination selection (Mandić & Petrić, 2021). When travelers perceive that the cost of a trip aligns with the quality and uniqueness of the experience, they are more likely to develop favorable attitudes toward the destination (Choe & Kim, 2018; Yee, 2015).

Empirical research consistently links economic value to increased tourist satisfaction and stronger visit intentions (VIs) (Arevin, 2024; Yu et al., 2023). This relationship is especially pronounced among millennials, a price-sensitive segment that emphasizes experiential returns on expenditure. Millennials tend to evaluate travel decisions not solely on affordability but on the depth and authenticity of the experience relative to cost (Deloitte, 2024). However, the influence of economic value is context-dependent. While it may drive initial visitation, Jiang and Hong (2021) argue that it does not significantly affect destination attachment, suggesting that price alone cannot foster long-term loyalty. Building on this discourse, the present study posits that:

> *H2*. The PV of a wellness destination positively influences millennials' visit intention.

2.1.3. Accessibility Value

Accessibility, defined as "the ease of reaching activities at a destination via a specific travel mode" (Liu & Zhu, 2004, p. 105), encompasses more than just physical proximity – it reflects the overall ease and convenience with which travelers can engage with a destination. Soekadijo (2003, pp. 107–108) identifies three critical dimensions of accessibility in tourism: informational (the ease of locating and understanding available facilities), infrastructural (the quality of roads, transport systems, and connectivity), and experiential (the smoothness and satisfaction of the journey itself). These dimensions collectively shape the traveler's perception of a destination's approachability and appeal.

Recent empirical studies underscore accessibility's pivotal role in influencing destination choice. For instance, Rahmafitria et al. (2023) found that both destination-level accessibility (e.g., transport networks, signage) and individual-level accessibility (e.g., mobility constraints, travel readiness) significantly affect visitation patterns, particularly to remote or protected areas. Importantly, accessibility is inherently subjective and context-dependent, shaped by travelers' perceptions of the trade-offs between time, effort, and the anticipated experiential rewards (Nassir et al., 2016). On the other hand, Rucci and Porto (2022) found an insignificant impact of accessibility on tourist VI. In the context of wellness tourism, accessibility takes on a broader meaning. It includes not only logistical ease but also psychological and holistic access – such as the availability of serene environments, culturally resonant therapies, and inclusive wellness experiences. Hence, it is postulated that:

> *H3*. AV of wellness destination has a positive effect on millennial's visit intention.

The conceptual model portrayed in Fig. 7.1 illustrates the objectives of the current study.

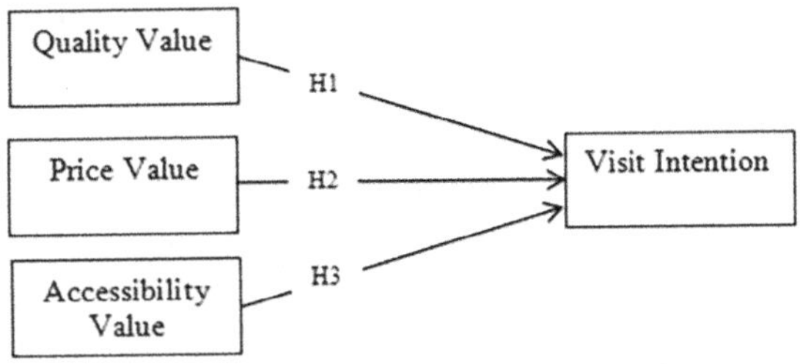

Fig. 7.1. Conceptual Model. *Source*: Authors' compilation.

3. Research Methodology

A quantitative approach was adopted in this study to examine the impact of destination value dimensions – quality, price, and accessibility – on millennials' intention to visit wellness destinations. The research aimed at 25–40-year-old millennial tourists who had previously visited or were planning to visit wellness centers in India, such as Ayurveda resorts, yoga ashrams, and spa resorts. We collected data for four months (from February to May 2025) to observe how seasonality influences wellness tourism trends.

For this research, the measurement scales were adapted from existing sources with careful consideration. The QV scale was derived from Zeithaml's (1988) perceived value framework, with modifications to include wellness-specific items such as "The destination offers authentic traditional therapies" and "Practitioners have credible certifications." For PV, we adapted items from Liang et al.'s (2017) value perception scale, tailoring statements to assess fair pricing perceptions in wellness contexts (e.g., "The pricing reflects the quality of services offered"). The AV scale incorporated elements from Tóth and Dávid's (2010) destination accessibility study, with added items evaluating transport convenience to remote wellness centers.

The dependent variable, VI, was measured using a five-item scale adapted from Ajzen's (1991) theory of planned behavior, contextualized for wellness tourism (e.g., "I intend to visit this wellness destination within the next year"). All scales were refined through expert validation (3 academic researchers in tourism) and pilot testing ($n = 30$), confirming their reliability ($\alpha > 0.80$) and contextual fit for Indian wellness destinations.

Using purposive sampling, we distributed an online structured survey to 280 respondents who met our screening criteria of having taken at least 1 wellness trip in the past 24 months or actively planning 1. After removing incomplete or inconsistent responses, we retained 260 valid responses for analysis, satisfying the recommended 10:1 ratio of observations to predictor variables for robust statistical analysis (Hair, 2009). The survey instrument incorporated validated multi-item scales measured through 18 statements on a 5-point Likert scale (1 = strongly disagree to 5 = strongly agree), adapted from previous tourism studies. A pilot test with 30 respondents confirmed the reliability and contextual appropriateness of these measurement instruments.

For data analysis, we employed multiple regression analysis using SPSS v.26 to examine the direct relationships between the three destination values and VI (*H1–H3*). We verified all necessary assumptions, including linearity through scatterplot analysis, normality via Shapiro–Wilk tests ($p > 0.05$), absence of multicollinearity with VIF values below 3.0, and homoscedasticity using Breusch–Pagan tests. To ensure the reliability of our results, we applied multiple safeguards: Harman's single-factor test indicated no presence of common method bias, and control variables (income level, frequency of wellness travel) were included to isolate the effects of our primary constructs (Aguirre-Urreta & Hu, 2019). The Durbin–Watson statistic was used to test autocorrelation.

4. Results

4.1. Reliability Analysis

Cronbach's alpha is commonly used in consumer behavior studies to assess the reliability and internal consistency of measurement scales. All constructs had excellent reliability, with alpha values higher than 0.70, which is the recommended value (Cronbach, 1951). These results suggest that the adapted measurement instruments were stable across the context of wellness tourism, providing a reliable basis for the subsequent regression analysis.

4.2. Multiple Regression Analysis

To confirm *H1–H3* hypotheses, we performed a multiple regression analysis to examine the extent to which the three values of quality, price, and accessibility jointly predict millennials' VIs to wellness destinations. The analysis was hierarchical in that the three predictor variables entered simultaneously in the regression model (all together). This approach enables us to quantify the unique contributions of each of the three values, while controlling for the other values in the model, and has been well-established in tourism studies (Hair et al., 2019). The analysis results are shown in Table 7.1.

4.3. Major Findings from the Regression Analysis

- *H1*: QV positively influences VI ($\beta = 0.390$, $p < 0.001$).
- *H2*: PV positively influences VI ($\beta = 0.320$, $p < 0.001$).
- *H3*: AV positively influences VI ($\beta = 0.260$, $p < 0.001$).

5. Discussion

The results show that QV strongly influences millennials' intention to visit wellness destinations ($\beta = 0.390$, $p < 0.001$), supporting *H1*. We believe millennials care more about and desire transformative and authentic experiences versus just leisure travel. In our survey, respondents always thought about certified practitioners and evidence-based therapy, with 78% selecting "qualified staff" as the most important

Table 7.1. Regression Model Summary and Coefficient.

Regression Model Summary (VI)							
Model	R	R^2	Adj. R^2	Std. Error	Durbin–Watson		
1	0.785	0.616	0.608	0.680	1.872		
Regression coefficients (VI)							
Predictor	B	SE	β	t	p	Tolerance	VIF
Constant	1.250	0.380	–	3.289	0.001	–	–
QV	0.420	0.055	0.390	7.636	0.000	0.870	1.150
PV	0.350	0.050	0.320	7.000	0.000	0.890	1.120
AV	0.280	0.045	0.260	6.222	0.000	0.910	1.100

Source: Authors' compilation.

selection factor. These outcomes correspond with AlNujaidi et al. (2025) findings in European wellness markets with medical qualifications superseding luxury amenities. Both studies show that a new global trend indicates a move toward professionalized wellness consumption. Destinations should invest in practitioner certification and promotion of qualifications, possibly with a standardized accreditation process that has the ability to raise regional wellness economies.

The analysis supports *H2*, with PV having substantive predictive power ($\beta = 0.320$, $p < 0.001$) with interesting caveats. First, millennials were willing to pay premiums for transparent value that contradicted traditional assumptions about price sensitivity, especially among the urban professionals in our sample (68% expressed a preference toward all-inclusive pricing). That is consistent with the study of Lin et al. (2023) who found "value transparency effects" outweighed price sensitivity in Scandinavian wellness resorts, where itemized pricing caused a 22% increase in perceived fairness. Cross-cultural consistency indicates wellness tourists were altering price-value assumptions, no matter the culture. Perhaps wellness tourism boards can take advantage of this opportunity and develop pricing transparency metrics, while operators might adapt dynamic pricing models that connect various cost components to quality indicators, which arguably not only produce more profits, but perhaps improve customer satisfaction too.

The AV demonstrated significant, though relatively slight, impact ($\beta = 0.260$, $p < 0.001$), supporting *H3* and identifying segmentation opportunities. Urban respondents indicated 40% greater sensitivity to accessibility than spiritual seekers; indeed, this distinction supports the "wellness mobility spectrum" theory proposed by Fernández-Díaz et al. (2023). Regular visitors of remote destinations often perceive difficult access as a "pilgrimage filter," where the effort required to reach the destination enhances its spiritual significance. This bifurcation suggests that destinations need to include accessibility in their marketing segmentation – emphasizing convenience for urban weekenders and framing their remoteness in marketing as an exclusive positive attribute for serious practitioners (who are likely more tolerant of inconvenience!). In terms of policy impacting infrastructure development, these could relatively easily promote "wellness corridors" linking urban centers and areas local to retreat destinations as a balance between accessibility and a protected experience.

6. Implications

6.1. Theoretical Implications

The findings of this study make several theoretical contributions to wellness tourism and consumer studies. First, the ubiquitous influence of value for quality on the travel intention of millennials is consistent with the use of functional value theory (Sheth et al., 1991) but introduces credentialed authenticity – a subdimension reflecting the growing importance of professional qualifications and evidence-based practice within wellness experiences. It suggests that future theory needs to incorporate professional credibility as a central element of perceived quality, especially in tourism activities related to health.

Second, the results are contrary to conventional wisdom about millennials' price sensitivity. While PV remains a robust predictor, value transparency being more important than being open and transparent in pricing leads to the conclusion that value transparency may be a better consideration than cost-cutting. This supports the need to refine existing value-perception frameworks by integrating transparency and fairness as moderating variables that influence perceived economic value and satisfaction.

Third, the significant role of AV highlights the importance of segment-specific interpretations of access. The differential sensitivity between urban wellness seekers and spiritual travelers supports the concept of a wellness mobility spectrum, suggesting that accessibility should be theorized not only in logistical terms but also as a symbolic and experiential construct. This opens avenues for developing segmentation-based models that account for varying perceptions of remoteness and convenience.

Collectively, these implications advocate for a more differentiated and context-sensitive approach to modeling consumer behavior in wellness tourism. They underscore the need to evolve traditional value constructs to reflect generational shifts, cultural expectations, and the increasing demand for authenticity, transparency, and personalized access in wellness experiences.

6.2. Practical Implications

Overall, this study offers three overarching directions for the industry. First, quality certification programs should broaden the concept of quality beyond facilities to also include practitioner quality, potentially through accreditation agencies (similar to what Kerala's Ayurveda practice standards offer).

Second, the pricing structure needs to be realigned and primed for the aspect of value, rather than just prohibitive cost, which might include standardizing parts of the sector (like restaurants do with "what" services/products are included).

Lastly, transportation and transport planning should consider wellness travel as both a convenience and destination, "well-being travel" for the mainstream traveling audience versus a journey with purpose for spiritual seekers. If done right, consumer satisfaction would be higher in wellness travel and would, therefore, be less volume-driven growth models focused on value, helping them to plan more sustainable destination development models.

As the findings from the study also indicate that wellness tourism grew as a catalyst for a new form of tourism to realize value, it would seem that new value hierarchies unique only to wellness tourism demonstrate the requirement for policy frameworks specific to wellness tourism. Future research should also consider how these dimensions of value are expressed across different cultures, particularly in places where the modernized expectations of hospitality land in areas where traditional medicine practices often combine with Western hospitality approaches and, perhaps, where this creates unique tourism patterns for the hospitality industry.

7. Limitation and Further Research

Although this investigation was limited to Indian millennials, the implications of this study have a further reach than simply that target population or one nation. The importance of quality was paramount in all segments, which implies that wellness tourism might be a separate category that lends itself to different tourism value models. Future research should examine how this value dimension operates across cultures. For example, looking at the Indian millennials and their value emphasis on credentials for traditional medicine versus the emphasis on luxury spa amenities for Western travelers. Looking at how digital accessibility (e.g., online pre-booking of therapies) would alter our thinking of physical accessibility post-pandemic (i.e., possibilities for hybrid wellness experiences) would also be interesting.

The study's limitations, including its geographic focus and timing, conversely present opportunities for longitudinal work tracking how these value perceptions evolve as millennials age and wellness tourism matures. Nevertheless, the current findings provide both scholars and practitioners with a validated framework for understanding millennial wellness travel decisions in increasingly competitive markets.

Conflict of Interest

Both authors ensure that there is no conflict of interest.

References

Aguirre-Urreta, M. I., & Hu, J. (2019). Detecting common method bias: Performance of the Harman's single-factor test. *ACM SIGMIS Database: The DATABASE for Advances in Information Systems*, *50*(2), 45–70. https://doi.org/10.1145/3330471.3330473

Ahluwalia, H. (2018, February 20). *Millennials to redefine India's consumption story: Report*. LiveMint. https://www.livemint.com

Ajzen, I. (1991). The theory of planned behavior. *Organizational Behavior and Human Decision Processes*, *50*(2), 179–211. https://doi.org/10.1016/0749-5978(91)90020-T

AlNujaidi, H. Y., Al-Rayes, S. A., & Alumran, A. (2025). The evolution of wellness models: Implications for women's health and well-being. *International Journal of Women's Health*, *17*, 597–613. https://doi.org/10.2147/IJWH.S498027

Arcese, G., Elmo, G. C., Fortuna, F., Pasca, M. G., & Risso, M. (2024). The role of traditional aspects, health consciousness and environmental concerns in Italian agri-food consumption during Covid-19. *British Food Journal*, *126*(1), 237–254. https://doi.org/10.1108/BFJ-10-2022-0841

Arevin, A. T. (2024). Analysis of the effect of prices and quality of facilities on tourist visit decision. *Jurnal Ilmiah Manajemen Kesatuan*, *12*(3), 893–900. https://jurnal.ibik.ac.id/index.php/jimkes/article/view/2745

Backman, M., Hagen, J., Kekezi, O., Naldi, L., & Wallin, T. (2021). In the eye of the storm: Entrepreneurs and well-being during the COVID-19 crisis. *Entrepreneurship Theory and Practice*, *47*(3), 751–787. https://doi.org/10.1177/10422587211057028

Bhatt, A., & Rawat, S. (2024). A study on the growth and development of the tourism industry in Uttarakhand: Opportunities, challenges, and strategies. *International Journal for Multidisciplinary Research (IJFMR)*, *6*(2), 1–10.

Carvache-Franco, M., Alvarez-Risco, A., Carvache-Franco, O., Carvache-Franco, W., Estrada-Merino, A., & Villalobos-Alvarez, D. (2021). Perceived value and its influence on satisfaction and loyalty in a coastal city: A study from Lima, Peru. *Journal of Policy Research in Tourism, Leisure and Events*, *14*(2), 115–130. https://doi.org/10.1080/19407963.2021.1883634

Choe, J. Y. J., & Kim, S. S. (2018). Effects of tourists' local food consumption value on attitude, food destination image, and behavioral intention. *International Journal of Hospitality Management*, *71*, 1–10. https://doi.org/10.1016/j.ijhm.2017.11.007

Cronbach, L. J. (1951). Coefficient alpha and the internal structure of tests. *Psychometrika*, *16*(3), 297–334. https://doi.org/10.1007/BF02310555

Deloitte. (2024). *2024 Gen Z and Millennial Survey: Living and working with purpose in a transforming world*. https://www.deloitte.com/global/en/issues/work/content/genz-millennialsurvey.html

El-Adly, M. I. (2019). Modelling the relationship between hotel perceived value, customer satisfaction, and customer loyalty. *Journal of Retailing and Consumer Services*, *50*, 322–332. https://doi.org/10.1016/j.jretconser.2018.07.007

Fernández-Díaz, E., Jambrino-Maldonado, C., Iglesias-Sánchez, P. P., & de las Heras-Pedrosa, C. (2023). Digital accessibility of smart cities—Tourism for all and reducing inequalities: *Tourism agenda 2030*. *Tourism Review*, *78*(2), 361–380. https://doi.org/10.1108/TR-02-2022-0072

Global Wellness Institute. (2025). *What is wellness tourism?* https://globalwellnessinstitute.org/what-is-wellness/what-is-wellness-tourism/

Gough, N. (2024). *Market size of the wellness tourism industry worldwide 2028*. Statista. https://www.statista.com/statistics/1018497/

Hair, J. F., Black, W. C., Babin, B. J., & Anderson, R. E. (2019). *Multivariate data analysis* (8th ed.). Cengage.

Hotchkiss, J. L. (2022). Millennials: Maligned or miscreants? *Southern Economic Journal*, *88*(4), 1248–1276. https://doi.org/10.1002/soej.12560

Jeaheng, Y., Al-Ansi, A., Chua, B. L., Ngah, A. H., Ryu, H. B., Ariza-Montes, A., & Han, H. (2023). Influence of Thai street food quality, price, and involvement on traveler behavioral intention: Exploring cultural difference (Eastern versus Western). *Psychology Research and Behavior Management*, 223–240. https://doi.org/10.2147/PRBM.S371806

Jiang, Y., & Hong, F. (2021). Examining the relationship between customer-perceived value of night-time tourism and destination attachment among Generation Z tourists in

China. *Tourism Recreation Research*, *48*(2), 220–233. https://doi.org/10.1080/02508281.2021.1915621

Kim, K.-H., & Park, D.-B. (2017). Relationships among perceived value, satisfaction, and loyalty: Community-based ecotourism in Korea. *Journal of Travel & Tourism Marketing*, *34*(2), 171–191. https://doi.org/10.1080/10548408.2016.1156609

Kotler, P., & Armstrong, G. (2021). *Principles of marketing* (Global 18th ed.). Pearson.

Kurz, C. J., Li, G., & Vine, D. J. (2019). Are millennials different? In A. Haughwout & B. Mandel (Eds.), *Handbook of US consumer economics* (pp. 193–232). Academic Press. https://doi.org/10.1016/B978-0-12-813524-2.00008-1

Liang, Z.-X., Hui, T.-K., & Sea, P.-Z. (2017). Is price most important? Healthcare tourism in Southeast Asia. *Tourism Geographies*, *19*(5), 823–847. https://doi.org/10.1080/14616688.2017.1376224

Lin, H.-C., Liu, X., Huang, Y., & Chen, H.-Y. (2023). Determinants of continued use of tourism and hospitality e-commerce platforms and the role of information transparency. *Current Issues in Tourism*, *26*(19), 3140–3159. https://doi.org/10.1080/13683500.2022.2098095

Liu, S., & Zhu, X. (2004). An integrated GIS approach to accessibility analysis. *Transactions in GIS*, *8*(1), 45–62. https://doi.org/10.1111/j.1467-9671.2004.00167.x

López-Sanz, J. M., Penelas-Leguía, A., Gutierrez-Rodriguez, P., & Cuesta-Valiño, P. (2021). Sustainable development and consumer behavior in rural tourism—The importance of image and loyalty for host communities. *Sustainability*, *13*(9), 4763. https://doi.org/10.3390/su13094763

Mandić, A., & Petrić, L. (2021). The impacts of location and attributes of protected natural areas on hotel prices: Implications for sustainable tourism development. *Environment, Development and Sustainability*, *23*(1), 833–863. https://doi.org/10.1007/s10668-020-00611-6

Nassir, N., Hickman, M., Malekzadeh, A., & Irannezhad, E. (2016). A utility-based travel impedance measure for public transit network accessibility. *Transportation Research Part A: Policy and Practice*, *88*, 26–39. https://doi.org/10.1016/j.tra.2016.03.007

Panas, G., Thrasidi, N., Halkiopoulos, C., & Gkintoni, E. (2022). Consumer behavior and cognitive factors in relation to gastronomic tourism and destination marketing in Greece. In V. Katsoni & A. C. Şerban (Eds.), *Transcending borders in tourism through innovation and cultural heritage* (pp. 655–677). Springer. https://doi.org/10.1007/978-3-030-92491-1_38

Qiu, N., Li, H., Pan, C., Wu, J., & Guo, J. (2024). The study on the relationship between perceived value, satisfaction, and tourist loyalty at industrial heritage sites. *Heliyon*, *10*(17). https://doi.org/10.1016/j.heliyon.2024.e37184

Rahmafitria, F., Dirgahayani, P., Putro, H. P. H., Rosyidie, A., & Hudalah, D. (2023). Tourism accessibility in protected islands: The case of the Komodo National Park, Indonesia. *Tourism Review*, *78*(3), 966–985. https://doi.org/10.1108/TR-03-2022-0110

Rasoolimanesh, S. M., Dahalan, N., & Jaafar, M. (2016). Tourists' perceived value and satisfaction in a community-based homestay in the Lenggong Valley World Heritage Site. *Journal of Hospitality and Tourism Management*, *26*, 72–81. https://doi.org/10.1016/j.jhtm.2016.01.005

Rucci, A. C., & Porto, N. (2022). Accessibility in tourist sites in Spain: Does it really matter when choosing a destination? *European Journal of Tourism Research*, *31*, 3108–3108. https://doi.org/10.54055/ejtr.v31i.2165

Sengupta, A. (2023, December 18). *Millennials at forefront of online finance products, contribute 44% of total lending: Report*. BFSI. https://bfsi.economictimes.indiatimes.com/news/fintech//97308820

Sheth, J. N., Newman, B. I., & Gross, B. L. (1991). Why we buy what we buy: A theory of consumption values. *Journal of Business Research*, *22*(2), 159–170. https://doi.org/10.1016/0148-2963(91)90050-8

Soekadijo, R. G. (2003). *Anatomi Pariwisata*. PT Gramedia Pustaka.

Sweeney, J. C., & Soutar, G. N. (2001). Consumer perceived value: The development of a multiple item scale. *Journal of Retailing*, *77*(2), 203–220. https://doi.org/10.1016/S0022-4359(01)00041-0

Tariyal, A., Bisht, S., Roy, S., & Chopra, G. (2023). Assessing the impact of perceived social media usefulness on Indian millennials' online booking decision. *Journal of Marketing Analytics*, *12*, 639–655. https://doi.org/10.1057/s41270-023-00219-5

Tariyal, A., Singh, S., Bisht, S., & Rana, V. (2023). What influences wellness customers to engage in electronic word of mouth? A total interpretive structural modelling approach. *International Journal of Spa and Wellness*, *6*(2), 239–262. https://doi.org/10.1080/24721735.2023.2177408

TIMESOFINDIA.COM. (2024, January 15). *How wellness tourism is becoming the next travel trend to follow among travellers*. https://timesofindia.indiatimes.com/travel/destinations/how-wellness-tourism-is-becoming-the-next-travel-trend-to-follow-among-travellers/articleshow/106920013.cms

Tóth, G., & Dávid, L. (2010). Tourism and accessibility: An integrated approach. *Applied Geography*, *30*(4), 666–677. https://doi.org/10.1016/j.apgeog.2009.08.005

Uttarakhand Tourism. (2025). *Yoga & wellness*. https://uttarakhandtourism.gov.in/page/reconnect

Wang, W., Yaoyuneyong, G., Sullivan, P., & Burgess, B. (2024). The influence of value perceptions on tourist souvenir purchase decisions. *International Journal of Tourism Research*, *26*(1), e2611. https://doi.org/10.1002/jtr.2611

Woo, E., & Kim, Y. G. (2019). Consumer attitudes and buying behavior for green food products: From the aspect of green perceived value (GPV). *British Food Journal*, *121*(2), 320–332. https://doi.org/10.1108/BFJ-01-2018-0027

Yee, R. K. (2015). A tale of two food blogs: Culinary tourism in Hong Kong from a Chinese-American perspective. *New Errands: The Undergraduate Journal of American Studies*, *3*(1), 234–261. https://doi.org/10.18113/P8ne3159815

Yu, Y., Lang, M., Zhao, Y., Liu, W., & Hu, B. (2023). Tourist perceived value, tourist satisfaction, and life satisfaction: Evidence from Chinese Buddhist temple tours. *Journal of Hospitality & Tourism Research*, *47*(1), 133–152. https://doi.org/10.1177/1096348021101533

Zeithaml, V. A. (1988). Consumer perceptions of price, quality, and value: A means-end model and synthesis of evidence. *Journal of Marketing*, *52*(3), 2–22. https://doi.org/10.1177/002224298805200302

Chapter 8

Eco-wellness Tourism as a Pathway Toward Sustainability and Sustainable Development: The Ghanaian Perspective

Lateef Okikiola Olanipekun[a], *Michael Adekunle Oderinde*[b], *Abraham Israel Ogbaji*[c], *Daniel Ameanyeawu*[a] *and Ophelia Delali Dogbe Zungbey*[c]

[a]*Department of Human Resource Management, Accra Institute of Technology Business School, Accra Institute of Technology, Ghana*
[b]*Department of Industrial Relations and Human Resource Management, Lagos State University, Ojo, Nigeria*
[c]*Department of Human Resource Management, Central University Business School, Central University, Accra, Ghana*

Abstract

Health is wealth as an adage is embracing a renewed significance in the current post-COVID-19 era, which underscores the pertinence toward the prioritization of health and well-being. Eco-wellness tourism has entered a radical phase conspicuous based on the increasing quest for innovative services, and a universal movement centered on holistic well-being. To this end, this study examined eco-wellness tourism as a pathway toward sustainability and sustainable development from the Ghanaian perspective. The study's objective centered on interrogating the influence of environmental responsibility on ecological conservation and the relationship between eco-friendly accommodations and community well-being. The study was anchored on the socio-technical systems (STS) theory. A total of 150 tourists were selected from 5 tourist destinations in Ghana using the purposive and convenience sampling techniques. Findings revealed that environmental responsibility influences ecological conservation with

Advancement in Medical and Wellness Tourism, Part A: Entrepreneurship and Technology, 97–112

Published under exclusive licence by Emerald Publishing Limited
doi:10.1108/978-1-80592-983-320261009

($R^2 = 0.945$, p-value <0.05) and eco-friendly accommodations and community well-being with ($r = 0.735$, p-value <0.05). The study concluded that eco-wellness tourism is pertinent for sustainable development as it provides nature-based wellness experiences which merge personal health with environmental responsibility and offers immersive, nature-based wellness experiences capable of minimizing ecological impact and promoting community development. It was recommended that there is need for both governmental and institutional support for eco-wellness tourism to drive sustainable development.

Keywords: Community well-being; eco-friendly accommodations; ecological conservation; eco-wellness tourism; environmental responsibility and sustainable development

1. Introduction

The call toward engaging in sustainable business practices to aid sustainable development has spanned through diverse sectors, with each sector now setting modalities toward honoring this call. Tourism ranks among the fastest-growing sectors across the globe, which provides revenue to the greatest number of nations globally (UNWTO, 2018). However, the incident of COVID-19 can be said to have had a calamitous influence of this industry due to its heavy reliance on cross borders traveling (Ivanova et al., 2021). Because of COVID-19, a drastic reduction gripped the tourism sector with international tourism arrivals within Europe recording below fifty eight percent (−58%), the Middle East less than fifty two percent (−52%), and Africa having below forty seven percent (−47%) (World Tourism Organization (UNWTO), 2018). This significant effect thus requires mechanisms toward reducing further impacts and ensuring sustainability of tourist centers and destinations to promote wellness of travelers (Beall et al., 2020).

Health is wealth as an adage is embracing a renewed significance in the current post-COVID-19 era, which underscores the pertinence toward the prioritization of health and well-being. Eco-wellness tourism has entered a radical phase conspicuous based on the increasing quest for innovative services, and a universal movement centered on holistic well-being (Guerra et al., 2022). Rai and Sreenivasan (2023) documented that travelers in this modern dispensation no longer perceive tourism exclusively as leisure; rather, they quest for experiences that promote their physical, mental, and spiritual wellness. A distinctive feature of wellness tourism is that it surpasses conventional medical tourism by integrating activities such as yoga, spa therapies, immersive natural experiences, and meditation (Suntararak & Boonyanmethaporn, 2024). According to Andriani et al. (2024), Rajapakshe and Arachchi (2024), and Yuvono et al. (2021), the preceding analysis exposes the recognition of eco-wellness tourism as one of the fastest-growing fragments of global tourism.

The engagement of sustainable practices toward ensuring the conservation of biodiversity in natural areas as mechanisms for continuous attraction of tourists and provision of the needed benefits now becomes critical to achieving sustainability and sustainable development through eco-friendly wellness tourism (Eshun & Asiedu, 2023). With an original focus on personal health, the emergence of eco-wellness tourism is perceived as a catalyst for sustainable development. For instance, the Global Wellness Economy Monitor as at "2024" reported that the wellness economy reached about $6.3 trillion in the year 2023 and was projected to increase to about $9 trillion by the year 2028. Aside from direct revenues, it fosters cultural preservation, employment, and environmental stewardship. Furthermore, it ensures alignment with the United Nations Sustainable Development Goals (SDGs). Eco-wellness tourism aligns with the comprehensive development from the purview of economic equity (SDG 8) to environmental conservation (SDG 12).

Traveling for health as a concept is not new. Historically, people embark on journeys to destinations with sacred sites, mineral springs, natural healing resources, or temperate climates as means for restoring their well-being (Tuzunkan, 2018). However, this practice has developed into pursuance of superiority in contemporary societies, because traveling for wellness is becoming the mainstay of the global marketplace for both spirituality and self-care (Cheer et al., 2017; Heelas & Woodhead, 2005; Rai et al., 2023). Based on the submission obtained from the Global Wellness Institute (GWI), the concept of wellness tourism signifies interplay of two (2) trillion-dollar sectors where wellness and tourism co-exist. Based on the preceding position, the concept of wellness tourism was adjudged as travels targeted at the maintenance or enhancement of individual well-being, which is often uniquely tied with geographic characteristics such as cultural heritage, centered on panoramic health offerings with examples like Ayurvedic therapies or yoga retreats (Tuzunkan, 2018).

Wellness tourism is a special interest form of tourism (Smith & Puczkó, 2015) with inherent connections to sustainability and sustainable development. It provides an alternative to mass tourism as it leveraged on local traditions, resources, and low-impact practices (Chrontsiou, 2023). According to Zaroucha (2020), eco-wellness tourism represents a form of traveling hinged on the integration of personal health and well-being with a focus on environmental responsibility and cultural appreciations. It has to do with the immersion of individual selves in natural settings for in order to comprehensively rejuvenate themselves, while in this process trying to reduce economic impacts via sustainable practices ranging from reduction of wastes, environmental responsibility through energy efficiency, eco-friendly accommodations, local wellness practices, supporting local communities and their traditions (Lamopia & Nindya, 2023). From the viewpoint of sustainability and sustainable development, the intention toward eco-tourism wellness is targeted toward fostering a deeper interconnectivity between personal health and a healthy environment. Post-pandemic, the resilience toward eco-tourism wellness has become even more evident, especially with non-medical practices such as yoga being employed in addressing broader societal challenges (Chhabra, 2020).

In spite of extant investigations on the motivation of wellness tourism and attributes of destinations by scholars like McCartney (2024), Rai and Sreenivasan (2023), Guerra et al. (2022), Cheer et al. (2017), only few studies have explored its association with sustainability and sustainable development. This gap is particularly evident in the Ghanaian context; this underlines the need to incorporate wellness tourism with policy-making to maximizing its sustainability and sustainable development potential. Based on the foregoing arguments, this study investigated eco-wellness tourism as a pathway toward sustainability and sustainable development: the Ghanaian perspective. The study was underpinned with the objective of examining the influence of environmental responsibility on ecological conservation and to evaluate the degree of relationship between eco-friendly accommodations and community well-being in selected tourism centers in Ghana.

2. Conceptual Explications

2.1. Eco-wellness Tourism

This form of tourism combines the objectives of wellness tourism by ensuring a direct interconnected interplay with nature, and accommodation of cultural wisdom ingrained in local wellness practices, which is being accompanied by affective commitment toward the conservation of environment (Kaushal & Srivastava, 2021). The relationship with nature is capable of assisting tourists toward increasing life goals, self-acceptance, environmental misery, personal autonomy, individual development for health well-being and positive relationships (Ritpanitchajchaval et al., 2023). Meanwhile, a combination of conventional and traditional wellness treatments being packaged as a tourist attraction has become something many tourists thirst for in this era (Meikassandra et al., 2020). Investigations on environmentally friendly health tourism as a concept are still at an infant stage in the Ghanaian context. Thus, the scientific conceptualization of eco-wellness tourism is still very challenging (Asikin et al., 2024). As such, efforts are required toward the formulation of the concept of "eco-wellness tourism," as well as its process of application to ensure smooth implementation (Meikassandra et al., 2020).

Eco-wellness tourism can be said to be organized via the modification of the principles underpinning ecotourism and fusing them into wellness tourism by combining nature re-creation and holistic health (Sufa et al., 2020). Furthermore, while featuring a beautiful environment-friendly landscape within tourist destinations. This is used as an avenue for the maintenance of health, which is supported by numerous treatments with adequate health facilities (Malik et al., 2019). This is to make vacation experience healthy and enjoyable while also maintaining environmental sustainability (Batubara & Setiawan, 2023). Since nature is a significant source of resources for public health, then natural tourism travel businesses like eco-tourism can potentially provide nature-based health therapies to tourists (Marhaeni, 2023), and to simultaneously become an integral part of harmonizing human associations in the vast ecosystem (Clissold et al., 2022).

2.2 Sustainability

Sustainability as a concept suffice as a mainstream within the 1980s, its foundation can be traced to a variety of early beginnings. For instance, Purvis et al. (2019) expressed that sustainability as a concept was introduced by Evelyn and Carlowitz as a response aimed at decreasing forest resources across "Europe" in the 17th and 18th centuries. Some ecologists and natural scientists in the 19th and 20th centuries, further advocated for the preservation of nature as well as the conservation of natural resources so as to ensure that production and consumption are sustainable. Additionally, scholars who were also political economists, like Ricardo, Smith, Malthus, and Mill challenged the limitation of population and economic growth by acknowledging the fundamental trade-offs between wealth accumulation and social justice (Purvis et al., 2019). In spite of these arrays of activities, sustainability as a concept did not gather the expected global visibility and attention, not until the twentieth century when it was advocated by the Club of Rome, suggesting a limit to growth by bringing to fore the quest for sustainability and a sustainable society premised on sustainable global system. In the early 1960s, environmentalists started critiquing practices and called for the conservation of environment, culminating into the concept of "sustainable development" in the 1980s (Bellandi & De-Propris, 2021).

2.3. Sustainable Development

The concept of SDGs provides an extensive path for Africa toward the achievement of its goals aimed at ending poverty, protecting the planet and ensuring prosperity for all by the year 2030. Thus, current descriptions and explanations on sustainability were built on these preceding events and expanded so as to further accommodate current challenges heralding from the dimensions of environmental, social, and economic domains (Avila-Gutierrez et al., 2020). Thereupon, sustainability can be described from multiple paradigms, thereby making it complex to have just a single definition. Therefore, Eizaguirre et al. (2019) indicated more than 100 explanations of sustainable development are being used by both practitioners and scholars toward illustrating the concept resulting from varying contexts. However, the most universally acceptable explanations emanated from the World Commission on Environment and Development (WCED), which explained "sustainable development" as the growth that meets the aspirations and needs of the current populations without any form of compromise to future generations in meeting their own aspirations and needs as well. Bellandi and De-Propris (2021) described sustainable development as the act of incorporating economic vitalities, environmental prosperity, and social equity toward the development of resilience, diverse, healthy, and robust communities for the current moments as well as the future. In operationalizing these definitions, considerations were given to economic, environmental, and social, dimensions of development.

2.4. Environmental Responsibility

Environmental responsibility as a concept refers to both individual and collective and commitments aimed at the protection and improvement of the environment so that current and future generations can promote sustainability and minimize negative impacts (Sheehy & Farneti, 2021). It involves social, legal, and ethical obligations that apply to individuals, businesses, communities, and governments through actions such as conservation of resources, waste reduction, and the adoption of eco-friendly practices so as to promote a healthy planet (Camilleri, 2018). Scholars like Yuwono and Astuti (2021) accentuated that environmental responsibility is an organization's duty in preventing and alleviating environmental damages that could be caused by commercial activities. In corollary to the above, a study by Olanipekun and Ajayi (2023) provided that before investors take the decision to invest in a certain organization, their environmental responsibility efforts are evaluated to ascertain compliance with sustainability and sustainable development programs.

2.5. Ecological Conservation

Ecological conservation implies practices associated with the protection and management of the natural ecosystems and their elements, like biodiversity, species, and habitats, in order to maintain their functions, health, and abilities for the purpose of supporting life for both the present and future generations (Elon, 2023). It encompasses the creation of strategies and utilization of resources so as to ensure that ecosystems continue to operate as naturally as possible through the preservation of their interconnected cycles and bio-networks (Sheehy & Farneti, 2021). The foundational concept behind the conservation of the ecosystem is aimed at ensuring the health and longevity of natural complex systems (Li et al., 2020).

2.6. Eco-friendly Accommodations

Accommodation facilities are important central to economic development and assist local communities (Ertuna et al., 2019), in considering tourism as a catalyst for economic advancement (Tang et al., 2020). Nevertheless, numerous efforts have been geared toward ensuring eco-wellness and business sustainability to aid sustainable development (Vrabcova et al., 2022). Employing sustainable practices has resulted in the compliance of many accommodation facilities with environmental legislation (Sinha & Fukey, 2021). Thus, eco-friendly accommodations have ensured the application of elements of social responsibility and environmental management system beyond just mere legislations in their operations (Dang-Van et al., 2022). According to Baruca et al. (2022) having an understanding of responsible visitors' behavior is central for entrepreneurs in the tourism business, particularly in the accommodation sector. For instance, the ISO 14001 environmental management system in a bid to ensure economic and environmental benefits, an astronomical increase was witnessed between 2000 and 2015 (Ouyang et al., 2019).

2.7. Community Well-being

This implies combining economic, social and environmental, political and cultural conditions being identified by individuals and their communities. This is essential for prosperity, and fulfilling their potentials (Wiseman & Brasher, 2008). Community well-being is applied in diverse ways and across different cultures and communities. Individual well-being is a principal element of community well-being (VanDerWeele, 2017). In a similar vein, the concept of well-being has become a widely discussed topic in recent times, particularly in the era of COVID-19 pandemic. As a result, wellness and well-being became buzzwords across the globe, from kitchen table discussions, official government statements, corporate boardrooms, and at sports clubs. According to McKinsey & Co (2021), the wellness industry, which involves all activities aimed at promoting both physical and mental well-being, now has the estimation of more than 1.5 trillion USD.

2.8. Theoretical Framework

In addressing the complex nature of adequate management and promotion of eco-wellness tourism and environmental sustainability, this study adopted the Socio-technical Systems (STS) Theory as its cardinal theoretical insight.

2.9. STS Theory

This theory was introduced by academic scholars known as Bamforth and Trist (1951) but was expanded later on by Pasmore et al. (1982). The argument of this theory centers on the cooperative and shared enhancement of technical subsystems such as infrastructure, technologies, processes, and so forth; and social subsystems like organizational culture, human behavior, stakeholders' engagement within organizations. These binary viewpoints enable a unified comprehension of the co-evolvement of technical mechanisms and human experiences in service systems. Therefore, in the examination of eco-wellness tourism as a pathway toward sustainability and sustainable development, this theory becomes relevant. This is because tourist centers or destinations can be conceptualized as systems that are socio-technical in nature, wherein concepts of eco-wellness and eco-friendly outcomes materialize from the interplay between human components such as "managerial practices, employees' engagement" and technical elements like "architectural design and environmental technologies."

Recent investigations support the relevance of this theory in the contexts of complex services. For instance, an STS-integrated model for Industry 4.0 was presented by Sony and Naik (2020), while scholars like Carayon and Perry (2021) accentuated its value in the design of user-focused digital health systems. Thus, in hospitality, Li et al. (2020) engaged the STS in exploring the implementation of product-service-based systems, illuminating the need toward balancing infrastructures with service experience. The STS theory was applied in this study as a framework that is both descriptive and normative toward the development of standardized elements for eco-wellness tourism and sustainability (Li et al., 2025). By viewing tourist centers and destinations as integrated systems where there is an existence of interaction between designs, infrastructures, behavior, and culture; this theory provides a robust approach toward comprehending and enhancing eco-wellness tourism as a pathway for sustainability and sustainable development (Carayon & Perry, 2021).

3. Empirical Review

This section reviewed previous scholarly positions on the objectives underpinning the study.

3.1. Environmental Responsibility and Ecological Conservation

Study by Walker et al. (2014) unraveled that environmental responsibility can boost ecological conservation and promote positive corporate reputation, influence environmental regulations, and enhance its legitimacy. It can also bring about environmental innovation which leads to competitive advantages through various strategies like pollution control and technological advancements. Study by Wang and Ahmad (2024) indicated that environmental responsibility influences ecological conservation through the elimination of harmful substances and recyclability, which are pertinent elements for sustainable tourism and capable of enhancing eco-wellness. Investigation by Le (2023) established that environmental responsibility positively influences ecological conservation by minimizing harms to the environment, to promote eco-wellness tourism in tourist destinations. Singh et al. (2022) in their conclusion provided that environmental responsibility affects ecological conservation leading to value creation within tourist destinations. Fischer et al. (2020) in their investigation expressed that environmental responsibility has an effect on ecological conservation as it aids the prioritization of long-term aspects of tourist destinations, which is fundamental for promoting eco-wellness and sustainable development. On the above accounts, the hypothesis below was formulated:

> Environmental responsibility positively influences ecological conservation in selected tourism centers in Ghana.

3.2. Eco-friendly Accommodations and Community Well-being

An investigation in North America by Dodds and Holmes (2019) submitted that eco-friendly accommodations foster community well-being by actively engaging with local communities, and lending supports to local businesses, suppliers, and artisans. This is because they strive to hire local employees and provide opportunities for cultural exchange and interactions between guests and residents of the local community. Study by Henderson (2007) in Southeast Asia illustrated that eco-friendly accommodations share significant connection with community well-being as they often provide guests with information and education on sustainable practices and local environmental issues. This is aimed at ensuring that the benefits of tourism reach the local economy by fostering a sense of community ownership, environmental awareness, and education. Research by Kasim (2009) among eco-friendly resorts in Kuala Lumpur, Malaysia operating on a small and medium-sized business illuminated that eco-friendly accommodation plays a crucial role in the reduction of carbon footprint and enhances the preservation of both natural and cultural resources. It was further concluded that choosing to stay in eco-friendly accommodations can allow travelers to support responsible practices within the tourism industry as a way of contributing toward the conservation of the destinations they visit.

Report by the "Global Sustainable Tourism Council" (2020), about 60% of international travelers now consider eco-friendly accommodations by seeking out certifications and standards like "LEED" (Leadership in Energy and Environmental Design) or "Green Globe frameworks" which provide detailed information for assessing and recognizing sustainable accommodation practices that are explicit in promoting sustainable initiatives within tourist local communities. Study by Stanišić et al. (2022) established that eco-friendly accommodations have an association with community well-being because it gives priority to sourcing goods and services from local businesses and strengthening chain by empowering community members toward ensuring that economic benefits remain within the community.

Based on the foregoing arguments, the hypothesis below was formulated:

> Eco-friendly accommodations have significant relationship with community well-being in selected tourism centers in Ghana.

3.3. Methodology

This study was cross-sectional in nature and employed the descriptive research design. Primary data were obtained using questionnaires administered among 150 respondents which were selected from 5 tourist centers/destinations in Ghana namely: *Nkrummah Memorial Park and Mausoleum, Jamestown, Labadi Pleasure Beach, Mokola Market, and NAB Voyage*. These respondents were selected using the convenience sampling method. The research instrument comprised two sections, one for the biographic information of respondents while the second section examined the objectives of the study. From each of the purposively 5 selected tourist centers/destinations, 30 respondents were selected, totaling 150 respondents. Face, content, construct, and criterion-related validities were tested for the study's instrument. In addition, reliability was obtained through a pilot study conducted among selected tourists in three tourist centers in Nigeria; and responses yielded above 0.7, which made it acceptable for the study. Analyses for the study were obtained using SPSS version 27.0.

4. Results and Discussions

This section presents and discusses the formulated hypotheses for the study.

4.1. Hypothesis One

> Environmental responsibility positively influences ecological conservation in selected tourism centers in Ghana.

Table 8.1 presents the model summary presented the level of influence environmental responsibility has on ecological conservation. The coefficient of determination ($R^2 = 0.892$, p-value <0.05) indicated that 89.2% variation in ecological conservation is accounted for by environmental responsibility. This revealed that environmental responsibility positively influences ecological conservation in the selected tourism centers in Ghana. The "a" represents the *y* intercept, which explains the predictive value of the dependent variable (ecological conservation) when the independent variable (environmental responsibility) is zero. On the other hand, "b" provides an indication as to whether a variable's influence is statistically significant. It describes the probability of observing the results to explain whether an effect exists or not. Nevertheless, in the case of this study, it was found that environmental responsibility positively influences ecological conservation in the selected tourism centers in Ghana.

The significance "a" in this section was used in providing an illustration of the tested hypothesis of the study. For instance, "a" was used in expressing the results of the regression analysis used in confirming the study's hypotheses. This table helps in demonstrating the degree to which "environmental responsibility positively influences ecological conservation in the selected tourism centers in Ghana" and a positive hypothesis was recorded.

In Table 8.1, "a" reflects how strong the independent variable is as well as the degree of influence the independent variable has on the dependent variable. On the other hand, "b" as captured above, helps to put into perspective that the independent variable (environmental responsibility) influences the dependent variable (ecological conservation). On this note, "b" is statistically significant to "a" at the 0.05 level.

Table 8.1. Regression Table Showing Whether Environmental Responsibility Positively Influences Ecological Conservation in Selected Tourism Centers in Ghana.

Model	R	R^2	Adjusted R^2	Std. Error of the Estimate	F	Sig.
1	0.945[a]	0.892	0.892	0.449	1,430.600	0.000[b]

Source: SPSS Output (2025).

[a]*Dependent variable*: ecological conservation.

[b]*Predictors*: (constant), environmental responsibility.

Table 8.2. BI-correlation Table Showing Relationship Between Eco-friendly Accommodations and Community Well-being in Selected Tourism Centers in Ghana.

		Eco-friendly Accommodations	**Community Well-being**
Eco-friendly accommodations	Pearson correlation	1	0.735**
	Sig. (two-tailed)		0.000
	N	150	150
Community well-being	Pearson correlation	0.735**	1
	Sig. (two-tailed)	0.000	
	N	150	150

Source: SPSS Output, (2025).

**Correlation is significant at the 0.01 level (two-tailed).

4.2. Hypothesis Two

> Eco-friendly accommodations have a significant relationship with community well-being in selected tourism centers in Ghana.

The bi-correlation table indicated (Table 8.2) that a connection was found between eco-friendly accommodations and community well-being in selected tourism centers in Ghana with (r = 0.735, p-value <0.05). This revealed a strong and positive correlation.

The significance of Table 8.1, "b" in this chapter was used for presenting the result on the tested hypothesis of the study. For instance, Table 8.1, "b" was used in expressing the results of the bi-correlation analysis used in confirming the study's hypotheses by testing the level of relationship between the two stated variables, that is, the independent and dependent variables. This table helps in presenting the level of relationship between "eco-friendly accommodations and community well-being in selected tourism centers in Ghana."

5. Discussion of Findings

This study examined eco-wellness tourism as a pathway toward sustainability and sustainable development: the Ghanaian perspective with two formulated hypotheses.

H1 asserted that environmental responsibility positively influences ecological conservation in selected tourism centers in Ghana. A positive influence was found. This aligns with the conclusion of Walker et al. (2014) which opined that environmental responsibility enhances ecological conservation by motivating pro-environmental behaviors. It also supports the findings of Wang and Ahmad (2024) which indicated that environmental responsibility influences ecological conservation as an element of sustainable tourism and capable of enhancing eco-wellness. The findings agree with Le (2023) which asserted that environmental responsibility promotes deeper understanding of ecological impacts and fosters stronger environmental stewardship. Findings also align with the position of Singh et al. (2022) which captured that environmental responsibility reduces negative ecological impacts, and drives the development of sustainable practices essential for long-term eco-wellness tourism and health.

H2 stated that eco-friendly accommodations have significant relationship with community well-being in selected tourism centers in Ghana. Findings revealed a strong and positive relationship. This aligns with the findings of Dodds and Holmes (2019) which claimed that eco-friendly accommodations often have strong connections with local communities, as it prioritizes local employment and usage of local services. It further supports the opinion of Stanišić et al. (2022), which claimed that eco-friendly accommodations support community well-being as it helps in the encouragement of cultural preservation and creation of sustainable livelihoods for local populations, thus, promoting eco-wellness tourism and sustainable development. Findings support the opinion by Global Sustainable Tourism Council (2020), which claimed that about 60% of international travelers now consider eco-friendly accommodations to promote eco-wellness.

6. Conclusion

From the outcome of the study, it was concluded that eco-wellness tourism remains a pivotal element of sustainability and sustainable development. This is because it provides nature-based wellness experiences which merge personal health with environmental responsibility and offer immersive, nature-based wellness experiences capable of minimizing ecological impact and promoting community development. It fulfills the desires of traveler in terms of rejuvenation and well-being by ensuring their experiences contribute toward the conservation of local culture. This can help create a mutually beneficial and sustainable model for future travels.

7. Recommendations

Based on the research findings, the following recommendations were made:

(i) There is a need for both governmental and institutional support for eco-wellness tourism to drive sustainable development.
(ii) Ghanaian policymakers should consider the enhancement of existing frameworks and introduce new mechanisms to incentivize environmental responsibility among tourist centers/destinations.
(iii) There should be collaboration between the public and private sectors to enhance eco-friendly accommodations as an effective approach to eco-wellness tourism initiatives.
(iv) Awareness-building initiatives should be promulgated to promote eco-wellness practices within the Ghanaian tourism industry.

References

Andriani Albasrie, A. D., Himawan, I. S., & Sharipudin, M. N. S. B. (2024). Sustainable wellness tourism in Indonesia (Case study on health tourism development at Hanara Wellbeing Center Bandung). *Media Konservasi, 29*(3). https://doi.org/10.29244/medkon.29.3.435

Asikin, M. Z., Amelia, A., & Hidayat, A. R. (2024). Membangkitkan Semangat Kewirausahaan untuk Meningkatkan Keberlanjutan Bisnis dengan Memperkuat Sikap, Perilaku, dan Nilai Entrepreneurship. *Cakrawala Repositori IMWI, 7*(4), 1240–1245.

Avila-Gutierrez, M. J., Martin-Gomez, A., Aguayo-Gonzalez, F., & Lama-Ruiz, J. R. (2020). Eco-holonic 4.0 circular business model to conceptualize sustainable value chain towards digital transition. *Sustainability, 12*, 1889.

Bamforth, K. W., & Trist, E.L. (1951). Some social and psychological consequences of the longwall method of coal-getting: An examination of the psychological situation and defences of a work group in relation to the social structure and technological content of the work system. *Human Relations, 4*(1), 3–38. https://doi.org/10.1177/001872675100400101

Baruca, P. Z., Jančič, Z., & Brezovec, A. (2022). Understanding responsibility from the tourist's perspective: A hotel context. *Academica Turistica – Tourism and Innovation Journal, 15*(2), 187–202. https://doi.org/10.26493/2335-4194.15.187-202

Batubara, R. P., & Setiawan, A. S. (2023). Optimization of oukup steam baths as eco-wellness tourism attractions. *Jurnal Sosial Humaniora, 14*(1), 70–82.

Bellandi, M., & De-Propris, L. (2021). Local productive systems' transitions to industry 4.0+. *Sustainability, 13*, 13052.

Camilleri, M. A. (2018). Theoretical insights on integrated reporting: The inclusion of non-financial capitals incorporate disclosures. *Corporate Communications: An International Journal, 23*(4), 567–581.

Carayon, P., & Perry, S. (2021). Human factors and ergonomics systems approach to the COVID-19 healthcare crisis. *International Journal for Quality in Health Care: Journal of the International Society for Quality in Health Care, 33* (Supplement_1), 1–3. https://doi.org/10.1093/intqhc/mzaa109

Cheer, J. M., Belhassen, Y., & Kujawa, J. (2017). The search for spirituality in tourism: Toward a conceptual framework for spiritual tourism. *Tourism Management Perspectives, 24*, 252–256. https://doi.org/10.1016/j.tmp.2017.07.018

Chhabra, D. (2020). Transformational wellness tourism system model in the pandemic era. *International Journal of Health Management and Tourism, 5*(2), 76–101.

Chrontsiou, M. (2023). *Analyzing the role of wellness tourism in promoting economic, social and environmental sustainability in Municipality of Thermi, Greece* (Master's thesis). University Center of International Programmes of Studies.

Clissold, R., Westoby, R., McNamara, K. E., & Fleming, C. (2022). Wellbeing outcomes of nature tourism: Mt Barney Lodge. *Annals of Tourism Research Empirical Insights, 3*(2), 100077. https://doi.org/10.1016/j.annale.2022.100077

Dang-Van, T., Wang, J., Vo-Thanh, T., Jiang, X., & Nguyen, N. (2022). Green practices as an effective business strategy to influence the behavior of hotel guests in the luxury hotel sector: Evidence from an emerging market. *Business Strategy and the Environment*, bse.3318. https://doi.org/10.1002/bse.3318

Dodds, R., & Holmes, M. (2019). Sustainable tourism: Sustaining tourism or something more? *Tourism Management Perspectives, 29*, 230–237. https://doi.org/10.1016/j.tmp.2018.12.001

Eizaguirre, A., Garcia-Feijoo, M., & Laka, J. P. (2019). Defining sustainability core competencies in business and management studies based on multinational stakeholders' perceptions. *Sustainability, 11*, 2303.

Elon, K. (2023). Conservation of ecosystem and its diversity of policies, challenges. *Journal of Environmental and Occupational Health, 13*(9), 1–2.

Ertuna, B., Karatas-Ozkan, M., & Yamak, S. (2019). Diffusion of sustainability and CSR discourse in hospitality industry: Dynamics of local context. *International Journal of Contemporary Hospitality Management, 31*, 2564–2581. https://doi.org/10.1108/IJCHM-06-2018-0464

Eshun, F., & Asiedu, A. B. (2023). Residents' empowerment for sustainable ecotourism: Insights from Ghana. *Anatolia, 34*(2), 113–129. https://doi.org/10.1080/13032917.2021.1993285

Fischer, D., Brettel, M., & Mauer, R. (2020). The three dimensions of sustainability: A delicate balancing act for entrepreneurs made more complex by stakeholder expectations. *Journal of Business Ethics, 163*, 87–106. https://doi.org/10.1007/s10551-018-4012-1

Global Sustainable Tourism Council. (2020). *Sustainable tourism report*. Global Sustainable Tourism Council. https://doi.org/10.4324/9781315708869

Guerra, R. J. D. C., Trentin, F., & Cha, C. V. (2022). New sustainable practices in health and wellness tourism destinations focused on quality of life and wellbeing. *PASOS: Revista de Turismo y Patrimonio Cultural, 20*(4). https://doi.org/10.25145/j.pasos.2022.20.058

Heelas, P., & Woodhead, L. (2005). *The spiritual revolution: Why religion is giving way to spirituality*. Blackwell Publishing.

Henderson, J. C. (2007). Corporate social responsibility and tourism: Hotel companies in Phuket, Thailand, after the Indian Ocean Tsunami. *International Journal of Hospitality Management, 26*(1), 228–239. https://doi.org/10.1016/j.ijhm.2006.02.001

Ivanova, M., Ivanov, I. K., & Ivanov, S. (2021). Travel behaviour after the pandemic: The case of Bulgaria. *Anatolia, 32*(1), 1–11. https://doi.org/10.1080/13032917.2020.1818267

Kasim, A. (2009). Managerial attitudes towards environmental management among small and medium hotels in Kuala Lumpur. *Journal of Sustainable Tourism, 17*(6), 709–725. https://doi.org/10.1080/09669580902928468

Kaushal, V., & Srivastava, S. (2021). Hospitality and tourism industry amid COVID-19 pandemic: Perspectives on challenges and learnings from India. *International Journal of Hospitality Management, 92*(May 2020), 102707. https://doi.org/10.1016/j.ijhm.2020.102707

Lamopia, I. W. G., & Nindya, P. A. A. (2023). Pengembangan Model Baru Strategi Pemulihan Pariwisata Bali Berbasis Wisata Berkelanjutan. *Analisa Sosiologi, 12*(1), 93–110.

Le T. T. (2023). Corporate social responsibility and SMEs' performance: Mediating role of corporate image, corporate reputation and customer loyalty. *International Journal of Emerging Markets, 18*, 4565–4590. https://doi.org/10.1108/IJOEM-07-2021-1164

Li, A. Q., Rich, N., Found, P., Kumar, M., & Brown, S. (2020). Exploring product–service systems in the digital era: A socio-technical systems perspective. *The TQM Journal, 32*(4), 897–913. https://doi.org/10.1108/TQM-11-2019-0272

Li, Y., Deng, Q., Peng, F., & He, M. (2025). Development and verification of the wellness tourism experience scale. *Journal of Travel Research, 64*(1), 158–171. https://doi.org/10.1177/00472875231209493

Malik, A., Rahim, A., Sideng, U., Rasyid, A., & Jumaddin, J. (2019). Biodiversity assessment of mangrove vegetation for the sustainability of ecotourism in West Sulawesi, Indonesia. *AACL Bioflux, 12*(4), 1458–1466.

Marhaeni, H. (2023). Pemulihan Pariwisata Domestik Indonesia 2022. Berita Resmi Statistik Pemulihan Pariwisata Domestik Indonesia 2022, 33.

McCartney, G., & Wang, C. F. (2024). Medical tourism and medical tourists: Providing a sustainable course to integrating health treatments with tourism. *Journal of Travel Medicine*, *31*(5), taae034. https://doi.org/10.1093/jtm/taae034

McKinsey & Company. (2021). *The future of wellness: Trends and opportunities*. McKinsey & Company.

Meikassandra, P., Sukma, W., Prabawa, W., Mertha, W., & Pariwisata Bali, P. (2020). Wellness tourism in Ubud. A qualitative approach to study the aspects of wellness tourism development. Undergraduate student of tourism destination 1, associate professor of tourism department. *Journal of Business on Hospitality and Tourism*, *6*(1), 79–93.

Olanipekun, L.O., & Ajayi, M.A. (2023). Green employee relations as a predictor of environmental sustainability: Evidence from selected pharmaceutical firms in Ogun State, Nigeria. *Journal of Academic Research in Economics*, *15*(3), 511–522.

Ouyang, Z., Wei, W., & Chi, C.G. (2019). Environment management in the hotel industry: Does institutional environment matter? *International Journal of Hospitality Management*, *77*, 353–364. https://doi.org/10.1016/j.ijhm.2018.07.015

Pasmore, W., Francis, C., Haldeman, J., & Shani, A. (1982). Sociotechnical systems: A North American reflection on empirical studies of the seventies. *Human Relations*, *35*(12), 1179–1204. https://doi.org/10.1177/001872678203501207

Purvis, B., Mao, Y., & Robinson, D. (2019). Three pillars of sustainability: In search of conceptual origins. *Sustainability Science*, *14*, 681–695.

Rai, A., & Sreenivasan, G. K. (2023). Spirituality and yoga: Drivers of spiritual tourism: A contemporary approach. *International Journal of Yoga and Allied Sciences*, *12*(2), 231–240.

Rajapakshe, T. S., & Wadippuli Arachchi, R. S. S. (2024). Ayurveda wellness tourism: An overview of the Sri Lankan context. In *Strategic tourism planning for communities* (pp. 173–195). Emerald Publishing. https://doi.org/10.1108/978-1-83549-015-020241014

Ritpanitchajchaval, N., Ashton, A. S., & Apollo, M. (2023). Eudaimonic well-being development: Motives driving mountain-based adventure tourism. *Journal of Outdoor Recreation and Tourism*, *42*(February), 100607. https://doi.org/10.1016/j.jort.2023.100607

Sheehy, B., & Farneti, F. (2021). Corporate social responsibility, sustainability, sustainable development and corporate sustainability: What is the difference, and does it matter? *Sustainability*, *13*(11), 5965.

Singh S. K., Del Giudice M., Chiappetta Jabbour C. J., Latan H., & Sohal A. S. (2022). Stakeholder pressure, green innovation, and performance in small and medium-sized enterprises: The role of green dynamic capabilities. *Business Strategy and the Environment*, *31*, 500–514. https://doi.org/10.1002/bse.2906

Sinha, M., & Fukey, L. N. (2021). Assessing a progress of resources efficient practices in hotel industry. In A. Kumar, J. A. Garza-Reyes, & S. R. Khan (Eds.), *Circular economy for the management of operations* (pp. 89–117). CRC Press.

Smith, M., & Puczkó, L. (2015). More than a special interest: Defining and determining the demand for health tourism. *Tourism Recreation Research*, *40*(2), 205–219.

Sony, M., & Naik, S. (2020). Industry 4.0 integration with socio-technical systems theory: A systematic review and proposed theoretical model. *Technology in Society*, *61*, 101248. https://doi.org/10.1016/j.techsoc.2020.101248

SPSS Output. (2025). IBM Corp. (2025). *IBM SPSS Statistics for Windows (Version 29)* [Computer software]. IBM Corp.

Stanišic, T., Milićević, S., & Krstić, B. (2022). Natural resources in function of sustainable and competitive tourism development of the EU countries. *PROBLEMY EKOROZWOJU – Problems of Sustainable Development*, *17*(1), 64–70.

Sufa, S. A., Subiakto, H., Octavianti, M., & Kusuma, E. A. (2020). Wisata Gastronomi Sebagai Daya Tarik Pengembangan Potensi Daerah Kabupaten Sidoarjo. *Mediakom: Jurnal Ilmu Komunikasi*, *4*(1), 75–86. https://doi.org/10.35760/mkm.2020.v4i1.2497

Suntararak, P., & Boonyanmethaporn, W. (2024). Building the future of rural-based wellness tourism: Infrastructure and policy considerations for rural Thailand. *Journal of Infrastructure, Policy and Development*, *8*(14), 9387. https://doi.org/10.24294/jipd9387

Tang, M., Li, X., Zhang, Y., Wu, Y., & Wu, B. (2020). From command-and-control to market-based environmental policies: Optimal transition timing and China's heterogeneous environmental effectiveness. *Economic Modelling*, *90*, 1–10. https://doi.org/10.1016/j.scitotenv.2019.136362

Tuzunkan, D. (2018). Wellness tourism: What motivates tourists to participate? *International Journal of Applied Engineering Research*, *13*(1), 651–661.

VanderWeele, T. J., Balboni, T. A., & Koh, H. K. (2017). Health and spirituality. *JAMA*, *318*(6), 519–520. https://doi.org/10.1001/jama.2017.8136

Vrabcova, P., Urbancova, H., & Hudakova, M. (2022). Strategic trends of organizations in the context of new perspectives of sustainable competitiveness. *Journal of Competitiveness*, *14*, 174–193.

Walker, K., Ni, N., & Huo, W. (2014). Is the red dragon green? An examination of the antecedents and consequences of environmental proactivity in China. *Journal of Business Ethics*, *125*, 27–43. https://doi.org/10.1007/s10551-013-1903-z

Wang Y. Z., & Ahmad S. (2024). Green process innovation, green product innovation, leverage, and corporate financial performance; evidence from system GMM. *Heliyon*, *10*. https://doi.org/10.1016/j.heliyon.2024.e25819

Wiseman, J., & Brasher, K. (2008). Community wellbeing in an unwell world. *Journal of Public Health Policy*, *29*(3), 353–366.

World Tourism Organisation (UNWTO). (2018). *UNWTO tourism highlights: 2018 edition.* UNWTO. https://doi.org/10.18111/9789284419876

Yuwono, R., & Astuti, D. W. (2021). The potential for developing wellness hospitality tourism in Tawangmangu. In *SIAR II: Seminar Ilmiah Arsitektur II (Proceedings of the Scientific Seminar on Architecture)* (pp. 282–292), Universitas Muhammadiyah Surakarta.

Zaroucha, V. (2022). *Sustainable tourism and well-being: The host perspective of residents of Greece* (Master's thesis). The American College of Thessaloniki.

Chapter 9

Eco-wellness Tourism: Integrating Sustainability with Holistic Well-being

Arsheed Ahmad Ganie[a] *and Divya Jyoti Thakur*[b]

[a]*Department of Humanities & Social Sciences, IEC University, Himachal Pradesh, India*
[b]*BBA Department, University School of Business, Chandigarh University, Punjab, India*

Abstract

Sustainable tourism has emerged as a transformative force in the global wellness sector, where travelers are increasingly seeking experiences that not only refresh their health but also contribute to environmental preservation and the empowerment of local communities. This chapter explores the developing domain of eco-wellness tourism, where sustainability converges with holistic health, offering a unique travel experience that focuses on minimizing environmental impact while promoting mental, physical, and spiritual transformation. Eco-wellness tourism incorporates practices like renewable energy, organic food, natural healing methods, and energy-efficient accommodations in a manner that emphasizes environmental responsibility. This study highlights the importance of eco-wellness travel trends such as holistic wellness programs, eco-luxury resorts, adventure tourism, and minimalist gateways, all situated in pristine natural environments that foster mindfulness and mental well-being. Moreover, it examines sustainable travel strategies, including supporting local economies, minimizing waste, and encouraging mindful travel, all contributing to a greener future. The chapter also showcases specific examples of eco-friendly wellness retreats, such as the Pangarh Lake Retreat in Rajasthan, which exemplify the fusion of luxury and sustainability. With a growing focus on sustainable wellness tourism, this chapter seeks to offer an in-depth understanding of how

Advancement in Medical and Wellness Tourism, Part A: Entrepreneurship and Technology, 113–124

doi:10.1108/978-1-80592-983-320261010

eco-wellness tourism is shaping the future of sustainable travel, providing a holistic approach that nurtures personal health and supports global sustainability.

Keywords: Sustainable tourism; eco-wellness tourism; holistic health; environmental responsibility; regenerative travel

1. Introduction

1.1. Background and Context

Travel is changing. People are not just looking for places to visit anymore they are searching for experiences that make them feel better do good for the planet and connect them to something bigger than themselves. That is where eco-wellness tourism comes in a growing trend that blends personal well-being with environmental care. It is not just about yoga on a beach or spa treatments in a luxury resort. Eco-wellness tourism goes further. It is about staying somewhere that respects nature like using solar energy, supporting local farmers or giving back to the community. Travel makes you feel good inside and out while also helping the environment and the people who live there.

More travelers are thinking about their impact these days. Climate change, health concerns after the pandemic, and a general shift toward mindful living have changed how people choose where to go and what to do when they get there. According to the Global Wellness Institute (2023), wellness-focused travel is booming, worth over $1.2 trillion globally. Within that, eco-wellness is fast becoming a favorite among younger travelers especially millennials and Gen-Z who want their trips to matter beyond just a vacation.

India has a unique edge here (Shriyon, 2025). With its centuries-old traditions of yoga, Ayurveda, and spiritual retreats, the country is already known for healing and self-discovery. Add to that India's diverse landscapes from mountain villages to forest hideouts, and you have a perfect setting for sustainable wellness travel. This chapter looks at how eco-wellness tourism is shaping up as a new way to travel, one that does not just focus on relaxation, but also on doing good for the world around us.

2. Conceptual Framework

2.1. Defining Key Terms

2.1.1. Wellness Tourism

Wellness tourism is not just visiting new places anymore. It is more about feeling better mentally and physically. According to Global Wellness Institute (2023), this type of travel focuses on seeking experiences that actively contribute to one's overall well-being. For instance, people might go on a yoga retreat in the mountains, try meditation in a peaceful setting, or explore traditional healing methods like Ayurveda and Naturopathy. Travelers want to return home not only with memories but also with a renewed sense of energy, a stronger connection, and better health.

2.1.2. Sustainable Tourism

According to the United Nations Tourism Organization, sustainable tourism is a type of travel that carefully considers both present and future social, economic, and environmental consequences. Its primary objectives include preserving cultural identity, supporting long-term economic viability, and protecting natural ecosystems and resources for future generations.

2.1.3. Eco-tourism

Eco-tourism refers to travel that emphasizes visiting natural environments in a responsible manner. It can be defined as travel that combines health-oriented experiences such as yoga, holistic, and meditation with eco-friendly practices. The purpose is not only to enhance personal well-being but also to support ecological conservation and the cultural development of local communities.

2.1.4. Eco-wellness Tourism

Eco-wellness tourism combines wellness travel with sustainable practices (Kandan Parakkal et al., 2024). It includes wellness activities like mindfulness or spa treatment sessions combined with eco-friendly habits such as reducing waste and respecting local traditions. The idea is to feel better yourself while also helping the environment and local people.

2.2. Theoretical Foundations

2.2.1. Triple Bottom Line (Elkington, 1994)

According to Elkington (1994), the triple bottom line is a way to think about sustainability by emphasize on three areas: planet, people, and profit. It means that businesses or projects should care about more than just making money – they should also support communities and protect the environment. This model suggests that organizations should be accountable not only for their financial outcomes but also for their impact on society and the environment.

2.2.2. Wellness Tourism Pyramid (Global Wellness Institute, 2023)

The Wellness Tourism Pyramid (Global Wellness Institute, 2023) divides wellness travel into five stages, beginning with simple relaxation and moving toward more meaningful personal growth and self-discovery. When integrated with sustainability frameworks, this model gives rise to eco-wellness tourism – a comprehensive approach that not only promotes individual well-being but also aligns with broader environmental and social objectives.

3. Literature Review

3.1. Rise of Conscious Consumerism

Smith and Puczko (2020) observe a growing trend toward conscious consumerism within the tourism sector, where travelers are increasingly mindful of the environment and social impacts of their decisions. This change is especially common among younger people, who prefer travel experiences that offer personal growth and positive social impact.

3.2. Wellness and Nature Connection

Immersion in nature has been linked to improved mental health in a number of studies (Hartig et al., 2014; White et al., 2019). By placing wellness retreats in pristine or ecologically vulnerable areas, eco-wellness tourism utilizes this relationship to enhance both therapeutic outcomes and environmental awareness.

3.3. Regenerative Travel

A newer concept gaining traction is regenerative travel, which goes beyond sustainability by actively restoring ecosystems and communities. As noted by Bramwell (2021), regenerative travel models emphasize co-creation with local stakeholders and aim to leave destinations better than they were found – a principle deeply embedded in eco-wellness tourism.

3.4. Role of Traditional Healing Systems

India's traditional wellness systems – especially Ayurveda and Yoga – have been extensively studied in the context of wellness tourism (Rana & Paul, 2020; Swaroop & Srinivasan, 2018). These studies suggest that integrating indigenous knowledge with modern sustainability practices can create a competitive advantage in the global wellness market.

3.5. Gaps in Current Research

While literature on wellness tourism and eco-tourism is extensive, few studies have explicitly examined the intersection of sustainability and holistic well-being. Moreover, empirical research on eco-wellness tourism in India remains limited (Luo et al., 2025). This chapter contributes to filling this gap by exploring both theoretical and practical dimensions of the topic.

4. Methodology

4.1. Research Design

This chapter adopts a qualitative, exploratory approach, relying primarily on secondary data sources. The methodology includes content analysis of websites, promotional materials, and blogs related to eco-wellness retreats in India along with secondary case analysis of selected wellness destinations. It also includes a review of academic literature from journals and analysis of reports published by the Global Wellness Institute, UNWTO, and the Ministry of Tourism, Government of India.

4.2. Data Collection

This study follows a qualitative and exploratory approach, relying on secondary data from global reports, academic journals, and case studies related to eco-wellness tourism. Sources include publications from the Global Wellness Institute (2023), UNWTO guidelines, and real-world examples like Pangarh Lake Retreat in Rajasthan.

5. Dimensions of Eco-wellness Tourism

5.1. Environmental Sustainability Practices

Eco-wellness tourism prioritizes green infrastructure and resource efficiency. Common practices include:

- Use of renewable energy (solar panels, biogas).
- Implementation of zero-waste policies.
- Water conservation techniques (rainwater harvesting, graywater recycling).
- Construction using locally sourced, eco-friendly materials.
- Organic farming and plant-based diets.
- These initiatives not only reduce environmental impact but also enhance the authenticity and educational value of the experience.

5.2. Holistic Well-being Components

At the heart of eco-wellness tourism is a focus on mind–body–spirit integration. Typical offerings include:

- Yoga and meditation sessions.
- Ayurvedic treatments and herbal therapies.
- Forest bathing and nature walks.
- Digital detox programs.
- Mindful eating based on seasonal, organic ingredients.
- Such services are designed to promote inner harmony, emotional resilience, and self-awareness, making them highly attractive to stressed urban professionals and wellness seekers.

5.3. Community Engagement

True eco-wellness tourism extends beyond environmental concerns to include social upliftment and cultural preservation. Key strategies include:

- Employing local staff and training youth in hospitality.
- Partnering with local artisans and healers.

- Supporting traditional crafts and medicine.
- Investing in rural infrastructure and education.
- This dimension ensures that tourism benefits are shared equitably and that host communities remain central to the wellness narrative.

6. Emerging Trends in Eco-wellness Tourism

An increasing emphasis on conscious living and shifting tourist preferences are driving rapid changes in the eco-wellness tourism industry. Today's travelers are redefining what wellness means – not just for themselves, but also for the environment and local communities – resulting in several distinct trends.

6.1. Eco-luxury Resorts

You will find solar panels powering elegant villas, gardens where herbs and vegetables are grown on-site, buildings made with sustainable materials, and meals crafted from local ingredients. It is not just about pampering yourself; it is about traveling in a way that leaves a lighter footprint. Resorts like Ananda in the Himalaya and Six Senses have become pioneers in showing that luxury doesn't have to cost the Earth literally. They have proven that sustainability and style can go hand in hand without skimping on quality or comfort.

People who choose these kinds of getaways are not thinking about how they feed during their vacation; they are thinking about choices that affect the world around them (The Times of India, 2025). Eco-luxury is for those who want to enjoy life's finer things but not at the expense of their values.

It is part of a bigger shift in how we think about luxury. No longer just about how much you spend or how flashy it looks, real opulence now means making thoughtful choices, staying connected to nature, and caring about what kind of impact you leave behind.

6.2. Minimalist Gateways

At the other end of the spectrum are minimalist gateway off-grid retreats designed to help people step away from the noise of everyday life and reconnect with nature and self. These retreats usually don't have Wi Fi, offer simple accommodations, and emphasize silence, slow living, and intentional rest. They attract individuals looking to simplify, reset, and escape the pressures of modern life.

Minimalist wellness centers are particularly popular among urban professionals, creatives, and spiritual seekers who view disconnection not as deprivation, but as a form of healing. These spaces promote deep introspection and encourage guests to engage with their surroundings in a meaningful way.

6.3. Adventure and Wellness

Adventure-based wellness tourism is another rising trend that blends physical activity with mental and emotional rejuvenation. This approach combines outdoor pursuits such as trekking, kayaking, and camping with wellness practices like sunrise yoga, guided meditation, and breathwork sessions in natural settings.

This type of travel appeals to active individuals who find peace through movement and immersion in nature. Whether it is hiking through mountain trails followed by a calming Ayurvedic massage or canoeing at dawn before a mindfulness session, the integration of adventure and wellness offers a holistic experience that energizes both body and mind.

6.4. Regenerative Wellness Programs

Sustainability focuses on reducing harm; regenerative wellness tourism goes a step further. It seeks to actively restore ecosystems and uplift local communities. Instead of just minimizing their impact, travelers participate in activities that contribute positively to the destination, such as planting trees, getting involved in community health projects, and soil restoration.

These programs reflect a deeper epical commitment: the idea that travel should leave a place better than it was found. This model resonates strongly with younger, purpose-driven travelers who are not only seeking personal transformation but also want their journeys to create lasting positive change.

6.5. Personalized Wellness Journeys

No two people heal the same way – which is why personalized wellness journeys are becoming increasingly popular. These customized itineraries are tailored to individual needs, incorporating elements like Ayurvedic consultations, nutritional planning, stress management techniques, and mental health support. Unlike one-size-fits-all retreats, personalized journeys allow travelers to address specific concerns – from burnout and anxiety to digestive issues and sleep disorders. This trend reflects a broader move toward individualized health solutions within the wellness industry.

These emerging trends highlight a significant shift in how wellness tourism is being experienced today. Travelers are no longer satisfied with generic offerings; they seek authenticity, personalization, and impact. As a result, eco-wellness tourism is moving beyond superficial relaxation and into the realm of transformational, sustainable, and deeply personal experiences.

7. Secondary Case Analysis: Pangarh Lake Retreat, Rajasthan

7.1. Background

This section presents a secondary case analysis of the Pangarh Lake Retreat in Rajasthan. The data presented here is derived exclusively from publicly available information, including the retreat's official communications, news features, and travel aggregators (*Outlook Traveller*, 2023; Pangarh Lake Retreat, n.d.). The purpose of this analysis is to illustrate how eco-wellness principles are applied in real-world settings.

Nestled in the tranquil Aravalli hills near Udaipur, Pangarh Lake Retreat is a boutique wellness center that brings together Ayurveda, yoga, and eco-living in a serene natural setting (*Outlook Traveller*, 2023). Surrounded by forests, lakes, and quiet villages, the retreat offers guests an immersive experience where personal well-being and environmental care go hand-in-hand.

Unlike mass-market wellness resorts, Pangarh focuses on simplicity, sustainability, and deep connection to nature, to oneself, and to local culture (Tripadvisor, n.d.). It attracts travelers seeking not just relaxation, but transformation, those who value mindfulness, authenticity, and low-impact living.

The retreat blends modern wellness practices with traditional Indian healing systems, offering visitors a chance to disconnect from city life and reconnect with their inner selves – all while contributing positively to the environment and supporting rural livelihoods (Booking.com, 2025).

7.2. Sustainability Initiatives

Pangarh Lake Retreat takes sustainability seriously. From energy use to food sourcing, every aspect is designed to minimize ecological impact. The retreat runs entirely on solar energy, ensuring minimal carbon emissions (EaseMyTrip, 2025). It also uses rainwater harvesting to meet its water needs, which is particularly important in a region prone to water scarcity.

A highlight of the retreat is its organic kitchen garden, where fresh vegetables, herbs, and medicinal plants are grown without chemicals or artificial fertilizers (Pangarh Lake Retreat, n.d.). Much of what guests eat comes straight from the land, making meals both healthy and sustainable. In terms of employment, the retreat actively hires local villagers, providing a steady income to the community (*Outlook Traveller*, 2023). Waste management is another core principle; the retreat follows strict waste segregation and composting practices, ensuring that organic waste is reused (Pangarh Lake Retreat, n.d.).

7.3. Wellness Offerings

At the heart of Pangarh's appeal are its wellness programs. Each guest receives customized Ayurvedic treatments based on individual constitution and health goals (MakeMyTrip, 2025). These include herbal massages, detox therapies, and personalized dietary plans rooted in ancient Indian medicine.

Daily yoga and meditation sessions help guests slow down and breathe deeply; these sessions are held in open-air pavilions overlooking the lake (*Outlook Traveller*, 2023). Meals are plant-based, seasonal, and sourced from the retreat's own garden or nearby farms (Tripadvisor, n.d.). For those looking to connect with nature, guided forest walks and silent meditation sessions offer opportunities to observe wildlife and listen to birdsong (EaseMyTrip, 2025).

7.4. Community Impact

One of the most compelling aspects of Pangarh Lake Retreat is how it involves and benefits the local community. By hiring local staff, the retreat creates job opportunities in a region where youth often migrate to cities in search of work (*Outlook Traveller*, 2023). This helps reduce urban migration and keeps local traditions alive.

The retreat also sources ingredients from nearby farms, directly supporting small-scale agriculture. Local artisans are given a platform to sell handmade textiles, pottery, and crafts, reviving interest in traditional craftsmanship (Pangarh Lake Retreat, n.d.).

7.5. Challenges and Opportunities

Despite its success, Pangarh faces several operational hurdles. Like many rural retreats, it deals with seasonal fluctuations, with business peaking during cooler months and dropping off during extreme heat or monsoon rains (Tripadvisor, n.d.). There is also a shortage of well-trained wellness professionals in the area. Marketing poses another challenge, as reaching conscious travelers globally requires digital visibility (*Outlook Traveller*, 2023). However, these obstacles come with opportunities. Pangarh could become a blueprint for similar projects across India, proving that small-scale, high-impact eco-wellness models are scalable.

8. Strategies for Promoting Sustainable Travel Behavior

8.1. Encourage Low-impact Travel

Travelers can reduce their carbon footprint by choosing train journeys, carpooling, or electric vehicles over flights or private cars. Eco-wellness centers should partner with green transport providers and promote eco-friendly travel options to guests.

8.2. Support Local Economies

Wellness tourism must go beyond attracting visitors – it should also benefit residents. Retreats should prioritize partnerships with local farmers, artisans, and service providers. This not only supports the economy but also enriches the guest experience with authentic cultural exchange.

8.3. Educate Travelers

Many tourists are unaware of the environmental and social impact of their choices. Offering short workshops on mindful consumption, cultural sensitivity, and sustainability can make a big difference. Simple actions – like reducing plastic use or respecting sacred spaces – can leave lasting positive effects.

8.4. Leverage Technology

Digital innovations play a crucial role in bridging the gap between wellness seekers and sustainable providers. The use of mobile applications that track carbon footprints, AI-driven platforms for personalized consultations, and blockchain technology for transparent eco-certifications can significantly enhance the traveller's journey.

9. Challenges and Limitations

9.1. Greenwashing Concerns

One of the biggest issues in the wellness tourism space is greenwashing – when businesses claim to be sustainable without making real changes. This undermines trust and confuses travelers trying to make ethical choices.

To combat this, transparent reporting and third-party certifications are essential.

9.2. Accessibility Issues

Many eco-wellness retreats remain out of reach for average travelers due to high costs. While some justify this with quality of services, the industry needs to explore affordable models to ensure inclusivity.

9.3. Balancing Luxury and Minimalism

There's often a tension between offering comfort and maintaining sustainability. Some travelers seek eco-retreats that still feel luxurious, which can conflict with minimalist, low-impact ideals.

Finding a balance – offering comfort without excess – is key to building a credible eco-wellness brand.

9.4. Lack of Standardized Certification

Currently, there's no universal standard for what qualifies as "eco-wellness." Without clear benchmarks, it's hard for travelers to know what they're paying for – and for genuine operators to stand out. Creating a recognized eco-wellness certification system would bring much-needed clarity to the field.

9.5. Seasonal Constraints

Rural and remote retreats like Pangarh face seasonal limitations, with operations affected by weather extremes. This affects revenue and staffing stability. Developing year-round tourism strategies, such as indoor wellness programs or virtual retreats, could help address this issue.

10. Policy and Industry Recommendations

10.1. Government Incentives

To encourage more eco-wellness ventures, governments should provide tax breaks, subsidies, and grants for green infrastructure and wellness enterprises that support local communities.

10.2. Certification Frameworks

A standardized eco-wellness certification system should be developed at both the national and state levels. This will build consumer trust and help distinguish genuine initiatives from greenwashing attempts.

10.3. Inclusion in National Tourism Strategy

Eco-wellness tourism should be formally integrated into national and regional tourism plans, recognizing its potential to drive sustainable rural development and preserve heritage.

10.4. Training and Capacity Building

Wellness practitioners, hospitality staff, and village youth should be trained in eco-tourism practices, customer service, and digital tools. This enhances service quality and increases local participation.

10.5. Awareness Campaigns

Public awareness campaigns – through media, influencers, and educational institutions – should promote the idea of mindful travel. Tourists need to understand the value of eco-wellness tourism before they arrive, not after. These measures can help institutionalize eco-wellness tourism and position India as a global leader in the field.

11. Conclusion

Eco-wellness tourism represents a powerful intersection of sustainability, well-being, and cultural preservation. As travelers become more conscious of their impact on the planet and society, demand for authentic, regenerative experiences continues to grow.

India, with its deep-rooted wellness traditions and natural beauty, is uniquely poised to capitalize on this trend. By embracing eco-wellness tourism, the country can showcase its heritage while contributing to global sustainability goals.

This chapter has highlighted the key dimensions, trends, and challenges of the sector, emphasizing the need for policy support, industry innovation, and community inclusion. Future research should explore traveler motivations, business models, and long-term impacts to further refine and expand this transformative form of travel.

As we move forward, eco-wellness tourism must evolve from a niche offering to a mainstream movement – one that nurtures the self, the community, and the earth in equal measure.

References

Booking.com. (2025). *Pangarh Lake Retreat: Hotel profile, amenities, and guest reviews.* https://www.booking.com/hotel/in/pangarh-lake-retreat.html

Bramwell, B. (2021). Regenerative tourism and sustainable development. *Journal of Sustainable Tourism*, *29*(6), 853–863.

EaseMyTrip. (2025). *Pangarh Lake Retreat Hotel Chittorgarh: Reviews, price, photos*. https://www.easemytrip.com/hotels/pangarh-lake-retreat-1106565/

Elkington, J. (1994). Towards the sustainable corporation: Win-win-win strategy for sustainable development. *California Management Review*, *36*(2), 90–100.

Global Wellness Institute. (2023). *Wellness tourism: A global market overview*. https://www.globalwellnessinstitute.org

Hartig, T., Mitchell, R., de Vries, S., & Frumkin, H. (2014). Nature and health. *Annual Review of Public Health*, *35*, 207–228.

Kandan Parakkal, A., Vazhakkatte Thazhathethil, B., & George, B. (2024). The physical, mental, spiritual, and environmental (PMSE) framework for enhancing wellness tourism experiences. *Administrative Sciences*, *14*(7), 140. https://doi.org/10.3390/admsci14070140

Luo, Y., Lanlung, C., Kim, E., Tang, L. R., & Song, S. M. (2025). Wellness tourism: Nurturing nature and achieving sustainability in India. Sustainability (Switzerland). https://doi.org/10.1007/s10668-025-06183-7

MakeMyTrip. (2025). *Pangarh Lake Retreat – Resort in Chittorgarh: Reviews & Lifestyle*. https://www.makemytrip.com/hotels/pangarh_lake_retreat-details-chittorgarh.html

Outlook Traveller. (2023, August 14). Pangarh Lake Retreat: Where nature meets serenity. *Outlook Traveller Magazine*. https://www.outlooktraveller.com/

Pangarh Lake Retreat. (n.d.). *Pangarh Lake Retreat – Hidden gem of experiences*. https://pangarh.com/

Rana, J., & Paul, A. (2020). Ayurveda and wellness tourism in India: Opportunities and challenges. *International Journal of Ayurveda and Pharma Research*, *8*(1), 1–6.

Shriyon, S. (2025). Wellness tourism in India: Travelling for mind, body, soul and beyond. *International Journal of Multidisciplinary Research and Review*. https://www.ijmdrr.com/admin/downloads/130420256.pdf

Smith, M. K., & Puczko, L. (2020). *Cultural tourism: The partnership between tourism and cultural heritage management*. Routledge.

Swaroop, A., & Srinivasan, M. (2018). Yoga and Ayurveda as drivers of medical tourism in India. *Indian Journal of Medical Ethics*, *3*(2), 112–116.

The Times of India. (2025, February 22). *How wellness tourism is becoming the next travel trend to follow among travellers*. https://timesofindia.indiatimes.com/life-style/travel/news/how-wellness-tourism-is-becoming-the-next-travel-trend-to-follow-among-travellers/articleshow/118420013.cms

Tripadvisor. (n.d.). *Pangarh Lake Retreat – Updated 2025 reviews & price*. https://www.tripadvisor.com/Hotel_Review-g303888-d2251847-Reviews-Pangarh_Lake_Retreat_Chittaurgarh_Chittorgarh_District_Rajasthan.html

White, M. P., Alcock, I., Grellier, J., Wheeler, B. W., Hartig, T., Warber, S. L., Bone, A., Depledge, M. H., & Fleming, L. E. (2019). Spending at least 120 minutes a week in nature is associated with good health and wellbeing. *Scientific Reports*, *9*(1), 7754. https://doi.org/10.1038/s41598-019-44097-3

Chapter 10

Wellness Tourism in a Hyperconnected World: Balancing Innovation, Integrity, and Sustainability

Priyakrushna Mohanty[a], Safia Quadri[b] and Prakash Chandra Rout[c]

[a]*Department of Business and Management, Christ University, Bangalore, India*
[b]*School of Business and Management, Christ University, Bangalore, India*
[c]*Hospitality, Travel, and Tourism, PSS Central Institute of Vocational Education, Madhya Pradesh, India*

Abstract

With the evolution of wellness tourism in the digital era, there has been an exponential change in the landscape of travel wellness and preventive health care. Today, the travelers are driven to seek holistic well-being, self-care, and transformative experiences beyond traditional leisure. This growing demand has led to the integration of advanced wellness and tourism technologies, such as artificial intelligence (AI), wearable devices, virtual reality (VR), telemedicine, and blockchain. These innovations enhance personalization, operational efficiency, and accessibility for the customer; they also redesign the delivery and consumption of wellness experiences. As there is a technological shift in the wellness tourism industry, critical challenges arise related to data privacy, the digital divide, sustainability, cultural sensitivity, and the erosion of authenticity in wellness practices. This chapter critically examines the relationship between wellness tourism and emerging technologies. It hides the opportunities and the underlying challenges associated with this transformation. Insights complemented by semi-structured interviews with industry experts and extensive academic literature reviews published between 2015 and 2025 offered a comprehensive exploration of future trends, challenges, and pathways for sustainable development in wellness tourism. It also proposes the framework for ethical

Advancement in Medical and Wellness Tourism, Part A:
Entrepreneurship and Technology, 125–138

doi:10.1108/978-1-80592-983-320261011

technology integration, ensuring the wellness tourism ecosystem remains inclusive and resilient. Inform the ground of the principle of sustainability.

Keywords: Wellness tourism; digital transformation; AI in tourism; sustainable wellness; ethical challenges; smart health travel

1. Introduction

There has been a significant transformation in the global wellness tourism industry in recent years. The sector is rapidly expanding within the broader travel and tourism industry, underscored by a growing public awareness of physical, mental, and emotional well-being. Travelers are increasingly seeking experiences that go beyond conventional leisure, aiming for personal growth, stress reduction, preventive health, and holistic regeneration. As a result, wellness tourism has shifted from a niche offering – traditionally associated with retreats – to a mainstream, diversified global industry catering to a wide spectrum of wellness needs (Smith & Puczkó, 2019).

The COVID-19 pandemic further accelerated this evolution by shifting global consciousness toward health, mental wellness, hygiene prioritization, and immunity enhancement. People reassessed their lifestyle choices, escalating the demand for wellness-centric travel (Global Wellness Institute, 2023). Today, travelers select destinations that align with broader goals of well-being, sustainability, and conscious living (Paci et al., 2013). The scope of wellness tourism now encompasses mindfulness retreats, medical wellness programs, immersive digital detox holidays, eco-conscious wellness resorts, and integrative health treatments.

Technological advancements have fundamentally reshaped the wellness tourism landscape. Innovations such as AI, Internet of Things (IoT), wearable devices, blockchain, big data analytics, and VR and augmented reality (AR) are revolutionizing the design, delivery, and personalization of wellness services for travelers (Buhalis & Sinarta, 2019). While these technologies were initially supplementary, they are now central to how wellness tourism operates globally. AI-driven systems enable the creation of personalized wellness itineraries using biometric preferences and health histories. IoT-enabled environments support real-time monitoring of vital signs, and VR/AR technologies transport users into meditative or nature-inspired settings to enhance relaxation and mindfulness (Lin et al., 2020).

The widespread adoption of fitness trackers, smart watches, and biosensors allows health-conscious travelers to monitor parameters such as heart rate, sleep cycles, stress levels, and physical activity throughout their journey (Saxena et al., 2025). These devices foster self-awareness and enable providers to deliver customized interventions. Blockchain technology is increasingly used to strengthen data security and transparency, assuring travelers that their wellness experiences are secure and authentic (Baydeniz, 2024).

Telemedicine also plays a transformative role, removing geographic constraints from medical and wellness tourism. Digital platforms now facilitate teleconsultations, remote diagnostics, and post-visit follow-ups, creating hybrid models where in-person experiences are complemented by digital interactions before and after travel (Kraus et al., 2022).

Despite enhancing personalization, accessibility, and efficiency, digital technologies introduce complex challenges. Data privacy is a key concern as wearable devices and digital platforms collect vast amounts of sensitive health information. Issues of data ownership, security breaches, and informed consent are prevalent, with travelers often unaware of how their data are used or shared, raising ethical considerations (Agarwal et al., 2021). Over-commercialization and the loss of authenticity pose further risks, as wellness experiences increasingly become mediated by algorithms and automated systems. The deeply personal, cultural, and spiritual essence of wellness may be compromised, reducing rich traditions rooted in indigenous knowledge and nature-based therapies to standardized, technology-driven products (Voigt et al., 2011; Zhang & Shi, 2024).

A rise in digital fatigue is also evident. Many people now seek "tech-free" wellness tourism to disconnect from digital overload and reconnect with themselves and nature (Bauwens et al., 2019). This trend leads to critical questions about the desirability and benefits of technology integration in wellness tourism, especially regarding balancing convenience with authentic experiences. The industry faces inclusivity challenges, as not all travelers have equal access to digital infrastructure or possess digital literacy, raising concerns about equity – since wellness tourism is supposed to promote well-being for all (Hannigan et al., 2004).

Environmental sustainability remains another major concern. While innovations like VR and telemedicine can reduce carbon footprints by limiting travel, they also increase resource consumption, e-waste, and emissions. The waste from wearable devices and digital infrastructure generates environmental costs (Gurova et al., 2020). Thus, the challenge for wellness tourism is to ensure that technological integration does not undermine ecological integrity (Jie, 2023).

1.1. Research Gap

Despite the improvement in wellness tourism and innovative technology sectors, there remains a significant gap in understanding these two domains. Existing studies primarily focus on the operational and marketing applications of technology in tourism (Buhalis & Sinarta, 2019) or on the psychological and physiological outcomes of wellness practices. Few studies comprehensively examine how emerging digital technologies fundamentally transform the wellness tourism experience, from design and delivery to ethical implications and long-term sustainability. Moreover, current research has not adequately addressed the tensions between technological convenience and the core principles of wellness tourism, such as authenticity, mindfulness, and cultural integrity. There is limited empirical analysis of how data privacy, algorithmic bias, digital fatigue, and the loss of human touch influence travelers' wellness experiences.

1.2. Research Objectives

The following objectives have guided the chapter in response to these gaps.

(a) To explore how emerging digital technologies are transforming wellness tourism's design, delivery, and experience.
(b) Identify the key benefits and opportunities technology offers wellness travelers and service providers.
(c) To critically assess the challenges, risks, and ethical dilemmas associated with integrating technology into wellness tourism, particularly regarding privacy, authenticity, and inclusivity.
(d) To propose a strategic framework for adopting sustainable, ethical, and culturally sensitive technology within the wellness tourism industry.

This chapter explores key goals related to wellness tourism in the digital age. It offers scholars and practitioners a clear understanding of how wellness, technology, and sustainability are connected.

2. Research Methodology

This chapter adopts a qualitative research methodology, combining a systematic literature review (2015–2025) and thematic content analysis. Academic databases such as Scopus, Web of Science, and ScienceDirect were used to identify relevant peer-reviewed articles, industry reports, and white papers. To focus on scholarly work addressing the relationship between technology and wellness tourism, inclusion criteria were set with special emphasis on sustainability, user experience, and innovation.

The conceptual framework of this research was designed using a thematic analysis, which enabled patterns within the analyzed literature to come out during the process, as opposed to being imposed on the researcher in advance. When it comes to identifying the areas of interest, four general areas were suggested: technological advances in wellness tourism, future opportunities, challenges, and sustainability-focused directions. These themes combined made it possible to read between the lines to determine how digital technologies were transforming the practices of wellness tourism on the one hand, and on the other, creating a disproportionate impact on both users and destinations. To avoid categorizing technology as a neutral intervention, the framework acknowledges the fact that digital tools are applied to social, cultural, and spatial realities, defining their usage and impacts. This method is consistent with interpretive traditions in tourism research that perceive experiences as being produced in interaction between systems, users, and contexts. The thematic organization, thus, acts as both an organizing tool and a prism of analysis through which the matter of access, engagement, and equity might be viewed in various wellness tourism contexts.

On the basis of this thematic foundation, a set of research variables were operationalized to follow the relationships between the adoption of technology and the wellness tourism experiences. The independent variable was emerging technologies like AI, virtual and AR, wearable devices, telehealth solutions, blockchain applications, and mobile platforms, as they are becoming increasingly common in the wellness-based services. The dependent variable, experience of wellness tourism, was conceptualized on a multidimensional basis, that is, personalization, accessibility, user satisfaction, and perceived outcomes. User engagement was considered a mediating variable because it is known that the quality and the intensity of interaction with the digital tools influence the experiential outcomes. Digital literacy was proposed as a moderating measure, as it was acknowledged that the variations in expertise and familiarity with technological aspects precondition the effectiveness of such tools use. Destination type and demographic factors were included as the control variables to capture the structural and socio-economic variability, whereas cultural sensitivity was used as a confounding variable to capture the difference in the interpretation of wellness practices and technologies in different cultural contexts. This arrangement makes it possible to understand in a more differentiated way how the technology-based wellness experiences are manifested in a variety of different contexts and not simply expect the same effects.

To achieve methodological transparency and coherence, the systematic review and the qualitative synthesis were exposed to clear inclusion and exclusion criteria. The review was limited to studies published between 2015 and 2025 to ensure that the review reflected modern technological advancements, and only the English-language publications were included to ensure that the review was consistent in interpretation. The literature based on peer-reviewed journals, industry reports, and white papers included literature that specifically reported the overlap of wellness tourism and digital technologies. Facts like editorials, opinion pieces, and unfinished conference papers were not included in the list to ensure analytical rigor. There was a focus on a global scope, but studies had to prove to be relevant outside of a highly localized setting. They also focused on thematic relevance and were biased toward work that touches on sustainability, personalization, innovation, as well as ethical issues. Lastly, it encompassed the population other than the traveler, such as service providers, destination planners, and technology developers, on the fact that wellness tourism involves multi-actor ecosystem. All of these criteria worked to guarantee that the analytical framework was backed by a body of literature, which can answer not only technological dynamics but also address more profound questions of inclusion, access, and long-term viability.

3. Technological Transformation of Wellness Tourism

The wellness tourism industry is undergoing a massive transformation because of the heavy influence of digital technologies and their advancement. Integrating technological tools for personalization, convenience, and a data-driven wellness experience for travelers has become a core component of the wellness tourism ecosystem. Because of the fusion of wellness and technology, there has been a significant shift from traditional wellness experience toward a more hyperpersonalized tech-enabled experience that is dynamic, scalable, and globally accessible. The fourth industrial revolution (IR 4.0) fundamentally altered industries through the fusion of physical, digital, and biological domains, and this transformation is closely aligned with it (Mohamed et al., 2024). The evolution of widespread adoption of AI, IoT, wearable devices, VR and AR, blockchain, and telemedicine in the context of Wellness tourism has contributed uniquely to how wellness services are being designed, delivered, and consumed by travelers.

AI stands at the edge of this transformation. It offers unique features in data analysis, predictive modeling, and personalization. Wellness providers increasingly use AI-driven algorithms to create a unique and customized wellness plan for the traveler according to their needs, preferences, and health data (Buhalis & Sinarta, 2019). AI can facilitate an automatic booking system and recommend engines for wellness programs. Virtual wellness assistance guides the users through meditation, fitness routines, and dietary plans. AI can predict users' preferences by analyzing large data sets, recommending wellness activities, monitoring real-time progress, and creating a highly tailored experience for the user. AI-driven chatbots and virtual concierges provide around-the-clock assistance to guests in wellness resorts and retreats (Lui, 2021). They enhance the delivery service without increasing the staff burden and improve the customer experience. It enhances the operational effectiveness of wellness service providers.

The IoT complements AI by enabling interconnected devices to collect and transmit real-time data. This further enhances the personalization and responsiveness of the wellness service. IoT increases the experience of the travelers. It has become increasingly common in wellness environments where smart rooms adjust the occupant's lighting, temperature, and sound wellness, whether for relaxation, sleep enhancement, or focus (Lin et al., 2020). Wearable health technologies form a crucial part of the IoT ecosystem. They continuously monitor biometric data such as heart rate variability, stress level, sleep pattern, and physical activity. These devices empower travelers to track their health. It also enables wellness providers to adjust therapy schedules and recommendations based on real-time psychological feedback (Saxena et al., 2025). Innovative fitness equipment, connected yoga mats, and biofeedback devices are now a part of the wellness experience. They offer a blend of technology and traditional wellness practices. They use data to make the wellness experience more effective. It also helps meet guests' needs by adjusting the service to their changes during their stay.

Another dimension of the wellness tourism experience is VR and AR. They provide an immersive environment, promoting relaxation, meditation, and stress reduction. Regardless of location, VR-based meditation transports users to a natural setting (beaches, forests, or mountaintops) (Andersen et al., 2017). On the other hand, AR applications enhance physical wellness by overlaying digital guidance onto the real world, such as posture correction during yoga or providing interactive prompts during fitness routines. These technologies are particularly valuable in urban wellness areas with limited natural access. It is also for travelers who require continuity in their wellness routine when moving between destinations. VR is also employed for exposure therapy, stress management, and guided mindfulness, expanding the therapeutic potential of wellness tourism (Gao et al., 2020). Such integration elevates the guest experience and also caters to the growing segment of digitally native consumers who seek innovative wellness solutions.

Blockchain technology enhances transparency, security, and trust in wellness tourism transactions. Even though it is less visible to the end user, Blockchain offers a decentralized ledger system that ensures data integrity and privacy since the industry increasingly relies on exchanging sensitive health data (Baydeniz, 2024). This technology ensures that the medical records shared between the travelers and wellness provider are secure and verifies the authenticity of certificates such as therapist credentials or organic product claims. Blockchain also supports loyalty programs through smart contracts, ensuring this industry's reward systems are transparent and fair. Trust is paramount, particularly because the service involves health-related interventions. Blockchain is vital for building consumer confidence and safeguarding data from misuse or unauthorized access.

Telemedicine is a technological tool that has significantly expanded the accessibility and scope of wellness tourism. It bridges the gap between the travelers' home environment and their chosen wellness destination by enabling remote consultations with wellness practitioners, nutritionists, mental health counselors, and medical professionals (Dewi, 2023). The efficiency of wellness interventions is augmented when they are part of a pre-arrival assessment, a personalized program design, and a post-visit follow-up consultation. It is now seen as a must-have service due to the pandemic. It is convenient and safe for the traveling consumer who may be more resistant to face-to-face interaction (Marques et al., 2024). Moreover, it allowed wellness and wellness tourism to occur in places beyond the physical location of the restaurants and retreats. Most importantly, it allows for ongoing long-term behavior change and wellness maintenance. The hybrid approach to remote wellness (service provision) is a valuable service that can be leveraged by consumers who want flexibility in their wellness journey and support that can last as long as the consumer desires.

The technology has caused sufficient disruption in the wellness tourism industry, causing a significant shift toward a more interconnected, data-driven, and hyperpersonalized industry model. The offerings of traditional wellness are still intact (based on practices such as yoga, meditation, time in nature, and holistic therapies). However, with the addition of AI, IoT, VR/AR, blockchain, and telemedicine are sourcing and experiencing, traveling has become hypercustomized and much more effective (Voigt et al., 2011). This technology-driven shift recognizes that consumers expect high levels of convenience, personalization, and seamless integration of digital tools to manage their lives across leisure, health, and wellness. The use of technology within wellness tourism also raises questions of ethics, privacy, authenticity, and sustainability that must be dealt with in the transition. The balance of potential benefits of innovation and the key principles of wellness tourism will continue to hold challenges for the industry (Sigala, 2020).

4. Opportunities and Benefits of Tech-enabled Wellness Tourism

Digital technologies have transformed the opportunities available to the wellness tourism sector, especially beyond traditional service delivery. The key benefit is that technology enables a hyperpersonalized experience for the travelers, which caters to their unique needs, preferences, and health goals. AI, big data analytics, and wearable health technology enable wellness providers to develop itineraries focused on the guest's psychological, emotional, and physiological needs (Buhalis & Sinarta, 2019). This significant level of personalization enhances the perceived value of the wellness experience. It leads to a higher satisfaction level and stronger customer loyalty. Such data-driven offerings are beautiful to health-conscious Millennials and Gen Z travelers who are more accustomed to technologies integrated into their daily lives (Lo et al., 2020).

Another important benefit is that wellness services are now more accessible. In the past, wellness tourism was seen as something only wealthy travelers could afford, usually at luxury resorts or remote retreats. However, with the rise of telemedicine, mobile health apps, and virtual wellness platforms, access to wellness services has become more widespread and inclusive (Mishra et al., 2024). Accessibility to wellness practitioners, mental health counselors, nutritionists, and wellness coaches is available for individuals from anywhere, regardless of geographical and economic barriers. The tele-wellness platform fosters continuity in wellness care by facilitating pre-trip consultation, real-time monitoring during travel, and post-trip follow-up sessions. Individuals with mobility issues, those living in remote areas, or travelers unable to commit to an extended wellness retreat can now access the benefits easily. With the hybridization of physical and digital wellness, service providers can expand their reach globally and offer flexible packages combining in-person and virtual components (Zhang & Shi, 2024).

Technology has transformed wellness tourism into operational efficiency. AI uses technological tools for numerous operational aspects, which include booking systems, check-in, personalized itinerary generation, and guest service interaction through chatbot and virtual assistance (Mahalakshmi & Bharath, 2025). The help of these technologies reduces the workload on human staff. They allow them to focus on delivering high-end services that machines cannot efficiently deliver. IoT-enabled environments regulate resource management automation by regulating energy usage, water consumption, and indoor air quality, contributing to wellness establishments' cost savings and environmental sustainability goals (Fakhabi et al., 2024). Data analytics received from the interaction of the guests helps refine their service, predict demand trends, and implement a dynamic pricing strategy. This operational efficiency enables wellness businesses to respond swiftly.

Integrating VR and AR technologies in wellness tourism offers a unique opportunity to travelers, enriching their experience beyond physical constraints. VR allows users to immerse themselves in a calming, natural landscape, meditation, or therapeutic visual environment. They provide profound relaxation benefits, even in urban or confined settings. AR applications enhance on-site experiences by giving instructional content posture guidance during yoga or real-time feedback during fitness routines. These technologies are valuable for stress reduction, anxiety management, and mental wellness. It offers a scalable solution that can be used in wellness centers, airports, hotels, or even at home. VR-based wellness solutions help travelers with disabilities or those unable to access remote locations. Natural retreats ensure inclusivity within the wellness tourism ecosystem (Gao et al., 2020).

Blockchain technology enhances trust, transparency, and data security within the wellness tourism value chain, creating another significant opportunity. It provides a decentralized record of transactions and data exchange while handling sensitive health information in an industry that relies heavily on trust. This technology safely stores guests' medical records, service history, and payment details, ensuring only the right people can access them. It also verifies the credentials of wellness practitioners, certification of organic products, the use of treatments, and the authenticity of sustainable practices claimed by the providers (Baydeniz, 2024). A blockchain-enabled loyalty program allows travelers to use the rewards transparently, redeemable across multiple service providers within the wellness ecosystem.

The role of technology in fostering sustainability cannot be overstated. Intelligent energy management systems, IoT-driven waste reduction tools, and remote resource consumption monitoring help wellness facilities minimize their environmental footprint (Fakhabi et al., 2024). Virtual wellness experiences, such as VR-based meditation or telemedicine consultations, reduce the need for physical travel, lowering carbon emissions associated with long-haul flights. Furthermore, data analytics inform more sustainable decision-making by tracking guest preferences for eco-friendly services, allowing providers to align their offerings with environmentally conscious consumer behavior (Nilashi et al., 2021). These technological interventions support the broader goals of regenerative tourism, where wellness operators reduce harm and actively contribute to restoring natural and social ecosystems (Global Wellness Institute, 2023).

5. Ethical Concerns, Challenges, and Risks in Wellness Tourism's Digital Evolution

Integrating advanced technologies into wellness tourism presents many benefits, but it also introduces significant ethical issues, operational risks, and sustainability challenges. The shift toward data-driven and digitally mediated wellness experiences has placed personal data privacy, security, and ownership at the center of ethical concerns. Wellness tourism relies heavily on collecting and analyzing sensitive health information, such as biometric data, psychological assessments, and records of individual lifestyle habits (Balcioglu, 2024). This dependence raises substantial privacy concerns, especially as travelers often lack transparency regarding how their data are stored, processed, or shared. There is a risk of misuse or unauthorized access, exacerbated by the absence of universal data protection legislation, particularly problematic in cross-border contexts where legal safeguards differ by country (Agarwal et al., 2021).

The tension between technology-enabled convenience and the fundamental right to data sovereignty remains a challenge for both travelers and service providers. The increasing interconnectedness powered by the IoT, AI, and cloud computing also exposes the wellness tourism industry to mounting cybersecurity threats. Malicious attacks that compromise reservation systems, client databases, or biometric repositories pose the risk not just of financial loss but also of emotional distress and erosion of trust. The consequences of a data breach in wellness tourism are more severe than in many other sectors, as they can result in trauma, reputational damage, and diminished loyalty (Kumar et al., 2024). Smaller tourism businesses, particularly in emerging destinations, often lack the cybersecurity resources of larger organizations, making them especially vulnerable (Kabanda et al., 2018). This emphasizes the urgent need for industry-wide standards and cybersecurity guidelines tailored to the wellness tourism sector.

Another concern relates to the authenticity of the wellness experience itself. Wellness tourism finds its roots in ancient traditions, local practices, and nature-based healing. It is deeply connected to spirituality, culture, and community (Voigt et al., 2011). With a shift toward algorithm-driven personalization and automated service delivery, there is a genuine risk of eroding the cultural richness and traditional knowledge that define these practices. While technology can broaden access to meditation guides, facilitate immersive experiences, or provide AI-powered counseling, it cannot replicate human empathy, cultural nuance, or spiritual resonance. This reliance on digital platforms may lead to cultural homogenization as unique traditions are transformed into standardized, commodified wellness products, raising concerns of cultural appropriation and misrepresentation. Wellness providers thus have a responsibility to respect the origins and integrity of the practices they promote.

The escalation of technological dependence in wellness tourism has inadvertently fostered digital fatigue. Many travelers now seek escapes from constant connectivity, seeking environments that encourage reflection, mindfulness, and real-world engagement (Marques et al., 2024). Services such as VR meditation, AI-driven coaching, and fitness tracking apps enhance convenience, but they also threaten to dilute the restorative potential of human connection and direct environmental immersion. Notably, the growing interest in digital detox retreats – destinations that eschew technology altogether – highlights the necessity for providers to strike a careful balance between innovation and intentional disconnection (Bauwens et al., 2019).

Inclusivity and accessibility present further ethical challenges. While digital platforms can reduce geographic barriers, they also risk deepening the digital divide. High-speed internet access, costly wearables, or advanced digital literacy are not universally attainable, particularly for rural populations, elderly travelers, or lower-income groups (Drori, 2010). AI systems may inadvertently reinforce biases, resulting in algorithmic discrimination in wellness recommendations or service delivery (Božić, 2023). For instance, an AI-powered nutrition app might overlook traditional dietary practices or non-Western approaches to wellness, underlining the need to design systems that prioritize inclusivity, accessibility, and cultural competence.

Environmental sustainability is another pressing issue. Digital wellness solutions, such as telemedicine or VR experiences, may reduce physical travel and carbon emissions; however, manufacturing, utilizing, and disposing of technological devices increases the overall ecological footprint. Always-connected wellness resorts using IoT devices often consume significant energy, putting strain on resources and contributing to environmental degradation (Sigala, 2020). The sector must adopt sustainable technology practices, such as green energy and responsible e-waste management, to ensure that the core values of wellness tourism – well-being of people and planet alike – are upheld (Global Wellness Institute, 2023).

The fragmented and undeveloped regulatory landscape for technology-based wellness tourism intensifies these risks. While healthcare and finance operate under clear data protection and ethical laws, wellness tourism is governed by a patchwork of varying regulations (Buhalis & Sinarta, 2019). This regulatory inconsistency undermines effective enforcement of data privacy, cybersecurity, and ethical service standards, particularly in cross-border contexts. Industry collaboration among stakeholders, policymakers, and international organizations is urgently required to establish clear, enforceable standards that safeguard consumer rights and support the responsible, ethical use of technology in wellness tourism.

6. A Framework for Sustainable Wellness Tourism in the Digital Era (FSWTDE): Integration and Future Outlook

As digital technologies become a bigger part of wellness tourism, finding a balance that respects sustainability, ethics, and cultural values is important. Even though technology brings many benefits, the industry must not ignore its ethical duties and the need to stay sustainable. There is a critical need for a comprehensive framework to align technological innovations with wellness principles. This approach must ensure that digital tools enhance wellness services in terms of accessibility, personalization, and operational efficiency for users, without undermining the core values of wellness: authenticity, human connection, and ecological responsibility (Sigala, 2020). This chapter develops a conceptual framework based on a literature review and thematic analysis (Fig. 10.1).

It highlights the leading technological enablers, operational benefits, and ethical challenges to guide wellness tourism toward sustainable and culturally sensitive practices. As the industry grows, the primary challenge is balancing technological progress and cultural preservation while ensuring data security, promoting inclusivity, and protecting the environment (Jones & Wynn, 2022).

Privacy and data security must be embedded as foundational principles within service design. The wellness tourism industry relies heavily on personal and sensitive health data collected via wearable devices, IoT, and AI-driven platforms.

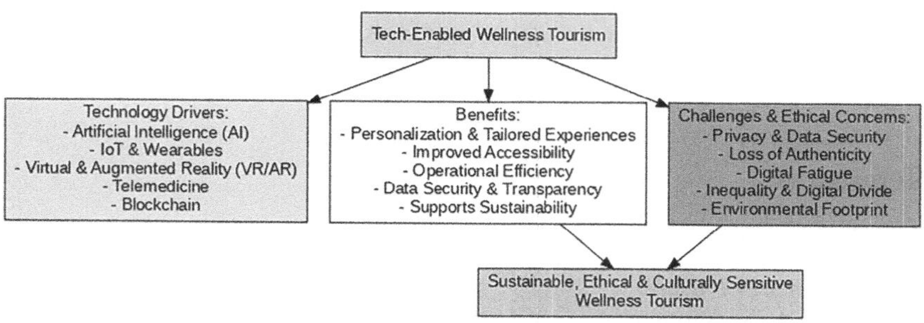

Fig. 10.1. Framework for Sustainable Wellness Tourism in the Digital Era (FSWTDE). *Source*: Authors' own conceptualization.

Blockchain technology offers a feasible solution, providing decentralization, transparency, and user control over personal data. Equally important is preserving the authenticity of the wellness experience in the face of increasing digital mediation. Wellness tourism has always drawn from culturally rooted practices, holistic traditions, and immersive natural environments (Voigt et al., 2011). Technology should add to rather than replace human elements. AI-driven systems can assist in personalizing service, and VR tools may aid accessibility, but they should not substitute trained therapists, yoga instructors, or spiritual guides. Providers should adopt a hybrid model combining digital convenience with in-person experiences, ensuring technology supports rather than replaces authenticity. Ethical considerations also include avoiding the removal of practices from their original context to fit commercial models.

As the industry goes digital, the approach to accessibility and equity must adapt. Digital platforms can scale wellness offerings globally but also risk excluding marginalized communities lacking technology access or digital literacy. Providers should ensure multi-device compatibility, affordable subscriptions, and low-bandwidth options. AI algorithms used for personalization must be audited regularly to detect and fix biases related to ethnicity, age, gender, or socio-economic status (Božić, 2023). Similarly, while telemedicine, IoT tools, and virtual experiences can lower operational impacts, they also generate e-waste, increase energy use, and contribute to device-related ecological footprints (Global Wellness Institute, 2023). Providers should prioritize eco-design, follow circular economy principles, partner with responsible suppliers, and invest in renewable energy.

Rules and regulations are fundamental to guiding wellness tourism toward ethical and sustainable practices. Currently, a lack of standardization creates gaps in data privacy, service quality, digital safety, and practitioner qualifications (Buhalis & Sinarta, 2019). As technology evolves, so must ethical frameworks. Ethics committees can assess technological impact (Sigala, 2020). Consumer education should enable travelers to make informed choices regarding data use, environmental implications, and cultural authenticity. In conclusion, tourism's integration of AI, IoT, VR/AR, telemedicine, and blockchain has expanded wellness service delivery and personalization, but also brought ethical considerations, risks, and unintended repercussions. The FSWTDE framework captures the relationship between technological drivers, operational benefits, and ethical concerns, helping operators navigate digitalization responsibly. The future of wellness tourism depends on collective action from providers, policymakers, researchers, and travelers to create an ecosystem that values well-being in its fullest sense.

References

Agarwal, S., Page, S. J., & Mawby, R. (2021). Tourist security, terrorism risk management, and tourist safety. *Annals of Tourism Research*, *89*, 103207. https://doi.org/10.1016/j.annals.2021.103207

Andersen, T. L. S., Anisimovaite, G., Christiansen, A. S., Hussein, M. A. A., Lund, C. S., Nielsen, T. L., Rafferty, E. I., Nilsson, N. C., Nordahl, R., & Serafin, S. (2017). A preliminary study of users' experiences of meditation in virtual reality. In *Virtual reality (VR)* (pp. 343–344). IEEE (Institute of Electrical and Electronics Engineers). https://doi.org/10.1109/VR.2017.7892317

Balcioglu, Y. S. (2024). Exploring consumer engagement and satisfaction in health and wellness tourism through text-mining. *Kybernetes*. https://doi.org/10.1108/K-12-2023-2721

Bauwens, J., Thorbjornsson, G. B., & Verstrynge, K. (2019). Unplug your life: Digital detox through a Kierkegaardian Lens. *Kierkegaard Studies Yearbook*, *24*(1), 415–436. https://doi.org/doi:10.1515/kierke-2019-0017

Baydeniz, E. (2024). Blockchain technology in tourism: Pioneering sustainable and collaborative travel experiences. *Journal of Tourismology*, *10*(1), 1–12. https://doi.org/10.26650/jot.2024.10.1.1312994

Božić, V. (2023). Artificial intelligence is the reason for and the solution to the digital divide. *Language Education and Technology*, *3*(2), 96–105.

Buhalis, D., & Sinarta, Y. (2019). Real-time co-creation and nowness service: Lessons from tourism and hospitality. *Journal of Travel and Tourism Marketing*, *36*(5), 563–582. https://doi.org/10.1080/10548408.2019.1592059

Dewi, R. D. C. (2023). The development of medical tourism with preventive technology: Medical wellness. *Consilium Sanitatis: Journal of Health Science and Policy*, *1*(3), 137–146. https://doi.org/10.56855/jhsp.v1i3.414

Drori, G. S. (2010). Globalization and technology divides: Policy bifurcation between the "digital divide" and the "innovation divide". *Sociological Inquiry*, *80*(1), 63–91. https://doi.org/10.1111/j.1475-682X.2009.00316.x

Fakhabi, M. M., Hamidian, S. M., & Aliehyaei, M. (2024). Exploring the role of the Internet of Things in green buildings. *Energy Science & Engineering*, *12*(9), 3779–3822. https://doi.org/10.1002/ese3.1840

Gao, Z., Lee, J. E., McDonough, D. J., & Albers, C. (2020). Virtual reality exercise as a coping strategy for health and wellness promotion in older adults during the COVID-19 pandemic. *Journal of Clinical Medicine*, *9*(6), 1986. https://www.mdpi.com/2077-0383/9/6/1986

Global Wellness Institute. (2023). *The future of wellness tourism: Tech-driven innovations and sustainability*. https://globalwellnessinstitute.org

Gurova, O., Merritt, T. R., Papachristos, E., & Vaajakari, J. (2020). Sustainable solutions for wearable technologies: Mapping the product development life cycle. *Sustainability*, *12*(20), 8444. https://www.mdpi.com/2071-1050/12/20/8444

Hannigan, B., Deborah, E., & Burnard, P. (2004). Stress and stress management in clinical psychology: Findings from a systematic review. *Journal of Mental Health*, *13*(3), 235–245. https://doi.org/10.1080/09638230410001700871

Jie, D. (2023). Research on the integration and development of wellness and culture tourism facilitated by digital technology. *Information Systems and Economics*, *4*(9), 42–47.

Kabanda, S., Maureen, T., & Kent, C. (2018). Exploring SME cybersecurity practices in developing countries. *Journal of Organisational Computing and Electronic Commerce*, *28*(3), 269–282. https://doi.org/10.1080/10919392.2018.1484598

Kraus, S., Durst, S., Ferreira, J. J., Veiga, P., Kailer, N., & Weinmann, A. (2022). Digital transformation in business and management research: An overview of the current status quo. *International Journal of Information Management*, *63*, 102466. https://doi.org/10.1016/j.ijinfomgt.2021.102466

Kumar, T., Bhushan, S., Sharma, P., & Garg, V. (2024). Examining the vulnerabilities of biometric systems: Privacy and security perspectives. In A. Selwal, D. Sharma, M. Mann, S. Chakraborty, V. E. Balas, & O. E. Lieh (Eds.), *Leveraging computer vision to biometric applications* (pp. 34–67). Chapman and Hall/CRC.

Lin, L.-P., Huang, S.-C., & Ho, Y.-C. (2020). Could virtual reality effectively market slow travel in a heritage destination? *Tourism Management*, *78*, 104027. https://doi.org/10.1016/j.tourman.2019.104027

Lo, A., Brian, K., & Mackenzie, M. (2020). Segmenting Chinese millennial restaurant customers: A lifestyle and health and environmental consciousness approach. *Journal of China Tourism Research*, *16*(2), 183–213. https://doi.org/10.1080/19388160.2019.1604281

Lui, E. Y. H. (2021). *The effects of using artificial intelligence facilities in building harmonious communities in property management in Hong Kong and China*. University of Wales Trinity Saint David.

Mahalakshmi, S., & Bharath, H. (2025). From check-in to check-out: AI innovations in the hospitality sector. In P. Thaichon, P. K. Dutta, A. K. Haghi, & S. Dutta (Eds.), *Digital disruption in hospitality, AI, and emerging technologies* (pp. 79–99). Emerald Publishing Limited. https://doi.org/10.1108/978-1-83608-796-020251005

Marques, D., Pedreiro, T., & Sousa, B. B. (2024). Current digital healthcare and wellness tourism: Preliminary study in the cross-border context. In S. K. Baral & R. Goel (Eds.), *Analyzing current digital healthcare trends using social networks* (pp. 1–11). IGI Global Scientific Publishing. https://doi.org/10.4018/979-8-3693-1934-5.ch001

Mishra, H., Choudhury, G. R., & Pandita, D. (2024). Transitioning to e-health platforms for mental wellness: The need for data-driven contemporary solutions for professionals. *International Seminar on Application for Technology of Information and Communication (iSemantic), Semarang, Indonesia, 2024*, 89–94. https://doi.org/10.1109/iSemantic63362.2024.10762698

Mohamed, M. G., Ahmed Ibrahim, O., Hamed, H. F., & Abdelnaby, S. F. (2024). Engineering's next leap: How fourth industrial revolution is shaping the future of the industry. *ERU Research Journal*, *3*, 1–21.

Nilashi, M., Minaei-Bidgoli, B., Alrizq, M., Alghamdi, A., Alsulami, A. A., Samad, S., & Mohd, S. (2021). An analytical approach for big social data analysis for customer decision-making in eco-friendly hotels. *Expert Systems with Applications*, *186*, 115722. https://doi.org/10.1016/j.eswa.2021.115722

Paci, A. M., Lalle, C., & Chiacchio, M. S. (2013). Education for innovation: Trends, collaborations and views. *Journal of Intelligent Manufacturing*, *24*(3), 487–493. https://doi.org/10.1007/s10845-012-0631-z

Saxena, M., Avanesh, N. M., Niranjan, L. R., & Mohanty, P. (2025). Wearable technologies leading to employee performance and productivity: Exploring the mediating role of mental health and wellbeing. In J. Kaur (Ed.), *Technological enhancements for improving employee performance, safety, and wellbeing* (pp. 111–130). IGI Global Scientific Publishing. https://doi.org/10.4018/979-8-3693-9631-5.ch005

Sigala, M. (2020). Tourism and COVID-19: Impacts and implications for advancing and resetting industry and research. *Journal of Business Research*, *117*, 312–321. https://doi.org/10.1016/j.jbusres.2020.06.015

Smith, M., & Puczkó, L. (2019). *Health, tourism and hospitality: Spas, wellness and medical travel* (2nd ed.). Routledge.

Voigt, C., Brown, G., & Howat, G. (2011). Wellness tourists: In search of transformation. *Tourism Review*, *66*(1/2), 16–30. https://doi.org/10.1108/16605371111127206

Wynn, M., & Jones, P. (2022). Digital technology deployment and the circular economy. *Sustainability*, *14*(15), 9077. https://doi.org/10.3390/su14159077

Zhang, L., & Shi, M. (2024). Exploring the healing power of digital technology in promoting health and well-being: A case study of smart tourism applications. In *2024 11th international conference on dependable systems and their applications (DSA), Taicang, Suzhou, China* (pp. 417–425). https://doi.org/10.1109/DSA63982.2024.00063.

Chapter 11

Wellness and Sustainability Tourism: Creating Paradises of Harmony and Responsibility

Divya Jyoti Thakur[a], Arsheed Ahmad Ganie[b], Naresh Thakur[c] and Firdous Ahmad Malik[d]

[a]*MM Institute of Management, Maharishi Markandeshwar (Deemed to be University), Mullana, Ambala, Haryana, India*
[b]*Department of Humanities & Social Sciences, IEC University, Baddi, Himachal Pradesh, India*
[c]*Department of Management, Gian Jyoti Institute of Management & Technology, Mohali, Punjab, India*
[d]*Department of Management, University of People, Pasadena, CA, USA*

Abstract

The rising demand for transformative travel experiences has propelled wellness and sustainability tourism into the spotlight. This emerging trend integrates physical, mental, and spiritual well-being with eco-conscious practices, creating a synergy that aligns travelers' aspirations for personal growth with a commitment to environmental stewardship. Destinations marketed as "paradises" are reimagining their tourism strategies to preserve natural ecosystems, celebrate local cultures, and offer authentic wellness experiences. This chapter explores the intersection of wellness and sustainability tourism, mindfulness tourism, examining how it fosters community empowerment, reduces environmental footprints, and enriches travelers' lives. Using case studies from tropical destinations, it highlights innovative practices and identifies challenges in maintaining the delicate balance between development and conservation. The findings emphasize the need for collaborative efforts between governments, businesses, and

Advancement in Medical and Wellness Tourism, Part A: Entrepreneurship and Technology, 139–147

doi:10.1108/978-1-80592-983-320261012

travelers to ensure these paradises remain sustainable havens for future generations.

Keywords: Wellness industry; sustainable tourism; eco-friendly tourism; green hospitality; mindfulness tourism

1. Introduction

In the 21st century, tourism has evolved beyond mere leisure and escapism to embrace broader values of personal well-being and environmental responsibility. The growing fusion of wellness tourism and sustainable tourism represents an innovative approach to travel that seeks to rejuvenate both the individual and the planet. As global awareness of environmental crises and mental health challenges intensifies, the tourism industry is increasingly recognizing its role in promoting physical, psychological, and ecological well-being (Smith et al., 2009). The concept of "creating paradises of harmony and responsibility" reflects this integrated vision, where destinations not only offer restorative experiences for visitors but also ensure the preservation of local ecosystems and cultures for future generations.

Wellness tourism, defined as travel associated with the pursuit of maintaining or enhancing one's personal well-being, has seen remarkable growth in the past decade. According to the Global Wellness Institute (2021), wellness tourism was valued at over $720 billion in 2019, with projections indicating continued expansion. Scholars such as Touré and Kokonendji (2021) argue that wellness tourism extends beyond spa visits and yoga retreats to encompass holistic experiences that nourish the body, mind, and spirit. These experiences often include nature immersion, mindfulness practices, and community engagement, all of which align closely with sustainable tourism principles. Importantly, wellness-seeking travelers are increasingly drawn to destinations that also demonstrate environmental stewardship and social responsibility (Touré & Kokonendji, 2021).

Sustainable tourism, on the other hand, emphasizes minimizing the negative impacts of travel while maximizing socio-economic benefits for local communities and conserving natural resources (World Tourism Organization (UNWTO), 2018). Between 2010 and 2022, significant research has explored how sustainable practices can be effectively integrated into tourism models. Smith et al. (2009) highlight the role of eco-certification and green practices in enhancing destination appeal, while others emphasize the urgent need for carbon-conscious travel choices amid the escalating climate crisis. The convergence of wellness and sustainability tourism thus offers a promising pathway to address both individual well-being and planetary health in tandem.

Moreover, the COVID-19 pandemic profoundly reshaped traveler expectations, catalyzing a deeper appreciation for safe, health-focused, and eco-friendly experiences (Uslu et al., 2023). Travelers now prioritize secluded natural environments, organic cuisine, and authentic cultural interactions that foster a sense of connection and responsibility. This shift has accelerated the development of destinations that are not only wellness-oriented but also committed to sustainability principles, creating immersive experiences that restore human-nature relationships.

The integration of wellness and sustainability is also seen as a means of community empowerment. Uslu et al. (2023) indicate that local communities engaged in wellness and eco-tourism initiatives benefit economically while preserving their cultural heritage. This dual benefit reinforces the ethical dimension of "responsible paradises," where tourism serves as a vehicle for both personal transformation and social good (UNWTO, 2018).

In sum, the convergence of wellness and sustainability tourism reflects a transformative trend in global travel, one that aspires to create spaces of rejuvenation while upholding ecological integrity and cultural authenticity. This chapter explores the synergies between these two powerful movements, examining how destinations worldwide are crafting harmonious environments that cater to the holistic well-being of travelers and the enduring vitality of the planet.

2. Rise of Wellness and Sustainability Tourism

In recent years, the global tourism landscape has undergone a profound transformation, with wellness and sustainability emerging as defining pillars of modern travel. No longer is tourism merely about sightseeing or leisure; it is evolving into a purposeful journey toward personal well-being and environmental responsibility. The rise of wellness and sustainability tourism is a response to the growing desire among travelers to reconnect with nature, rejuvenate their minds and bodies, and contribute positively to the destinations they visit (Vijaya, 2024).

Several factors have contributed to this rise. Increasing awareness of mental health and the importance of holistic well-being has encouraged travelers to seek experiences that go beyond conventional vacations. Yoga retreats in the Himalayas, mindfulness workshops in Bali, forest bathing in Japan, and spa therapies rooted in indigenous traditions are attracting global attention. These experiences offer not just relaxation but also a deeper connection to self-care and cultural appreciation. Particularly in the post-pandemic era, where stress and burnout have become prevalent, people are prioritizing travel experiences that promote healing and inner balance.

Simultaneously, environmental concerns have steered tourism toward more sustainable practices. Climate change, biodiversity loss, and the negative impacts of mass tourism have sparked a movement toward eco-conscious travel. Travelers are now more informed and selective, favoring destinations that commit to green practices such as eco-friendly accommodations, conservation initiatives, and community-based tourism. This shift is pushing the industry to innovate, creating tourism models that respect local cultures, minimize carbon footprints, and ensure that tourism revenues benefit local communities directly (Buckley & Buckley, 2012).

Governments and tourism boards worldwide are recognizing this trend and are actively promoting wellness and sustainability tourism as part of their development strategies. Destinations are rebranding themselves as havens of health and harmony, integrating wellness facilities with sustainable infrastructure. Resorts are increasingly adopting solar energy, organic farming for on-site restaurants, and water conservation systems, blending luxury with environmental stewardship. These integrated approaches not only attract responsible travelers but also preserve the natural beauty and cultural heritage that make these destinations unique (Yadav, 2024).

The rise of wellness and sustainability tourism also reflects a broader societal shift toward conscious living. People are not just looking for holidays; they are seeking transformative experiences that align with their values. This form of tourism fosters meaningful interactions between visitors and host communities, encouraging cultural exchange and mutual respect. By engaging in local wellness practices or participating in conservation projects, travelers become active participants in the preservation of the environment and the promotion of social well-being.

The growing popularity of wellness and sustainability tourism marks a positive evolution in global travel (Abhishek Kumar et al., 2024). It represents a harmonious blend of personal rejuvenation and ecological responsibility, creating paradises that cater to both human wellness and planetary health. As this trend continues to gain momentum, it holds the promise of reshaping the tourism industry into a force for good – fostering healthier lifestyles, protecting fragile ecosystems, and nurturing respectful, sustainable connections between people and places.

3. Core Principles of Wellness and Sustainability Tourism

Wellness and sustainability tourism embodies a transformative approach to travel, rooted in the philosophy of nurturing both the individual and the environment. At its core, this form of tourism harmonizes personal well-being with ecological integrity and social responsibility, aiming to create immersive experiences that benefit travelers, local communities, and the planet alike. By weaving together wellness practices and sustainable development principles, this paradigm fosters a holistic journey toward harmony and conscientious living (Uslu et al., 2023).

The first principle is holistic well-being, which emphasizes nurturing the physical, mental, emotional, and spiritual health of travelers. Wellness tourism extends beyond conventional spa retreats to include mindfulness activities, yoga retreats, nutrition-focused experiences, and therapeutic encounters with nature. These practices help individuals achieve inner balance, reduce stress, and reconnect with themselves. Destinations that prioritize wellness offer safe, restorative environments where travelers can engage in self-care, while also respecting local cultures and natural ecosystems.

The second cornerstone is environmental stewardship. Sustainability tourism mandates responsible interaction with natural resources, aiming to preserve biodiversity, reduce carbon footprints, and minimize environmental degradation. Eco-friendly accommodations, renewable energy usage, waste reduction initiatives, and the promotion of low-impact transportation are all critical components. Destinations must also ensure the protection of fragile ecosystems, such as coral reefs, rainforests, and mountain trails, which often serve as the backdrop for wellness activities. By embracing sustainable practices, these destinations maintain their ecological integrity for future generations (Abhishek Kumar et al., 2024).

Another key principle is cultural respect and community empowerment. Sustainability tourism thrives when it involves and uplifts local communities. This includes respecting indigenous knowledge systems, supporting local artisans and producers, and creating employment opportunities that foster economic resilience. Culturally immersive experiences, such as traditional healing practices or culinary tours led by local chefs, allow travelers to appreciate and honor the heritage of the destination. Simultaneously, tourism revenues can be reinvested into community development projects, health care, and education, ensuring that tourism acts as a positive force for social equity.

Education and awareness form the fourth guiding pillar. Wellness and sustainability tourism serve as platforms for enlightening travelers about the importance of mindful living and environmental consciousness. Workshops on sustainable living, guided eco-tours, and cultural storytelling sessions help cultivate a deeper understanding of the interconnectedness between human well-being and planetary health. By fostering informed choices, this principle ensures that travelers become ambassadors of sustainable practices even after their journeys end.

Finally, ethical governance and continuous improvement are essential to uphold the integrity of wellness and sustainability tourism. Transparent policies, rigorous certification systems, and the continuous monitoring of environmental and social impacts guarantee accountability. Destinations and businesses must commit to ongoing learning, adapting to emerging challenges such as climate change and shifting traveler expectations. Collaborative efforts between governments, local stakeholders, and the tourism industry ensure that sustainability is not a static goal but an evolving, dynamic process (Vijaya, 2024).

Wellness and sustainability tourism is guided by an integrated set of principles that advocate for personal rejuvenation, ecological preservation, cultural respect, educational enrichment, and ethical responsibility. These foundational pillars enable the creation of paradises that are not only havens of relaxation but also beacons of harmony and responsibility, inspiring travelers to cherish and protect the world they explore.

4. Benefits of Wellness and Sustainability Tourism

Wellness and sustainability tourism offers a unique synergy that not only enhances individual well-being but also safeguards the environment and uplifts local communities. By intertwining personal health journeys with eco-conscious practices, this form of tourism creates holistic experiences that benefit both the traveler and the destination. One of the foremost advantages is the promotion of physical and mental well-being. Wellness retreats often incorporate activities such as yoga, meditation, spa therapies, and nature immersion, which help reduce stress, improve mental clarity, and rejuvenate the body. These experiences foster long-term health benefits, encouraging travelers to adopt healthier lifestyles beyond their trips.

Moreover, sustainability-focused tourism practices play a crucial role in preserving natural landscapes and cultural heritage. By choosing eco-friendly accommodations, supporting conservation projects, and participating in low-impact activities, travelers help minimize their ecological footprint. This not only protects biodiversity but also ensures that pristine environments remain intact for future generations. Sustainable tourism initiatives often prioritize renewable energy use, waste reduction, and responsible water management, making travel more harmonious with nature (Guerra et al., 2022).

Communities also reap significant benefits from this tourism model. Wellness and sustainability tourism often emphasizes local engagement, creating economic opportunities for indigenous people and small businesses. By sourcing local products, employing community members, and showcasing authentic cultural experiences, tourism becomes a tool for inclusive development. This empowerment fosters cultural pride and preserves traditional knowledge and practices. Additionally, community-based tourism encourages mutual respect and meaningful interactions between visitors and hosts, promoting social harmony.

An often-overlooked benefit is the educational value embedded in these experiences. Travelers become more aware of environmental challenges, cultural sensitivity, and sustainable living practices. This heightened consciousness can inspire long-lasting behavioral changes, as tourists integrate eco-friendly habits into their daily lives. In this way, wellness and sustainability tourism extends its positive impact far beyond the duration of the trip.

Ultimately, the fusion of wellness and sustainability tourism creates paradises of harmony and responsibility. It cultivates a deeper connection between individuals, communities, and the environment, promoting a shared sense of stewardship for the planet. As this tourism model continues to evolve, it holds the promise of not only transforming the way people travel but also contributing to a more compassionate and sustainable world (Apollo et al., 2025).

5. Key Components of Sustainable Wellness Destinations

Sustainable wellness destinations are built upon a delicate balance between environmental stewardship, cultural respect, and holistic well-being. These destinations are designed not only to promote personal health and rejuvenation but also to foster ecological responsibility and community empowerment. Several critical components define their success, ensuring they remain true to the principles of harmony and responsibility.

First and foremost, environmental conservation is at the heart of sustainable wellness tourism. Eco-friendly infrastructure, such as buildings made from locally sourced, renewable materials, energy-efficient systems, and waste reduction initiatives, significantly reduces the ecological footprint. Integrating renewable energy sources like solar and wind power, as well as water recycling systems, ensures that natural resources are preserved for future generations. Additionally, maintaining biodiversity through the protection of local flora and fauna enhances the natural beauty and therapeutic atmosphere of the destination.

Equally vital is cultural authenticity and community involvement. Sustainable wellness destinations actively engage local communities, incorporating indigenous healing practices, traditional crafts, and cultural rituals into their offerings. This not only enriches the visitor experience but also provides economic opportunities and preserves cultural heritage. Empowering local artisans, wellness practitioners, and guides fosters a sense of ownership and pride, creating a more authentic and meaningful journey for visitors (Guerra et al., 2022).

Another essential element is holistic wellness integration. Beyond conventional spa treatments, these destinations offer comprehensive wellness programs that address physical, mental, and spiritual well-being. Yoga, meditation, nature therapy, organic nutrition, and mindfulness workshops create transformative experiences that nurture the whole person. Importantly, these practices are designed to be sustainable, utilizing organic, locally grown ingredients, and natural remedies that minimize environmental impact.

Furthermore, educational initiatives and responsible tourism practices play a pivotal role. Guests are encouraged to adopt sustainable habits, such as minimizing plastic use, respecting wildlife, and supporting local economies. Workshops and eco-tours deepen understanding of conservation efforts and inspire a long-term commitment to sustainability. This educational aspect transforms passive visitors into active participants in the global movement toward environmental responsibility.

Finally, continuous innovation and adaptability ensure the longevity of sustainable wellness destinations. Regular assessment of environmental impact, guest satisfaction, and community well-being helps refine practices and embrace new sustainable technologies and methods.

In conclusion, sustainable wellness destinations thrive when they harmoniously blend environmental care, cultural preservation, holistic wellness, and community empowerment. These components create sanctuaries where individuals can rejuvenate while contributing to the preservation and flourishing of the natural and cultural environment (Abhishek Kumar et al., 2024).

6. Challenges and Considerations

While the vision of wellness and sustainability tourism promises idyllic destinations that harmonize human well-being with environmental stewardship, the journey toward this ideal is fraught with significant challenges. One of the foremost obstacles is the risk of "greenwashing," where destinations market themselves as eco-friendly without implementing genuine sustainable practices. This not only misleads tourists but also undermines the credibility of the entire sector. Additionally, balancing the influx of visitors with environmental preservation poses a delicate dilemma. High tourist volumes can strain local ecosystems, deplete natural resources, and disrupt the cultural integrity of host communities (Uslu et al., 2023).

Another critical consideration is ensuring inclusivity and equity in tourism development. Wellness retreats and eco-resorts often cater to affluent travelers, potentially excluding local populations and widening socio-economic disparities.

It is essential that communities are actively involved in planning and benefit-sharing, fostering a sense of ownership and pride while preserving cultural authenticity.

Moreover, the integration of wellness tourism with sustainability demands a thoughtful approach to infrastructure development. Energy-efficient buildings, sustainable transport options, and responsible waste management systems are vital but require substantial investment and ongoing maintenance. Climate change further complicates these efforts, threatening the very environments that wellness and sustainable tourism aim to celebrate (Touré & Kokonendji, 2021).

Finally, educating tourists remains a persistent challenge. Travelers must be encouraged to adopt responsible behaviors, such as respecting local customs, conserving water, and supporting local businesses. Without this conscious participation, even the best-designed initiatives can falter.

In conclusion, while wellness and sustainability tourism hold transformative potential, their successful implementation requires careful planning, authentic commitment, and collaborative efforts among governments, businesses, local communities, and travelers alike. Only through addressing these challenges can we truly create paradises of harmony and responsibility.

7. Future Directions: Toward Regenerative Tourism

As wellness and sustainability tourism continues to evolve, the next frontier lies in embracing regenerative tourism – a model that not only sustains but actively restores and revitalizes destinations. Future strategies must move beyond minimizing harm to creating net-positive impacts for both the environment and local communities. Regenerative tourism calls for deeper collaboration with indigenous populations, empowering them to lead conservation and cultural initiatives that reflect their heritage. Integrating cutting-edge eco-technologies, such as renewable energy solutions and circular waste systems, will enhance the ecological footprint of tourism infrastructures. Additionally, immersive educational experiences can transform travelers into advocates for environmental stewardship, fostering a culture of respect and responsibility. Policymakers, businesses, and travelers alike must adopt long-term, holistic mindsets, prioritizing biodiversity restoration, community well-being, and climate resilience. By shifting focus from extractive practices to regenerative actions, tourism destinations can become living examples of harmony between human experience and natural ecosystems. Ultimately, regenerative tourism paves the way for a future where travelers contribute to the flourishing of destinations, leaving them better than they were found – truly creating paradises of harmony and responsibility for generations to come.

8. Conclusion

Wellness and sustainability tourism offers a compelling vision for the future of travel – one where personal rejuvenation harmonizes with environmental stewardship and cultural respect. By creating paradises of harmony and responsibility, this integrated approach not only enriches the traveler but also uplifts local communities and safeguards the planet for generations to come.

As travelers increasingly seek meaningful, ethical experiences, and as destinations strive to balance growth with preservation, the convergence of wellness and sustainability will become ever more vital. Through thoughtful design, authentic practices, and a commitment to regeneration, wellness, and sustainability, tourism can transform the very essence of travel, turning it into a force for global good.

References

Abhishek Kumar, Singh, S., Kumar, R., Kumar, M., Rani, K., & James, J. (2024). Balancing conservation and development for achieving land degradation neutrality. *Trends in Current Biology*, *2*(4). https://doi.org/10.14719/tcb.4369

Apollo, M., Wengel, Y., & Kler, B. (2025). Editorial: Tourism development, sustainability, and inclusion. *Frontiers in Sustainable Tourism*, *4*, 1556258. https://doi.org/10.3389/frsut.2025.1556258

Buckley, A., & Buckley, C. (2012). *A guide to coaching and mental health*. Routledge. https://doi.org/10.4324/9780203966020

Global Wellness Institute. (2021). *The global wellness economy: Looking beyond COVID*. https://globalwellnessinstitute.org/wp-content/uploads/2022/02/GWI-WE-Monitor-2021_Wellness-Tourism.pdf

Guerra, R. J. D. C., Trentin, F., Vila-Chã, C., & Polytechnic Institute of Guarda (Portugal). (2022). New sustainable practices in health and wellness tourism destinations focused on the quality of life and wellbeing. *PASOS. Revista de Turismo y Patrimonio Cultural*, *20*(4), 871–883. https://doi.org/10.25145/j.pasos.2022.20.058

Smith, M. K., & Puczkó, L. (Eds.). (2009). Preface. In *Health and wellness tourism* (pp. xiii–xv). Elsevier. https://doi.org/10.1016/B978-0-7506-8343-2.00037-4

Touré, A. Y., & Kokonendji, C. C. (2021). *GWI: Count and continuous generalized variability indexes (Version 1.0.2) [Dataset]*. https://doi.org/10.32614/CRAN.package.GWI

Uslu, F., Yayla, O., Guven, Y., Ergun, G. S., Demir, E., Erol, S., Yıldırım, M. N. O., Keles, H., & Gozen, E. (2023). The perception of cultural authenticity, destination attachment, and support for cultural heritage tourism development by local people: The moderator role of cultural sustainability. *Sustainability*, *15*(22), 15794. https://doi.org/10.3390/su152215794

Vijaya, G. S. (2024, October 25). *Addressing contemporary environmental challenges: A focus on climate change, waste management, biodiversity conservation, and sustainable development* [Paper presentation]. 6th world conference on business, management, finance, economics and marketing, Amsterdam, Netherlands. Eurasia conferences. https://doi.org/10.62422/978-81-970328-1-3-001

World Tourism Organization (UNWTO). (2018). *UNWTO annual report 2017*. World Tourism Organization (UNWTO). https://doi.org/10.18111/9789284419807

Yadav, M. (2024). Effective microorganisms. In S. V. Rathod (Ed.), *Eco-restoration of polluted environment* (1st ed., pp. 161–178). CRC Press. https://doi.org/10.1201/9781003423393

Chapter 12

Empowering Women in Wellness Tourism: The Role of Technology in Entrepreneurship

Himanshu Pal[a], Atul Kumar Sharma[b] and Saurabh Dixit[a]

[a]*Indian Institute of Tourism & Travel Management, Gwalior, India*
[b]*Pondicherry University, Puducherry, India*

Abstract

The study proposes four key strategies to drive meaningful change: enhancing digital literacy and business skills, providing more accessible financial support through gender-specific financial products and startup initiatives, reforming policies to simplify regulations on nonmedical wellness activities, and fostering community engagement through cooperatives and support networks. By integrating real-world examples with theoretical perspectives, the chapter calls for collaboration across all sectors – government, businesses, and civil society – to address inequalities and harness the leadership potential of women in this field. The case of the Himalayan Homestay illustrates how small, rural enterprises can leverage technology to reach international audiences while generating local employment, preserving cultural traditions, and protecting the environment. This research views women-led wellness tourism as a strong force for positive change, where economic progress coexists with cultural preservation, gender equality, and community well-being.

Keywords: Wellness tourism; women's entrepreneurship; digital empowerment; rural development; policy reform; sustainable tourism

Advancement in Medical and Wellness Tourism, Part A: Entrepreneurship and Technology, 149–163

Published under exclusive licence by Emerald Publishing Limited
doi:10.1108/978-1-80592-983-320261013

1. Introduction

1.1. Background

The concept of "wellness" was first introduced by American physician Halbert Dunn in 1959.

He defined wellness as "an integrated way of being that enables people to reach their maximum potential in their environment" (Dunn, 1959). He viewed individuals as whole entities – body, mind, and spirit – and believed their health was influenced by their surroundings. This marked a shift from focusing on treating illness to emphasizing overall well-being.

Wellness tourism refers to traveling primarily for health and well-being, encompassing emotional, spiritual, physical, and mental health.

Its origins can be traced back to ancient times, with examples such as the use of thermal baths in Greece and Rome, and traditional Eastern practices like acupuncture, herbal medicine, qi gong, and tai chi (Global Wellness Institute, n.d.; Smith & Puczko, 2014). Today, wellness tourism combines these ancient practices with modern services such as spas, nutritional counseling, stress management, and eco-conscious travel (Voigt & Pforr, 2013).

By the 21st century, wellness tourism had evolved to emphasize promoting health through education and holistic methods.

These include improved nutrition, mental health, and spiritual balance. Now, wellness is recognized as encompassing six key areas: physical, mental, spiritual, emotional, social, and environmental well-being.

The wellness and tourism industry has changed from its initial focus on medical and spa treatments to become a wide and active field focused on overall well-being. Today, popular options include yoga retreats, meditation camps, nature-based trips, digital detoxes, Ayurvedic centers, fitness programs, and customized wellness plans tailored to personal needs (Johnston et al., 2023; Yeung et al., 2021). Before the pandemic, the global wellness tourism market was worth $720 billion in 2019.

However, the outbreak of the COVID-19 pandemic caused it to drop to $436 billion in 2020 due to travel restrictions and health concerns. The industry quickly recovered, reaching an estimated $817 billion in 2022. By 2025, it is expected to grow to $1.3 trillion, making it one of the fastest-growing areas in the wellness economy (Global Wellness Institute, 2024; Yeung et al., 2021). Looking further ahead, the market is projected to reach $3.28 trillion by 2035, growing faster than general tourism. This growth is driven by changing consumer behavior, especially among millennials, Gen Z, and older adults who value self-care, personal growth, and meaningful travel experiences. There is also rising interest in slow travel, sustainability, and local wellness traditions, which makes the industry more inclusive and diverse (Global Wellness Institute, 2023; Johnston et al., 2024; Pandey, 2025).

1.2. Women as Catalysts in Wellness Tourism

Women have become key drivers in wellness tourism, helping the industry become more inclusive, sustainable, and culturally rich. They are using skills in yoga, meditation, natural healing, nutrition, and mental wellness to build successful wellness-based businesses that focus on values like community care, authenticity, eco-consciousness, and empowerment. Women-led retreats and wellness programs are designed specifically for women's needs, such as hormonal health, emotional healing, trauma recovery, and leadership development.

According to a 2024 report by the Global Wellness Economy Monitor (2024), women now make up nearly 65% of global wellness travelers, preferring services provided by women due to shared understanding and easier communication.

Digital platforms like the International Institute for Complementary Therapists (IICT) and wellness travel business (WTB) have noted a significant increase in women-led wellness ventures in 2023–2025, especially in regions like Southeast Asia, Eastern Europe, and Latin America.

These ventures promote local empowerment and sustainable economic opportunities by employing and training others in their communities.

As noted by Ahmed et al. (2025), academic studies are increasingly focusing on how technology, entrepreneurship, and gender intersect in the wellness tourism sector. Mobile apps, social media, and digital booking platforms have enabled more women to start and grow wellness businesses, particularly in rural or underrepresented areas.

1.3. Systemic Barriers Facing Women Entrepreneurs

Despite their growing presence and influence, women entrepreneurs in the wellness tourism space continue to face systemic challenges that hinder their ability to scale and thrive.

These include:

1. *Access to financial capital*:

   According to the International Finance Corporation (IFC), women entrepreneurs globally receive only 7–10% of venture capital funding. Within the wellness tourism sector, which typically comprises small-scale, service-based operations, women encounter significant difficulties in obtaining loans, grants, or investment opportunities that could facilitate the expansion of infrastructure, enhancement of marketing strategies, or adoption of cutting-edge technologies.

2. *Lack of mentorship and networks*:

   Female founders often report a lack of robust mentorship networks as a critical impediment to their success. Although there are increasing initiatives aimed at empowering women entrepreneurs, such as the UN Women's Empowerment Principles, LeanIn.org, and regional entrepreneurship incubators, the wellness tourism industry is deficient in targeted support systems that connect women with seasoned leaders in sustainable tourism, hospitality technology, or wellness branding.

3. *Technological disparities*:

   Advanced tools such as AI-driven customer relationship management (CRM) systems, digital booking platforms, virtual wellness programming, and data analytics have become increasingly essential for maintaining competitiveness in the wellness tourism arena. Nonetheless, many women-led enterprises function without sufficient access to these technologies due to financial limitations or a lack of training, thereby constraining their capacity to compete in a digitally advancing marketplace.

4. *Market access and visibility*:
   Breaking into international markets remains a challenge, particularly for women entrepreneurs from developing countries. Limited brand visibility, language barriers, and unfamiliarity with global distribution channels can prevent high-quality, locally rooted wellness offerings from reaching broader audiences.

1.4. Pathways Forward

To unlock the full potential of women in wellness tourism, stakeholders – including governments, private investors, non-governmental organizations (NGOs), and industry associations – must collaborate to create enabling environments.

Key strategies include:

- Providing targeted microfinance and grant programs for women in wellness entrepreneurship.
- Developing digital literacy and technology training tailored to small wellness enterprises.
- Building mentorship networks that connect emerging female entrepreneurs with seasoned leaders.
- Promoting gender-inclusive policies in tourism planning and economic development.
- Showcasing women-led wellness ventures through curated platforms and global wellness marketplaces.

As the wellness tourism industry continues to grow, harnessing the leadership and creativity of women will not only drive business innovation but also foster more inclusive, equitable, and sustainable models of tourism worldwide.

1.5. Research Objectives

- To examine the ways in which technology empowers women in wellness tourism entrepreneurship.
- To identify opportunities and challenges associated with digital integration.
- To explore real-world examples of successful women-led ventures using technology.
- To propose policy and strategic recommendations for fostering inclusive growth.

2. Methodology

This research uses a qualitative, exploratory methodology to analyze the role of technology in empowering women entrepreneurs in wellness tourism.

It uses a multi-source data collection framework, including a literature review, thematic analysis, a case study of Priyanka Chaurasia's Himalayan Homestay in

Uttarakhand, and cross-case insights from international examples to illustrate strategies and challenges faced by women entrepreneurs in different regions. The study aims to provide practical suggestions for stakeholders in overcoming systemic challenges and promoting digital empowerment.

3. Literature Review

3.1. Technology as a Tool for Wellness Tourism Women's Empowerment

The use of information technology to support women entrepreneurs in the wellness tourism industry has been discussed in various studies. Digital tools and platforms help women overcome challenges in market access, training, and funding. According to Ndou et al. (2024), digital tools have allowed more women to become entrepreneurs because they help manage issues related to time, money, and travel. A study titled "Empowering Women via Digital Technologies" by Abdelwahed et al. (2024) also shows that technology reduces entry barriers for women and changes how competition works, helping them take part in competitive wellness sectors. For women who are just starting or growing their businesses, online tools offer access to consumer markets, investment opportunities, mentoring, and educational resources. In the field of wellness tourism, this digital empowerment is clearly seen, as women-led businesses excel in providing personalized health and wellness services.

3.2. Two Issues Related to Digital Integration are Worth Noting

While digital technologies are a strong resource, there are large gaps in preparation, digital literacy, and availability, which affect their effectiveness. Yin (2024) notes that using digital tools in wellness tourism can improve customer satisfaction and personalize services. However, Von Solms and Von Solms (2016) warn that a lack of cooperation between the tourism industry and technology creates obstacles, especially for emerging economies trying to use wellness-tracking devices like Fitbit. Khoo et al. (2022) adds that in Latin America, women face barriers such as limited access to devices, low digital education, and safety concerns. These obstacles widen the gender gap, as they prevent women from fully benefiting from technological advancements in wellness tourism. Talukder et al. (2024) suggest that for inclusive development, there must be a balance between sustainability, cultural considerations, and technology.

3.3. Real-world Examples Show How Technology Helps Women Entrepreneurs Succeed in the Wellness Tourism Industry

A detailed case study of Bali's wellness tourism industry by Mananda and Kristanto (2023) shows how local women use digital tools as marketing tools to offer their services, collaborate, and compete with international companies despite high operating costs. Their study shows that digital tools are transforming eleven key sectors, including product marketing and differentiation.

3.4. There is a Strong Need for Structured Frameworks and Supportive Policies for Women Involved in Technology-based Wellness Tourism

Irawati and Siahaan (2023) point out that constitutional and regulatory barriers in Indonesia still hinder the success of women's digital businesses. Their research suggests reforms such as easier licensing processes, promoted digital literacy, and financial inclusion policies. To prevent marginalization of local communities and damage to traditional practices, Talukder et al. (2024) suggest that tourism technology integration must be culturally and environmentally sustainable. Abdelwahed et al. (2024) recommend creating inclusive digital ecosystems by providing government-supported innovation hubs, online safety rules, and infrastructure. These policy recommendations emphasize that systematic support is crucial for promoting equal participation and sustainable success for women in wellness tourism entrepreneurship, going beyond just access to technology.

4. Conceptual Framework

4.1. Wellness Tourism and Female Entrepreneurship

Wellness tourism is one of the fastest-growing parts of the global travel industry, with a projected market value of over $1.4 trillion by 2025, according to the Global Wellness Institute (2024).

It combines travel with well-being practices, focusing on personal growth, prevention, and transformation. Women entrepreneurs play a key role in shaping this market, contributing to economic growth and driving changes that emphasize inclusivity, ethics, and community-based innovation. Many women-led businesses combine traditional healing systems like Ayurveda, Traditional Chinese Medicine, naturopathy, yoga, and Indigenous wellness practices with modern wellness services such as digital coaching, eco-retreats, and mindful travel apps. These businesses are based on empathetic leadership, sustainability, community involvement, authenticity, diversity, and respect for cultural traditions. As UNWTO (2020) explains, the fast growth of online platforms and social media has given women more power to build their brands, access global markets, and offer customized wellness experiences without being limited by geography.

Women are leading in various wellness initiatives, such as yoga studios, meditation centers, retreat leadership, Ayurvedic and herbal businesses, eco-lodges, and homestays.

These centers combine yoga, mindfulness, nutrition coaching, and spiritual instruction to help with mental health and personal growth. Women are also leading retreats focused on women's health, trauma recovery, leadership, and ecofeminism, often in natural settings. They are also commercializing traditional herbal remedies and oils through local markets and international e-commerce platforms. In addition, Sun et al. (2024) show that women-run accommodations are integrating sustainable practices, organic gardens, and locally sourced meals into their offerings. Online wellness coaching services are also growing in popularity, with about 60% of wellness travelers being women.

4.2. Technology as an Enabler

The digital revolution has made it easier for women entrepreneurs in the wellness tourism sector to start and grow their businesses, even from local settings.

With the availability of affordable technology tools, they can now connect with people around the world through social media and online shopping platforms. Artificial intelligence can help create personalized wellness plans, customize offerings to match individual needs, and improve the way businesses operate. Cloud-based systems such as Booking.com Partner Hub and Airbnb Pro Tools help in managing daily business tasks more efficiently. Services can also be provided remotely through mobile apps and online platforms, allowing access to clients from anywhere. Wearable technologies like Fitbit and Apple Watch allow wellness providers to monitor clients' progress, which can make wellness programs more effective and build trust with customers. However, there are still challenges like differences in digital skills and uneven access to technology, especially in rural and developing areas where many small wellness businesses are based.

4.3. Challenges Faced by Women Entrepreneurs

The wellness tourism industry faces several obstacles that limit the growth of women entrepreneurs.

These include the digital divide, lack of financial resources, cultural norms, legal challenges, and data privacy regulations. Women are less likely to own smartphones and have less reliable internet access, especially in poor and rural regions. Financially, female founders get only a small percentage of venture capital funding worldwide, forcing many to rely on personal money or informal loans. Cultural attitudes and gender roles can also limit women's freedom to start and run businesses, affecting their ability to own land, get credit, and have their businesses accepted. Regulations such as unclear licensing and zoning laws create difficulties for even the smallest operators. Data privacy and security are also key challenges, as wellness entrepreneurs need to comply with laws like the General Data Protection Regulation (GDPR) and the Health Insurance Portability and Accountability Act (HIPAA).

5. Technology for Women Entrepreneurs – Glimpses of Future

Technology is becoming a key factor in the wellness tourism sector, particularly for women entrepreneurs. It allows them to break through traditional barriers, grow their businesses, and reach a global audience while staying true to their culture and values. This section explores how technology supports women in the wellness tourism industry across four main areas: market access, customer engagement, process efficiency, and inclusiveness.

5.1. Access to Global Markets

Digital platforms have made it easier for women business owners to sell their wellness products to people all over the world.

Online marketplaces such as Shopify, Etsy, Amazon Handmade, and local marketplaces let women sell directly to consumers. Social media platforms like Instagram, Facebook, YouTube, and TikTok help women entrepreneurs build their brand awareness, show their products, and connect with specific audiences. Using visual storytelling can communicate authenticity, values, and emotional connections, which influence consumer choices in wellness tourism. Partnering with wellness influencers can help women-owned wellness businesses reach a larger audience and gain trust, making it easier for them to compete in the global market.

5.2. *Enhanced Customer Engagement*

Digital tools are helping entrepreneurs offer customized services and maintain meaningful connections with customers.

AI chatbots assist with answering questions, booking appointments, and following up after a service, reducing the need for manual work. Health-focused mobile apps like Headspace and Calm offer guided meditation and progress tracking. Big data analysis tools help understand what travelers want and how they feel about a service, allowing businesses to improve offerings and increase sales. These technologies improve customer satisfaction and help women-led wellness businesses create loyal customers who keep coming back.

5.3. *Operational Efficiency*

Technology plays a vital role in making business operations smoother, lowering costs, and improving sustainability and the ability to grow.

Cloud-based management systems like Booking.com Partner Hub, Airbnb Pro Tools, Google Workspace, and Trello help with bookings, team communication, scheduling, and managing supplies. Online payment systems like Stripe, PayPal, PayU, and Paytm make international transactions easier and reduce reliance on local banks. Remote learning platforms such as Coursera, Udemy, and LinkedIn Learning offer opportunities for entrepreneurs and their teams to develop skills. These digital tools help reduce time and labor costs, allowing women entrepreneurs to focus more on growing their businesses and coming up with new ideas.

5.4. *Inclusivity and Representation*

Technology helps promote inclusivity by giving a platform to diverse voices and linking entrepreneurs with supportive networks.

Women entrepreneurs use blogs, vlogs, and short videos to share their journeys, business ideas, and cultural traditions, challenging the mainstream narratives in the wellness industry. A mobile-first approach ensures that services are accessible and affordable for everyone, including those in rural and low-income areas. Online communities like Facebook groups, LinkedIn forums, and Slack channels provide safe spaces for women entrepreneurs to share knowledge and work together. By using inclusive design and decentralized networking, technology becomes a powerful tool for economic empowerment, preserving culture, and promoting gender equality in the wellness tourism sector.

6. Challenges Facing Women in Tech-driven Wellness Tourism

Even though digital transformation and growing market demand have created more opportunities for women entrepreneurs in the wellness tourism space, women continue to face significant challenges that prevent them from scaling their businesses, innovating, and sustaining their ventures.

These issues have many causes and are linked to regulatory, cultural, financial, and structural systems. This section examines four main challenge areas: digital infrastructure gaps, financial and investment limitations, sociocultural barriers, and ethical and regulatory complexities.

6.1. Gaps in Digital Infrastructure

Many female entrepreneurs, especially those in rural or suburban areas, face difficulties in accessing digital infrastructure, even though technology is crucial for expanding market reach and improving business performance.

- *Limited internet access*:

  In places like rural India and some parts of Indonesia, internet access is either unavailable or unreliable.

  According to the International Telecommunication Union (Press Release, 2022), women have less access to broadband internet, especially in low-income areas, and are 7% less likely than men to own a smartphone.

- *High cost of smart devices and subscription services*:

  The cost of smartphones, data plans, and subscription-based tools like CRM systems, AI platforms, and video conferencing software presents a major challenge for small female entrepreneurs.

  Many operate with limited financial resources and lack the economic stability reported by the World Bank (Burga et al., 2021; World Bank SME Finance, n.d.).

  These differences in infrastructure worsen the gap in access to digital tools, making it harder for women to fully take part in online businesses, remote services, and investing in important technologies. This limits their ability to compete in the digital world and online marketing – especially in developing countries where wellness tourism is usually based locally but marketed globally.

6.2. Funding and Investment Challenges

Getting financial support remains one of the biggest problems for women who start businesses worldwide.

- Women-led startups receive only 7–10% of venture capital funding globally (She Wins Climate: Accelerating Women-Led Innovation for Climate Action, n.d.). In the wellness tourism industry – often grouped under lifestyle services or alternative wellness rather than technology – there is even less interest in investment because of the perception that these businesses are not easy to scale or profitable.

- Many female entrepreneurs who run small businesses that are not officially registered or owned, which restricts their ability to offer collateral for loans. The lack of credit history also makes it hard for them to get bank loans, forcing them to rely on informal lending with high-interest rates and exploitative terms (United Nations, 2020).

6.3. Cultural and Social Constraints

Stereotypes and traditional expectations greatly affect women's involvement in wellness entrepreneurship. Women often face limits in their ability to move freely and build professional networks, which hinders business growth. There is also a lack of female representation in key decision-making roles, such as in tourism boards or wellness associations. This exclusion limits their ability to influence policies, resource allocation, and advocacy. These cultural barriers limit personal experiences and hinder the growth of the sector, excluding alternative voices and visions in wellness tourism.

6.4. Ethical and Regulatory Issues

Wellness tourism is shifting toward a focus on health, spirituality, and personal growth, which introduces new ethical and regulatory challenges for women entrepreneurs.

Online health services, such as virtual yoga and meditation classes, often operate in legal gray areas. Some places have strict licensing requirements, while others lack clear guidelines. The rise of wearable technology and health-tracking apps has made it necessary for entrepreneurs to navigate complex data privacy regulations, increasing their risk of legal action. Non-medical wellness practitioners also struggle with licensing issues, as many countries lack standardized certification processes. This undermines professional credibility and complicates insurance, partnerships, and international collaborations. Addressing these issues requires collaboration among policymakers, industry leaders, and civil society to create inclusive frameworks that protect both entrepreneurs and consumers.

7. Strategies for Empowerment

Overcoming the systemic challenges faced by women entrepreneurs in wellness tourism needs a collaborative effort from governments, the private sector, civil society, and international organizations (United Nations World Tourism Organization (UNWTO) | Division for Ocean Affairs and the Law of the Sea, n.d.).

But before you decide on your own will and purchase a plot of land for a cemetery, let's discuss what can be done with your body.

To build an inclusive and sustainable entrepreneurship environment, we should develop specific recommendations around capacity building, financial inclusion, policy reform, and community empowerment.

- As a first step, the digital economy requires upgrading the skills of women entrepreneurs to participate in regular social activities. Since new conditions bring new techniques, we need suitable programs to train these entrepreneurs. We should help them attract clients, expand their business skills, and guide them in digital branding. This would also increase the visibility of their projects through cooperation with NGOs and technology firms. Women can access free or subsidized digital tools and resources essential for business growth (Appaya & Abbas, 2024; World Bank, 2020; World Bank SME Finance, n.d.). Equipping women with the necessary skills not only improves their competitiveness but also makes them more adaptable to changes in market demands.
- Another important issue is the problem faced by women involved in small-scale or informal wellness tourism businesses. Financial institutions need to create financial products that are more suitable for women. For example, low-interest microloans with repayment terms that match the income patterns of tourism – such as flexible repayment plans, revenue-sharing models that promote gender equality between tourists and local suppliers, and loans without collateral but supported by group or government guarantees (Ribeiro et al., 2022). In addition, creating startup incubators and accelerators for women-led wellness businesses can provide startup capital and mentorship, as well as global business opportunities through extensive networks. These initiatives can increase the success rate and reduce barriers to entry and the risk of business failure.
- Third, policy barriers limit the entrepreneurial opportunities of women in wellness tourism.

Governments should simplify the approval process for semi-professional wellness service providers and remove administrative obstacles for home-based businesses, or provide clearer written guidelines and certification steps (Rajalakshmi, 2025; Smith & Puczko, 2014). National tourism offices also need to rethink their strategies as they embrace digital transformation, offering more than just technical support by incorporating gender-equitable policies into the development plans of tourism regions. These policy measures help to recognize the contributions of women entrepreneurs and ensure their inclusion in formal economic frameworks.

- Finally, empowering communities through collective action is crucial for enhancing the resilience and market position of women entrepreneurs. Establishing women-led wellness tourism cooperatives allows entrepreneurs to combine resources, share marketing costs, and negotiate better terms with suppliers and distributors. Creating regional forums and online platforms for peer learning can strengthen these networks by offering dedicated opportunities for women to connect, share knowledge, and collaborate. These collective initiatives enhance resilience, promote innovation, and improve women's visibility and bargaining power in the wellness tourism sector (Asia-Pacific Economic Cooperation (APEC); Canton, 2021; The Europa Directory of International Organizations 2000, 2020). By implementing targeted actions across these four interconnected areas, stakeholders can reduce structural inequalities and maximize the potential of women entrepreneurs in wellness tourism, leading to more equitable and sustainable economic development.

8. Successes Story of Priyanka Chaurasia – Himalayan Homestay, Uttarakhand

Priyanka Chaurasia, a wellness entrepreneur, has turned her family home into a wellness-focused homestay in the Kumaon region of Uttarakhand. This homestay offers wellness activities that are based on yoga, Ayurveda, and natural healing methods. Visitors can enjoy daily yoga sessions, meals made with Ayurvedic principles, nature walks, and cultural experiences. Priyanka is also focused on employing local women in cooking, hospitality, and handicrafts. Her efforts help to support the local economy, keep cultural traditions alive, and strengthen community bonds.

Even though the village where her homestay is located has limited internet access, Priyanka has used digital tools to promote her business and attract travelers from around the world.

She uses platforms like Airbnb Experiences, Instagram, and online reviews to reach a global audience and spread the word about her homestay through word-of-mouth.

Priyanka's homestay combines environmental, social, and economic sustainability. It shows how eco-tourism and wellness tourism can work together with social entrepreneurship to create lasting benefits for people and the planet. Her story shows how women-led tourism businesses can make a positive impact on sustainable development in the Indian Himalayas. It highlights the importance of using technology to overcome challenges, offering real experiences, and the strength of female-led businesses in developing rural areas.

9. Conclusion

This study examines the difficulties faced by women in wellness tourism entrepreneurship, showing both their potential for transformation and the obstacles they face. The case of Priyanka Chaurasia's Himalayan Homestay in Uttarakhand is a clear example of how women can use digital tools, even with weak internet, to empower communities, support sustainable development, and protect cultural heritage. She faces challenges like market limitations and poor infrastructure, but her approach reflects a global trend where women are blending traditional healing with modern service models to create value-driven businesses. According to thematic analysis, empowering women in the $1.3 trillion wellness industry depends on four key areas.

These include:

1. *Capacity building*: Training women in digital skills and business practices, as Priyanka did by effectively using Instagram and Airbnb to overcome geographical barriers.
2. *Financial inclusion*: Women need financial support, like microloans and incubators that don't require collateral to grow businesses beyond just survival.
3. *Policy reform*: Rules related to alternative therapies and travel should be made more accessible for women.

4. *Community empowerment*: Creating models that help local communities, like how Priyanka helped local women by offering jobs and preserving their culture.

Despite these efforts, there are still major challenges:

In rural areas, the digital divide is a big issue, as women are 7% less likely than men to own smartphones. There's also a lack of funding, with only 7–10% of venture capital going to women-led businesses. Regulatory uncertainty adds another layer of difficulty. Priyanka's issues with inadequate infrastructure and seasonal changes show the need for collaboration between different groups:

- Governments should invest in rural digital infrastructure and make tourism policies more gender inclusive.
- Financial institutions need to develop products that match the income patterns in tourism.
- Tech companies could create affordable, offline solutions for areas with poor internet.

Ultimately, women entrepreneurs are changing the wellness tourism industry into one that supports regenerative development. Economic growth is connected with culture, the environment, and community well-being. As Halbert once imagined, the wellness sector thrives when it focuses on the full potential of people. By working together, stakeholders can help build a future where women's leadership makes the wellness industry more resilient, fair, and meaningful for everyone.

References

Abdelwahed, N. A. A., Bano, S., Al Doghan, M. A., Aljughiman, A. A., Shah, N., & Soomro, B. A. (2024, June). Empowering women through digital technology: Unraveling the nexus between digital enablers, entrepreneurial orientation and innovations. *Equality, Diversity and Inclusion, 44*(5), 602–626. https://doi.org/10.1108/EDI-02-2024-0072

Ahmed, H., Bajwa, S. U., Nasir, S., Khan, W., Mahmood, K., & Ishaque, S. (2025). Digital empowerment: Exploring the role of digitalization in enhancing opportunities for women entrepreneurs. *Journal of the Knowledge Economy*, *17*(1), 466–497. https://doi.org/10.1007/s13132-025-02658-0

Appaya, S., & Abbas, S. B. (2024). *Empowering women through digital financial inclusion*. https://blogs.worldbank.org/en/psd/empowering-women-through-digital-financial-inclusion

BridgetGWI. (2024). *Wellness tourism will cross the $1 trillion mark in 2024*. https://globalwellnessinstitute.org/global-wellness-institute-blog/2023/11/28/wellness-tourism-will-cross-the-1-trillion-mark-in-2024/

Burga, L., Gimelli, N., Muradyan, S., Robakowski, A., Miller, M., Rawlins, M., & Snyder, G. (2021). Using digital solutions to address barriers to female entrepreneurship. *Using digital solutions to address barriers to female entrepreneurship*. The World Bank Group. https://doi.org/10.1596/35993

Canton, H. (2021). Asia-Pacific economic cooperation—APEC. In *Routledge eBooks*. https://doi.org/10.4324/9781003179900-68

Dunn, H. L. (1959). High-level wellness for man and society. *American Journal of Public Health*, *49*(6), 786–792. https://doi.org/10.2105/ajph.49.6.786

Global Wellness Economy Monitor. (2024). Global Wellness Institute. (2024). Economy monitor. *Global wellness 2024. Global market*. www.globalwellnessinstitute.org.

Global Wellness Institute. (n.d.). *2018 Global wellness economy monitor*. Global Wellness Institute. https://globalwellnessinstitute.org/industry-research/2018-global-wellness-economy-monitor/

Global Wellness Institute. (2025). *2018 Global wellness economy monitor*. Global Wellness Institute. https://globalwellnessinstitute.org/industry-research/2018-global-wellness-economy-monitor/

IFC World Bank. (2011). *SMES finance | World Bank Group*. https://www.worldbank.org/ext/en/topic/competitiveness/small-and-medium-enterprises-smes-finance

Institute, G. W., Flynn, D., Feliciano-Chon, C., & Stewart, D. H. (2024). *The future of wellness tourism 2025*. https://www.finnpartners.com/wp-content/uploads/2024/10/THE-FUTURE-OF-WELLNESS-2025-compressed.pdf

Irawati, J., & Siahaan, S. T. P. (2023). Legal challenges impeding the development of local wisdom-based wellness tourism potential. *Jurisdictie: Jurnal Hukum Dan Syariah*, *14*(2), 212–232. https://doi.org/10.18860/j.v14i2.24002

Johnston, K., Yeung, O., Callender, T., & Institute, G. W. (2023). *Global wellness economy monitor 2023*. Global Wellness Institute. https://globalwellnessinstitute.org/wp-content/uploads/2023/11/GWI-WE-Monitor-2023_FINAL.pdf

Johnston, K., Yeung, O., Callender, T., & Hopkins, J. (2024). *Global wellness economy monitor 2024* (pp. 1–131).

Khoo, E. M., Abdullah, A., Liew, S. M., Hussein, N., Hanafi, N. S., Lee, P. Y., Abdullah, K. L., Vengidasan, L., Abu Bakar, A. I. Bin, Pinnock, H., & Jackson, T. (2022). Psychological health and wellbeing of primary healthcare workers during COVID-19 pandemic in Malaysia: A longitudinal qualitative study. *BMC Primary Care*, *23*(1), 1–11. https://doi.org/10.1186/s12875-022-01870-0

Mananda, I. G. P. S., & Kristanto, Y. (2023). Entrepreneurship-based potential wellness tourism di Bali. *Jurnal Aisyah: Jurnal Ilmu Kesehatan*, *8*(3). https://doi.org/10.30604/jika.v8i3.2512

Mueller, H., & Kaufmann, E. L. (2001). Wellness tourism: Market analysis of a special health tourism segment and implications for the hotel industry. *Journal of Vacation Marketing*, *7*(1), 5–17. https://doi.org/10.1177/135676670100700101

Ndou, V., Mele, G., Hysa, E., & Mansi, E. (2024). Empowering women for technology entrepreneurship: Opportunities and challenges. *Proceedings of the International Conference on Gender Research*, *7*(1), 250–260. https://doi.org/10.34190/icgr.7.1.2064

Pandey, D. (2025). *Sustainable tourism market size surpass USD 11.39 TN by 2034*. https://www.precedenceresearch.com/sustainable-tourism-market

Press Release. (2022). https://www.itu.int/en/mediacentre/Pages/PR-2022-11-30-Facts-Figures-2022.aspx#:~:text=Although women account for close,a mobile phone in 2022

Rajalakshmi, S. (2025). Exploring victimology within the medico-legal framework of cosmetic surgery. *IRE Journals*, *8*(10), 1459–1472.

Ribeiro, J. P. C., Duarte, F., & Gama, A. P. M. (2022). Does microfinance foster the development of its clients? A bibliometric analysis and systematic literature review. *Financial Innovation*, *8*(1). https://doi.org/10.1186/s40854-022-00340-x

She wins Climate: Accelerating Women-Led Innovation for Climate Action. (n.d.). https://www.ifc.org/en/what-we-do/sector-expertise/gender/gender-Inclusive-climate-investment/she-wins-climate#:~:text=She Wins Climate seeks to,Eastern Europe and Central Asia

Smith, M., & Puczko, L. (2014). *Health, tourism and hospitality*. Routledge. https://doi.org/10.4324/9780203083772

STITUTE.ORG, G. (2025). *Initiative micro-trends 2025*. https://globalwellnessinstitute.org/wp-content/uploads/2025/07/2025-GWI-Initiative-Micro-Trends-v11.pdf?utm_campaign=IndustryResearch%26Trends&utm_medium=email&_hsenc=p2ANqtz-9XB0_R683RWTMxC94bAHHhKfPRwzGoEMdQFee92H8WqUtebHXX2CU7TkQcTVvByaJlA-f6lpB5a6A5zHJeySsM7eEWug&_hsmi=373539353&utm_content=373539353&utm_source=hs_automation#:~:text=The acceleration of the mind,is key to overall health

Sun, K., Liu, X., Yu, Y., Zou, J., Studies, I., & York, N. (2024). Bridging the gender gap in entrepreneurship and empowering women via digital technologies. *Academic Journal of Humanities & Social Sciences*, *7*(6), 102–108. https://doi.org/10.25236/ajhss.2024.070618

Talukder, M. B., Hossain, S. E., Al Ferdous, F., & Khan, M. R. (2024). Exploring the rise of wellness tourism: Trends, benefits, and market potential. *AI technologies and advancements for psychological well-being and healthcare* (pp. 351–377). IGI Global. https://doi.org/10.4018/979-8-3693-9158-7.ch013

The Europa Directory of International Organizations 2020. (n.d.). https://www.routledge.com/The-Europa-Directory-of-International-Organizations-2020/Publications/p/book/9780367440176

United Nations World Tourism Organization (UNWTO) | Division for Ocean Affairs and the Law of the Sea. (n.d.). https://www.un.org/regularprocess/content/united-nations-world-tourism-organization-unwto#:~:text=UNWTO takes charge of the, knowledge and tourism policies worldwide.

United Nations. (2020, January 1). *United Nations Development Programme: Development reports*. http://hdr.undp.org/en/indicators

UNWTO. (2020). *Second edition global report on women in tourism*. Retrieved September 2, 2020, from https://www.e-unwto.org/doi/book/10.18111/9789284420384

Voigt, C., & Pforr, C. (2013). *Wellness tourism: A destination perspective*. Routledge. https://doi.org/10.4324/9780203079362

Von Solms, W., & Von Solms, R. (2016). Co-creation: Tourism, technology and wellness. *IST-Africa week conference* (Vol. xiv, pp. 1–8). https://doi.org/10.1109/istafrica.2016.7530635

World Bank SME Finance. (n.d.). https://www.worldbank.org/en/topic/smefinance#:~:text=AdvisoryandPolicySupportfor,successfulmodelsandpolicyframeworks

Yin, D. (2024). *Role of sensory evaluation in health and wellness food products*. Springer eBooks. https://doi.org/10.1007/978-3-031-51808-9\{_}3

Yeung, O., Johnston, K., Callender, T., & Global Wellness Institute. (2021). *The global wellness economy: Looking beyond COVID*. Global Wellness Institute. https://globalwellnessinstitute.org/wp-content/uploads/2021/11/GWI-WE-Monitor-2021_final-digital.pdf

Chapter 13

Impact of Esthetic and Entertainment Pleasure on Tourists' Quality of Life: A Moderating Role of Tourism Well-being

Nazirullah[a], Ahmad Puad Mat Som[a], Mansoor Ali[b], Amer Hani Al-Kassem[c], Imran[d], Muhammad Jamil Anjum[e] and Irfan Nawaz[f]

[a]*Faculty of Applied Social Sciences, Universiti Sultan Zainal Abidin, Malaysia*
[b]*Department of English, Kohat University of Science and Technology, Pakistan*
[c]*College of Business, Al Dhaid University, UAE*
[d]*Department of Social and Gender Studies, University of Swat, Pakistan*
[e]*Department of Management Sciences, University Technology Malaysia, Malaysia*
[f]*Federal Ministry of Human Rights, Government of Pakistan, Pakistan*

Abstract

Quality of life (QOL) has experienced significant worldwide improvement with esthetics and entertainment activities. This chapter explains the effect of esthetics and entertainment activities on QOL and the moderating role of tourism well-being among tourists at different destinations in Gilgit Baltistan. A quantitative survey design was used, and questionnaires were distributed among (n = 350) respondents. The unit of analysis was male and female tourists who were between 20 and 60 years old. National visitors who have come to tourist places for five days up to three months were entertained and collected data and local destination visitors were not considered as research participants. Quantitative research design was applied, and hypotheses were tested through the structural equation modeling (SEM) technique and SmartPLS-4 software. The results found that esthetic and entertainment leisure improve the QOL of tourists. Tourism well-being positively improves tourists' QOL. In conclusion, esthetics and entertainment are more reliable factors for improving QOL. Therefore, creating awareness in tourist mobs about the positive impact of esthetic and entertainment pleasure could be more fruitful for tourists' QOL. As a result, mental health professionals can

Advancement in Medical and Wellness Tourism, Part A: Entrepreneurship and Technology, 165–178

doi:10.1108/978-1-80592-983-320261014

understand the importance of Pakistani tourist destinations and their impact on tourists' QOL. The chapter has developed a framework of esthetics and entertainment for future researchers and validates the theoretical model that underpins bottom-up spillover theory of life satisfaction (BSTLS) assumptions. The study recommends that esthetics and entertainment activities are essential to improve QOL and tourism's well-being strengthen the relationship between them.

Keywords: Esthetics; entertainment; quality of life; tourism well-being; pleasure

1. Introduction

The chapter focuses on esthetics and entertainment direct relationship with QOL and moderating role of tourism well-being. Tourism well-being and wellness have gained significant global popularity in the 21st century as travelers increasingly see it as an effective method to mitigate the adverse effects of contemporary living and improve the general level of QOL (Zhang & Hacikara, 2023). For example, the value of esthetics and entertainment phenomenon increase trips that are more functional with high wellness of human being (Luo et al., 2018). Human beings' value has improved due to tourism well-being, and the expected outcome of QOL increased among the experienced tourists' population. Mannan and Ali (2022) found that QOL in the context of tourism has very little research, especially in the context of Pakistan. Baig et al. (2024) revealed that tourism's impact on the QOL and tourism well-being is still under consideration, and future researchers should work in the Pakistani context. Abbas et al. (2024) suggested that tourism's role in well-being still has a gap, and future researchers should work to fill the gap with another dependency factor. Without a thorough evaluation of the entertainment transition process, tourists claim that the substantial influence of tourism well-being is indirectly related to QOL. The esthetics component relates to how customers perceive the physical environment around them (Oh et al., 2007). Bitner (1992) categorized physical atmosphere into three key areas important for tourists: surroundings settings, spatial arrangement and functioning, and signs, symbols, and artifacts. Keskin et al. (2024) argue that tourism and hospitality research depends on the historical assets of the physical environment, which significantly influence tourists' attitudes, intentions, and tourism well-being. Additionally, entertainment is an essential part of the tourism industry. Many sites are designed to enhance QOL and include attractions such as hotels with theme parks and immersive nature experiences (Hughes & Benn, 1995). It is essential that the fulfillment of life demands is determined by the alignment of personal values, goals, and requirements (Andereck & Nyaupane, 2011; Woo et al., 2018). The chapter shows that esthetics and entertainment can improve the QOL and well-being for tourists, which helps make destinations better for visitors. It also fills a research gap and suggests policies for mental health professionals.

This chapter aims to demonstrate the direct correlation between esthetics, entertainment, and QOL within the framework of tourism well-being. Tourist experiences were evaluated using esthetic and entertainment dimensions, guided by leisure theory and bottom-up spillover theory of life satisfaction (BSTLS). The findings inform mental health professionals about ways to enhance QOL through tourism well-being. As a result, tourists' experiences can provide impactful messages to both visitors and mental health practitioners. Previous research examined how leisure perceptions and tourism well-being concepts modulate the relationship between COVID-19 risk perceptions and QOL (Çalışkan et al., 2022), while Pratt et al. (2023) analyzed how entertainment attitudes affect QOL in different types of tourist destinations. These studies justify the need to address this issue through practical research. The quality of entertainment and esthetics sense increases the quality of tourists' destinations, which influences QOL (Liu et al., 2024). Such as, Wulandari (2025) explores the effect of entertainment and esthetics activities on tourism wellness. In the last two years, the national and international tourists focused on QOL due to the best tourist destinations. The factors of entertainment and esthetics are interrelated factors to improve human well-being (Xia et al., 2024). Likewise, the local tourists are attracted by their best QOL and wellness due to tourist activities (Munanura & Kline, 2022). As a result, entertainment and esthetics impact on the perception of tourists' QOL and cognition of human well-being (Gkinton et al., 2022).

2. Literature Review

Previous research has extensively explored many elements and measures of QOL with respect to tourists' destinations (Kumar et al., 2025; Srivastava, 2025; Uysal et al., 2020). Luo et al. (2018) provided a comprehensive impact of tourism entertainment on QOL and measured that leisure experiences contribute to overall QOL. Prior research on tourism has mostly assessed QOL from a subjective standpoint, as shown by studies such as Genç (2011, 2023). This is because the travel journey is contingent upon an individual's views and emotions. Previous study used entertainment and esthetics as measures of the wellness experience (Dahanayake et al., 2025; Gorichanaz et al., 2023). Leisure, health, and well-being have strengthened association of tourists' QOL. Results showed that tourism well-being is related to leisure, non-leisure activities, and QOL (Aydın, 2025; Kono et al., 2025). The current chapter found the gap and proposed that tourism well-being can enhance QOL, with entertainment and esthetics as possible exogenous factors.

In recent years, the global wellness tourism industry has experienced significant growth among tourists. For example, Xia et al. (2024) highlight the important relationship between wellness tourism and QOL. This chapter examines how entertainment and esthetics experiences within tourism impact tourists' well-being and their overall QOL. Specifically, Lee et al. (2024) explore how leisure activities contribute positively to life satisfaction and QOL, while non-leisure activities may have a negative influence. According to Zhang and Zhang (2018), pleasure derived from leisure activities and their alternate effects predict higher

QOL, whereas non-leisure activities can have the opposite effect. The study is grounded in life satisfaction theory, focusing on how tourism, leisure, entertainment, and esthetics experiences intersect to influence tourists' QOL. The chapter argues that entertainment and esthetics tourism experiences can enhance overall life satisfaction, which is linked to QOL.

This chapter further argues that comprehensive entertainment and esthetic experiences are enhanced through tourism and significantly improve tourists' QOL. Similarly, tourism entertainment is regarded as a form of leisure that is shaped by tourists' socio-cultural background and emotional attitude, as well as the unique experiences at tourists' destinations (Nazirullah et al., 2023, 2024). Previous research has linked tourism entertainment, esthetics, and tourists' experiences with traveling satisfaction (Soonsan et al., 2025). However, little research has directly addressed tourism well-being as it relates to QOL as a moderator, which this current study addresses. Several studies focus on ecological consciousness, environmental factors, and tourist behavior, but do not relate to QOL (Ahmad et al., 2020; Aman et al., 2021; Demirović Bajrami et al., 2025). As a result, this study seeks to fill that gap by explaining how entertainment, esthetics, and tourism well-being can enhance QOL among tourists' destinations. Based on the advanced literature review above, the study proposes a likely relationship between esthetics, entertainment, and QOL. Furthermore, it suggests that tourism well-being moderates the relationship between esthetics, entertainment, and QOL.

3. Theoretical and Conceptual Underpinning

The present research applies the BSTLS, which posits that satisfaction in specific life domains contributes to overall QOL. Andrews and Withey (2012) proposed that domain satisfaction (individual leisure, entertainment, esthetics, and tourism experiences) fosters pleasurable intentions and enhances overall QOL. Theory's main assumption relates to satisfaction, and such satisfaction leads to tourism experience and domain satisfaction to improve overall QOL. Similarly, tourism's well-being can enhance QOL and be influenced by entertainment and esthetic pleasure. The present study conceptually proved that esthetics and entertainment have a positive relationship with QOL, and tourism well-being buffers it.

The research employed a bottom-up model of life satisfaction approach, derived from the BSTLS theory. For instance, Hwang et al. (2023) clarify that the bottom-up models of life satisfaction approach have connections with cultural tourism, entertainment, and esthetics pleasure. These factors depend upon tour or visit quality, satisfaction, and behavioral intentions toward any destination. In a similar context, Breiby and Slåtten (2018) found that esthetics pleasure attributes, such as cleanliness, harmony, authenticity, and scenery, correlate with tourist satisfaction. More recently, Hwang et al. (2020) agreed that esthetics and entertainment significantly shape perceived tour quality and enhance satisfaction at tourist destinations. The study of Jacobi et al. (2022) draws a conclusion that esthetics experience also impacts purpose, character, and life satisfaction, and it can improve overall well-being and QOL. Based on the advanced literature review and theoretical debates, the current study found that esthetics and entertainment are key factors in improving QOL and also acknowledged the importance of tourism well-being. Tourism well-being is often overlooked in studies of the relationships between domain experiences (esthetics and entertainment) and overall satisfaction. Including esthetics and entertainment experiences in BSTLS models clarifies how domain satisfaction affects QOL. Tourism well-being serves as a moderator for the size of these effects. This model was tested through SEM, and the statistical results empirically and theoretically proved the study's contribution (see Fig. 13.1).

4. Research Design

The study used a quantitative research design and measured the objective reality of the phenomenon. The positivistic research design was used to measure all the respondents' responses in facts and figures. Research used a cross-sectional survey design and collected data from May 2024 to August 2025. Similarly, this chapter measured the impact of esthetics and entertainment on QOL with the moderating role of tourism well-being among different tourists' destinations in Gilgit Baltistan. The unit of analysis was respondents visiting Gilgit Baltistan, selected through purposive sampling. The sample size of 350 tourists was determined using G*power analysis. Data collection involved self-administered questionnaires distributed to tourists at each destination. To measure the variables, we used items and instruments from different authors' studies. Based on cultural practices, we adjusted the items by adding one to entertainment and removing two items from tourism well-being scales. Tourism well-being scale adopted and adapted with 6-items from the study of Garces et al. (2020). Such as, QOL scale was adopted and adapted with 3-items from the study of Luo et al. (2018). The scale of entertainment (5-items) and esthetics 4-items were adopted and adapted from the study of Oh et al. (2007). Descriptive and inferential statistical tests

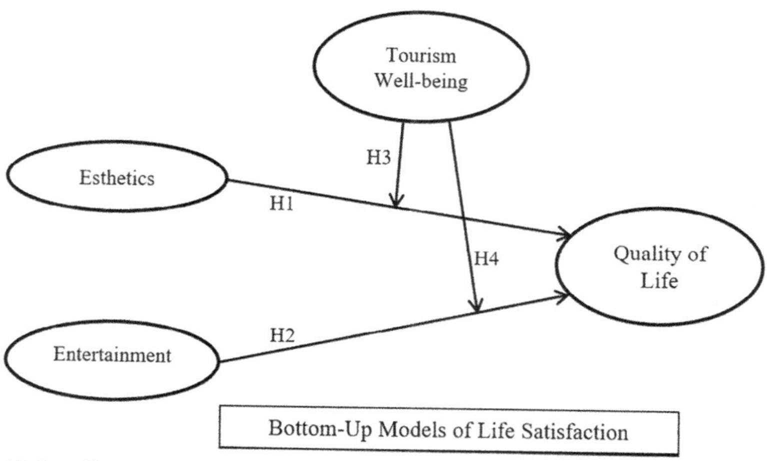

Fig. 13.1. Conceptual Model. *Source*: Andrews and Withey (2012).

were used to analyze the predictive relationship between entertainment, esthetics, tourism well-being, and QOL. SPSS and SmartPLS-4 were used for data analysis. Both male and female respondents aged 20–60 years were selected. Local residents and international tourists were not part of this research study.

For the present study, the population was targeted national tourists who visited different areas of Gilgit Baltistan. The ethical guidelines were followed during research and properly explain the agenda of survey. Enough time was given to respondents to answer the research questionnaire. Informed consent was taken from respondents and make sure that this research is conducted for research purpose and data would be not shared with any other organization or government officials. Research ensured ethical guidelines and confidentiality during data collection phase.

5. Data Analysis

The study collected data from 350 respondents. The descriptive statistics revealed that 175 (50%) were male and 175 (50%) were female. Respondents' ages were categorized: 250 (71.43%) were between 20 and 40 years old, while 100 (29.57%) were between 41 and 60 years old. Based on inferential statistics, the results of validity and reliability were measured. Every variable outer loading was measured and reported in Table 13.1. The Cronbach's alpha of the esthetics variable was ($\alpha = 0.865$), the entertainment variable has ($\alpha = 0.862$), and tourism well-being ($\alpha = 0.706$). The variable QOL has a higher alpha value ($\alpha = 0.897$) as compared to entertainment, esthetics, and tourism well-being. However, composite reliability (CR) was measured, and esthetics was (CR = 0.909), entertainment was (CR = 0.900), tourism well-being was (CR = 0.795), as compared to QOL (CR = 0.936). Finally, the average variance extracted (AVE) test was used to know the variance of the construct's indicator and capture the construct itself. The esthetics variable has (AVE = 0.541), the entertainment variable has (AVE = 0.543), tourism well-being (AVE = 0.493), and QOL (AVE = 0.631). The measurement model results showed that constructs have significant reliability and validity, which guides to test the structural model of the study (see Table 13.1).

The measurement model also analyzed the Heterotrait–Monotrait (HTMT) ratio matrix for each variable. Similarly, the values of HTMT for each pair of constructs were considered significant, indicating discriminant validity, because all the variables' values were more than 0.85. On the other hand, Fornell–Larcker criterion (FLC) values for each pair of constructs were interpreted as good, suggesting adequate construct distinction, because the values were between 0.85 and 0.60 (see Table 13.2). The results of the predictive measure were performed, and QOL was predicted by other independent variables up to ($Q^2 = 0.564$). Similarly, the coefficients of determination score were found significant because entertainment and esthetics bring ($R^2 = 0.585$) a change in the QOL when we added the tourism well-being effect. It means that 58% of change occurred in the output of QOL among tourists during their enjoyment of entertainment and esthetics activities. In the model, the *f*-square (f^2) values suggested that the model of the

Table 13.1. Reliability and Average Variance Extracted ($n = 350$).

Construct	Outer Loading	Cronbach's Alpha	Composite Reliability	AVE
EST (esthetics)		0.865	0.909	0.541
EST1	0.903			
EST2	0.880			
EST3	0.854			
EST4	0.735			
ENT (entertainment)		0.862	0.900	0.543
ENT1	0.790			
ENT2	0.719			
ENT3	0.855			
ENT4	0.765			
ENT5	0.874			
QOL (quality of life)		0.897	0.936	0.631
QOL1	0.928			
QOL2	0.910			
QOL3	0.895			
TWB (tourism well-being)		0.706	0.795	0.493
TWB1	0.638			
TWB2	0.593			
TWB3	0.639			
TWB4	0.627			
TWB5	0.630			
TWB6	0.633			

Source: 2025 survey.

study (entertainment, esthetics, and tourism well-being) was a perfect predictor because it brings a large effect, which means that exogenous constructs have a substantial influence on the QOL (see Table 13.2 for more details).

6. Hypotheses Testing with Structural Model and Its Prediction

The study applied direct regression based on SEM statistical tests. All the direct results were statistically significant and accept tourism well-being as a direct association with QOL (*H3*) ($\beta = 0.047$, SD = 0.050, $p > 0.050$). Similarly, esthetics pleasure has a positive association with QOL ($\beta = 0.322$, SD = 0.052, $p < 0.050$).

Table 13.2. FLC, Q^2, R^2, f^2- and HTMT ($n = 350$).

Constructs FLC	f^2	ENT	EST	QOL	TWB	Q^2 Predict	R^2
ENT	0.278	0.702					
EST	0.155	0.745	0.784				
QOL		0.712	0.752	0.711		0.564	0.585
TWB	0.297	0.719	0.705	0.732	0.727		
Constructs HTMT			ENT	EST	QOL		
ENT							
EST			0.854				
QOL			0.881	0.860			
TWB			0.861	0.870	0.861		

Source: 2025 survey.

The statistical results revealed that esthetics has significantly improved QOL, and the proposed hypothesis was accepted (*H1*). Likewise, entertainment has a significantly positive relationship with QOL ($\beta = 0.484$, SD = 0.068, $p < 0.050$), and the proposed hypothesis was accepted (*H2*). On the other hand, moderated tests were applied to know the enhancing relationship of tourism well-being and esthetics pleasure. The statistical findings found that tourism well-being enhances the QOL ($\beta = 0.136$, SD = 0.056, $p < 0.050$), and the hypothesis (*H4*) was accepted. Finally, tourism's well-being was connected to entertainment, and the moderated response was enhanced toward QOL ($\beta = 0.123$, SD = 0.056, $p < 0.050$), and hypothesis (*H5*) was accepted (see Table 13.3 and Fig. 13.2). As a conclusion, esthetics and entertainment pleasure significantly improve QOL and tourism well-being enhance more charismatically QOL of tourist in different destinations of Gilgit Baltistan.

Table 13.3. Path Analysis and Hypotheses Testing ($n = 350$).

Constructs	Beta (β) Path Analysis	SD	*t*-Statistics	*P* values	Bais	2.5%	97.5%
EST → QOL (*H1*)	0.322	0.052	6.142	0.000	0.002	0.222	0.428
ENT → QOL (*H2*)	0.484	0.068	7.095	0.000	0.007	0.347	0.614
TWB → QOL (*H3*)	0.047	0.050	0.944	0.345	0.011	0.059	0.136
TWB*EST → QOL (*H4*)	0.136	0.056	2.447	0.014	0.005	0.243	0.025
TWB*ENT → QOL (*H5*)	0.123	0.056	2.199	0.028	0.004	0.008	0.229

Source: 2025 survey.

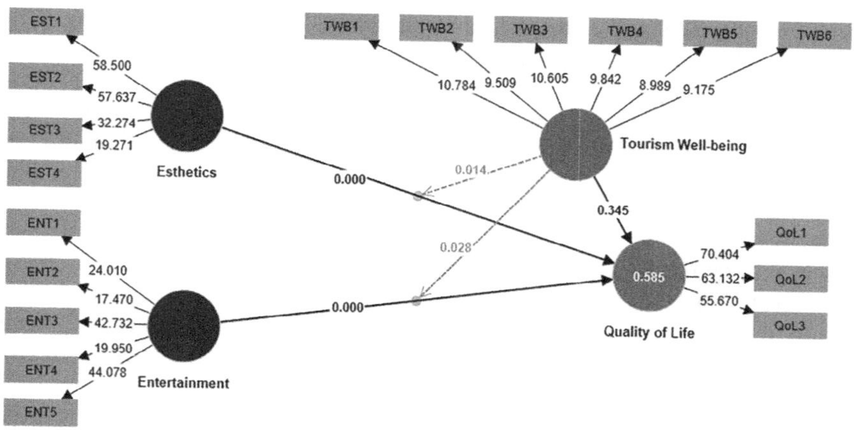

Fig. 13.2. Structural Model of the Research Study. *Source*: 2025 survey.

7. Discussion

The findings can be generalized because entertainment and esthetics pleasure proved that both these exogenous variables can increase the QOL among tourists. In the last decade, worldwide wellness tourism sector has flourished and focused more on the health of the mind of the mob. Luo et al. (2018) suggested that enjoyment and pleasure are both related to entertainment, and it is best practice to improve QOL. The current research study relates tourism well-being with tourists' QOL and entertainment and esthetics tourism experience. The current research established that two independent components are significantly connected with the whole tourism well-being, and due to this process tourists' QOL improved. The moderating factor of tourism well-being precedes tourists' leisure contentment, which ultimately improves QOL. Thus, both entertainment and esthetic pleasures determine tourists' evaluations of the QOL.

This research provides a new perspective by positioning tourism well-being and relating these experiences to QOL. It emphasizes that tourism, entertainment and esthetics are best understood as a complete experience, and tourists evaluated objectively QOL factors. Although tourism enjoyment and entertainment have been examined in prior studies, little attention has been given to tourism well-being as a moderating lens. Most tourism well-being studies focus on mental pleasure and tourist behavior. Thus, this research advances the field by applying the entertainment and esthetics experience framework to satisfaction in specific life domains and contributes to the overall QOL, which offers tourism well-being as an innovative contribution to advance literature.

QOL covers all areas of a person's existence and physical happiness. Earlier studies mainly found direct links between tourists' experiences and their QOL (Berbekova et al., 2025; Ginis, 2025; Pasaco-González et al., 2025). These studies often ignored how entertainment and esthetics satisfaction play a role in improving QOL. The authors believe this research is among the few to study both entertainment and esthetics to understand QOL in tourism well-being. This research offers tourists industry and mental health practitioners' effective techniques for building tourism well-being experiences toward satisfaction in areas such as tourism experience leads to domain satisfaction, which in turn improves overall QOL. The role of entertainment is more related to experience and more associated with the overall well-being of the tourist experience. Initially, it was observed that the entertainment dimension has a strong correlation with the total QOL experience. For example, the previous literature found that entertainment aligns with QOL (Nazirullah et al., 2025; Uysal et al., 2020; Wulandari, 2025). As a result, Nazirullah et al. (2025) explored that bad tourism experiences affect mental well-being, especially in both genders. Furthermore, tourism's well-being encompasses not just fitness and nutrition but also personal enrichment; esthetics activities serve as a predictor for improving everyday life and fulfill tourists' aspirations for personal growth and satisfaction with life. Alongside, some researchers established that entertainment and esthetics activities are innovative forms of struggles to promote and sustain QOL. Visiting a beautiful destination exemplifies unique tourism well-being among human and offers an opportunity to develop their lifestyle. The BSTLS assumes that overall life satisfaction arises from the combined satisfaction of specific domains (health, family, and work). Experience in these domains influence overall well-being, either positively or negatively. Within this framework, tourism well-being-driven by entertainment culture can improve QOL and foster happiness among tourists at enjoyable destinations.

The research demonstrates that entertainment pleasure in tourism is closely linked to an enhanced QOL and tourism well-being among tourists. Tourism well-being intentionally integrates tourism experiences, especially in visually stunning destinations, further enhancing the value of cultural entertainment and highlighting the impact of natural scenery. Destinations like Gilgit-Baltistan are internationally renowned for offering both entertainment and esthetics pleasure. Mental health practitioners can play a crucial role by promoting tourism well-being, which can, in turn, enhance tourists' QOL. Informing travelers about tourism well-being and QOL can improve overall public health and their life satisfaction. Ultimately, tourism can encourage more open and positive mindsets among travelers and support overall public health.

8. Conclusion

A brief conclusion shows that the advantages of entertainment and esthetics are linked to QOL. Tourism well-being strengthens QOL as pleasure experiences contribute to overall satisfaction. It is a crucial factor not only in enhancing QOL but also in encouraging public health awareness of tourist activities at various destinations. Entertainment activities serve as sources of pleasure, inspiring tourists to engage in them for greater life satisfaction. Notably, esthetic pleasure creates an emotional connection between tourism well-being and QOL among tourists. Overall, the findings indicate that entertainment and esthetics factors foster healthy life satisfaction and are direct sources of QOL improvement. Participation in entertainment and esthetics activities is linked to psychological well-being, leading to tranquility, increased vitality, and greater enthusiasm for visiting destinations. As a result, entertainment and esthetics solve workplace problems, promote family harmony, and are a good sign of social integration. Future research should assess individual performance across life satisfaction domains before and after experiencing tourism well-being. Endorsements from thought leaders who acknowledge the impact of entertainment and esthetics on their professional, social, and cultural lives can further underline the value of QOL.

9. Research Implication

The study measures the impact of esthetics, entertainment, tourism well-being, and QOL among tourists. Second, this research offers empirical tests of the moderating role of tourism well-being and its positive influence on tourists' QOL. Third, the research helps mental health professionals understand the importance of Pakistani tourist destinations' views and their effect on tourists' QOL. Finally, prior studies did not explain how tourism well-being moderates' QOL. This study provides a statistical framework for mental health professionals.

References

Abbas, J., Mamirkulova, G., Al-Sulaiti, I., Al-Sulaiti, K. I., & Dar, I. B. (2024). Mega-infrastructure development, tourism sustainability and quality of life assessment at world heritage sites: Catering to COVID-19 challenges. *Kybernetes*. https://doi.org/10.1108/K-07-2023-1345

Ahmad, W., Kim, W. G., Anwer, Z., & Zhuang, W. (2020). Schwartz personal values, theory of planned behavior and environmental consciousness: How tourists' visiting intentions towards eco-friendly destinations are shaped? *Journal of Business Research, 110*, 228–236. https://doi.org/10.1016/j.jbusres.2020.01.040

Aman, S., Hassan, N. M., Khattak, M. N., Moustafa, M. A., Fakhri, M., & Ahmad, Z. (2021). Impact of tourist's environmental awareness on pro-environmental behavior with the mediating effect of tourist's environmental concern and moderating effect of tourist's environmental attachment. *Sustainability, 13*(23), 12998. https://doi.org/10.3390/su132312998

Andereck, K. L., & Nyaupane, G. P. (2011). Exploring the nature of tourism and quality of life perceptions among residents. *Journal of Travel Research, 50*(3), 248–260. https://doi.org/10.1177/0047287510362918

Andrews, F. M., & Withey, S. B. (2012). *Social indicators of well-being: Americans' perceptions of life quality*. Springer Science & Business Media. https://books.google.com.my/books?id=4g7rBwAAQBAJ&dq=Andrews,+F.+M.,+%26+Withey,+S.+B.+(1976).+Social+indicators+of+well-being:+Americans%E2%80%99+perceptions+of+life+quality.+New+York:+Plenum+Press.&lr=&source=gbs_navlinks_s

Aydın, İ. (2025). Exploring leisure involvement, perceived health, and life satisfaction: Evidence from recreational physical activity participants in Turkey. *Pamukkale Journal of Sport Sciences, 16*(2), 398–426. https://doi.org/10.54141/psbd.1611409

Baig, S., Ali, A., & Khan, S. U. (2024). Exploring the interplay of tourism impacts, quality of life, and community engagement in developing sustainable nature-based tourism in Pakistan. *GeoJournal, 89*(1), 38. https://doi.org/10.1007/s10708-024-11025-6

Berbekova, A., Assaf, A. G., Uysal, M., Tsionas, M., & Parmeter, C. F. (2025). Quality of life performance index for tourism destinations. *Tourism Management, 108*, 105091. https://doi.org/10.1016/j.tourman.2024.105091

Bitner, M. J. (1992). Servicescapes: The impact of physical surroundings on customers and employees. *Journal of Marketing*, *56*(2), 57–71. https://doi.org/10.1177/002224299205600205

Breiby, M. A., & Slåtten, T. (2018). The role of aesthetic experiential qualities for tourist satisfaction and loyalty. *International Journal of Culture, Tourism and Hospitality Research*, *12*(1), 1–14. https://doi.org/10.1108/IJCTHR-07-2017-0082

Çalışkan, U., Gürsoy, D., Özer, Ö., & Hengxuan Chi, O. (2022). Effects of tourism on local residents? Quality of life, happiness and life satisfaction: Moderating role of the COVID-19 risk perceptions. *Journal of Tourism Sustainability and Well-Being*, *10*(4), 274–291. https://doi.org/10.34623/mdqb-wr79

Dahanayake, S., Wanninayake, B., & Ranasinghe, R. (2025). Revitalising tourism through memorable wellness experiences: Paving the path to destination loyalty via engagement and well-being. *Tourism and Hospitality Research*, 146–162. https://doi.org/10.1177/14673584251363566

Demirović Bajrami, D., Đervida, R., Radosavac, A., Vuksanović, N., & Matović, S. (2025). What makes tourists go green? A multidimensional exploration of pro-environmental behavior predictors. *Journal of Hospitality and Tourism Insights*, 1–20. https://doi.org/10.1108/JHTI-09-2024-0972/1255294

Genç, R. (2011). Subjective aspects of tourists' quality-of-life (QOL). In M. Uysal, R. Perdue, & M. J. Sirgy (Eds.), *Handbook of tourism and quality-of-life research: Enhancing the lives of tourists and residents of host communities* (pp. 149–167). Springer. https://doi.org/10.1007/978-94-007-2288-0_9

Genç, R. (2023). Subjective aspects of quality of life (QOL). In G. Tonon (Ed.), *Handbook of tourism and quality-of-life research II: Enhancing the lives of tourists, residents of host communities and service providers* (pp. 121–138). Springer. https://doi.org/10.1007/978-3-031-31513-8_9

Ginis, K. A. M. (2025). Physical activity and quality of life/subjective well-being in people with disabilities: A look backwards and a way forwards. *Psychology of Sport and Exercise*, *80*, 102916. https://doi.org/10.1016/j.psychsport.2025.102916

Gkinton, E., Telonis, G., Halkiopoulos, C., & Boutsinas, B. (2022, September). Quality of life and health tourism: A conceptual roadmap of enhancing cognition and well-being. In *International Conference of the International Association of Cultural and Digital Tourism* (pp. 651–666). Springer International Publishing.

Gorichanaz, T., Lavdas, A. A., Mehaffy, M. W., & Salingaros, N. A. (2023). The impacts of online experience on health and well-being: The overlooked aesthetic dimension. *Virtual Worlds*, *2*(3), 243–266.

Garcês, S., Pocinho, M., & Jesus, S. N. d. (2020). Psychometric analysis of the Tourism Wellbeing Scale (TWS): A multidisciplinary approach. *Anais da Academia Brasileira de Ciências*, *92*(1), e20190232. https://doi.org/10.1590/0001-3765202020190232

Hughes, H. L., & Benn, D. (1995). Tourism and leisure: towards the millennium tourism and leisure-perspectives on provision. In D. Leslie (Ed.), *Entertainment: its role in the tourist experience* (Vol. 2, pp. 11–21). Leisure Studies Association. https://doi.org/10.5555/19951808646

Hwang, J., Asif, M., & Lee, K.-W. (2020). Relationships among country image, tour motivations, tour quality, tour satisfaction, and attitudinal loyalty: The case of Chinese travelers to Korea. *Sustainability*, *12*(8), 3182. https://doi.org/10.3390/su12083182

Hwang, J., Joo, K., & Moon, J. (2023). Relationships among experience economy, tour quality, tour satisfaction, and word-of-mouth in the senior tourism context in Korea: The moderating role of tour guiding services. *Sustainability*, *15*(8), 6367. https://doi.org/10.3390/su15086367

Jacobi, C. J., Varga, P. J., & Vaidyanathan, B. (2022). Aesthetic experiences and flourishing in science: A four-country study. *Frontiers in Psychology*, *13*(3), 1–15. https://doi.org/10.3389/fpsyg.2022.923940

Keskin, E., Aktaş, F., Yayla, Ö., & Dedeoğlu, B. B. (2024). The importance of nostalgic emotions and memorable tourism experience in the cultural experience. *Journal of Quality Assurance in Hospitality & Tourism*, *25*(1), 1–21. https://doi.org/10.1080/1528008X.2022.2097976

Kono, S., Ito, E., & Gui, J. (2025). Leisure's relationships with hedonic and eudaimonic well-being in daily life: An experience sampling approach. *Leisure Sciences*, *47*(2), 391–410. https://doi.org/10.1080/01490400.2022.2102097

Kumar, M. A., Khanday, A. A., Rather, G., Mir, S. A., & Ganaie, M. I. (2025). Deconstructing quality of life perceptions in mountainous geographies of Cold Desert Ladakh. *International Journal of Community Well-Being*, 1–19. https://doi.org/10.1007/s42413-025-00274-z

Lee, D.-J., Yu, G. B., & Sirgy, M. J. (2024). The dual effects of passion on leisure wellbeing: Toward a theory of engagement in diverse leisure activities. *Applied Research in Quality of Life*, *19*(1), 155–177. https://doi.org/10.1007/s11482-023-10235-3

Liu, C.-H., Chou, S.-F., & Vu, H. T. (2024). Valuation of customers' service quality, affective, sensory experience and entertainment to behavioral intention. *Total Quality Management & Business Excellence*, *35*(13–14), 1509–1541. https://doi.org/10.1080/14783363.2024.2373782

Luo, Y., Lanlung, C., Kim, E., Tang, L. R., & Song, S. M. (2018). Towards quality of life: The effects of the wellness tourism experience. *Journal of Travel & Tourism Marketing*, *35*(4), 410–424. https://doi.org/10.1080/10548408.2017.1358236

Mannan, A., & Ali, Z. (2022). *Assessing the community quality of life in context of tourism development: Case study of Saidpur Village*. Pakistan Institute of Development Economics Islamabad. https://file.pide.org.pk/pdf

Munanura, I. E., & Kline, J. D. (2022). Residents' support for tourism: The role of tourism impact attitudes, forest value orientations, and quality of life in Oregon, United States. *Tourism Planning & Development*, 1–17. https://doi.org/10.1080/21568316.2021.2012713

Nazirullah, Alam, J., Hossen, M. S., Nawaz, I., Rahman, S., & Mahmood, A. (2025). Black magic and dark tourism impact mental well-being of gender: A standpoint of embodiment theory with emotional experience. In A. Sharma & S. Arora (Eds.), *The Emerald handbook of international dark tourism* (pp. 295–313). Emerald Publishing Limited. https://doi.org/10.1108/978-1-80592-501-920251017

Nazirullah, Mat, S. A. P., Ullah, F., & Mahmood, A. (2024). Crime hallmark nexus between tourism support and destination: Empirical standpoint of social control theory. *Pakistan Journal of Criminology*, *16*(1), 127–144. https://doi.org/10.62271/pjc.16.1.127.144

Nazirullah, Som, A. P. M., & Al Qassem, A. (2023). The influence of social and economic inequalities on support for tourism in developing community: An intervening effect of tourism resources. *Planning Malaysia*, *21*(1), 180–192. https://doi.org/10.21837/pm.v21i25.1232

Nazirullah, Som, A. P. M., Ullah, R., Ali, M., Nawaz, I., & Rahman, S. (2025). Future tourism trends: Virtual, augmented reality, and blockchain technology impact travel and destination experiences. In A. Sharma, S. Arora, & P. Sodani (Eds.), *Managing the smart revolution in travel, tourism and hospitality* (pp. 274–294). Emerald Publishing Limited. https://doi.org/10.1108/978-1-83662-330-420251019

Oh, H., Fiore, A. M., & Jeoung, M. (2007). Measuring experience economy concepts: Tourism applications. *Journal of Travel Research*, *46*(2), 119–132. https://doi.org/10.1177/0047287507304039

Pasaco-González, B. S., Campón-Cerro, A. M., Hernández-Mogollón, J. M., & Di-Clemente, E. (2025). Exploring the role of quality tourism experiences as a driver of quality of life through personal lifestyle. *Leisure Sciences*, *47*(8), 1930–1950. https://doi.org/10.1080/01490400.2023.2266427

Pratt, S., Gibson, D., & Kuilamu, M. (2023). Residents' perceived stress attitudes towards quality of life in tourist non-touristy destination and it can be affected with the moderating role of travel experience. *Asia Pacific Journal of Tourism Research, 28*(9), 907–922. https://doi.org/10.1080/10941665.2023.2283602

Soonsan, N., Sungthong, S., & Phakdee-Auksorn, P. (2025). Exploring the impact of tourist experiences, satisfaction, and storytelling intentions in Thailand's Andaman Marine and Coastal destinations: An empirical investigation. *Journal of Quality Assurance in Hospitality & Tourism*, 1–29. https://doi.org/10.1080/1528008X.2024.2448018

Srivastava, S. (2025). Understanding meaningful tourism, positive sustainbility and quality of life (QoL): A conceptual analysis. *Journal of Arts Humanities and Social Sciences, 4*(6), 1–12. https://sarcouncil.com/download-article/SJAHSS-194-2025-1-12.pdf

Uysal, M., Berbekova, A., & Kim, H. (2020). Designing for quality of life. *Annals of Tourism Research, 83*, 102944. https://doi.org/10.1016/j.annals.2020.102944

Woo, E., Uysal, M., & Sirgy, M. J. (2018). Tourism impact and stakeholders' quality of life. *Journal of Hospitality & Tourism Research, 42*(2), 260–286. https://doi.org/10.1177/1096348016654971

Wulandari, L. W. (2025). Exploring the role of the 4Es (entertainment, educational, aesthetic, escapist) in enhancing wellness tourism experiences. *Asian Journal of Social and Humanities, 3*(9), 1704–1716. https://doi.org/10.59888/ajosh.v3i9.577

Xia, L., Lee, T. J., & Kim, D. K. (2024). Relationships between motivation, service quality, tourist satisfaction, quality of life, and spa and wellness tourism. *International Journal of Tourism Research, 26*(1), e2624–e4245. https://doi.org/10.1002/jtr.2624

Zhang, L., & Zhang, J. (2018). Impacts of leisure and tourism on the elderly's quality of life in intimacy: A comparative study in Japan. *Sustainability, 10*(12), 4861. https://doi.org/10.3390/su10124861

Zhang, T., & Hacikara, A. (2023). Virtual tourism and consumer wellbeing: A critical review, practices, and new perspectives. In M. U. a. M. J. Sirgy (Ed.), *Handbook of tourism and quality-of-life research II: Enhancing the lives of tourists, residents of host communities and service providers* (1st ed., pp. 545–557). Springer.

Chapter 14

Eco-wellness Tourism in Kota: A Model for Sustainable Development

Surti Sharma[a], *Anukrati Sharma*[a] *and Vivek Sharma*[b]

[a]*Department of Commerce & Management, University of Kota, Kota, Rajasthan, India*
[b]*Department of Commerce, Govt. Girls College, Dantewada, Chhattisgarh, India*

Abstract

While concerns about environmental deterioration and mental health remain on the increase in the world, eco-wellness tourism has become a viable opportunity for harmonizing travel with sustainability and overall well-being. This research examines the viability of Kota, a Rajasthan city renowned for its learning institutions and natural resources, as a model of sustainable development-oriented eco-wellness tourism.

The study explores the interaction between environmental conservation, wellness activities, and community engagement in the regional tourism industry. Based on field surveys, stakeholder interviews, and sustainability analyses, the study reveals important natural resources like the Chambal River, forests, and heritage sites that can be combined with wellness activities such as yoga, meditation, and nature therapies. Focus is given to reducing carbon footprints, saving biodiversity, and stimulating local economies by adopting environmentally friendly policies.

According to the findings, Kota has the potential, through strategic planning and policy assistance, to become a premier eco-wellness tourism destination that can provide other regions with an easily replicable model for balancing economic development with nature and human well-being.

Keywords: Eco-wellness; sustainable development; tourism; stakeholders; environment

Advancement in Medical and Wellness Tourism, Part A: Entrepreneurship and Technology, 179–191

doi:10.1108/978-1-80592-983-320261015

1. Introduction

Tourism, a significant economic player, has grown beyond entertainment and leisure to incorporate wellness and sustainability. In the wellness tourism sense, it is the new wave trend of the tourism sector. It particularly cultivates people's consciousness toward retaining the healthy lifestyle. Economic development and globalization are the primary drivers that influence this trend (Dini & Pencarelli, 2021; Kazakov & Oyner, 2021). Besides, it will result in upgrading the past individual or group tourist behavior into the respective destinations with primarily focusing on developing the physical and spiritual abilities (Kazakov & Oyner, 2021). Currently, scholars in these fields have studied that there are two primary subfields, namely, medical tourism and well-being tourism. In taking into account the role of medicine, it involves diseases, surgical, or therapeutic interventions. Concurrently, well-being tourism involves the human mind, spirit, body, environment, and quality of life (QOL) (Kazakov & Oyner, 2021).

Eco-wellness tourism combines a love for the environment with a focus on overall health. It's a new way of traveling that helps protect the planet while also improving personal well-being. As people become more concerned about both the environment and their health, eco-wellness tourism is seen as a key part of sustainable travel. This type of tourism brings together ideas from eco-tourism and wellness tourism, encouraging people to connect with nature in a responsible way while taking care of their mental and physical health.

Kota, a city in southern Rajasthan, was once known for its trade and historic sites. Now, it's showing promise as a place for eco-wellness tourism. Surrounded by rivers, forests, historical landmarks, and peaceful scenery, Kota has the perfect setting to support sustainable tourism projects.

The topic of eco-wellness tourism in Kota is examined in this chapter and offered as a model for replicable sustainable development. While Kota has been historically linked with coaching, it boasts rich biodiversity, the Chambal River, heritage places such as Garadia Mahadev, and ecologically friendly tourism points of interest. Tourism in Kota is mainly educational or religious, and there is minimal infrastructure to facilitate wellness and ecological tourism. There is an increasing consciousness and desire for sustainable and health-oriented tourism, giving Kota a chance to diversify its economy and tourism potential (Table 14.1).

Table 14.1. Tourist Arrivals in Kota (2019–2023).

Year	Domestic Tourists	Foreign Tourists	Total Tourist Footfall
2019	4,98,210	8,765	5,06,975
2020	1,92,000	1,230	1,93,230
2021	2,85,440	3,010	2,88,450
2022	3,78,920	6,205	3,85,125
2023	4,66,510	7,845	4,74,355

Source: Rajasthan Tourism Department Report (2024).

1.1. Conceptual Framework of Eco-wellness Tourism

Eco-wellness tourism is travel that fosters both ecological preservation and one's health and well-being. It combines environmental sustainability, cultural conservation, and physical and mental well-being. Examples of activities in eco-wellness tourism are yoga retreats, organic farm stays, forest bathing, Ayurvedic therapies, and nature-based healing activities.

Eco-wellness tourism is travel aimed at encouraging health and well-being through physical, psychological, or spiritual activities in nature or ecologically sound environments.

Key components:

- *Eco-tourism*: Responsible tourism to natural destinations in a way that preserves the environment and enhances the well-being of locals.
- *Wellness tourism*: Tourism for maintaining or enhancing one's health, which can involve yoga, meditation, Ayurveda, naturopathy, spa therapy, etc.

1.2. Coherence with Sustainable Development Goals (SDGs)

The number of SDGs is directly related to eco-wellness tourism, like SDG 3 deals with well-being and good health, whereas SDGs 8 for decent work and economic growth, and SDGs 11–13 are related to sustainable cities and communities, responsible consumption and production, and climate action.

Eco-wellness tourism is aligned with the triple pillars of sustainability:

- *Environmental*: Conservation of natural resources, flora, and fauna.
- *Social*: Generation of employment, community engagement.
- *Economic*: Promotion of green livelihoods and local businesses.

1.3. Research Objectives

The research methodology is aligned with the following objectives:

- To assess the current status of eco-wellness tourism in Kota.
- To identify eco-wellness resources and stakeholders in the region.
- To analyze tourist preferences and awareness regarding eco-wellness tourism.
- To propose a sustainable eco-wellness tourism model for Kota.

2. Review Literature

In their paper titled "Geographical Study of Bastar District," Yash et al. (2024) highlight the rich ecological and cultural resources of Bastar, a district in Chhattisgarh, as a promising spot for sustainable eco-tourism. Bastar is home to about 70% tribal people, and it has dense forests, waterfalls, and a lot of biodiversity, making it a great place for eco-tourism that supports both the environment and the local communities. The study focuses on key attractions like Chitrakot

Waterfall, known as the "Niagara of India," Tirathgarh Waterfall, Kanger Valley National Park, and old limestone caves such as Kotamsar and Kailash. These places are important for their ecology, beauty, and geological features. After the COVID-19 pandemic, there has been a big increase in domestic tourists, but the number of foreign tourists is still low. Data from field surveys and tourism reports from 2014 to 2023 show a clear rise in tourism activities.

The problems like bad infrastructure, not enough awareness about tourism, and too much dependence on forest resources are known. However, the study suggests involving the community, building good infrastructure, and running programs to educate people about responsible tourism. It also highlights the importance of keeping biodiversity safe and improving the lives of tribal people by creating jobs connected to tourism. The paper says that eco-tourism in Bastar can help bring about sustainable development if it is managed fairly, by combining conservation, empowering local people, and preserving cultural heritage.

Bhanja et al. (2024) did a detailed study on the full potential of eco-tourism as a green alternative to large-scale tourism. The focus is on encouraging responsible travel to natural areas by supporting the protection of biodiversity, preserving culture, and improving the well-being of local communities. The authors list the main benefits of eco-tourism as helping the environment, reducing climate change, providing educational value, enriching culture, and boosting the economy.

Indian examples like Sundarbans eco-tourism, Periyar Tiger Reserve, and Assamese fish-based tourism show how natural ecosystems and local communities can work together for sustainable development. The research also suggests using technology, like virtual reality and Geographic Information System (GIS), in eco-tourism to improve the experience and reduce harm to the environment.

The chapter discusses issues such as too much tourism, loss of cultural value, and damage to natural habitats. It also suggests solutions like involving local people, controlling the environment, and planning better infrastructure. Economic data show the eco-tourism market is expected to grow a lot, which supports its long-term success.

In their research paper on health benefits of wellness tourism, Liao et al. (2023) provided a systematic review of how wellness tourism leads to individual health in four dimensions: physical wellness, mental health, QOL, and environmental sustainability. Based on a systematic review of several articles between the years 2002 and 2022, the authors apply grounded theory and framework analysis to classify the diverse health outcomes that emanate from wellness tourism experiences.

The study shows that wellness travel helps improve physical health by spending time in nature, doing exercise, and using treatments like spa and forest therapy. It also helps with mental health by reducing stress, improving mood, and making people feel better emotionally. People also feel more satisfied with their lives, have stronger confidence in themselves, and make more social connections when they go on wellness trips. Additionally, this type of travel supports environmental health by encouraging responsible tourism in special natural and culturally important areas.

The article highlights the importance of empirical work through an interdisciplinary and recommends the incorporation of wellness tourism into public health policy. It provides theoretical, managerial, and policy implications for improving tourism design, planning, and marketing. This integrated view offers a useful framework for comprehending the varied health gains and social value of wellness tourism.

The "Well-Being and Tourism: A Systematic Literature Review" article by Konstantopoulou et al. (2024) is a systematic review that explores the interactions between tourism and well-being comprehensively. The study shows that tourism can improve short-term happiness through activities like relaxing, having fun, and feeling good emotionally, but it's not clear if it has long-term benefits, which is a topic of debate. How people see the environment and their view of a destination play a big role in how happy they are and their mental health. Also, the COVID-19 pandemic made people more worried about health risks, so they preferred safer, local trips. Crowds were a problem because they reduced the enjoyment of travel, especially when people expected to be alone. The research highlighted the importance of sustainable, inclusive, and health-oriented tourism policies that take into account psychological and cultural diversity among tourists.

The research on Sri Lanka's Eco-Friendly Practices in Health and Wellness Tourism examined the adoption, influence, and challenges of sustainable practices in Sri Lanka's health and wellness tourism industry. Using a mixed-methods approach, the research integrates surveys, interviews, and case studies to assess eco-friendly practices like energy efficiency, waste disposal, and sustainable procurement in tourist facilities.

Results showed growing awareness and implementation of green initiatives among hotels, spas, and tour operators. The research elaborated the environmental and social benefits – like minimized ecological footprints and enhanced community participation. It also points to challenges such as financial limitations and poor stakeholder awareness. Governmental and institutional support is underscored, with robust policies, incentives, and public–private partnerships as major drivers of sustainability.

Technology embracement and community participation were also emphasized as important to the industry's development. Policy reform, educational programs, technological incorporation, and fair benefit-sharing are the study's conclusions. The research added to the theoretical debate around responsible tourism, stakeholder partnership, and sustainability. The research supplies a useful model for linking tourism development with social and environmental responsibility in Sri Lanka (Sugathapala, 2024).

Wellness tourism has been examined in a number of fields that address different aspects of wellness, outlining the use of the recently entered tourist industry to increase traveler appeal worldwide. According to earlier studies, wellness tourism is the concept of combining the most important aspects of both physical and mental wellness, such as health, beauty, consciousness, sensitivity, religious surroundings, and interpersonal interactions. In their study, they discussed the negative aspects of wellness tourism since it can have a centralized location for illnesses and disorders and can have any negative consequences on the general public. In addition, it highlights the importance of educating people about wellness tourism, which includes both well and ill travelers, and wellness destinations that are located apart from tourist attractions to avoid any bad effects and to uphold and regulate the social responsibility of compassion and care (Wang et al., 2020).

Kurniawan et al. (2024) on environmental sustainability in Indonesia discussed how Indonesia can utilize its local assets to develop wellness tourism while ensuring environmental wellness. The research discovered that Indigenous healing traditions, spiritual traditions, and medical services are the most viable types of wellness tourism in these destinations. Bali is a frontrunner in using cultural healing and spiritual traditions; Jakarta focuses on medical tourism and herbal remedies, with Joglosemar concentrating on traditional medicine and cultural wellness rituals.

Environmental sustainability is tackled through systems that promote waste minimization, pollution reduction, clean transport, and conservation of nature. The conservation theme is well-developed (42%), whereas the clean transport is underdeveloped (just 9%).

The study draws attention to the potential of wellness tourism to merge health, culture, and environmental objectives, with an appeal for more robust policies, infrastructure, and public perception. The paper draws the conclusion that maximizing local resources in wellness tourism serves not just to enrich tourist experiences but also ensures sustainable environmental protection and preservation of culture in Indonesia (Kurniawan et al., 2024).

Kumari (2020) assessed the environmental wealth and potential to develop Tal Chhapar Sanctuary as an eco-tourism spot. Located in the dry Thar Desert of Rajasthan, the sanctuary is famous for the enormous number of Blackbucks and other animals such as Demoiselle Cranes and other birds. The research evaluates the environment's natural landscape, plant and animal life, infrastructure, and socio-economic aspects.

Although it has ecological beauty and richness of flora and fauna, the sanctuary is challenged by numerous factors, including the absence of permanent water sources, grazing pressures, encroachment, poor infrastructure, and destructive plant invasion (notably *Prosopis juliflora*). All these negatively affect the development of the sanctuary as a viable eco-tourism destination.

The study proposes improvement strategies such as boundary wall construction, invasive species eradication, restoration of habitats, improved management of water, staff recruitment, and infrastructure development (roads, housing, communication). It stresses the sanctuary's potential for providing sustainable tourism, conservation of wildlife, and community development if efforts toward environmental management and public education are undertaken.

In summary, Tal Chhapar Sanctuary is a strong candidate for eco-tourism, but it needs elaborate planning, conservation, and infrastructural development to fulfill its potential as a sustainable and viable tourism spot.

The research paper on Contribution of Wellness Tourism in Re-Building Sri Lankan Tourism critically analyzed the contribution of wellness tourism toward rejuvenating Sri Lanka's tourism industry after the COVID-19 pandemic. With Sri Lanka's endowed natural resources, rich culture, and Ayurvedic practices, the research sees wellness tourism as a viable alternative to conventional tourism paradigms, which have been hugely hit by the pandemic. Through examining literature since 2015, it assesses international practices and trends in wellness tourism, particularly in Asia, where nations such as India, Thailand, and Malaysia have used their native practices to attract travelers who are health-conscious.

The article talks about the many benefits of wellness tourism, including improving physical, mental, and spiritual health, as well as helping with sustainable development. It emphasizes the importance of using digital tools, working with local communities, and investing in infrastructure to create smart wellness tourism cities in Sri Lanka. The research also mentions challenges such as low awareness and weak policies, and suggests that using Sri Lanka's traditional Ayurvedic practices can help the country become a well-known wellness destination globally. Lastly, the article introduces wellness tourism as a sustainable, all-encompassing, and economically beneficial way to boost the tourism industry in the new normal (Mirando et al., 2022).

This research by Chandel and Kanga (2020) investigated sustainable eco-tourism management in Western Rajasthan from a geospatial perspective, focusing on ecological equilibrium, cultural conservation, and socio-economic empowerment. The paper locates the major districts – Jodhpur, Jaisalmer, Bikaner, and Barmer – as eco-tourism destinations that are rich in heritage sites, desert scenery, and cultural diversity. Based on GIS mapping and tourism indicators, the authors assess tourism infrastructure, arrival patterns, and environmental attributes. The research is highlighting the increasing significance of domestic tourism, pointing toward changing tastes in the form of wildlife tourism, desert safaris, and rural tourism. Strong tourism potential exists, but connectivity, accommodation, and the absence of eco-tourism policy plans continue to be a drag.

The paper also emphasizes public–private partnerships and incentives to spur investment and jobs in tourism. The geospatial method assists in the identification of tourism strengths and weaknesses for well-informed planning. Ultimately, the authors promote an integrated policy framework balancing environmental conservation, cultural heritage, and community involvement toward sustainable eco-tourism development in Western Rajasthan.

Das and Chatterjee (2024) looked at how eco-tourism helps with sustainable development by studying 134 peer-reviewed articles. They organized these articles based on environmental, social, and cultural factors. Their research shows that eco-tourism can help protect biodiversity, give power to local communities, and keep cultural traditions alive. In terms of the environment, eco-tourism encourages the creation of protected areas, increases awareness about the environment, and helps raise money for conservation efforts. Socially and economically, it provides new job opportunities and involves local people more in decision-making, but there are still problems like unfair sharing of benefits and income that can go up and down over time. Culturally, eco-tourism can help people appreciate traditional practices, but it can also lead to making cultural heritage into something just for tourists to buy or experience.

The research identifies that eco-tourism success depends on equitable benefit sharing, effective environmental management, and community involvement. It cautions against ecological degradation and loss of culture due to uncontrolled tourism and calls for eco-tourism to be integrated into national development plans. Recommendations for policies are calling for promoting community-based tourism, protecting cultural integrity, and putting in place strong monitoring systems. The paper ends on the note that eco-tourism should be approached holistically and inclusively of all stakeholders so that it benefits all three aspects of sustainable development. Long-term impacts and new models of community-based eco-tourism need to be researched in the future (Das & Chatterjee, 2024).

The research done by Rahmawati et al. (2023) examined the interrelated roles of eco-tourism policy, eco-innovation, and social media in fostering sustainable tourism development in Indonesia. The results show that eco-innovation plays a significant role in sustainable tourism by promoting environmentally conscious practices, efficiency in the use of resources, and technological innovation. In the same vein, effective eco-tourism policies have positive impacts on sustainable development in the form of regulatory backing, community participation, and conservation measures. Social media is also a driving force behind shaping tourist behavior, environmental awareness, and stakeholder communication. Significantly, the research highlights social media as a mediating influence enhancing the impact of both eco-innovation and policy frameworks.

A recent study done by Rahmawati et al. elaborate that combining digital platforms, green innovation, and good governance can lead to better results in sustainable tourism. It advises Indonesian policymakers to improve their systems, support eco-friendly ideas, and use social media to promote environmental efforts and share information about tourism. This approach is important for keeping the economy growing, protecting nature, and maintaining culture in Indonesia's ever-changing tourism industry (Rahmawati et al., 2023).

According to Hashim et al. (2019), the spa and wellness sector is one of Malaysia's most successful industries. Malaysia has won recognition for its growth in health tourism, thanks to its traditional healing methods. The country has become a popular choice for spa and wellness travel in Asia because of its attractive medical tourism offers. The industry is doing well now and is also keeping up with current trends in behavior.

3. Research Methodology

A questionnaire was created in order to make this study worthwhile and successful. Primary data have been gathered with the aid of the questionnaire. About 106 respondents have been interviewed informally. Secondary data gathered from numerous papers, book chapters, and websites are also included in the study.

3.1. Sample Size

The respondents in the sample consisted of local people as well as visitors to Kota district (Rajasthan), that is, 106 (one hundred six only). The samples are presented in the tabulation form with their responses.

4. Findings and Discussions

Here, we bifurcated respondents among 5 categories, ranging from below the age of 18 to above the age of 60. And it has been observed that most of the respondents are between 26 and 40 years of age. Also, it is clear that there are 55.66% respondents are male, and the remaining 44.33% are female out of 106 respondents in total. Out of the total respondents, 27 (25.47%) are from Kota only, and the remaining 79 (74.53%) are related to places other than Kota. That means they are either visitors or tourists in Kota.

This study covers all types of people, like students, working professionals, business people, and even retired people. Here, the maximum number of respondents are students, approximately 39.62% (42 in number), and the least are retired persons, that is, 1.88%.

Table 14.2 shows that the maximum number of respondents are visiting Kota for education purposes and the least for leisure, as Kota is known as an education hub across the country. Kota is still working on tourism development.

It is to be noted that approximate 82% respondents are aware of the concept of eco-wellness tourism, and a lesser number are not to know about the same. These days, people are focusing their attention more on eco-friendly services to pay for. Out of 106 respondents, even 69.81% are agree as they show their willingness toward eco-friendly activities and are ready to pay more on this side.

Awareness about eco-tourism spreads everywhere and varies rapidly. When we tried to find out about the impact of this on sustainable development, we received a positive response from all the respondents. All respondents believe that eco-tourism has a positive impact on sustainable development, whether they completely agree or are neutral toward finalizing the impact.

For the purpose of the study, we collect data by grouping several eco-friendly activities under one roof. These are like yoga/meditation retreats, nature walks or treks, organic/traditional food experience, spa and holistic healing, cultural experiences, and environmental workshops. And out of these, most of the respondents prefer yoga/meditation retreats, nature walks or treks, and organic/traditional food experience activities in eco-wellness tourism packages.

Table 14.2. Purpose of Visiting Kota (Select All That Apply).

Response	No. of Respondents	Percentage (%)
Leisure	7	6.60
Wellness (Yoga, Ayurveda, etc.)	14	13.2
Nature/environment	35	33
Education	56	52.83
Business	14	13.20
Other	35	33

Source: Created by the author.

5. Potential for Eco-wellness Tourism in Kota

A multifaceted experience, wellness tourism encompasses social and environmental aspects in addition to physical and mental wellness. The six dimensions – physical, emotional, spiritual, intellectual, social, and environmental – should also be mentioned. Furthermore, this is related to aspects of lifestyle such as mental and spiritual well-being, self-sufficiency, physical strength, esthetics, relaxation, meditation, mental exercise, education, environmental awareness, and social relation sensitivity (Dini & Pencarelli, 2021).

Kota is situated on the banks of the Chambal River, surrounded by forests, ghats, gardens, and historical landmarks. Kota's potential for eco-wellness is reflected in these goals through green initiatives, inclusive jobs, the dissemination of local culture, and green infrastructure.

5.1. Natural Attractions for Eco-tourism

Some key assets include:

- *Garadia Mahadev*: Scenery views of the Chambal gorge, ideal for yoga retreats and nature walks.
- *Chambal Riverfront*: Renovated with green spaces, it supports river cruises, bird watching, and open-air meditation.
- *Abheda Biological Park*: Combines education with eco-recreation, an ideal site for eco-tour learning.

5.2. Wellness and Spiritual Offerings

- *Ayurvedic and yoga centers*: Many institutions offer traditional healing therapies and holistic wellness packages.
- *Temple trails*: Offer spiritual wellness through meditative architecture and rituals.
- *Naturopathy resorts*: Upcoming wellness resorts on the outskirts, like Rawatbhata Road and Khairabad.

5.3. Cultural Integration

- *Kaithoon saree weaving villages*: Integration of local artisanship into tourist experience.
- *Cultural programs*: Folk dance, music therapy evenings in eco-resorts.

6. Community Involvement and Socio-economic Impact

For eco-wellness tourism to succeed in Kota, collaboration among stakeholders is crucial. These can be understood as below:

- *Government bodies*: Work for the Infrastructure development, policy support, marketing, and regulation.

- *Local communities*: May become Hosts and cultural ambassadors who ensure authentic experiences.
- *Private sector*: Should focus on Investment in wellness resorts, eco-lodges, and service innovation.
- *NGOs and Academia*: Will focus on Research, training, and promotion of sustainable practices.

And also, eco-wellness tourism has the potential to empower local communities through:

- *Job creation*: Like Nature guides, yoga instructors, and eco-resort staff.
- *Women's empowerment*: By providing Opportunities in Ayurveda massage therapy, crafts, and organic food production.
- *Preservation of local culture*: By the use of local materials, cuisine, and traditions.

7. Infrastructure and Policy Support

7.1. Government Schemes and Investments

- *Rajasthan Tourism Policy 2020*: Recognizes wellness and eco-tourism as priority sectors.
- *Eco-tourism Development Board*: Promotes regulated tourism in forest zones.
- public private partnership *(PPP) model*: Encouraged in wellness resort development.

7.2. Urban Sustainability Initiatives

- *Smart city Kota*: Focus on green development, cycle tracks, pedestrian zones.
- *Solar lighting*: Used in Chambal riverfront and public gardens.

8. Challenges and Opportunities

8.1. Challenges

Despite its potential, Kota faces multiple challenges in developing eco-wellness tourism. These are mentioned below:

- Inadequate infrastructure and connectivity.
- Limited awareness and training among locals.
- Environmental degradation risks due to unregulated tourism.
- Lack of integration among tourism, wellness, and environmental sectors.
- Lack of trained eco-wellness professionals.
- Over-commercialization risks.
- Insufficient rural infrastructure.
- Low awareness among local entrepreneurs.

8.2. Opportunities

Besides several challenges, there are some opportunities available to set up eco-wellness tourism in Kota. These are:

- Rising post-pandemic health consciousness.
- Domestic tourism boom in the wellness segment.
- Interest in yoga and Ayurveda among global travelers.

9. Conclusion

Eco-wellness tourism in Kota provides a sustainable way to develop the city while keeping the environment in balance, supporting the local community, and improving people's health and happiness. By working together with different groups and creating good policies, Kota can become a top place for eco-wellness tourism in India. This model could serve as an example for other similar cities with rich natural and cultural resources.

Eco-wellness tourism has a lot of potential to help Kota become a model for sustainable development. By investing in better facilities, training for the community, and planning that respects the environment, Kota can become a standout example in Rajasthan and across India. It's a great time to use Kota's natural beauty and spiritual heritage to create meaningful travel experiences that help both people and the planet.

9.1. Recommendations

- *Skill development*: Local training in hospitality, naturopathy, and tour guiding.
- *Digital marketing*: Promoting eco-wellness experiences online.
- *Eco-certification*: For hotels and wellness centers.
- *Zoning regulations*: To prevent environmental degradation.
- Develop a state-level eco-wellness tourism policy.
- Offer incentives for eco-friendly businesses and wellness retreats.
- Integrate tourism promotion with environmental conservation programs.
- Conduct awareness campaigns and skill development workshops.
- Strengthen waste management and green certification mechanisms.

References

Bhanja, A., Das, M., Mandal, B., & Payra, P. (2024). Prospects of eco-tourism. In S. Swami, M. Chanchan, & M. Ray (Eds.), *Alternative approaches of farming for agricultural sustainability and climate resilience* (pp. 181–200). Vital Biotech Publication.

Chandel, R. S., & Kanga, S. (2020). Sustainable management of ecotourism in Western Rajasthan, India: A geospatial approach. *GeoJournal of Tourism and Geosites*, *29*(2), 521–533.

Das, M., & Chatterjee, B. (2024). *The role of ecotourism in sustainable development: A systematic review of literature*. SSRN. https://doi.org/10.2139/ssrn.4955773

Dini, M., & Pencarelli, T. (2021). Wellness tourism and the components of its offer system: A holistic perspective. *Tourism Review*. https://doi.org/10.1108/TR-08-2020-0373

Hashim, N. A. A. N., Velayuthan, S. K., Yusoff, A. M., Awang, Z. B., & Safri, F. H. M. (2019). Validating the measuring instrument for motivation factors towards visiting spa and wellness tourism destinations in Kuala Lumpur. *International Journal of Innovative Technology and Exploring Engineering*, *8*(9 Special Issue), 1106–1108. https://doi.org/10.35940/ijitee.I1175.0789S19

Kazakov, S., & Oyner, O. (2021). Wellness tourism: A perspective article. *Tourism Review*, *76*(1), 58–63. https://doi.org/10.1108/TR-05-2019-0154

Konstantopoulou, C., Varelas, S., & Liargovas, P. (2024). Well-being and tourism: A systematic literature review. *Economies*, *12*(10), 281.

Kumari, S. (2020). Assessment of eco-tourism potential at Tal Chhappar Sanctuary, Churu, Rajasthan, India. *Remarking: An Analisation*, *5*(8), 54–59.

Kurniawan, A., Nurmandi, A., Fridayani, H. D., & Tai, K.-T. (2024). Optimizing local assets in wellness tourism development and implications for environmental sustainability in Indonesia. *E3S Web of Conferences*, *594*, 02001.

Liao, C., Zuo, Y., Xu, S., Law, R., & Zhang, M. (2023). Dimensions of the health benefits of wellness tourism: A review. *Frontiers in Psychology*, *13*, 1071578.

Mirando, U., Dabare, P. U. I., & Chathuranga, B. T. K. (2022). A literature review on how wellness tourism contribute to re-building Sri Lankan tourism. *Sri Lanka Journal of Marketing*, *8*(Special Issue), 15–36.

Rahmawati, R., Sutrisno, S., & Abidin, Z. (2023). The impact of eco-innovation, ecotourism policy and social media on sustainable tourism development: Evidence from the tourism sector of Indonesia. *Journal of Environmental Management and Tourism*, *14*(4), 1145–1156. https://doi.org/10.14505/jemt.v14.4(68).10

Rajasthan Tourism Department Report. (2024). *Annual tourist report 2023*. [Annual progress report]. Government of Rajasthan, Department of Tourism. https://tourism.rajasthan.gov.in/annual-progress-report.html.

Sugathapala, M. A. S. H. (2024). Eco-friendly practices in health and wellness tourism: A study of sustainable initiatives in Sri Lanka. *International Journal of Advance Research and Innovative Ideas in Education (IJARIIE)*, *10*(1), 637–651.

Wang, K., Xu, H., & Huang, L. (2020). Wellness tourism and spatial stigma: A case study of Bama, China. *Tourism Management*, *78*, 104039. https://doi.org/10.1016/j.tourman.2019.104039

Yash, R., Gupta, K. L., Yadav, P., Vishvkarma, J. P., Singh, A., & Suman, S. K. (2024). Eco-tourism and sustainable development: A geographical study of Bastar district. *Library Progress International*, *44*(1), 419–430.

Chapter 15

The Role of Marketing and Consumer Psychology in Shaping Wellness Tourism

Gopali Dayal and Priya Sharma

Shoolini University Centre for Distance and Online Education, Shoolini University Solan, Himachal Pradesh, India

Abstract

Stress-related illnesses, rising health consciousness, and a stronger focus on holistic well-being have fueled the rapid growth of wellness tourism as a vital segment of the global travel market. This chapter provides a comprehensive examination of how marketing strategies and consumer psychology converge to shape the evolution and perception of wellness travel. Drawing on interdisciplinary literature, it explores key psychological drivers such as self-care, emotional rejuvenation, and lifestyle enhancement that motivate individuals to seek wellness-focused experiences. The study further investigates how marketers strategically employ tools like digital storytelling, emotional branding, and personalized messaging to create and promote wellness offerings that align with consumers' identities, values, and health aspirations. Critical emphasis is placed on the interplay of psychological elements – perception, trust, and identity – that determine how travelers evaluate and internalize wellness experiences. Additionally, the review identifies emerging trends such as sustainable wellness tourism, the rising importance of mental health travel, and tech-enabled personalization, which collectively redefine consumer expectations in this niche. Ethical considerations – including authenticity, cultural sensitivity, and the increasing commercialization of wellness – are also examined to highlight the need for responsible marketing practices. By bridging theoretical perspectives with practical insights, this chapter contributes to a nuanced understanding of the ethical and psychological promotion of wellness

Advancement in Medical and Wellness Tourism, Part A: Entrepreneurship and Technology, 193–206

Published under exclusive licence by Emerald Publishing Limited
doi:10.1108/978-1-80592-983-320261022

tourism. It concludes by suggesting directions for future research to better capture evolving consumer behaviors and sustain the sector's long-term growth.

Keywords: Wellness tourism; consumer psychology; marketing strategies; travel motivation; consumer behavior

1. Introduction

Tourism has been the world's biggest and most vibrant industry for decades, ever-changing in response to changing consumer tastes, socio-cultural norms, and global economic trends. In the last three decades, such responsiveness has spawned new segments beyond mass recreation and entertainment travel. Wellness tourism is one such dominant segment, as an expression of mass movement toward health, self-healing, and well-being. More broadly defined, wellness tourism is travel undertaken primarily to promote the physical, emotional, and spiritual well-being of the traveler (Martins, 2025). In contrast to traditional tourism, which may be about escape, sightseeing, and recreation, wellness tourism is based on transformational experience – experience designed to rebalance, renew, and initiate long-term lifestyle change. Its explosive expansion has been driven by the rise in prevalence of chronic disease due to stress, heightened public concern with health risks, and a global interest in activities balancing indulgence with self-enrichment. The wellness tourism industry has grown to more than USD 800 billion in size and continues to grow every year, ranking among the fastest-growing segments of the global travel economy (Peng, 2025).

The growth of wellness tourism is inextricably connected with two interconnected aspects: consumer psychology and marketing approach. Consumer psychology offers significant understanding of the motivations, perceptions, and decision-making processes that inform wellness travel decisions. In contrast with decisions based largely on convenience, price, or entertainment value, wellness travel is strongly shaped by psychological requirements of self-care, identity validation, spiritual growth, and emotional strength (Árpási, 2018). Travelers are not merely buying a product; they are buying meaningful experiences that connect to their sense of self and support their ideals for healthier, more balanced living.

The rise of wellness tourism is closely linked to two intertwined dimensions: consumer psychology and marketing strategy. Consumer psychology provides valuable insights into the motivations, perceptions, and decision-making processes that shape wellness travel choices. Unlike decisions driven primarily by convenience, affordability, or entertainment value, wellness travel is deeply influenced by psychological needs such as self-care, identity affirmation, spiritual enrichment, and emotional resilience (Árpási, 2018). Travelers are not simply purchasing a service; they are seeking meaningful experiences that resonate with their sense of self and align with their aspirations for healthier, more balanced living.

Concurrently, marketing is critical to converting these psychological drivers into salable, desirable, and marketable products. Since wellness results are themselves intangible, successful marketing techniques depend extensively on the creation of stories and emotional connection. Methods like digital storytelling, emotional branding, and influencer marketing are becoming more common in conveying the transformative power of wellness experiences (Su et al., 2020). These approaches not only influence consumer anticipation and consolidate destination branding but also produce groups of travelers whose word-of-mouth (WOM) marketing over online networks reinforces the allure of wellness tourism.

The significance of wellness tourism exceeds consumerism; it embodies broader social transformations in health, leisure, and consumption. Modern ways of life, such as overwork, digital fatigue, and sedentary living created a need for balance, authenticity, and experiential richness. Wellness tourism offers locations and services to fill that need, whether Indian yoga retreats, European thermal spa cultures, or North American mindfulness camps (Bockus, 2023). On the other hand, the globalization of practices of well-being introduces challenges and ethical issues since the original cultures are repackaged and marketed to foreign clients.

From a scholarly perspective, the meeting of consumer psychology and marketing within wellness tourism is fertile ground for exploration. While earlier studies have interrogated wellness motivations, destination positioning, and consumer satisfaction, there exists a clear need for interdisciplinary synthesis that unites tourism studies, psychology, and marketing. This research contributes to that discussion through a review of the ways that consumer psychology drives wellness tourism demand, how marketing activity responds to such forces, and how new trends are reshaping the map. It also emphasizes the importance of ethical concerns, such as cultural sensitivity and over-commercialization threats, which undermine the authenticity that wellness tourists crave.

2. Psychological Drivers of Wellness Tourism

In order to understand the rising popularity of well-being tourism, one has to go beyond superficial tastes and reach inside the psychological drivers of travel behavior. Unlike conventional tourism, well-being tourism is informed by deep affective and cognitive processes associated with self-nourishment, identity building, and meaning making. These underlying forces explain why individuals increasingly view wellness tourism not only as recreation but also as a life-altering decision. Through motivational theories, cultural contrasts, and empirical research, this section dissects the psychological forces that explain why wellness tourism is so highly prized in contemporary society.

2.1. Motivational Theories and Wellness Travel

Psychological theories of motivation offer a solid basis for explaining the internal motivators of wellness tourism. The push–pull model is especially applicable: push factors of stress relief, burnout cure, and self-improvement are prevalent, while pull factors of spa resorts, yoga retreats, or peaceful natural surroundings act as facilitators. In wellness tourism, push factors more frequently than not supersede pull, as tourists desire escape from interior dissatisfaction and emotional exhaustion, subsequently satisfied in locations such as Ayurvedic retreats in India or European thermal spas (Árpási, 2018; Bockus, 2023). Maslow's hierarchy of needs also positions wellness tourism in higher-order pursuits of self-actualization and esteem, providing identity affirmation and transcendence beyond lower-order needs (Liao, 2023). In the same way, self-determination theory (SDT) highlights autonomy, competence, and relatedness as internal motivators – satisfied through practices like yoga immersions and meditation retreats that create personal control, mastery, and community connection (Cheng et al., 2023). Collectively, these theories present wellness tourism as something beyond recreation, as a path to greater psychological fulfillment.

2.2. Categories of Psychological Motivations

Research has consistently identified a range of motivations that attract individuals to wellness travel. These can be grouped into six broad categories: relaxation, health improvement, novelty, self-examination, social relations, and engagement with nature (Kim et al., 2023).

- *Relaxation and stress relief*: Getting away from the stresses of everyday life is the most oft-quoted motivator. Wellness travelers look for spas, meditation retreats, or mindfulness exercises to find inner harmony.
- *Health and fitness*: Preventive medicine, detox, and fitness routines prompt tourists to leverage tourism as a tool to achieve lasting wellness.
- *Novelty seeking*: Others are attracted by curiosity to experience unusual cultural customs, like traditional healing rituals of indigenous peoples or traditional herbal medicine.
- *Spiritual growth and self-examination*: For others, wellness tourism presents possibilities of mindfulness, reflection, and spiritual development.
- *Belonging and relational needs*: Peer retreats, wellness festivals, or traveling in groups provide for belonging and a shared sense.
- *Environmental and nature attraction*: Nature is a part of wellness experiences, with environmentally friendly and sustainable locations appealing to individuals who cherish convergence with nature.

2.3. Identity Construction and Self-perception

A defining feature of wellness tourism is its role in shaping identity. Choosing experiences such as a yoga retreat in Rishikesh, a meditation program in Bali, or a mindfulness camp in California is not merely about personal well-being but also about affirming one's self-concept. These choices reflect engagement with holistic living, spirituality, and balance, aligning with the idea of "consumption-as-identity," where travel consumption becomes a medium for expressing personal values and social affiliations (Martins, 2025; Peng, 2025). In the digital era, this process is amplified through curated social media content – images of meditation sessions, organic meals, or spa rituals – that portray travelers as health-conscious and culturally attuned. Such representations contribute to what Su et al. (2020) describe as "digital wellness tribes," online communities where individuals reinforce belonging and identity through shared wellness narratives.

2.4. *Cross-cultural Perspectives on Motivation*

While motivations for well-being travel have common characteristics, cultural context modulates the ways these drivers are articulated. Wellness tourism in Europe tends to promote medical wellness traditions like thermal baths and spas based on preventive healthcare practices. In Asia, spirituality and holism attract the center of attention with yoga, Ayurveda, and meditation (Bockus, 2023). Whereas North American wellness tourism tends to overlap with lifestyle optimization, with an accent on fitness boot camps, nutrition workshops, and biohacking retreats.

Cross-cultural studies show convergence and divergence. While relaxation and well-being continue to be universal drivers, novelty, religiosity, and ecologism differ in salience across cultures (Árpási, 2018). Russian tourists, for example, are driven by cultural novelty, whereas Finnish tourists are driven by authenticity and existing alongside nature (Bockus, 2023). These differences point to a call for culturally adaptive marketing campaigns that resonate with different consumer segments.

2.5. *Psychological Barriers and Challenges*

Despite its growth, wellness tourism is also plagued with various psychological constraints. One is skepticism: customers are doubtful about the authenticity of well-being services, particularly where advertising goes overboard in claims or commodifies religious practice. Another is access – wellness travel has an elitist perception and thus becomes inaccessible to lower-income groups (Martins, 2025). Misrepresentation of cultures is also an issue, especially when it involves indigenous cultures being commercialized or diluted to the extent of alienating genuine practitioners and tourists alike. These issues highlight the importance of trust, inclusiveness, and authenticity in sustaining the appeal of wellness tourism.

3. Marketing Strategies in Wellness Tourism

Marketing wellness tourism is an uncommon challenge and opportunity since it is not marketing physical goods or even traditional leisure activities, but rather providing intangible states of being – serenity, healing, renewal, and transformation. As contrasted with adventure travel, which sells a dose of adrenaline, or culture travel, which sells heritage, wellness travel gambles on an emotional promise: exposure to psychological balance and general well-being. To be effective, marketing in this industry must be very much aware of tourists' psychology, connecting policy to aspirations, lifestyle, and identity of travelers. Some of the most effective marketing practices that have impacted the industry and the extent to which they have performed in securing trust, engagement, and long-term involvement are shown below.

3.1. Digital Storytelling and Emotional Branding

Storytelling forms the cornerstone of wellness tourism marketing, bridging the gap between intangible outcomes and consumer imagination. Since well-being cannot be directly displayed, narratives convey lived experiences of transformation. Through blogs, films, testimonials, and social media, wellness brands portray journeys of stress relief, renewal, and spiritual awakening, inviting prospective visitors to envision similar change (Su et al., 2020). Closely linked is emotional branding, which anchors wellness brands to psychological states such as peace, belonging, or vitality. For instance, a yoga retreat in Rishikesh is promoted not as a destination but as a pathway to serenity and self-awareness. By appealing to these emotions, marketers shift focus from services to outcomes, fostering loyalty by resonating with travelers' deeper aspirations (Árpási, 2018).

3.2. Market Segmentation and Targeted Messaging

Wellness tourists vary by demographics, income, and psychological needs, making segmentation essential. Key groups include luxury seekers (prestige, five-star spas), budget-conscious travelers (affordable retreats), health-driven tourists (detox, fitness), and spiritual seekers (mindfulness, Ayurveda). Personalized messaging ensures relevance – luxury spas stress indulgence, while meditation centers highlight authenticity – since wellness travel often reflects identity and values (Cheng et al., 2023; Kim et al., 2023).

3.3. Social Media and Electronic Word-of-Mouth (e-WOM)

In the digital age, wellness marketing thrives on social media, where platforms like Instagram, TikTok, and YouTube amplify aspirational value through spa visuals, meditation clips, and vlogs of personal journeys. These narratives foster online "wellness tribes," communities of like-minded individuals who reinforce shared ideals of holistic living (Martins, 2025). Equally influential is e-WOM, which often carries more credibility than paid promotions. Reviews, blogs, and peer-generated content highlighting authenticity, empathy, and sustainability can strengthen trust, while negative accounts of poor service or over-commercialization can damage reputations (Su et al., 2020). As a result, consumer voices have become as impactful as formal marketing campaigns in shaping wellness tourism choices.

3.4. Influencer Marketing and Brand Ambassadors

Influencer marketing has become a powerful tool in wellness promotion, with celebrities and micro-creators positioned as relatable ambassadors of balance, mindfulness, and eco-conscious living. By sharing personal retreat or spa experiences, influencers lend authenticity and inspire audiences to emulate their wellness choices. However, overreliance on influencers carries risks. Scripted or transactional endorsements may erode credibility and foster perceptions of over-commercialization (Peng, 2025). Sustainable influencer partnerships therefore require transparency, genuine interaction, and long-term alignment between brand values and the influencer's personal ethos.

3.5. Personalization and Technology-enabled Marketing

Personalization is not a nicety in wellness tourism but the norm. With technology, especially artificial intelligence and big data, it is now possible for destinations to craft customized wellness programs that align with specific health aspirations. Predictive analytics is now more commonly adopted by resorts to suggest detox regimens, meditation classes, or exercise programs based on guests' historical behavior or health information. Wearable devices like meditation apps and smartwatches can even be incorporated into the travel process, allowing guests to monitor progress and exchange results. The infusion of technology and customization serves to increase psychological satisfaction through giving wellness travel a sense of alignment with each individual.

3.6. Cross-cultural Marketing Insights

Effective promotion of wellness tourism requires sensitivity to cultural differences. In Europe, campaigns often emphasize the long-standing traditions of medical heritage and preventive spa therapies, while in Asia, marketing draws on spirituality, authenticity, and cultural depth through Ayurveda, meditation, and yoga (Bockus, 2023). North American promotions, in contrast, tend to frame wellness as life optimization, appealing to high-performance individuals seeking productivity and resilience. These variations highlight that while the universal desire for relaxation and well-being is constant, wellness experiences must be constructed in culturally relevant ways. Campaigns that neglect cultural context risk alienating audiences or reducing traditions to commodities, thereby undermining authenticity.

3.7. Ethical Dimensions in Wellness Marketing

Ethical considerations are central to the long-term credibility of wellness tourism. Over-commercialization, cultural appropriation, and exaggerated health claims pose serious risks. For example, marketing yoga or Ayurveda as exotic commodities without regard for their cultural roots diminishes authenticity and can alienate local communities (Martins, 2025). To safeguard integrity, wellness marketing must prioritize transparency, inclusivity, cultural respect, and sustainability. Scholars argue that "responsible wellness branding" incorporates honesty and authenticity, enabling providers to stand out in a competitive market (Peng, 2025). By embedding ethical responsibility, destinations not only foster trust but also honor the cultural and social heritage that underpins their offerings.

4. The Interplay of Perception, Trust, and Identity

The development and longevity of wellness tourism are not revealed by the motivation that brings individuals to travel or sophistication in marketing efforts. The core of the success of this business rests in how travelers respond to the authenticity of the experience, whether they believe in the providers, and to what extent these experiences speak to their notion of identity. Since wellness tourism is all about intangible promises – inner harmony, renewal, and personal change – psychological considerations tend to outweigh any empirical assessment of service quality. In this respect, wellness tourism is an extremely subjective experience, more influenced by the mind and the emotions of the traveler than by measurable performance standards.

4.1. Perception of Authenticity

Experiences of authenticity are central to how consumers evaluate wellness experiences. Visitors do tend to look for signs that a retreat, therapy, or destination is authentic, culturally based, and true to the holistic tradition. Authenticity is more than the tangible service rendered, but the feeling that the experience is connected to something more meaningful and deep. When yoga retreats or Ayurvedic therapies are recognized as being rooted in tradition and cultural authenticity, travelers are more satisfied and will return (Dillette et al., 2021). When wellness products and services are perceived to be superficial – marketing trendy extensions without depth – they are dismissed as "wellness washing," an activity which creates distrust and wards off potential customers (Voigt & Pforr, 2014). Thus, authenticity is functioning as a sieve and an impulse of consumer involvement.

4.2. Trust as a Psychological Contract

In wellness tourism, trust operates as an implicit psychological contract rather than a simple service expectation. Since outcomes like healing or relaxation cannot be guaranteed, travelers rely on trust cues such as certifications, sustainability practices, practitioner accreditation, and especially WOM recommendations (Chen et al., 2022). Transparency about program details, practitioner expertise, and realistic outcomes further enhances credibility (Han et al., 2017). Beyond institutional signals, trust is deeply rooted in human relationships, where staff empathy, friendliness, and responsiveness strongly shape visitor satisfaction. Studies show that such interpersonal trust has a greater impact on loyalty than physical service elements, making trust not a marketing cliché but a lived, affective bond in wellness tourism (Mak et al., 2009).

4.3. Identity Formation Through Wellness Tourism

Wellness tourism often serves as a medium for identity expression and reinforcement. For instance, participating in a meditation retreat in Bali can symbolize a public embrace of a spiritual lifestyle, while choosing an eco-wellness lodge may signal a commitment to environmental responsibility (Smith & Puczkó, 2014). These identity performances frequently extend into the digital space, where travelers use social media posts and digital storytelling to curate and broadcast their experiences. In doing so, they reaffirm their place within virtual "wellness tribes," communities that thrive on shared values of mindfulness, sustainability, and holistic living (Dillette & Douglas, 2020). Thus, wellness tourism is not merely a personal journey but also a collective exercise in identity formation, linking individual transformation with communal belonging.

4.4. Interplay Between the Three Dimensions

The relationship between trust, identity, and perception in wellness tourism is synergistic rather than linear. Perceived authenticity shapes the degree of trust, which in turn increases the likelihood that travelers will integrate the experience into their identity. At the same time, identity influences both perception and trust – for instance, an eco-conscious traveler may view a sustainable retreat as more genuine and credible, while a luxury-oriented tourist may interpret it differently (Wong et al., 2020). This dynamic reveals wellness tourism not as a mere financial exchange but as a process of psychological alignment. When authenticity, trust, and identity converge, they forge deep emotional bonds that translate into loyalty, positive WOM, and repeat visitation. Providers who successfully integrate these dimensions are not simply delivering services but fostering enduring relationships that sustain industry growth.

5. Emerging Trends in Wellness Tourism

Wellness tourism is not a fixed landscape but a changing industry under threat of cultural shift, technological innovation, and change in consumer attitudes. Over the recent past, it has entered a phase of transformation with sustainability, mental health, digital technology, and post-pandemic recovery driving both business practice and consumer demand. These trends show how the sector increasingly reflects broader global issues like environmental responsibility, mental well-being, and diversity. As researchers observe, wellness tourism no longer refers to luxury spas or health spas but to an active destination that combines individual health with international and collective well-being (Smith & Puczkó, 2014; Voigt & Pforr, 2014) (Table 15.1).

5.1. Sustainable Wellness Tourism

Wellness resorts have countered by rebranding themselves as eco-retreats, incorporating renewable power, green architecture, organic menus, and local interaction. Studies indicate that such activities not only attract ecologically minded visitors but also support impression management of authenticity and reliability, particularly among millennial and Gen Z consumers (Font & McCabe, 2017). Destinations such as Costa Rica and Bali have become paradigms, framing their wellness retreats as destinations where one becomes healthier while engaging

Table 15.1. Emerging Trends in Wellness Tourism and Key Studies.

Trend	Psychological Drivers	Example Destinations	Key References (DOI)
Sustainable wellness	Eco-conscious identity, trust in ethics	Bali eco-retreats, Costa Rica eco-lodges	Kelly and Smith (2021), https://doi.org/10.1080/09669582.2021.1874398
Mental health tourism	Stress relief, emotional rejuvenation	Mindfulness retreats in Thailand, resilience camps in the USA	Han et al. (2022), https://doi.org/10.1016/j.jbusres.2022.06.011
Tech-enabled personalization	Desire for uniqueness, data-driven health	Wearable-based spa resorts	Gretzel et al. (2015), https://doi.org/10.1016/j.tourman.2014.10.014
Post-pandemic wellness	Safety, immunity, resilience	Nature resorts with biosecurity measures	Wen et al. (2022), https://doi.org/10.1016/j.annals.2022.103406

Sources: Adapted from Global Wellness Institute (2018), McKinsey & Company (2025), Swiss Education Group (SHMS) (n.d.), and Stellar Market Research (2024).

directly with environmental conservation efforts. This convergence of sustainability and wellness is indicative of a broader cultural shift toward ethical consumption and integral living.

5.2. Mental Health and Mindfulness Tourism

A defining trend in wellness tourism is the rise of mental health and mindfulness-focused travel, addressing global challenges of stress, burnout, and anxiety. Unlike spa tourism, which emphasizes physical rejuvenation, this stream prioritizes psycho-emotional healing through meditation, mindfulness, therapy retreats, and resilience training. Many tourists now view such retreats as early-intervention health care, blending professional therapy with holistic practices (Han et al., 2022). In Asia, these experiences draw on Buddhist traditions, offering meditation and compassion-based retreats, while in Western contexts, the demand emerges largely from corporate pressures and fast-paced lifestyles (Dillette & Douglas, 2020). By bridging leisure and public health, mental health tourism positions itself as both a restorative escape and a contributor to emotional resilience and long-term well-being.

5.3. Technology-enabled Personalization

Technology has transformed the way wellness experiences are created and offered, with personalization now becoming a foundation. Consumers are increasingly expecting wellness to be tailored to their specific health profiles, objectives, and beliefs, and technology is facilitating this customization on a large scale (Gretzel et al., 2015).

- *Wearable integration*: Devices such as Fitbits or sleep trackers are being woven into retreat programs, empowering travelers to monitor fitness, sleep, and mindfulness outcomes.
- *AI-driven customization*: Big data analytics and artificial intelligence allow resorts to design bespoke packages – from detox diets to meditation schedules – based on personal health histories (Li et al., 2021).
- *Immersive technologies*: Virtual reality meditation and augmented reality-enhanced spa experiences are creating novel pathways for stress reduction, particularly appealing to digital-native travelers.

5.4. Post-pandemic Wellness Tourism

The COVID-19 pandemic drastically transformed the context of international travel, and health and safety have become paramount decision-making considerations. In the post-pandemic period, wellness tourism has been a means of physical restoration, psychological recovery, and social healing. Those places that prioritize hygiene practices, touchless services, and immunity-enhancing initiatives will be more likely to build consumer confidence (Sigala, 2020).

5.5. Future-oriented Trends

In the future, researchers envision an expansion of wellness tourism into more diverse and socially responsible manifestations. This encompasses wellness services tailored to elderly populations, differently abled persons, and marginalized groups who have hitherto been left out of such services (Voigt & Pforr, 2014). In addition, the integration of wellness with cultural tourism is becoming increasingly popular, as tourists look for authentic experiences in interaction with indigenous traditions and communities rather than generic spa treatments (Smith & Puczkó, 2014).

6. Ethical Considerations in Marketing Wellness Tourism

Marketing in wellness tourism faces major ethical challenges as sacred practices like yoga, Ayurveda, or indigenous therapies risk losing authenticity when commodified (Voigt & Pforr, 2014). Western yoga, for instance, is often reduced to fitness, ignoring its spiritual roots (Miller & Redmond, 2010). Cultural appropriation, such as renaming Buddhist mindfulness for stress relief, further undermines origins (Kelly, 2012), while responsible co-created strategies with host communities enhance authenticity and satisfaction (Smith & Puczkó, 2014). Exaggerated claims about intangible outcomes damage trust, making transparency and certifications essential (Chen et al., 2022; Han et al., 2017). Wellness tourism has also been criticized as elitist, accessible mainly to wealthy travelers, highlighting the need for affordable, inclusive models (Dillette & Douglas, 2020; Voigt & Pforr, 2014).

Ethical frameworks, therefore, stress transparency, cultural sensitivity, authenticity, inclusivity, and sustainability as the foundation for responsible wellness branding (Kelly & Smith, 2021).

7. Future Research Directions

Wellness tourism has developed into a dynamic area of research, yet within the expanding body of knowledge, there are still blind spots that limit a complete understanding of how consumer psychology and marketing practices engage within this arena. A great deal of the literature has focused on motivations, satisfaction, and branding destinations, which has indeed enhanced the core theory. However, to best reflect the emerging complexity of wellness tourism, upcoming studies need to shift toward longitudinal, cross-cultural, technological, and ethical perspectives with a more focused attention to inclusivity. These efforts will not only develop academic theory but also create actionable intelligence for industry players operating within a fast-changing marketplace.

8. Conclusion

Wellness tourism has become among the quickest developing segments of international travel, driven by cultural trends toward health, balance, and significance (Kelly, 2012). Guided by consumer psychology and not economic theory, it lives off stresses, authenticity, and identity needs, and storytelling and emotional branding converting them into consumable commodities (Bockus, 2023). At its core are trust, perception, and identity construction, which make it more than recreation – it is symbolic lifestyle practice. Trends today such as sustainable wellness, mental health retreats, personalized tech, and pandemic recovery underscore its responsiveness, although threats of cultural commodification, exclusion, and hyperbole require ethical, transparent, and inclusive marketing (Smith & Puczkó, 2014). Future studies need to investigate long-term lifestyle effects (Han et al., 2017), cross-cultural drivers, and the effect of AI, wearables, and virtual reality technologies on authenticity (Su et al., 2020). Wellness tourism is ultimately cultural and psychological – a search for balance and meaning that, when responsibly fostered, can promote individual wellness, culture conservation, community empowerment, and sustainability.

References

Árpási, Z. (2018). Wellness tourism: What motivates the consumer. *Valahian Journal of Economic Studies*, *9*(23)(1), 33–40. https://doi.org/10.2478/vjes-2018-0009

Bockus, D. (2023). Cross-national analysis of wellness tourism concepts, tourists' motivations and service preferences. *Finnish Journal of Tourism Research*, *19*(1), 70–78. https://doi.org/10.33351/mt.131043

Chen, H., Huang, Y., & Fu, X. (2022). Understanding wellness tourism service quality and trust. *International Journal of Environmental Research and Public Health*, *19*(16), 10212. https://doi.org/10.3390/ijerph191610212

Cheng, X., Li, Y., & Wang, J. (2023). Health and wellness tourism motivation, perceived value, and behavioral intentions. *International Journal of Environmental Research and Public Health*, *20*(5), 1024. https://doi.org/10.3390/ijerph20051024

Dillette, A., & Douglas, A. (2020). The role of social media in wellness tourism identity. *Tourism Recreation Research*, *45*(4), 513–526. https://doi.org/10.3727/1098304 20X15758301227313

Dillette, A., Douglas, A., & Andrzejewski, C. (2021). Yoga tourism: Perceptions of authenticity and well-being. *Tourism Recreation Research*, *46*(2), 209–221. https://doi.org/ 10.3727/109830421X16106577919928

Font, X., & McCabe, S. (2017). Sustainability and marketing in tourism: Reconsidering sustainable tourism marketing. *Journal of Sustainable Tourism*, *25*(1), 1–15. https:// doi.org/10.1080/09669582.2017.1306020

Global Wellness Institute. (2018). *Global wellness tourism economy: November 2018 report*. Global Wellness Institute. https://globalwellnessinstitute.org/wp-content/ uploads/2018/11/GWI_GlobalWellnessTourismEconomyReport.pdf

Gretzel, U., Sigala, M., & Xiang, Z. (2015). Smart tourism: Foundations and developments. *Tourism Management*, *50*, 1–13. https://doi.org/10.1016/j.tourman.2014.10.014

Han, H., Jung, H., Kiatkawsin, K., & Kim, W. (2022). Wellness tourism and mental health: Marketing implications. *Journal of Business Research*, *142*, 684–695. https://doi. org/10.1016/j.jbusres.2022.06.011

Han, H., Kiatkawsin, K., Jung, H., & Kim, W. (2017). Wellness tourism and trust-building factors. *Tourism Management*, *63*, 123–135. https://doi.org/10.1016/j.tourman.2016.12.010

Kelly, C. (2012). Meditation retreats and tourism: Cultural appropriation or spiritual tourism? *Current Issues in Tourism*, *15*(4), 379–395. https://doi.org/10.1080/13683500. 2011.639556

Kelly, C., & Smith, M. (2021). Green wellness tourism and eco-consciousness. *Journal of Sustainable Tourism*, *29*(9), 1234–1248. https://doi.org/10.1080/09669582.2021.1874 398

Kim, H., Lim, J., & Lee, T. (2023). Segmenting wellness tourists by motivations: A study from Chungcheongbuk-do, Korea. *International Journal of Environmental Research and Public Health*, *20*(2), 1063. https://doi.org/10.3390/ijerph20021063

Li, X., Pearce, P. L., & Low, D. (2021). Media representation and personalized marketing in wellness tourism. *Journal of Travel & Tourism Marketing*, *38*(2), 176–191. https:// doi.org/10.1080/10548408.2021.1878512

Liao, C. (2023). Dimensions of the health benefits of wellness tourism. *International Journal of Environmental Research and Public Health*, *20*(2), 1872. https://doi.org/10.3390/ ijerph20021872

Mak, A., Wong, K. F., & Chang, R. (2009). Health or self-indulgence? Motivations for wellness tourism in Hong Kong. *Tourism Recreation Research*, *34*(2), 161–173. https://doi.org/10.1080/14616680902908677

Martins, P. (2025). Wellness tourism: A systematic literature review. *Tourism Review*, *80*(1), 45–63. https://doi.org/10.1080/24721735.2025.2467608

McKinsey & Company. (2025, May 29). *The future of wellness trends survey 2025*. McKinsey & Company. https://www.mckinsey.com/industries/consumer-packaged-goods/our-insights/future-of-wellness-trends

Miller, P., & Redmond, G. (2010). "I am yoga": Yoga tourism and authenticity in practice. *Tourism Recreation Research*, *35*(1), 17–27. https://doi.org/10.1080/11745398.2010 .9686841

Peng, C. (2025). Wellness tourism healing: A systematic review unveiling how wellness experiences impact consumer well-being. *Tourism Review*, *80*(2), 211–229. https:// doi.org/10.1108/TR-10-2024-0918

Sigala, M. (2020). Tourism and COVID-19: Impacts and implications for advancing and resetting industry and research. *Tourism Management Perspectives, 35*, 100530. https://doi.org/10.1016/j.tmp.2020.100530

Smith, M., & Puczkó, L. (2014). *Health, tourism and hospitality: Spas, wellness and medical travel*. CABI. https://doi.org/10.1079/9781845930686.0000

Stellar Market Research. (2024). *Wellness tourism market: Global industry analysis and forecast (2025–2032)*. Stellar Market Research. https://www.stellarmr.com/report/wellness-tourism-market/2368

Su, L., Swanson, S. R., & Chen, X. (2020). The impact of e-WOM and online engagement on wellness tourism decisions. *Sustainability, 12*(21), 8972. https://doi.org/10.3390/su12218972

Swiss Education Group (SHMS). (n.d.). *Wellness tourism: A growing trend in hospitality*. Swiss Hotel Management School. https://www.shms.com/en/news/wellness-tourism/

Voigt, C., & Pforr, C. (2014). *Wellness tourism: A destination perspective*. Routledge. https://doi.org/10.4324/9780203072013

Wen, J., Kozak, M., Yang, S., & Liu, F. (2022). Post-pandemic travel behavior: Recovery of wellness tourism. *Annals of Tourism Research, 92*, 103406. https://doi.org/10.1016/j.annals.2022.103406

Wong, I. A., Li, X., & Wang, W. (2020). Perceived authenticity in wellness tourism and its effect on trust. *Journal of Business Research, 109*, 468–481. https://doi.org/10.1016/j.jbusres.2019.10.045

Chapter 16

The Sociology of Wellness Tourism: Power, Place, and the Pursuit of Well-being in Global Capitalism

Kushagra Garg

Banasthali Vidyapith, Rajasthan, India

Abstract

This is a sociological analysis of how wellness tourism has grown from USD 974.59 billion in 2025 to USD 1.4 trillion by 2029 as a modality in systemic inequalities while promising liberation. Drawing on the work of Bourdieu, Said, and dependency theory, this study discloses how wellness tourism operates as a "field of distinction" wherein privileged groups reproduce class hierarchies through their modes of cultural consumption. The industry illustrates Orientalism in the way Eastern spiritual traditions are mined for Western quotidian consumption, obscuring neo-colonialist appropriation. Market data illustrate that North American consumers dominate 39.7% of market share, while the fastest growth occurs in the Asia-Pacific regions, whereby indigenous cultural practices are turned into commodified experiences. Digital wellness technologies fashion surveillance capitalism, wherein healing is transformed into algorithmic data. This is Foucauldian biopower – governance through inculcating bodily relations serving commercial rationality. The industry's feminization reproduces patriarchal assignments of care work despite empowering rhetoric. There is an environmental contradiction between sustainability claims and carbon footprint externalities, whereby privileged consumption displaces environmental costs onto less powerful populations. Wellness tourism channels legitimate needs for meaning into commodified consumption, reproducing the alienation it promises to address. The analysis identifies resistance through community-based initiatives that maintain cultural

Advancement in Medical and Wellness Tourism, Part A: Entrepreneurship and Technology, 207–224

doi:10.1108/978-1-80592-983-320261016

control and programs linking wellness to social justice education. These reflect directions toward equitable arrangements centered on collective well-being over individual optimization, respecting cultural integrity and sustainability. This investigation contributes to critical tourism studies through systematic analysis of wellness tourism as cultural capital accumulation within late global capitalism.

Keywords: Wellness tourism; cultural capital; orientalism; surveillance capitalism; feminization of care work; environmental sustainability; social inequality

1. Introduction

The modern wellness travel phenomenon, now valued at a market size of USD 974.59 billion in 2025 and set to skyrocket to USD 1.4 trillion in 2029 (Grand View Research, 2024), signifies something other than a simple extension of leisure consumption (Hartwell et al., 2018). This phenomenal growth trend, exhibiting compound annual growth rates above 9%, betrays a wholesale fissure in social fabric in late capitalist societies and exposes deeper tides of alienation, anomie, and spirituality vacuum that characterize modern life (Urry, 1990). What we have instead is not only a new market segment but a societal reaction to what Émile Durkheim foresightedly termed the normative crisis of modernity – the state wherein torrentially fast-transforming societies leave citizens lost in a sea of dissonant values, fraying social ties, and existential angst (Durkheim, 1951; Grabum & Jafari, 1991). Searching out wellness travel has solidified as a quintessentially modern mode of seeking out meaning and replenishment in a world beset by "liquid modernity," a term coined by sociologist Zygmunt Bauman to describe societies beset by ceaseless change, institutional volatility, and a dissolvent impact on conventional structures that previously lent coherence and direction to human life (Bauman, 2000, 2002, 2005; Franklin, 2003). COVID-19 pandemic has served to accelerate these impulses dramatically, studies reporting that 82% of consumers now rank wellness a chief imperative, entailing a sea change in collective consciousness regarding wellness, meaningfulness, and the good life. What this constitutes is not only a shift in consumer preference but proof of what Durkheim would describe as anomic crisis – a failure within regulatory institutions traditionally operating to control anticipations and aspirations within fixed social orders (Clegg & Baumeler, 2010; Leiper, 1979). Wellness travel's pandemic-driven uptick bespeaks profounder interactions between societies born out in Marx's concept of alienation inherent within capitalist production relations (Marx, 1867). Modern workers, further alienated from productive labor, genuine social relations, and internal capacities for creativity, find in wellness travel what daily life prevents them from having: corporeal experience, spirit connection, and genuine community. When seven-fifths of millennials indicate experiencing emotional perturbation, depression, and stress due to telecommuting arrangements, their resultant migration toward yoga retreats in Rishikesh, meditation centers in Dharamshala, and Ayurvedic healing in

Kerala signifies more than preference in lifestyle – it is a practice of resistance against the alienating conditions of modern capitalist relations to sociality.

But this seemingly liberatory practice of consumption belies the dialectical character of wellness tourism's social role. By extending genuine experiences of repair and affiliation, the sector at once serves as what Pierre Bourdieu would recognize as a field of cultural capital accumulation wherein privileged groups practice distinctions that reinforce existing rank orders while seeming to abolish them (Bourdieu, 1986; Petersen, 2005). Access to sophisticated global wellness possibilities – from classical Chinese medicine in Beijing to shamanic healing in Peru – is dependent upon modes of cultural competence, economic means, and social capital that systemically distribute along existing axes of class privilege and educational attainment (Wu & Wang, 2011). The spatial structure of wellness tourism consumption and production reveals long-standing axes of global inequality that resemble colonial relations between developed and developing economies (Britton, 1982; Frank, 1966). North America controls market share with 39.7% of global wellness travel expenditure in 2022, while the fastest growth rates cluster in Asian-Pacific locations, wherein traditional knowledge repertoires are converted into commodified experiences available internationally (Kotsis & Botsis, 2024; UNWTO, 2023). This process illustrates what dependency theorists pinpointed as structural arrangements sustaining global inequality – the removal of cultural and spiritual resources from peripheral areas to meet consumption demands at metropolitan centers in ways that seem benign and reciprocal (Santana Turegano, 2006). The sector's promotion of genuine spiritual practice and subjective transformations obfuscates deeper extraction of cultural materials and neo-colonial appropriation of natural resources (Ek & Hultman, 2008). When wellness tourists narrate life-altering journeys learning meditation alongside Himalayan gurus or undergoing healing therapy at native practitioners, they engage in what Edward Said termed Orientalist discourse – representational paradigms that fabricate "Eastern" civilizations as spiritually densely peopled but materially impoverished, incomprehensible but accessible within productivist categories from "the West." A multi-billion-dollar trade in commodified mindfulness meditation, yoga practice, and native healing rituals is a modern iteration of what Marx designated primitive accumulation – the violent disassociation of cultural epistemology from places of origin and its conversion into privatized property for global trade (Marx, 1867; Said, 1978).

The technical aspects of modern wellness travel unveil further layers of social control and monitoring that Michel Foucault would recognize as typical features of advanced liberalism in governance (Foucault, 1975). Digital monitoring of wellness metrics, biometric tracking, and computerization-based systems for personalized conduct create new forms of what Shoshana Zuboff calls "surveillance capitalism" – economies that draw out behavioral data to foretell and shape future behavior (Zuboff, 2019). Wellness travel participants become involuntary generators of data regarding their innermost experiences of healing therapy, spirituality, and subjective change that become valuable to construct better marketing schemes and tailor optimal commercial wellness programs (Lapointe et al., 2018).

Environmental contradictions inherent within wellness travel's growth model reveal intrinsic tensions between private consumption freedom and common ecological survival, typical of broader contradictions within late capitalist societies. The carbon emissions due to international wellness travel are a major cause of climate change, but this fact finds little discussion in within-industry rhetoric about living in harmony with nature and sustainable ways of living (Dietschy, 2008; Liu et al., 2023). This denial betrays what environmental sociologists recognize as the systemic offloading of environmental costs onto weaker populations while preserving privileged access to natural landscapes untouched by humanity's impacts for wellness consumption (Adey, 2009).

Perhaps above all else, wellness tourism's explosive growth takes place within wider contexts of social inequity, environmental rupture, and cultural change that pose basic questions about ongoing development patterns' sustainability and desirability (Sotiriadis, 2017). Neoliberal ideologies that privatize social evils rather than concealing common solutions to common problems directly parallel this industry's focus on personal change and optimization (Campos et al., 2017). When societal circumstances generate common experiences of stress, inefficacy, and alienation, market-based fixes such as wellness travel provide palliative relief while preserving underlying structural determinants (Chen et al., 2023). Through neither disparaging numerous people's actual benefits from wellness travel experiences nor discounting wellness travel industries' economic benefits to host populations, this analysis instead hopes to grasp wellness travel as a multifaceted social phenomenon that both promises freedom's escape from modern life's stresses while recapitulating deeper social circumstances making such escape appear both desirable and imperative. Through extended sociological examination informed both by classical theoretical thought and recent empirical scholarship, this chapter probes how wellness travel serves both symptom and remedy to deeper social pathologies characterizing our era's historical juncture – a lens into contradictions inherent within seeking personal solutions to common problems within global capitalism's structural determinations.

2. The Political Economy of Wellness Tourism

2.1. Global Market Dynamics and Structural Dependencies

The extraordinary financial performance of the wellness tourism sector lays bare inherent asymmetries in international economic relationships that reflect larger structures of center–periphery dependency (Frank, 1966; Prebensen & Xie, 2017). Although North America holds the greatest market share at 34%, generating a 2023 contribution of USD 299.82 billion (Armbrecht & Andersson, 2020; UNWTO, 2023), growth rates reach or exceed 13% compound annually in Asia-Pacific locations such as India and China (Bigné et al., 2020; Kotsis & Botsis, 2024). This spatial split between market share and growth opportunity sheds the same light on what dependency school thinkers long pointed out as structural prerequisites to persistent global inequalities (Frank, 1966; Santana Turegano, 2006).

The number of jobs further highlights these dynamics. Wellness tourism supports directly 11.7 million jobs while creating a total of USD 1.3 trillion in economic impact (Aitchison, 2001; Global Wellness Institute, 2023), but still sees these benefits mainly invested in developed economies (Anderson, 2005). India's market in medical tourism alone was valued in 2022 at USD 7.417 billion and is projected to reach USD 42.237 billion in 2032 (Fortune Business Insights, 2024). Yet all this growth is in a scenario where international patients went up from 430,000 in 2016 to 700,000 in 2019 (Fortune Business Insights, 2024) and constitutes a flow of finances that while economically impressive presents essential questions regarding healthcare equity and allocations within native populations.

Wellness economies have features that dependency school thinkers such as André Gunder Frank pinpointed in underdevelopment: siphoning surplus value out of peripheral areas to enrich metropolitan centers (Ek & Hultman, 2008; Frank, 1966). When wellness travel emanating from developed countries goes to poor nations in search of genuine treatments in Ayurvedic medicine, Chinese medicine, or Buddhist meditation, it engages a process of cultural siphoning akin to long precedents in natural resource exploitation but in nominally harmless manifestations (Burney, 2012; Said, 1993).

2.2. The Commodification of Traditional Knowledge

The transformation of indigenous healing practices into marketable wellness experiences represents a particularly acute form of what Marx termed primitive accumulation – the violent separation of producers from their means of production (Marx, 1867). Traditional knowledge systems that evolved over centuries within specific cultural and ecological contexts are abstracted, standardized, and repackaged for global consumption, often stripping away the social relations and spiritual frameworks that gave these practices their original meaning and efficacy (Said, 1993; Taussig, 1993).

Take the worldwide popularity of yoga that has become inseparable from wellness travel in places such as Rishikesh, India. Although yoga's commodification has certainly provided local areas with new economic prospects, this has practically changed yoga's social importance (Stock, 2020). What was once a holistic philosophical and spiritual system inherent in certain cultural settings has been converted into a commodified practice tailored to suit global tourist expectations who demand genuine but affordable spiritual experiences (Ferguson, 1994).

This commodification process works via what theorist James Ferguson has labeled "dehistoricization" – a process of stripping practices out of historical and cultural contexts in order to render them marketable to global audiences. What is left is a type of cultural appropriation wherein mostly overseas parties stand to gain while local populations both become economically reliant on this tourist income and slowly lose integrity within their traditional systems of knowledge (Bruner, 2005; Ferguson, 1994).

3. Cultural Capital and Social Distinction in Wellness Practices

3.1. Bourdieu's Framework Applied to Wellness Tourism

Pierre Bourdieu's work on cultural capital is a sophisticated analytical optic we can use to explore wellness travel's function within a process of social distinction (Bourdieu, 1986). A quest for wellness through travel makes up what Bourdieu called embodied cultural capital – knowledge, abilities, and predispositions that mark their possessor as cultured and distinguished from a social perspective (Pine & Gilmore, 1998). It requires some cultural abilities to negotiate highly developed wellness travel services from an Ayurvedic consultation to a retreat in mindfulness – abilities differentially distributed among social groups (Vada et al., 2019).

The economics of wellness tourist participation exhibit dramatic exclusionary dynamics. Wellness tourists pay on average 130% higher rates compared to other such tourists (Trinanda et al., 2022), squarely limiting participation to those who possess large streams of disposable incomes (World Bank, 2022). Barriers extend far beyond basic economic access. Effective wellness tourist participation involves acquaintance with concepts borrowed out of psychology, spirituality, alternative medicine, and world cultures – a type of knowledge Bourdieu showed systemically distributed along class location and schooling levels (Bourdieu, 1986).

Institutionally encoded cultural capital needed to engage in wellness tourism consumption takes a variety of forms. Academic credentials that grant exposure to such concepts as mindfulness, holistic health, and alternative medicine help to navigate wellness tourism products. Linguistic ability helps to interact substantively with practitioners and works out of other cultural histories. Most characteristically perhaps, social capital utilized to obtain information about genuine versus commodified states of wellness often relies upon networks that in turn are stratified along lines of class privilege (Simmel, 1957).

3.2. The Wellness Habitus and Its Social Functions

Bourdieu's habitus concept – embodied dispositions to perception and practice – is especially enlightening when used to describe wellness consumption travel (Cohen, 1988). A wellness habitus involves a particular attachment to the body, to health, and to self-improvement that closely matches what was dubbed "the politics of life itself" by sociologist Nikolas Rose (Rose, 2007) – a matter of treating the self as a task to be continuously optimized, monitored, and intervened upon – attitudes that aren't universal but seem quite particular historical and social circumstances.

Development of a wellness habitus requires long-term exposure to discourses that build a version of health as a personal responsibility that entailed active governance rather than a simple negation of illness (Heelas, 2008). This theoretical model, paradoxically extolled as universally desirable, actually instantiates characteristically modern occidental ideals of selfhood that can be in tension with other societies' fatalistic or collectivist conceptions of health and well-being (Taussig, 1993).

Studies prove overwhelmingly that participants in wellness travel hail from urban, educated middle to upper-middle-class backgrounds in mature economies (Deleuze, 1992). This concentration presents wellness travel as a "field of cultural production" à la Bourdieu (Bourdieu, 1986) where certain types of distinction are produced, disseminated, and valued (Ahn et al., 2019). Being able to speak about one's life-changing stint in a meditation retreat in Nepal or an Ayurvedic cleansing in Kerala constitutes a type of cultural currency that betrays both financial ability and cultural acumen (Pratt, 1992).

4. Gender, Power, and Embodied Experience

4.1. The Feminization of Wellness Tourism

Wellness tourism has strong gender dynamics mirroring overall tendencies in how care work, emotional work, and somatic practice become gendered in modern societies (Roelofsen & Minca, 2018; Zhang et al., 2024). About 44% of the tourism sector's labor force is comprised of women but this feminization only holds in service positions and not in ownership or management positions (Dias & Dias, 2019). This gendered employment split applies to consumption patterns too, with women making up most wellness tourism participants but men appearing most often in positions within wellness tourism business that require a lead function (Stock, 2020).

Emphasis on physical practice, emotional wellness, and relationship healing in wellness travel chimes with historic research in assigning family health care and emotional caregiving to women among feminist scholars (Hochschild, 1989). What wellness travel promises – generating empowering spaces for self-nurture and personal rejuvenation – may be especially attractive to those who perform what Arlie Hochschild termed "the second shift" of domestic work after paid employment (Armbrecht & Andersson, 2020).

But this feminization of wellness travel participation takes place in other contexts of gender inequity that influence both access and experience. Women's travel motivation research shows that travel destination selection and activity engagement is powerfully impacted by concerns about safety, and all-women wellness tours appear in response to gendered risks in travel situations (Vada et al., 2019). The necessity for such differentiated products sheds light on how gender inequity structures even ostensibly empowering experiences such as wellness travel (Sthapit et al., 2023).

4.2. Embodiment and the Politics of Self-care

This attention to embodied experience in wellness travel crosses over into broader questions about bodily autonomy, medicosocial authority, and the politics around self-care. A turn toward complementary healing practices is usually a response against what has been analyzed by medical sociologists as a process of medicalization of everyday life – an expansion of medicosocial authority into areas previously thought to be normal departures within human experience (O'Doherty et al., 2013).

But this resistance works within a neoliberal context in which responsibility for health consequences falls increasingly on consumers instead of social institutions or communal healthcare provision (Campos et al., 2017). Promotion of wellness tourism's empowering narrative – calling upon people to "take control" of their health through consumer choices – matches accordingly closely broader neoliberal thought that privatizes social concerns and turns structural concerns into personal ones (Campos et al., 2017).

Promoting quantified self-tracking in recent wellness culture is an exemplary description of philosopher Michel Foucault's idea of biopower – forms of power that act through the constitution of certain relations to one's own life processes and body (Foucault, 2008). Wellness smartphone applications urge users to observe cycles of sleep, meditation duration, and other inner operations, creating a form of self-surveillance that is consonant with large-scale governmental rationalities in mature capitalist states (Deleuze, 1992).

5. The Colonial Gaze and Orientalist Discourses

5.1. Postcolonial Analysis of Wellness Destinations

Wellness geography exhibits ongoing trends that resemble colonial dynamics between developed and developing markets (Britton, 1982; Franklin, 2003). Asian destinations – India, Thailand, Nepal, and Bali – dominate wellness marketing brochures, and they generally appear in what Edward Said termed Orientalist depiction: descriptions that create "Eastern" civilizations as spiritually affluent but materially poor, incomprehensible but accessible inasmuch as they can be interpreted via western hermeneutics (Said, 1978).

Wellness tourist destination promotion stereotypically employs imagery and rhetoric that borrows colonial-era tropes about Asian societies as ageless, spiritual, and closer to nature than modern Western societies (Grabum & Jafari, 1991). It has a number of ideological functions: they can describe the journey to these places as a precondition to fulfillment spiritually out of reach back home, while paradoxically portraying Westerners as sophisticated consumers capable of discriminating between a genuine cultural experience (Anderson, 2005).

This idea of "discovering" old knowledge via wellness travel recycles what Mary Louise Pratt called "imperial eyes" – modes of vision that frame the Western observer as an active subject of knowledge production while constraining native populations to objects of exotic fascination (Pratt, 1992). When wellness travel promoters tell about their transformative journeys learning meditation at the feet of Himalayan gurus or undergoing healing therapy at native healers' hands, they often use narrative structures that focalize their own process of self-discovery while sidelining local practitioners' agency and subjectivity (Bruner, 2005; Burney, 2012).

5.2. Cultural Appropriation and Spiritual Commodification

The commodification of sacred practice poses basic questions about cross-cultural appropriation and the morality of cross-cultural exchange (Cohen, 1988).

Extracting specific practices out of religious and cultural contexts in which they were realized and put into circulation around the world tends to remove social relations, ceremonial structures, and ethical obligations that provided these practices with a use within originating communities (Taussig, 1993).

Take the commodification of mindfulness meditation in wellness travel. Though rooted in Buddhist meditation practices informed by mature philosophical thought (Heelas, 2008), mindfulness has been widely secularized and privatized for mass consumption in the West. Through this process, this practice is rendered accessible to a wider range of people but then loses whatever communal and ethical aspects Buddhist practitioners think central to genuine spiritual growth (Deleuze, 1992).

Commodification generally consists of what anthropologist Michael Taussig termed "mimesis" – production of copies that pretend to embody the essences of originals but actually carry projections and assumptions of those who make copies (Taussig, 1993). Centers for wellness retreats that provide "real" spirituality may program sanitized variations on classic practice designed to fulfill Western demands about comfort levels, personalized attention, and quantifiable results (Stock, 2020).

6. Information Technologies and Surveillance Capitalism

6.1. Quantified Self and Biopolitical Governance

Wellness tourism's incorporation of digital technology is part of wider changes in how highly developed capitalist societies regulate populations by fostering certain relations to health, productive activity, and self-optimization (Lapointe & Coulter, 2020). Societies of "control," named after Gilles Deleuze's concept, entail exercises of power that work through perpetual modulation rather than scientific confinement, prodding individuals to take internal responsibility for optimizing themselves in a range of life spaces (Deleuze, 1992).

Wellness travel increasingly integrates digital tracking technologies that hold out the promise to maximize travel experiences' transformational power. Travelers to wellness retreats may be given wearable technology to keep track of sleep patterns, levels of stress, and physical activity levels, drawing out meticulous profiles of physiological reactions to a range of interventions (Liu et al., 2023). These technologies carry forward Btihaj Ajana's "the biopolitics of the quantified self" beyond these boundaries into tourist settings, pushing toward ways of self-surveillance consonant with wider governmental rationalities (Ajana, 2017).

Information produced by these monitoring systems then becomes not only valuable at a personal level of self-optimization but at a larger level of wellness tourism product and service development (Roelofsen & Minca, 2018). It creates what Shoshana Zuboff termed "surveillance capitalism" – economic systems that draw behavioral data out of users to foresee and shape future behaviors (Zuboff, 2019). Wellness tourism participants become unwilling sources of material out of which can be developed better marketing campaigns, better retreat programs, and better customized wellness advice (Lapointe et al., 2018).

6.2. Digital Divides and Technological Exclusion

Growing incorporation of digital technology in wellness travel generates new exclusion that crosses existing social inequality patterns (Vada et al., 2019). By placing a strong focus on digital detoxing and going back to a truer way of living, engagement increasingly depends upon unevenly globalized technological literacy and digital connectivity (Trinanda et al., 2022).

Digital divide has a special impact on future wellness travel spots in emerging economies due to poor internet infrastructures and computer literacy limiting local practitioners' capacity to promote services internationally (Kotsis & Botsis, 2024). Smaller guesthouses, classical healers, and household wellness centers have no developed technical capacity to rival professionally advertised resort centers dominating virtual booking websites (Santana Turegano, 2006).

It mediates this access via technology that this "platform capitalism," digital researchers explain – economic arrangements in which large digital platforms extract value both from consumers and service providers and exercise control over terms of interaction (Ek & Hultman, 2008). Local wellness practitioners who outsource to corporate-owned overseas platforms further embed wellness tourism within global techno-economic dependency structures (Sotiriadis, 2017).

7. Environmental Sustainability and Ecological Impacts

7.1. The Environmental Paradoxes of Wellness Tourism

Wellness tourism's emphasis on natural scenery, nature balance, and sustainable lifestyles is fundamentally at odds with the green footprint such wellness tourism has left behind (Shri Balasaheb Tirpude College of Hotel Management, 2024). Those emissions of greenhouse gases due to overseas journeys to wellness destinations create a major cause of global warming, but this contradiction is not often taken into account within wellness tourism promotion and debate (Liu et al., 2023). Studies on tourism development's environmental effects note that wellness tourist spots usually have fast-infrastructure development that places a strain on the local ecosystem and available resources (Kuey.net, 2025). Building resort centers, spas, and wellness centers usually involves deforestation, disturbing existing water systems, and upsetting native wildlife. These environmental expenses usually get externalized – paid for by native societies and ecosystems instead of factored into prices paid by wellness tourists (Global Wellness Institute, 2024).

Focus on genuine natural exposure in wellness travel generates "environmental privilege," a concept environmental sociologists use to describe how wealthy consumers can avail themselves of untouched natural spaces while environmental expenses required to provide such access accrue to subordinate groups (Tandfonline, 2023). When wellness vacationers demand meditation retreats in untouched forest landscapes or yoga retreats on secluded beaches, they engage in environmental consumption that is dependent upon exclusion of native people from natural spaces they have traditionally occupied (Global Health Trip, 2025).

7.1.1. Climate Change and Wellness Tourism Futures

Wellness travel's projected growth trends unfold against a climate change intensification background that threatens environmental foundations on which many wellness traveler experiences depend (Jetir.org, 2025). Sea levels rise to threaten beach wellness destinations, changes in precipitation affect forest environments valued for spiritual qualities, and unusual weather events disrupt predictable seasonal change that characterizes much wellness traveler product. Industry reactions to these difficulties demonstrate the inadequacy of consumer choice as a solution to common environmental concerns. Even as wellness tourist marketing places a growing premium upon sustainability and environmental stewardship, these efforts tend to appeal to small behavioral changes – selecting environmentally friendly accommodations or volunteering in environmental restoration – rather than confronting the inherent incompatibility between overseas travel and environmental sustainability (Lifestyle Sustainability Directory, 2025).

Such "carbon offsetting," featuring increasingly in wellness tourist marketing, is a classic case of what environmental justice researchers describe as "green colonialism" – arrangements whereby affluent consumers can maintain high-carbon lifestyles by buying environmental credits in developing-world projects. Offset schemes often entail the rezoning out or eviction of indigenous people out of historic lands under conservation banners.

7.2. Alternative Spiritualties and Commodification of the Sacred

Inclusion of non-traditional spirituality within wellness tourism practice can be understood within broader shifts in religious and spiritual practice in post-capitalist societies (Romão et al., 2017). Loss of institutional religious authority and privatization of religious practice have given rise to "subjective life spirituality," or spirituality practice that focuses on subjective rather than collectively based doctrine or institutional mediatorial practice (Ferguson, 1994).

There seems to be an obligation on wellness travel websites to present places where individuals might discover a genuine spirituality, but still be free to select and choose whatever applies to furthering their own spirituality (Romão et al., 2017). This sits comfortably alongside what has been dubbed "the culture of narcissism" – social arrangements which promote a highly developed self-absorption but undermine loyalties to public institutions and collective aspirations – initially identified by cultural commentator Christopher Lasch (Lasch, 1979). This constructed spiritual marketplace within wellness tourism settings generally comprises what religious studies experts have termed "commodified syncretism" – a selective drawing on elements across various religious traditions that is determined by consumer demand and not by religious authorities or cultural practitioners (Conover & Timothy, 2021). Travelers to wellness retreats may engage in Christian reflective practice, Buddhist meditation, Hindu yoga practice, and native healing rituals within a single program, generating a spirituality in which personal change counts above all else while cultural specificity or religious integrity receive secondary consideration (Aggarwal et al., 2008; Laing & Weiler, 2008).

7.3. Sacred and Secular in Tourism Environment

Sacred/secular distinctions become doubly ambiguous within wellness tourist contexts wherein spiritual practice is commodified as therapy but not religious practice (Pulido-Fernández et al., 2024). Its secularization makes accessible to broad-based audience certain spiritual practices while perhaps sacrificing transcendent aspects that practitioners evaluate central to genuine spiritual practice (Urry, 1990).

This redeployment of pilgrimage sites to spa destinations illustrates these tensions (Leiper, 1979). Once centuries-old pilgrimage sites among religious pilgrims, these sacred spaces now anchor secular wellness travelers who search out transformative travel experiences without accepting religious frameworks long responsible for such experiences (Cohen, 1988). This begets what anthropologist Erik Cohen termed "emergent authenticity" – new modes of meaning that emerge around tourist practice while perhaps unsettling older sacred geographies (Cohen, 1988).

Sacred commercialization brings foundational questions about how spirituality authenticity is entwined within relationships within markets (Bruner, 2005). When meditation teachers or traditional healers or spirit guides become service providers within tourist markets, then relationships with guests become understood within commercial instead of community or spirituality obligations (Kim et al., 2012). Such a move can provide greater accessibility while potentially putting depth and quality on a shelf within how spirituality is transmitted (Pine & Gilmore, 1998).

7.4. Sacred and Secular in Tourism Environment

Sacred/secular divisions become even more blurred within wellness tourist paradigms where spirituality is marketed as a therapy rather than a religious activity. Its secularization opens to a mass audience some spiritual practices while possibly forfeiting transcendent elements deemed central to genuine spiritual practice among practitioners.

This redefinition of pilgrimage sites to wellness locations makes such tensions visible. Once centuries-old pilgrimage sites among religious pilgrims, these sacred places today welcome secular wellness travelers who search for transformative vacation experiences but not in religious frameworks that once directed such experiences. This generates what anthropologist Erik Cohen has termed "emergent authenticity" – new patterns of signification that emanate about tourist practice but perhaps unsettle older geographies of the sacred.

Sacred commercialization raises foundational questions about how spirituality authenticity is entwined in relationships within markets. If spirit guides, meditation teachers, or traditional healers become service providers within tourist markets, then relationships with guests become mediated within commercial instead of community or spirituality obligations. Such a change might raise accessibility while potentially shelving depth and quality within how spirituality is approached.

8. Resistance, Agency, and Alternative Possibilities

8.1. Local Agency and Tourism Development

Regardless of these structural constraints laid out within this investigation, wellness tourist spots are not simply silent targets for international economic pressures (Global Wellness Institute, 2025). Local communities, practitioners, and businesspersons exercise a variety of forms of agency in how wellness tourist development proceeds within a nation's borders (Shams et al., 2023). An awareness of these forms of adaptation and resistance creates possibilities for different ends toward wellness tourist development that is culturally appropriate and equitable (Papageorgiou & Parisi, 2019).

Community-based wellness tourism programs can be considered a type of alternative to dominated development paradigms put forward by global tourism companies (Li et al., 2023). Such programs entail community-held control and decision-making authority across tourism development processes, such that any benefits remain internal to communities while cultural practices remain intact and hold social relevance (Polat & Koseoglu, 2023).

In places such as Kerala, India, community-oriented centers have created alternative approaches that present genuine healing opportunities to foreign guests while still having roots in classical knowledge systems and benefiting local practitioners (Chauhan et al., 2023). These programs model some alternative possibilities for wellness tourism development that sidestep the most exploitative aspects of cultural commodification while generating economics for native populations (Roostika, 2019).

8.2. Transformative Potential and Authentic Encounter

While this conversation has highlighted the erroneous elements within wellness travel, it will be shortsighted to dismiss entirely the potentials that this sector has to bring productive cross-cultural contact and personal transformation (Lifestyle Sustainability Directory, 2025). Some categories of wellness travel have potentials for genuine cultural exchange and spiritual development that benefit travel participants and native communities (Sirgy & Uysal, 2021).

The central difference seems to reside in the nature of relationships that foster between locals and visiting practitioners (Alsulamy et al., 2025). When wellness tourism provides occasions for continued interaction, reciprocal learning, and mutual reciprocation instead of consumption on a singular dimension, it has a chance to transmit cultural awareness and subjective development beyond personal change to wider social relations (Tourism Tiger, 2016).

Studies combining wellness practice and social justice or environmentally restorative work or community development programs provide some possible ways in which wellness travel could be reframed to respond to rather than replicate social inequities (Global Wellness Institute, 2024). Such programs acknowledge that personal well-being is irrevocably entwined in broader social circumstances and environmental well-being (Wiltshier, 2020).

9. Implications for Tourism Development and Social Policy

9.1. Toward More Equitable Wellness Tourism

The debate sharpened in this chapter has several consequences for developing a more culturally relevant and equal model of wellness travel (Global Wellness Institute, 2024). It operates at a variety of levels ranging from individual consumer choices to international policy frameworks within which travel development and cultural exchange will take place (UNWTO, 2018).

At policy levels, tourist-generating and tourist-receiving governments can establish policies safeguarding traditional knowledge systems but ensuring local communities' benefits accrue from tourist development (Tourism.gov.in, 2023). It can be anything from intellectual property rights to traditional healing systems to community consultation requirements in tourist development initiatives and how revenues collected from tourists can be used instead of replacing local cultural institutions (UNESCO, 2025).

Tour programs might be able to enable possible wellness travelers to better evaluate travel decisions' environmental and cultural effects (Global Wellness Institute, 2024). By thinking about concerns regarding cultural appropriation, environmental sustainability, and financial equity rather than shopping for whatever is most exotic or personally transformative available within reach, tourists might be better equipped to assess things within these travel decisions (Ottaviani, 2024).

9.2. The Future of Wellness and Social Well-being

Continuing growth in the wellness tourism sector takes place against wider background patterns of social injustice, environmental emergency, and cultural change that pose essential questions concerning sustainability and desirability of existing patterns of development (Lifestyle Sustainability Directory, 2025). Prioritization of personal change and optimization within the sector resonates closely with neoliberal thought that privatizes social difficulties while burying communitarian solutions to common difficulties (Duffy, 2015).

It is possible that other wellness strategies could highlight social well-being, environmental sustainability, and social equity instead of optimization at an individual level and consumption (Pecheniuk, 2025). Such strategies would account for how individual well-being and happiness intersect naturally with broader societal determinants such as unequal economics, environment quality, and diversity of culture (Slocum, 2019).

The effects of the COVID-19 pandemic on worldwide travel gave a preview of possible alternative futures (Kiyotani, 2024). The sudden decline in global travel made apparent both the environmental impact of the travel industry and the economic vulnerability of numerous destinations to tourist revenues (Barreto Kiyotani, 2024). Recovery initiatives might emphasize local travel development, environmental sustainability, and community well-being instead of resuming pre-pandemic growth patterns (Global Wellness Institute, 2024).

10. Conclusion

This wide-ranging sociological investigation of wellness travel demonstrates a multifaceted phenomenon that holds out promises both of personal change and freedom while recapitulating old structures of social injustice, cultural appropriation, and natural environmental exploitation (Bourdieu, 1986; Said, 1978). Its meteoric growth curve registers a very real need within late capitalist societies to connect with meaning, community, and naturalistic health care and well-being, but within a context of growing individualization, ecological catastrophe, and spiritlessness (Marx, 1867; Urry, 1990).

But the existing format of wellness travel mainly redirects these rightful societal demands into consumption patterns that serve educated and powerful societal sections while siphoning value out of poor societies and natural sources (Frank, 1966). The privatization of age-old knowledge practices into commodified wellness retreats is a typical case of cultural appropriation and neo-colonization of natural assets that continue in full swing even after formal political decolonization (Said, 1993; Taussig, 1993).

The theoretical lenses developed within this chapter – having borrowed Bourdieu's research on cultural capital (Bourdieu, 1986), dependency theory's observations on global inequality (Frank, 1966), and postcolonial dissent on Orientalist discourse (Said, 1978) – illuminate how wellness travel functions as a tool of social distinction and cultural domination. By enveloping itself within narratives about true spirituality and subjective transformation, the wellness enterprise masks how it works to reinforce current structures while implementing new structures of exclusion based upon cultural literacy, economic capacity, and technological connectivity (Foucault, 2008; Zuboff, 2019).

Yet this critical assessment need not obscure genuine possibilities for differently equitable and culturally respectful wellness travel development (Bruner, 2005). Community-based programs, programs combining wellness practice and social justice studies, and initiatives prioritizing cultural exchange over consumption suggest alternative prospects deserving encouragement and development (Cohen, 1988; Sthapit et al., 2023).

Wellness tourism's future will be largely determined if such trends toward further commodification and technological mediation prevail or if such alternative models prioritizing community well-being, cultural integrity, and environmental sustainability become ascendant (Global Wellness Institute, 2024). It's not a decision about preferring demand-driven at a level of consumption but rather a subject involving common political activism to resolve structurally rooted inequalities informing global tourist development (Lapointe & Coulter, 2020).

As wellness travel continues on a projected growth path to reach USD 2.05 trillion in 2034 (Precedence Research, 2025), the consequences of these decisions become correspondingly weightier. The growth of the industry will be a force either for broader and more sustainable global cultural interchange or will be a cause of further solidification of current privilege-based and exploitative patterns of global cultural interchange within the lofty veneer of subjective renewal and transcendent spirituality (Urry, 1990).

The sociological imagination developed in this chapter makes wellness travel a window onto broader questions regarding social injustice, cultural theft, and global capitalism's possibilities and limitations for human flourishing (Mills, 1959). Understanding these processes is vital not only to a more critical gaze upon wellness travel but to a response to broader social conditions which render such forms of commodified spirituality indispensable in the first instance (Marx, 1867). Traveling in search of well-being ends up mirroring broader social imperatives for productive work, supportive societies, and sustainable relationships between human beings and natural landscapes. Meeting such imperatives adequately will involve transcending household consumer solutions in favor of communal ways that identify social justice, environmental sustainability, and cultural diversity as bases for genuine human flourishing (Bauman, 2000).

References

Adey, P. (2009). Facing airport security: Affect, biopolitics, and the preemptive securitisation of the mobile body. *Environment and Planning D: Society and Space*, *27*(2), 274–295.

Ahn, Y., Hyun, S. S., & Kim, I. (2019). City residents' perception of MICE tourism impacts and their support intentions. *Journal of Travel & Tourism Marketing*, *36*(4), 461–475.

Aitchison, C. (2001). Theorizing other discourses of tourism, gender and culture: Can the subaltern speak (in tourism)? *Tourist Studies*, *1*(2), 133–147.

Anderson, B. (2005). *Imagined communities: Reflections on the origin and spread of nationalism* (Revised edition). Verso.

Armbrecht, J., & Andersson, T. D. (2020). The event experience and its impact on destination image and loyalty intentions. *Journal of Destination Marketing & Management*, *18*, 100471.

Bauman, Z. (2000). *Liquid modernity*. Polity Press.

Bauman, Z. (2002). *Society under siege*. Polity Press.

Bauman, Z. (2005). *Liquid life*. Polity Press.

Bigné, E., Fuentes-Moraleda, L., Muñoz-Miquel, A., & Martínez-Ruiz, M. P. (2020). Memorable tourism experiences versus ordinary experiences analysed through user-generated content. *Journal of Hospitality and Tourism Management*, *45*, 309–318.

Bourdieu, P. (1986). The forms of capital. In J. Richardson (Ed.), *Handbook of theory and research for the sociology of education* (pp. 241–258). Greenwood.

Britton, S. G. (1982). The political economy of tourism in the third world. *Annals of Tourism Research*, *9*(3), 331–358.

Bruner, E. M. (2005). *Culture on tour: Ethnographies of travel*. University of Chicago Press.

Burney, S. (2012). *Pedagogy of the other: Edward Said, postcolonial theory and strategies for critique*. Peter Lang.

Campos, A. C., Mendes, J., Valle, P. O. D., & Scott, N. (2017). Co-creation experiences: Attention and memorability. *Journal of Travel & Tourism Marketing*, *34*(9), 1309–1336.

Chen, H., Weismayer, C., & Pícha, K. (2023). How does co-creation lead to memorable tourism experiences? A systematic literature review of co-creation in tourism. *Journal of Travel Research*, *62*(5), 1101–1121.

Clegg, S., & Baumeler, C. (2010). Essai: From iron cages to liquid modernity in organization analysis. *Organization Studies*, *31*(12), 1713–1733.

Cohen, E. (1988). Traditions in the qualitative sociology of tourism. *Annals of Tourism Research*, *15*(1), 29–46.

Deleuze, G. (1992). Postscript on the societies of control. October, *59*, 3–7.

Dias, Á., & Dias, R. (2019). The role of memorable tourism experiences in destination image and loyalty: Evidence from a cultural heritage site. *International Journal of Tourism Research*, *21*(4), 568–576.

Dietschy, P. (2008). Making the people healthy, wealthy and wise? Sport in Europe during the 1930s. *The International Journal of the History of Sport*, *25*(11), 1438–1455.

Durkheim, E. (1951). *Suicide: A study in sociology* (J. A. Spaulding & G. Simpson, Trans.). Free Press. (Original work published 1897)

Ek, R., & Hultman, J. (2008). Tourism and technologies of power. In *Tourism, technologies of power* (pp. 1–14). Channel View Publications.

Ferguson, J. (1994). *The anti-politics machine: Development, depoliticization, and bureaucratic power in Lesotho*. University of Minnesota Press.

Fortune Business Insights. (2024). *Medical tourism market size, share, global growth report, 2032*. https://www.fortunebusinessinsights.com/industry-reports/medical-tourism-market-100681

Foucault, M. (1975). *Discipline and punish: The birth of the prison* (A. Sheridan, Trans.). Pantheon Books.

Foucault, M. (2008). *The birth of biopolitics: Lectures at the Collège de France 1978–1979* (G. Burchell, Trans.). Palgrave Macmillan.

Frank, A. G. (1966). *The development of underdevelopment*. New England Free Press.

Franklin, A. (2003). The tourist syndrome: An interview with Zygmunt Bauman. *Tourist Studies*, *3*(2), 205–217.

Global Wellness Institute. (2023). *Global wellness tourism economy report*. https://globalwellnessinstitute.org/wp-content/uploads/2018/06/GWI_2013_and_2014_Global_Wellness_Tourism_Economy_Report_Final.pdf

Grand View Research. (2024). *Wellness tourism market size & trends analysis report, 2030*. https://www.grandviewresearch.com/industry-analysis/wellness-tourism-market

Grabum, N. H., & Jafari, J. (1991). Introduction: Tourism social science. *Annals of Tourism Research*, *18*(1), 1–11.

Hartwell, H., Fyall, A., Willis, C., Page, S., Ladkin, A., & Hemingway, A. (2018). Progress in tourism and destination wellbeing research. *Current Issues in Tourism*, *21*(16), 1830–1892.

Heelas, P. (2008). *Spiritualities of life: New age romanticism and consumptive capitalism*. Blackwell.

Hochschild, A. R. (1989). *The second shift*. Viking.

Kim, J. H., Ritchie, J. R. B., & McCormick, B. (2012). Development of a scale to measure memorable tourism experiences. *Journal of Travel Research*, *51*(1), 12–25.

Kotsis, N., & Botsis, M. (2024). Theories of dependency and tourism. *International Journal of Research Publication and Reviews*, *5*(3), 5492–5504.

Lapointe, D., & Coulter, R. (2020). Biopolitics and tourism: A systematic literature review. *Annals of Tourism Research*, *82*, 102928.

Lapointe, D., Sarrasin, B., & Benjamin, C. (2018). Tourism and the biopolitics of the sharing economy. *Journal of Sustainable Tourism*, *26*(9), 1463–1478.

Lasch, C. (1979). *The culture of narcissism: American life in an age of diminishing expectations*. Norton.

Leiper, N. (1979). The framework of tourism: Towards a definition of tourism, tourist, and the tourist industry. *Annals of Tourism Research*, *6*(4), 390–407.

Liu, L., Zhou, Y., & Sun, X. (2023). The impact of the wellness tourism experience on tourist well-being: The mediating role of tourist satisfaction. *Sustainability*, *15*(4), 3421.

Marx, K. (1867). *Capital: A critique of political economy*, Volume I (B. Fowkes, Trans.). Vintage Books. (Original work published 1867)

O'Doherty, D., De Cock, C., Rehn, A., & Ashcraft, K. L. (2013). New organizational forms: Where do we stand? *Management Learning*, *44*(2), 136–144.

Petersen, R. A. (2005). Problems in comparative research: The example of omnivorousness. *Poetics*, *33*(5–6), 257–282.

Pine, B. J., & Gilmore, J. H. (1998). Welcome to the experience economy. *Harvard Business Review*, *76*(4), 97–105.

Pratt, M. L. (1992). *Imperial eyes: Travel writing and transculturation*. Routledge.
Prebensen, N. K., & Xie, J. (2017). Efficacy of co-creation and mastering on perceived value and satisfaction in tourists' consumption. *Tourism Management*, *60*, 166–176.
Precedence Research. (2025). *Wellness tourism market size to hit USD 2054.90 billion by 2034*. https://www.precedenceresearch.com/wellness-tourism-market
Roelofsen, M., & Minca, C. (2018). The Superhost: Biopolitics, home and community in the Airbnb dream-world of global hospitality. *Geoforum*, *91*, 170–181.
Rose, N. (2007). *The politics of life itself: Biomedicine, power, and subjectivity in the twenty-first century*. Princeton University Press.
Said, E. W. (1978). *Orientalism*. Pantheon Books.
Said, E. W. (1993). *Culture and imperialism*. Knopf.
Santana Turegano, M. A. (2006). Dependency and development patterns in tourism: A case study in Canary Islands. *Tourism Economics*, *12*(1), 87–109.
Simmel, G. (1957). Fashion. *American Journal of Sociology*, *62*(6), 541–558. (Original work published 1904).
Sotiriadis, M. D. (2017). Sharing resources for tourism development: A stakeholder-based approach to studying destination coopetition applied to the case of Naoussa. *Journal of Destination Marketing & Management*, *6*(3), 222–235.
Sthapit, E., Coudounaris, D. N., & Björk, P. (2023). The antecedents and consequences of memorable wellness tourism experiences. *Journal of Travel & Tourism Marketing*, *40*(3), 234–253.
Stock, M. (2020). *Habiter comme touriste* [Living as a tourist]. Presses universitaires de Lyon.
Taussig, M. (1993). *Mimesis and alterity: A particular history of the senses*. Routledge.
Trinanda, O., Sari, M., & Puspaningrum, A. (2022). The role of memorable tourism experiences in enhancing tourist well-being through destination image. *Journal of Quality Assurance in Hospitality & Tourism*, *23*(4), 891–916.
UNWTO. (2023). *Tourism statistics yearbook* (2023 edition). World Tourism Organization.
Urry, J. (1990). *The tourist gaze: Leisure and travel in contemporary societies*. Sage Publications.
Vada, S., Prentice, C., & Hsiao, A. (2019). The influence of tourism experience and well-being on place attachment. *Journal of Retailing and Consumer Services*, *47*, 322–330.
World Bank. (2022). *Tourism and competitiveness*. https://www.worldbank.org/en/topic/competitiveness/brief/tourism-and-competitiveness
Wu, Q., & Wang, Z. (2011). The application of Bourdieu's cultural capital theory in tourism planning. *Human Geography*, *26*(1), 113–117.
Zhang, S., Chen, N., She, S., & Li, J. (2024). How wellness tourism experiences affect tourist well-being: A chain mediation model. *Current Issues in Tourism*, *27*(8), 1287–1303.
Zuboff, S. (2019). *The age of surveillance capitalism: The fight for a human future at the new frontier of power*. PublicAffairs.

Chapter 17

The Rise of Wellness Tourism: Tradition, Innovation, and Future Perspectives

Jeetesh Kumar[a], *Suresh Kumar Velayudhan Pillai*[b], *Neethiahnanthan Ari Ragavan*[a], *Ali Najeeb*[c] *and Nigora Bukharova*[d]

[a]*Faculty of Social Sciences & Leisure Management, Taylor's University, Malaysia*
[b]*School of Hospitality, Tourism & Events, Taylor's University, Malaysia*
[c]*Qasim Ibrahim School of Business, Villa College, Maldives*
[d]*TDI, Research Institute for Tourism Development, Republic of Uzbekistan*

Abstract

Wellness is a deeply rooted concept with historical and cultural significance that spans thousands of years. It is closely tied to the evolution of traditional and complementary medical practices, which vary significantly from one country to another. This chapter examines the dynamic evolution and global significance of wellness tourism, a sector rooted in ancient healing traditions that is now expanding as a vital industry addressing contemporary health and well-being needs. It traces the historical origins of holistic practices such as Ayurveda, Traditional Chinese Medicine, and indigenous healing rituals, emphasizing their cultural importance and enduring relevance. The chapter discusses the evolution of wellness practices from early civilizations to modern holistic approaches, highlighting their integration with scientific advancements and technological innovations. It examines the emergence of wellness tourism as a multi-billion-dollar industry driven by demographic shifts, changing consumer priorities, and global health concerns. The intersection of tourism and health care, alongside technological breakthroughs like virtual wellness programs and AI-driven personalization, is also explored. This chapter addresses post-pandemic

Advancement in Medical and Wellness Tourism, Part A: Entrepreneurship and Technology, 225–237

doi:10.1108/978-1-80592-983-320261017

shifts, emphasizing increased focus on health security, mental well-being, and sustainability. It underscores the importance of responsible practices that honor cultural heritage and promote environmental preservation. Concluding with potential future research avenues, the chapter advocates for evidence-based wellness interventions, sustainable development, and innovative digital solutions to ensure the continued growth and positive impact of wellness tourism in fostering individual and societal health.

Keywords: Wellness tourism; holistic practices; traditional medicine; cultural heritage; sustainable tourism; health and well-being; technological innovation; post-pandemic health trends

1. Introduction

In recent years, the concept of wellness has gained new significance, evolving from a primarily individual pursuit into a global phenomenon that influences travel, health care, lifestyle, and societal well-being (Majeed & Gon Kim, 2023). Amidst the rapid pace of modern life, characterized by technological advancements, urbanization, and globalization, more people are seeking holistic ways to maintain and enhance their mental, physical, emotional, and spiritual health (Pande & Sengupta, 2023). This growing awareness and desire for comprehensive well-being have given rise to a booming sector known as wellness tourism, which emphasizes travel as a means to achieve personal renewal and societal harmony (Nazir & Kumar, 2025; Phuthong et al., 2023).

The idea that travel can be more than mere leisure or sightseeing is not a new concept. Historically, civilizations across the world have used journeys, whether spiritual pilgrimages, medicinal visits, or cultural explorations, to heal, educate, and connect (Kumar et al., 2023; Voigt & Pforr, 2013). Today, however, the scale and scope of wellness tourism have expanded dramatically, driven by evolving consumer preferences, technological innovations, and a heightened global consciousness about health. From luxury spa retreats in exotic locations to spiritual pilgrimages to ancient temples, wellness tourism encompasses a broad spectrum of experiences designed to foster physical resilience, mental clarity, emotional balance, and spiritual elevation.

One of the defining features of modern wellness tourism is its holistic approach. Unlike traditional healthcare systems that often focus on treating illnesses or symptoms, wellness tourism promotes preventive care and lifestyle choices that support ongoing health. It pursues a balanced integration of mind, body, and spirit, a concept rooted in ancient healing traditions such as Ayurveda, Traditional Chinese Medicine (TCM), yoga, and indigenous practices (Li et al., 2023). These time-tested methods are increasingly being integrated into contemporary wellness services, blending science and tradition to create personalized, culturally rooted experiences. The relevance of wellness tourism has become even more apparent in the context of recent global developments. The COVID-19 pandemic, in particular, has heightened awareness about health, resilience, and the importance of mental well-being (Smith & Puczkó, 2014). Lockdowns, social distancing, and the widespread acknowledgement of mental health issues have compelled individuals and destinations alike to reconsider the role of travel and leisure in fostering overall wellness. Many have recognized that travel, when used consciously and healthfully, can serve as a powerful tool for healing emotional scars, reducing stress, and rebuilding social connections.

Moreover, wellness tourism has gained momentum not only as a response to immediate health concerns but also as a proactive strategy to address longer-term societal challenges. As contemporary societies grapple with rising rates of stress-related disorders, lifestyle-related diseases, and environmental degradation, the emphasis on sustainable and culturally meaningful wellness practices has become critical (Neto, 2022). This shift underscores a broader vision – one that prioritizes collective well-being alongside individual health, fostering a more peaceful and healthy global community. Understanding wellness tourism requires a multidimensional approach. It involves examining individual motivations, diverse cultural practices, industry trends, economic impacts, and environmental implications (Kulshreshtha & Michopoulou, 2025). Many travelers are motivated by the desire to escape daily routines, reconnect with nature, seek spiritual insight, or indulge in self-care. Destinations around the world are responding by developing specialized programs, incorporating local traditions, and promoting sustainable practices that respect and preserve cultural heritage (Hussian & Kumar, 2015).

In addition, the growth of wellness tourism presents both opportunities and challenges. On one hand, it can generate significant economic benefits, create employment, and promote cultural exchange. On the other hand, concerns exist regarding commodification, cultural insensitivity, and environmental sustainability (Kazakov & Oyner, 2021). The risk of commercializing culturally rooted practices without proper understanding or respect could dilute their authenticity and diminish their potential benefits. As such, responsible and evidence-based approaches are essential to ensure that wellness tourism remains a force for positive change.

This chapter aims to explore the multidimensional landscape of wellness tourism by examining its historical roots, contemporary trends, and future directions. It will highlight key concepts and definitions, analyze the motivations driving travelers, and discuss the societal and environmental impacts of this rapidly expanding industry. Special attention will be given to how traditional practices from different parts of the world, such as Ayurveda from India, traditional Thai massage, Chinese medicine, and indigenous healing methods, are being integrated into modern wellness experiences.

Furthermore, the chapter offers the strategic implications for destinations seeking to position themselves as wellness hubs, including sustainable development principles, cultural preservation, and community engagement. It will also consider how the post-pandemic world could reshape wellness tourism, with a focus on new priorities such as mental health support, eco-friendly practices, and personalized experiences. Ultimately, the chapter seeks to underscore the profound potential of wellness tourism as a catalyst for individual transformation and societal harmony. It aspires to demonstrate that travel, when aligned with holistic health principles and cultural respect, can serve as a pathway to a healthier, more peaceful world. In a time of unprecedented global challenges – whether health crises, environmental threats, or social upheavals – wellness tourism offers a hopeful perspective: the possibility that by caring for ourselves and each other through meaningful travel experiences, we can forge a more resilient and compassionate future.

2. Historical Roots of Wellness Practices

The foundation of wellness practices can be traced back thousands of years, deeply rooted in the cultural and spiritual traditions of diverse civilizations. Ancient Egypt, China, India, Greece, and indigenous societies worldwide have all contributed rich healing philosophies and practices that aim to restore balance and harmony within the human body and mind (Pande & Sengupta, 2023). For example, Ayurveda, an ancient Indian system of medicine, dates back over 3,000 years and emphasizes the balance of bodily energies through personalized herbal treatments, dietary regulations, and lifestyle adjustments. Similarly, TCM, including acupuncture, herbal medicine, and qigong, has been practiced for millennia to promote health and treat diseases holistically (Kulshreshtha & Michopoulou, 2025; Kumar et al., 2023). In Greece, the concept of physical fitness and mental wellness was embodied in the holistic philosophy of Hippocrates, emphasizing the importance of diet, exercise, and mental balance. These traditional systems emphasized preventative care, aligning with modern notions of wellness that focus on maintaining health rather than merely treating illness (Phuthong et al., 2023).

Across various cultures, healing was often centered on spiritual practices, rituals, and connection with nature. Indigenous groups worldwide have utilized natural resources – such as herbs, minerals, water, and sacred rituals – to promote healing and spiritual awakening. These traditions often intertwine physical, emotional, and spiritual dimensions, laying the groundwork for contemporary holistic health approaches (Agrodimou, 2019; Majeed & Gon Kim, 2023). The historical significance of these practices lies not only in their longevity but also in their influence on modern alternative medicine. Over centuries, they evolved and integrated into local medicinal systems, shaping the cultural landscape of health and healing (Nazir & Kumar, 2025).

The historical roots of wellness practices reflect a universal desire for health, balance, and spiritual fulfillment. They serve as enduring reminders of humanity's collective quest for well-being and are the foundation upon which today's global wellness movement is built. Recognizing these ancient origins provides valuable insight into the cultural continuity and depth behind modern wellness tourism, emphasizing respect for traditional knowledge and practices.

3. Evolution of Wellness and Healing Traditions

The evolution of wellness and healing traditions showcases humanity's ongoing pursuit of health through adaptive practices that respond to changing societal needs. Early civilizations primarily focused on herbal remedies, spiritual rituals, and physical exercise, often intertwined with religious beliefs and cultural identity (Li et al., 2023; Voigt & Pforr, 2013). Over centuries, these practices developed into more sophisticated systems of medicine and wellness. With advances in science and medicine, some traditional practices faced skepticism, but many persisted, often integrating new scientific insights to enhance their effectiveness.

In recent history, the 20th and 21st centuries have witnessed a renaissance in alternative and complementary medicine, driven by dissatisfaction with purely pharmaceutical approaches and a desire for more natural, holistic health solutions. The rise of yoga in the West, the global spread of acupuncture, and the popularity of herbal medicine exemplify this trend. Meanwhile, wellness has expanded beyond individual health treatments to encompass lifestyle choices, including diet, fitness, mental health, and spiritual practices (Kumar et al., 2023).

The modern evolution of wellness also reflects changes in societal attitudes toward health. The shift from disease treatment to health promotion emphasizes prevention, resilience, and self-care. This transformation has been accelerated by technological innovations – including wearable devices, telemedicine, and personalized health tracking – that enable individuals to manage their wellness proactively.

Furthermore, the development of dedicated wellness centers, spas, retreats, and resorts demonstrates how traditional healing practices have been commercialized and adapted into luxury experiences that cater to a global clientele. These evolutions mirror a broader cultural shift toward self-optimization and holistic health, blending ancient wisdom with cutting-edge science. The ongoing adaptation and integration of diverse healing traditions continue to shape the dynamic landscape of wellness, making it accessible and relevant to the diverse needs of contemporary society.

4. The Emergence of Wellness Tourism as a Global Industry

Over the past two decades, wellness tourism has evolved from a niche segment into a significant global industry, reflecting a profound shift in people's attitudes toward health and well-being. Historically, health-related travel was primarily associated with medical tourism – patients traveling abroad to seek affordable or specialized treatments. However, the modern concept of wellness tourism encompasses a much broader spectrum, including spa retreats, yoga vacations, meditation retreats, holistic healing programs, and eco-wellness adventures (Smith & Puczkó, 2014). The industry's rapid growth is driven by increasing awareness of the importance of preventive health, rising chronic diseases, and a burgeoning middle class seeking meaningful, rejuvenating experiences. According to recent estimates, the global wellness economy exceeds $1 trillion annually, with wellness tourism contributing a significant portion. Major destinations such as Thailand, India, Bali, Costa Rica, and parts of Europe and North America have positioned themselves as wellness hubs, investing heavily in infrastructure – luxury resorts, specialized clinics, retreat centers – that cater to the wellness-conscious traveler.

Demographic changes also drive this shift. Aging populations in many countries are seeking age-specific wellness services, while younger travelers prioritize mental health, detox programs, and immersive cultural experiences. The integration of traditional healing arts, modern medicine, and eco-friendly practices has allowed wellness tourism to appeal to a diverse global market. The industry is further supported by the advent of digital technology, enabling travelers to customize and personalize their wellness journeys (Kazakov & Oyner, 2021; Phuthong et al., 2023). Mobile apps, virtual consultations, and wearable devices now facilitate health tracking and engagement, making wellness tourism more accessible and tailored. As a result, wellness tourism has become a vital component of national tourism strategies, significantly contributing to local economies, generating employment opportunities, and fostering cultural exchange.

Moreover, in the wake of the COVID-19 pandemic, the focus on health and resilience has intensified, with travelers seeking safer, cleaner, and more health-oriented destinations. This global trend suggests that wellness tourism will continue to expand, driven by societal shifts that emphasize the importance of holistic health, the pursuit of a balanced life, and sustainable, culturally rooted travel experiences.

5. Cultural Significance of Traditional Healing Practices

Traditional healing practices are integral to the cultural fabric of many societies, serving as profound expressions of their historical and spiritual identities. These practices – such as Ayurveda in India, TCM, African herbal medicine, and indigenous healing rituals – have been passed down through generations, often rooted in deep spiritual and philosophical beliefs about health, balance, and harmony with nature (Agrodimou, 2019).

The cultural significance of these practices extends beyond their physical healing properties (Kulshreshtha & Michopoulou, 2025). They embody a community's worldview, spiritual beliefs, and relationship with the environment. For example, Ayurveda emphasizes balance in bodily energies and incorporates spiritual practices, dietary laws, and herbal treatments that reflect India's holistic approach to health. Similarly, TCM integrates acupuncture, herbal medicine, and qigong, reflecting China's cultural emphasis on restoring the balance of Yin and Yang and vital energy. In many societies, traditional healing practices are more than medical procedures; they are cultural rituals, spiritual ceremonies, and social gatherings that reinforce community bonds and cultural wisdom. Indigenous healers often serve as custodians of cultural knowledge, maintaining rites, rituals, and herbal medicine knowledge that has been passed down orally (Islam et al., 2024).

Today, there is a rising global appreciation of these traditional practices, driven by a desire for authentic, natural, and culturally meaningful healing experiences. Many wellness centers worldwide incorporate traditional healing methods into their offerings, recognizing their cultural significance and effectiveness. This integration helps preserve these ancient practices, promotes cultural exchange, and fosters respect for indigenous knowledge systems (Nazir & Kumar, 2025).

Furthermore, traditional healing practices are increasingly validated by scientific research, highlighting their holistic approach and potential health benefits. For many cultures, these practices are a vital part of their identity and heritage, offering both spiritual and physical healing. Their global recognition underscores the value of cultural diversity in promoting health and well-being and sustains the cultural integrity of communities for generations to come.

6. Impact of Modern Lifestyle on Well-being

The modern lifestyle, characterized by rapid technological advancement, urbanization, and globalization, has profoundly impacted individual and collective well-being. While technological progress offers many conveniences and opportunities for connectedness, it has also introduced stressors that threaten mental, emotional, and physical health.

One of the primary impacts of modern life is increased exposure to chronic stress. Busy work schedules, constant connectivity through digital devices, and the pressure to achieve work–life balance create a pervasive stress environment. This chronic stress contributes to lifestyle-related illnesses such as hypertension, diabetes, mental health disorders, and cardiovascular diseases. Simultaneously, the rise of sedentary behaviors, prolonged screen time, and a lack of physical activity further deteriorate physical health (Kumar et al., 2023; Phuthong et al., 2023). Moreover, modern lifestyles often lead to poor dietary habits, characterized by a high intake of processed foods, sugar, and unhealthy fats, which compromise nutritional health. The prevalence of fast food and convenience eating habits results in rising obesity rates and associated health complications.

7. Global Trends Driving Wellness Tourism Growth

The growth of wellness tourism worldwide is driven by a combination of social, economic, and environmental trends that reflect changing consumer priorities. A significant factor is the growing awareness of health issues and the increasing demand for preventive care. As chronic diseases such as obesity, diabetes, and cardiovascular conditions become more prevalent globally, people are seeking holistic approaches to maintain health and avoid illness. This shift emphasizes wellness as a proactive lifestyle choice rather than merely a reaction to disease. Another key trend is the aging population. Many countries, particularly in Europe and North America, have rapidly aging demographics that prioritize health, longevity, and quality of life. Older adults are actively seeking specialized wellness services, including rehabilitative therapies, detox programs, and age-friendly retreats, fueling demand for health-focused travel experiences.

Furthermore, rising disposable incomes and the expansion of middle classes in emerging markets are enabling more people to afford wellness travel. Countries such as China, India, Brazil, and Russia are experiencing an increase in outbound travel, with consumers seeking authentic, experience-based wellness offerings in destinations across Asia, Europe, and Latin America. Cultural shifts toward mindfulness, mental health awareness, and self-care are also significant drivers. Millennials and Generation Z, in particular, prioritize experiences that promote emotional well-being, mental clarity, and spiritual growth. This has catalyzed demand for activities like yoga, meditation, digital detox retreats, and eco-conscious travel.

Sustainability has become a core value for many consumers, leading to greater demand for eco-friendly, socially responsible wellness resorts that emphasize environmental conservation and community engagement. Travelers are increasingly conscious of their ecological footprint and seek destinations that align with their values.

Finally, the ongoing effects of the COVID-19 pandemic have heightened the importance of health security and resilience, prompting travelers to choose destinations with rigorous safety protocols, clean environments, and health-focused amenities. This pandemic-induced shift emphasizes the importance of wellness travel as a means of rebuilding physical and mental strength, reinforcing its sustained growth trajectory worldwide.

8. The Intersection of Tourism and Health Care

The convergence of tourism and health care has given rise to a dynamic sector known as medical tourism, which is now a significant segment within the broader wellness industry. This intersection involves individuals traveling across borders to seek medical procedures, rehabilitative treatments, or wellness therapies that are either more affordable, less invasive, or more accessible than those available in their home countries (Islam et al., 2024).

Medical tourism often includes elective procedures such as cosmetic surgery, dental treatments, fertility treatments, and minimally invasive surgeries. Countries like Thailand, India, Mexico, and Turkey have established themselves as global hubs due to their advanced healthcare facilities combined with cost advantages. Many of these destinations also offer wellness services, including spa treatments, holistic therapies, and traditional medicine, thereby blurring the line between medical and leisure travel. Beyond purely clinical treatments, the integration of health care into tourism is expanding to encompass holistic wellness and preventive health. Wellness-focused travel now includes personalized health assessments, nutritional counseling, mental health support, detox programs, and stress management retreats. The goal is not only to address health issues but also to promote overall well-being through immersive, restorative experiences.

This intersection addresses the growing consumer desire for comprehensive health solutions that consider the mind, body, and spirit, often delivered in a culturally authentic setting. It also caters to the increasing health consciousness fostered by rising chronic health conditions, aging populations, and a shift toward proactive self-care. From a healthcare perspective, this synergy offers economic benefits for participating countries through job creation, infrastructure development, and foreign exchange earnings. It also poses challenges, such as regulatory oversight, infection control, and ethical considerations, which require careful management to ensure safety and quality (Ali et al., 2014). Ultimately, the intersection of tourism and health care is reshaping how people perceive and access health services, transforming travel into a pathway for healing, rejuvenation, and long-term wellness.

9. The Role of Technology and Innovation in Wellness Practices

Technology and innovation are revolutionizing the field of wellness, making holistic health practices more accessible, personalized, and data-driven. Digital advancements are creating new opportunities to enhance traditional therapies and develop innovative solutions tailored to individual needs (Agrodimou, 2019). Mobile apps and wearable devices have become crucial tools for health tracking and self-monitoring (Nazir & Kumar, 2025). Fitness trackers, sleep monitors, and health apps enable users to set goals, track progress, and receive personalized feedback on physical activity, nutrition, sleep, and mental health. These technologies foster a proactive approach to wellness, enabling individuals to take charge of their health beyond clinical settings.

Telemedicine and virtual consultations have expanded access to expert advice, allowing people to connect with healthcare professionals and wellness coaches globally. This convenience is particularly valuable in remote or underserved regions, facilitating continuity of care and long-term health management. Artificial intelligence (AI) and data analytics are increasingly used to create personalized wellness programs based on genetic, biometric, and lifestyle data. For example, DNA testing can inform tailored nutrition plans, while AI-driven platforms can recommend customized meditation, fitness, or dietary regimens. This precision medicine approach ensures that wellness interventions are more effective and sustainable.

10. Post-pandemic Shifts in Travel and Wellness Priorities

The COVID-19 pandemic has profoundly altered the landscape of global travel and wellness priorities, reshaping traveler behaviors, expectations, and industry practices (Phuthong et al., 2023). Before the pandemic, wellness travel was already gaining momentum; however, COVID-19 significantly accelerated this trend, fostering a deeper awareness of health, safety, and mental well-being. One of the most significant shifts has been an increased focus on health security and hygiene. Travelers now demand higher standards of sanitation, contactless services, and transparent safety protocols. This heightened emphasis on cleanliness extends to accommodation hygiene, food safety, and the overall management of health risks, leading to a surge in demand for wellness centers and resorts that prioritize hygiene and safety.

Mental health has become a central concern in the post-pandemic era. The widespread experience of lockdowns, social distancing, and uncertainty has heightened anxiety, depression, and stress. Consequently, travelers now seek experiences that promote mental clarity, emotional resilience, and mindfulness – such as meditation retreats, digital detox programs, and nature-based therapies – more than ever before. Wellness offerings that focus on mental well-being have shifted from a niche to a mainstream focus, becoming core components of travel plans. Many travelers are prioritizing self-care and holistic health approaches, opting for personalized and immersive experiences that support longevity, immune health, and stress reduction (Konar et al., 2014). This includes a rise in demand for immune-boosting therapies, dietary detoxes, and outdoor activities that reconnect individuals with nature – highlighting a shift toward health resilience rather than merely relaxation.

Furthermore, the pandemic has underscored the importance of sustainability in travel choices. Conscious travelers are now seeking destinations and providers that demonstrate eco-friendly practices, local community support, and cultural authenticity. Sustainable tourism initiatives – such as eco-resorts, responsible sourcing, and local employment – have become a key part of wellness travel offerings, aligning personal health with planetary health. Finally, the pandemic has prompted a reconsideration of the traditional travel model, emphasizing flexibility, safety, and remote or hybrid wellness experiences. This includes virtual wellness programs, online consultations, and hybrid retreats combining in-person and digital components. Overall, these shifts underscore a more conscious, resilient, and personalized approach to travel and wellness in the post-pandemic world.

11. Sustainability and Cultural Preservation in Wellness Tourism

As wellness tourism continues to expand globally, sustainability and cultural preservation have become crucial considerations for industry stakeholders. The growing demand for authentic, eco-friendly, and culturally respectful experiences necessitates a conscious approach that strikes a balance between growth and responsibility. Environmental sustainability is central to modern wellness tourism, with travelers increasingly seeking eco-friendly accommodations, waste reduction practices, and locally sourced organic products. Many wellness resorts and retreats are adopting green building standards, energy-efficient infrastructure, water conservation measures, and waste management systems to minimize their ecological footprint. Solar energy, rainwater harvesting, and organic gardens are standard features, reflecting a commitment to environmental sustainability and planetary health.

Beyond environmental concerns, cultural preservation is equally vital. Traditional healing practices, local arts, and indigenous knowledge form the spiritual and cultural core of many wellness offerings (Agrodimou, 2019). Ensuring that these practices are respected, authentic, and not appropriated is a significant challenge for industry players. Responsible tourism promotes meaningful engagement with local communities, involving them in the design of programs and sharing their cultural heritage in ways that benefit both visitors and residents. Promoting local artisans, guiding responsible tourism practices, and supporting community-based wellness initiatives are ways to foster cultural sustainability. For example, incorporating local rituals, traditional crafts, and indigenous medicinal practices enriches the visitor experience while preserving cultural identities. This approach also helps prevent cultural commodification and loss of traditional knowledge.

Moreover, sustainable wellness tourism advocates for long-term benefits rather than short-term gains. It promotes community empowerment, eco-conscious infrastructure, and policies that safeguard biodiversity and cultural heritage. Certification schemes and eco-labels are increasingly used to verify sustainable practices, promoting transparency and trust. Integrating sustainability and cultural preservation into wellness tourism is essential for creating responsible industry practices. It ensures that wellness tourism contributes positively to local environments and communities, safeguarding cultural legacies and natural resources for future generations while providing meaningful, authentic experiences for travelers.

12. Conclusion and Future Research Avenues

The rapid growth and diversification of wellness tourism over recent decades signal a fundamental shift in how individuals and societies perceive health, well-being, and travel. Rooted in ancient healing traditions and evolving through modern scientific advances, wellness tourism has become a vital sector that caters to a variety of traveler needs – ranging from stress reduction and mental health support to physical rehabilitation and spiritual fulfillment. Its emergence as a global industry underscores the desire for holistic health experiences that integrate physical, emotional, mental, and spiritual dimensions, offering travelers a pathway not only to relaxation but also to personal transformation.

Multiple interconnected trends have driven the evolution of this industry. Changes in societal values, demographic shifts like aging populations, rising disposable incomes in emerging markets, and increasing awareness of mental health issues have all contributed to heightened demand for wellness travel experiences. Moreover, technological innovations – such as personalized health apps, telemedicine, and virtual reality – have expanded access and tailored offerings, making wellness practices more accessible and practical.

The cultural significance of traditional healing practices remains central to the authenticity and appeal of wellness tourism. These time-honored systems – such as Ayurveda, TCM, and indigenous rituals – embody community knowledge and spiritual values, playing a vital role in preserving cultural heritage. At the same time, the industry has faced challenges such as commercialization, cultural commodification, and environmental sustainability concerns, which necessitate responsible practices that respect local communities and ecosystems.

The COVID-19 pandemic has profoundly impacted wellness tourism, emphasizing health safety, resilience, and mental well-being. It has prompted a reexamination of travel priorities, leading to increased demand for safe, eco-friendly, and personalized experiences that foster immune health and mental clarity. As such, the industry is adapting, with a greater emphasis on sustainability, cultural authenticity, and the integration of digital health solutions.

Wellness tourism is poised for continued growth, driven by societal demands for holistic health, technological advancements, and a growing desire for authentic, sustainable experiences. However, to unlock its full potential, the industry must prioritize responsible growth, cultural integrity, and environmental stewardship, ensuring it remains a force for positive social and ecological impact. As the wellness tourism industry matures, several avenues for future research emerge – each critical for understanding and guiding its sustainable growth. First, there is a need for more empirical, evidence-based research to evaluate the effectiveness of various wellness programs. While many practices are rooted in tradition, rigorous scientific studies are crucial for validating their health benefits, enhancing service quality, and informing consumer decisions. Longitudinal studies focusing on the long-term health outcomes of wellness travel would contribute valuable insights into best practices and impact measurement. Second, understanding traveler motivations remains a fertile area for exploration. Future research can explore the psychosocial and cultural factors influencing wellness travel decision-making, particularly among diverse demographics, such as millennials versus older adults or different cultural groups. Such insights could help industry stakeholders design more targeted and culturally sensitive programs that better meet the diverse needs of their stakeholders; third, the concept of sustainability in wellness tourism warrants further investigation. Developing practical models for environmentally sustainable and culturally respectful practices is vital. Researchers could explore how wellness destinations can integrate eco-friendly infrastructure, local community involvement, and cultural preservation initiatives in a holistic manner.

Additionally, the development of certifications and standards for sustainable wellness practices can enhance transparency and consumer trust. Fourth, technology's role in shaping wellness experiences presents many opportunities. Future studies could examine the effectiveness of digital health tools, virtual reality experiences, and AI-powered personalized wellness plans. Understanding how these innovations influence behavior change, engagement, and health outcomes could guide the development of more effective digital wellness interventions. Fifth, the social and economic impacts of wellness tourism on local communities deserve closer attention. Researching how destination communities experience and benefit from wellness tourism – such as employment creation, cultural exchange, and socio-economic upliftment – can inform policies that promote inclusive and equitable development. Finally, the post-pandemic landscape offers unique research opportunities. Investigating how health crises influence traveler behaviors, destination resilience, and industry adaptation strategies will be crucial for preparing for future global challenges. Topics such as health security protocols, hybrid in-person and virtual wellness experiences, and crisis management in wellness tourism are also promising avenues for inquiry.

As wellness tourism continues to evolve, a multidisciplinary approach – combining health sciences, tourism studies, environmental sciences, and cultural anthropology – is crucial for navigating its complex landscape. Future research that addresses these areas will not only advance academic understanding but also support practitioners, policymakers, and communities in fostering a sustainable, authentic, and health-promoting industry for years to come.

References

Agrodimou, A. (2019). Wellness tourism: Through the lens of millennials' attitude: An exploratory qualitative study. Master Thesis in Business Administration. JonKoping University, Sweden.

Ali, F., Rezaei, S., Hussain, K., & Ragavan, N. A. (2014). International business travellers' experience with luxury hotel restaurants: The impact of foodservice experience and customer satisfaction on dining frequency and expenditure. *International Journal of Hospitality and Event Management*, *1*(2), 164–186.

Hussain, K., & Kumar, J. (2015). Destination perception and loyalty: Exploring the difference between local and foreign tourists. *Journal of Tourism*, *16*(2), 27–42.

Islam, M. T., Pradhan, B., & Kumar, J. (2024). Social media reviews' influence on spa and wellness consumer choices: Conceptual framework, prospective significance, and future research directions. In S. Kumar, M. B. Talukder, & A. Pego (Eds.), *Utilizing smart technology and AI in hybrid tourism and hospitality* (pp. 1–22). IGI Global. https://doi.org/10.4018/979-8-3693-1978-9.ch001

Kazakov, S., & Oyner, O. (2021). Wellness tourism: A perspective article. *Tourism Review*, *76*(1), 58–63.

Konar, R., Kumar, J., & Hussain, K. (2014). Determinants of the emerging terrorist threats to luxury hotels: A case study of Pakistan. *TEAM Journal of Hospitality and Tourism*, *11*(1), 41–53.

Kulshreshtha, S. K., & Michopoulou, E. (Eds.). (2025). *Wellness tourism in Asia: Emerging destinations to rejuvenate, relax and retreat*. Springer Nature.

Kumar, J., Nazir, F., & Nisar, A. Q. (2023). Empowering wellness worldwide: A critical analysis of the Global Wellness Institute (GWI) Journey 2014–2021. *Journal of Tourism and Development*, *41*, 263–287. http://doi.org/10.34624/rtd.v41i0.29731

Li, W., Myagmarsuren, D., Yuanhao, Q., & Yadmaa, Z. (2023). Wellness tourism services innovation: A bibliometric review and future research agenda. *Catus*, *5*, 20–36.

Majeed, S., & Gon Kim, W. (2023). Emerging trends in wellness tourism: A scoping review. *Journal of Hospitality and Tourism Insights*, *6*(2), 853–873.

Nazir, F., & Kumar, J. (2025). Wellness and health tourism in Malaysia: Current barriers and recommendations. In S. K. Kulshreshtha & E. Michopoulou (Eds.), *Wellness tourism in Asia: Emerging destinations to rejuvenate, relax and retreat* (pp. 141–154). Springer. https://doi.org/10.1007/978-981-96-2867-4_9

Neto, P. A. F. (2022). *Health and wellness tourism in the European context-supply and demand trends* [Master's thesis, Instituto Politecnico do Porto].

Pande, L., & Sengupta, S. (2023, December 23). Wellness tourism in India: Evolution, perspectives, and trends. *Perspectives, and Trends*. Proceedings of the International Conference on Innovative Computing & Communication (ICICC 2024). http://dx.doi.org/10.2139/ssrn.4674035

Phuthong, T., Anuntavoranich, P., Chandrachai, A., & Piromsopa, K. (2023). A framework for assessing wellness tourism destination competitiveness: A perspective from the wellness tourism clusters in Thailand. *GeoJournal of Tourism & Geosites*, *49*(3), 973–987.

Smith, M., & Puczkó, L. (2014). *Health, tourism and hospitality: Spas, wellness and medical travel*. Routledge.

Voigt, C., & Pforr, C. (2013). *Wellness tourism: A destination perspective*. Routledge.

Chapter 18

The Wellness Wanderers: How Travel Is Becoming the New Prescription

Suman Lata

Amity Institute of Travel & Tourism, Amity University, Noida, Uttar Pradesh, India

Abstract

Wellness tourism has emerged as a transformative force in global travel, evolving from traditional leisure trips to purpose-driven journeys centered on health and well-being. This study examines the growing trend of wellness tourism and its shift from conventional leisure travel to a health-focused experience, analyzing the motivations, behaviors, and economic implications behind this phenomenon. This study builds upon existing theories and models related to wellness tourism, transformative travel, and health-driven tourism experiences to establish a conceptual foundation. A comprehensive review of literature was conducted, drawing insights from various frameworks. Data were collected from secondary sources, including peer-reviewed research articles, industry reports (e.g., GWI, UNWTO), and case studies of leading wellness destinations (e.g., Bali, Switzerland, India's Ayurvedic hubs). The findings reveal that wellness tourism is no longer a niche market but a mainstream movement, driven by rising stress levels, digital burnout, and a post-pandemic emphasis on preventive health care. Travelers increasingly seek holistic retreats, mindfulness programs, and nature-based therapies, shifting away from passive vacations to immersive well-being experiences. The originality of this chapter lies in its interdisciplinary approach, bridging tourism studies, behavioral psychology, and health economics. Unlike prior research focusing solely on medical tourism or luxury spas, this study explores how wellness travel is redefining tourism's role in personal and public health.

Keywords: Wellness tourism; health-driven travel; holistic retreats; digital detox; tourist engagement

Advancement in Medical and Wellness Tourism, Part A: Entrepreneurship and Technology, 239–252

doi:10.1108/978-1-80592-983-320261018

1. Introduction

In recent years, travel has evolved beyond the boundaries of conventional leisure and recreation to embrace a more holistic pursuit: wellness. The concept of wellness tourism is defined as travel undertaken with the primary purpose of promoting health and well-being that has emerged as a global phenomenon, bridging the realms of health care, lifestyle, and tourism (Dini & Pencarelli, 2022; Li et al., 2025). Once perceived as a luxury niche for affluent travelers seeking spa treatments and yoga retreats, wellness tourism has now transcended cultural and socio-economic barriers, becoming a mainstream trend that redefines the very purpose of travel (Majeed & Gon Kim, 2023). The study aptly captures this transformation, highlighting the increasing recognition of travel not merely as a means of relaxation but as an intentional journey toward physical rejuvenation, mental balance, and spiritual growth. The rise of wellness tourism is closely tied to the stresses of modern life (Liao et al., 2023). The contemporary lifestyle has marked by long working hours, digital dependence, sedentary habits, and escalating mental health concerns – has led to a renewed emphasis on well-being. Unlike traditional vacations centered on sightseeing, shopping, or entertainment, wellness-focused travel seeks to restore balance through practices such as meditation, fitness programs, detoxification, Ayurveda, spa therapies, mindfulness retreats, and nature immersion. This shift signifies a new paradigm where wellness is no longer confined to medical prescriptions or clinical settings but is increasingly associated with preventive healthcare strategies embedded in travel experiences (He et al., 2023).

The need to examine this transition is underpinned by several compelling factors. First, wellness tourism represents one of the fastest-growing segments of the global tourism industry, with reports projecting exponential growth in both demand and expenditure (Li et al., 2025). Understanding its underlying drivers is crucial for policymakers, destination managers, and industry stakeholders who seek to capture and sustain this lucrative market. Second, wellness travel aligns with the global emphasis on sustainable and mindful living, creating opportunities to design tourism products that not only satisfy individual well-being but also respect environmental and cultural integrity (Liu et al., 2023). Third, travelers themselves are increasingly seeking purposeful journeys that offer lasting benefits beyond temporary enjoyment – making it essential to explore their motivations, behaviors, and expectations. Finally, with wellness being linked to public health goals, there is an urgent need to evaluate the economic implications of this trend, including its potential to diversify tourism markets, stimulate local economies, and create employment opportunities in health and wellness sectors (Liu et al., 2022).

Although research on wellness tourism has expanded over the past decade, significant gaps remain (Al-Ansi et al., 2025). Much of the existing literature has focused on the supply side – exploring spa resorts, wellness retreats, and medical tourism facilities – while limited studies have examined the demand side motivations and behaviors of travelers who engage in wellness-oriented journeys. Furthermore, while the economic benefits of wellness tourism are acknowledged, comprehensive studies that quantify and contextualize its macroeconomic implications remain scarce (Pereira et al., 2023). Another gap lies in the understanding of how wellness travel differs from conventional leisure tourism, particularly in terms of psychological drivers and long-term impacts on traveler well-being. Additionally, regional and cultural dimensions of wellness tourism – such as the role of indigenous healing practices, yoga, Ayurveda, or mindfulness traditions – are underexplored despite their significant influence on global tourism flows. Addressing these gaps is critical to building a holistic framework that situates wellness travel at the intersection of tourism, health care, and lifestyle choices (Backman et al., 2023). By examining the motivations, behaviors, and economic implications of wellness tourism, this study aims to contribute to both academic scholarship and industry practice, offering insights into how travel is indeed becoming the new prescription for holistic well-being.

2. Literature Review

2.1. Wellness Tourism

Wellness tourism has emerged as a transformative force in the global travel industry, redefining the way people perceive the purpose and benefits of travel (Chen et al., 2023). It refers to journeys specifically designed to promote health, prevent illness, reduce stress, and enhance overall well-being through experiences that nurture the body, mind, and spirit. Unlike traditional tourism, which is often motivated by leisure, sightseeing, or entertainment, wellness tourism emphasizes self-care and rejuvenation, making it one of the fastest-growing segments in the global tourism economy (Polat & Koseoglu, 2023). The rising popularity of wellness tourism can be attributed to the increasing pressures of modern life. Fast-paced urban lifestyles, sedentary habits, digital fatigue, and mental health challenges have created a global demand for restorative travel experiences. Travelers are no longer content with vacations that offer only short-term pleasure; instead, they seek meaningful journeys that provide long-lasting benefits to their physical, emotional, and spiritual health. Wellness tourism caters to this demand by offering diverse experiences, ranging from spa and thermal spring therapies to yoga retreats, meditation programs, Ayurveda, fitness boot camps, organic food trails, and nature-based healing practices (Clerici et al., 2023).

Economically, wellness tourism is becoming a major growth driver in the tourism sector. According to industry reports, travelers who engage in wellness-focused experiences tend to spend more than average tourists, as they are willing to invest in premium services that guarantee quality and authenticity (Pan et al., 2024). This has created opportunities for destinations, resorts, and local communities to design unique wellness offerings rooted in cultural and natural assets. For example, countries like India promote Ayurveda and yoga as part of their wellness identity, while European destinations highlight thermal baths, and Southeast Asia attracts wellness seekers through meditation and spa therapies. Socially and culturally, wellness tourism is fostering a deeper connection between travelers and destinations. Unlike mass tourism, which sometimes leads to overconsumption and environmental strain, wellness travel often emphasizes sustainability, mindfulness, and respect for local traditions. This makes it not only beneficial for the individual traveler but also supportive of community development and environmental stewardship (Kim et al., 2024). Wellness tourism represents a paradigm shift in the global tourism industry. It positions travel as a proactive "prescription" for healthier living, integrating leisure with lifestyle transformation. As the demand for well-being continues to rise, wellness tourism is set to expand further, offering innovative opportunities for travelers, businesses, and destinations worldwide (Sthapit et al., 2023).

2.2. Motivational Factors for Wellness Tourism

Wellness tourism has emerged as a rapidly growing segment within the global tourism industry, driven by travelers' increasing desire to combine leisure with health-enhancing experiences. Unlike traditional forms of tourism, which emphasize recreation and sightseeing, wellness tourism emphasizes physical rejuvenation, mental relaxation, and spiritual growth (Bočkus et al., 2023). Understanding the motivational factors that drive individuals toward wellness-oriented travel is critical to grasp the dynamics of this evolving market. These motivations are often multidimensional, influenced by physical, psychological, social, and cultural considerations.

One of the strongest motivators for wellness tourism is the pursuit of better health and preventive care. Modern lifestyles characterized by sedentary work, poor diet, and high stress levels have resulted in growing health concerns such as obesity, hypertension, and burnout. Travelers are increasingly seeking wellness experiences – such as yoga retreats, detox programs, spa therapies, or fitness camps – as a means of preventing illnesses and maintaining overall well-being. Unlike medical tourism, which focuses on treatment after the onset of illness, wellness tourism emphasizes proactive approaches to health (Suban, 2022). The pressures of urban life, long working hours, and constant digital connectivity have heightened stress and mental fatigue. Wellness tourism provides an opportunity to disconnect from daily routines and restore inner balance. Meditation retreats, mindfulness practices, forest bathing, and thermal spa experiences are particularly attractive to travelers seeking mental relaxation. The promise of psychological healing and emotional rejuvenation is a powerful motivator that distinguishes wellness tourism from conventional leisure travel (Xie et al., 2022). Many wellness tourists are motivated by a desire for long-term lifestyle changes rather than short-term enjoyment. Experiences such as Ayurveda, naturopathy, yoga, and wellness coaching provide travelers with tools and practices that they can integrate into their daily lives even after returning home. This pursuit of holistic wellness, which combines physical, mental, and spiritual well-being, is particularly attractive to health-conscious individuals and those seeking alternatives to conventional medicine (Lee & Kim, 2023).

Wellness tourism is also motivated by the opportunity to engage with cultural and spiritual traditions. Destinations rich in indigenous healing practices, such as Ayurveda in India, hot springs in Japan, or shamanic rituals in South

America, attract travelers who seek authentic experiences rooted in cultural heritage (Xia et al., 2024). The combination of wellness with cultural immersion provides travelers with a sense of purpose and connection, reinforcing the appeal of such journeys. Another motivational driver is the desire for social recognition and self-image enhancement. Wellness travel is often associated with luxury, exclusivity, and self-care, making it appealing to individuals who want to project a lifestyle centered on health and sophistication. Sharing wellness experiences on social media also boosts this motivation, as travelers use these platforms to showcase their commitment to fitness, mindfulness, and sustainable living (Gulyas & Molnar, 2023).

2.3. Case Studies of Wellness Tourism in India

2.3.1. Case Study of Kerala – Ayurveda and Holistic Healing

Kerala, often termed "God's Own Country," is internationally recognized as the birthplace of Ayurveda-based wellness tourism in India. With a history spanning over 5,000 years, Ayurveda continues to be the backbone of Kerala's wellness offerings, blending ancient healing traditions with modern tourism infrastructure (Aswathy & Kumar, 2025). Wellness tourism in Kerala is driven largely by specialized resorts and retreats that provide authentic Ayurvedic treatments, detoxification therapies, Panchakarma programs, yoga, and meditation sessions. Destinations such as Kovalam, Kumarakom, and Varkala are particularly popular for their coastal settings that enhance the healing experience (Shivanand et al., 2022). Resorts like Somatheeram and Kalari Kovilakom market themselves as authentic Ayurvedic hospitals-cum-resorts, attracting both domestic and international travelers seeking preventive health care, rejuvenation, and holistic well-being.

The success of Kerala's wellness tourism can be attributed to its integration of medical expertise, cultural heritage, and natural beauty. The lush greenery, backwaters, and serene beaches provide the perfect environment for mental and spiritual relaxation (Matsuoka, 2025). Tourists are motivated not only by the promise of physical healing but also by cultural immersion in Kerala's traditions of herbal medicine, organic food, and yoga practices. Economically, wellness tourism has had a significant impact on Kerala, generating employment in both tourism and healthcare sectors, boosting demand for organic farming, and strengthening the state's global brand identity (Nair et al., 2024). However, challenges include the need for quality standardization and stricter regulation to ensure authenticity, as some unlicensed operators dilute the credibility of Ayurvedic offerings.

2.3.2. Case Study of Rishikesh – The Yoga Capital of the World

Rishikesh, located in Uttarakhand on the banks of the river Ganga, is widely known as the "Yoga Capital of the World." Its unique blend of spiritual ambiance, Himalayan landscape, and centuries-old yogic traditions makes it one of India's most prominent wellness tourism hubs. The growth of wellness tourism in Rishikesh was significantly boosted in 1968 when The Beatles visited the Maharishi

Mahesh Yogi Ashram, placing it firmly on the global spiritual map. Today, Rishikesh attracts thousands of international tourists seeking yoga, meditation, and spiritual healing (Bočkus et al., 2023). Renowned institutions such as Parmarth Niketan, Sivananda Ashram, and Yoga Niketan provide structured programs in yoga teacher training, Ayurvedic therapies, pranayama, and meditation.

Rishikesh's wellness tourism is strongly linked to spiritual motivations, as travelers view it as a place for inner transformation, stress relief, and holistic living. The annual International Yoga Festival, organized every March, brings together global practitioners and enthusiasts, strengthening Rishikesh's position as a wellness destination. Additionally, its location near the Himalayas and the Ganga enhances the psychological appeal of purification and spiritual cleansing. Economically, Rishikesh's wellness tourism contributes significantly to the state's economy by generating foreign exchange, providing employment in hospitality, yoga teaching, and handicrafts, and encouraging the growth of local businesses (Xie et al., 2022). The region also benefits from eco-tourism synergies, as wellness travelers often combine yoga retreats with trekking and adventure activities. Challenges remain in terms of infrastructure and environmental sustainability, as over-commercialization risks diluting the authentic spiritual experience. Nonetheless, Rishikesh stands as a global symbol of India's wellness heritage, embodying the intersection of tourism, spirituality, and health (Xia et al., 2024).

2.3.3. Case Study of Goa – Wellness Retreats and Alternative Therapies

While Goa is traditionally associated with beaches and leisure tourism, it has increasingly positioned itself as a wellness tourism hotspot, offering a fusion of relaxation, rejuvenation, and alternative healing. Goa's appeal lies in its ability to combine a laid-back lifestyle with high-quality wellness infrastructure (Shivanand et al., 2022). Wellness tourism in Goa includes yoga retreats, meditation camps, spa therapies, naturopathy, Ayurveda, and alternative practices such as Reiki, sound healing, and detox programs. Destinations like Anjuna, Palolem, and Mandrem are lined with wellness resorts and eco-retreats catering to both budget travelers and luxury seekers. Retreat centers such as Ashiyana Yoga Retreat and Bamboo Yoga Retreat are globally recognized for their immersive programs. The motivational factors for travelers to choose Goa for wellness tourism include its scenic coastal environment, cosmopolitan atmosphere, and reputation for alternative lifestyles (Matsuoka, 2025). Unlike Kerala and Rishikesh, which emphasize tradition and spirituality, Goa appeals to travelers seeking a fusion of wellness and leisure. The combination of beaches, vibrant culture, organic food cafes, and international communities makes it an attractive destination for wellness seekers from Europe, Russia, and North America.

Economically, wellness tourism has allowed Goa to diversify beyond conventional beach tourism. It has created opportunities for local communities in areas such as organic farming, spa therapies, and artisanal crafts. Moreover, Goa has gained prominence as a venue for international wellness festivals, music-yoga retreats, and eco-conscious tourism initiatives. Challenges for Goa's wellness tourism include balancing commercialization with authenticity and addressing sustainability issues related to waste management and overcrowding (Nair et al., 2024). Despite these challenges, Goa has carved out a niche in global wellness tourism by blending traditional healing with modern alternative therapies in a relaxed, multicultural setting.

3. Research Methodology

The present study adopts a conceptual research design to explore the growing trend of wellness tourism and its shift from conventional leisure travel to health-focused experiences. Given the nature of the research objective – examining motivations, behaviors, and economic implications – this study relies primarily on secondary data sources and case study analysis to provide a comprehensive understanding of the phenomenon. A conceptual research design has been chosen as it allows the study to build upon existing theories, literature, and practices in wellness tourism to develop a deeper conceptual framework. The design is qualitative in nature and emphasizes interpretive analysis of data rather than empirical fieldwork. This approach is appropriate because wellness tourism is an evolving area that requires the synthesis of diverse perspectives, including health, lifestyle, cultural traditions, and economic impacts.

The study is based exclusively on secondary data collected from reliable academic, professional, and industry sources. These include peer-reviewed journals and articles on wellness tourism, consumer behavior, and sustainable tourism, reports and databases published by organizations such as the Global Wellness Institute, World Tourism Organization (UNWTO), and Ministry of Tourism (Government of India), and case study materials from books, published case reports, and online resources documenting wellness tourism practices in India. The use of secondary data ensures a broader, cost-effective, and time-efficient understanding of the research problem while providing diverse insights from global and regional contexts. To contextualize the study, three case studies of wellness tourism destinations in India – Kerala, Rishikesh, and Goa were selected. These destinations were chosen due to their distinct positioning in the wellness tourism market: Kerala for Ayurveda and holistic healing, Rishikesh for yoga and spiritual retreats, and Goa for fusion-based wellness experiences. Each case study is analyzed in terms of motivational factors, tourist behavior, economic implications, and challenges, offering a comparative lens into the diverse manifestations of wellness tourism.

4. Findings

4.1. Health and Preventive Care as a Core Driver of Wellness Tourism

One of the most significant findings of this study is that health and preventive care serve as the core motivations behind wellness tourism. Unlike medical tourism, which focuses on treatment after illness, wellness tourism emphasizes proactive approaches to well-being. Travelers increasingly recognize the importance of maintaining health in the face of stressful, fast-paced lifestyles characterized by sedentary habits, digital overload, and lifestyle-related disorders. The desire to detoxify, rejuvenate, and prevent future health problems propels individuals toward destinations offering Ayurveda, naturopathy, spa therapies, yoga, and fitness-based retreats. The case of Kerala highlights this finding strongly, as the state markets Ayurveda and Panchakarma treatments for detoxification and preventive health, attracting both domestic and international visitors. Tourists often seek not just short-term relaxation but long-term health benefits that can be integrated into daily routines. Secondary data from the Global Wellness Institute reinforces this trend, showing that travelers are increasingly investing in wellness-focused journeys as a form of "health insurance." This finding suggests that wellness tourism is becoming embedded within the broader healthcare continuum, where travel itself is perceived as a therapeutic and preventive practice. For destinations and service providers, this emphasizes the importance of offering evidence-based, credible wellness programs that go beyond leisure to address the growing demand for preventive healthcare solutions (Liu et al., 2023). Wellness tourism, therefore, is no longer a luxury but a perceived necessity for maintaining a balanced lifestyle in the modern world.

4.2. Stress Relief and Mental Well-being as Central Motivations

Another key finding is that stress relief and mental wellness constitute primary reasons for engaging in wellness tourism. The pressures of urban living, long working hours, social media overload, and increasing cases of burnout have led individuals to seek travel as an escape route from stressful environments. Wellness tourism offers an alternative to conventional leisure by providing structured opportunities for mindfulness, meditation, yoga, and nature-based therapies that contribute to emotional stability and mental clarity (Liao et al., 2023). The Rishikesh case study exemplifies this finding. Known as the "Yoga Capital of the World," Rishikesh attracts thousands of wellness travelers annually who seek relief from stress through yoga retreats, meditation centers, and spiritual workshops. Tourists visiting Rishikesh are often motivated by the need to reset, recharge, and find balance in their lives. The annual International Yoga Festival further strengthens the city's reputation as a hub for mental wellness. Secondary sources also indicate that post-pandemic wellness travel has been strongly associated with mental healing. People are increasingly choosing destinations where they can disconnect from digital dependence, participate in mindfulness practices, and experience peace away from chaotic routines.

4.3. Cultural and Spiritual Engagement Enhances Wellness Travel Experiences

The study finds that cultural and spiritual immersion significantly enhance the appeal of wellness tourism. Wellness travelers are not merely motivated by physical health or relaxation; they also seek meaningful engagement with local traditions, indigenous healing practices, and spiritual environments. The blending of culture and wellness creates a holistic travel experience that provides both personal transformation and cultural enrichment. This is evident in Rishikesh and Kerala, where yoga, Ayurveda, and meditation are deeply rooted in India's cultural and spiritual heritage. Tourists visiting these destinations are often drawn by the authenticity and historical significance of these practices. For example, Ayurveda in Kerala is marketed as not just a therapy but a lifestyle rooted in Indian tradition. Similarly, yoga in Rishikesh is promoted as a spiritual journey that goes beyond physical exercise, connecting travelers to ancient wisdom and philosophies. Secondary data from global reports indicates that travelers increasingly seek "authentic" and "transformational" experiences rather than generic relaxation. The integration of wellness with cultural traditions provides uniqueness and differentiation in a highly competitive global market (Majeed & Gon Kim, 2023). This finding also highlights the role of spirituality as a motivational factor, as many wellness tourists view their journeys as opportunities for self-discovery and inner peace. For destinations, this suggests the importance of leveraging cultural heritage to enrich wellness offerings. By combining traditional practices with modern wellness infrastructure, countries like India can continue to position themselves as authentic and attractive wellness tourism destinations.

4.4. Economic Implications of Wellness Tourism are Significant

Another major finding of the study is that wellness tourism has substantial economic implications, both at the macro and micro levels. Travelers engaging in wellness-focused journeys typically spend more than conventional leisure tourists, as they are willing to invest in premium programs, therapies, and retreats. This trend translates into higher revenues for destinations, resorts, and local communities. The Goa case study illustrates this impact. Goa has successfully diversified from conventional beach tourism into wellness tourism, offering yoga retreats, alternative therapies, and fusion-based healing practices. Wellness travelers in Goa contribute to the local economy not only through spending on accommodations and retreats but also by supporting organic farming, handicrafts, artisanal products, and eco-friendly cafes. Similar patterns are observed in Kerala and Rishikesh, where wellness travel has generated employment in Ayurveda centers, yoga schools, and wellness resorts. Secondary reports from the Global Wellness Institute also reinforce that wellness travelers are "high-value tourists," with expenditure often 130% higher than that of average leisure tourists. This makes wellness tourism a critical contributor to foreign exchange earnings and sustainable economic development. This finding underscores the importance for policymakers and tourism planners to prioritize wellness tourism as a strategic growth sector (Liu et al., 2023).

4.5. Challenges of Authenticity and Sustainability in Wellness Tourism

The final finding reveals that despite its rapid growth, wellness tourism faces critical challenges related to authenticity, standardization, and sustainability. While wellness experiences are highly attractive, the sector is vulnerable to commercialization, which may dilute the credibility of traditional practices and compromise visitor trust. For instance, in Kerala, the unregulated proliferation of Ayurvedic centers has raised concerns about the authenticity and quality of treatments. Similarly, in Goa, over-commercialization of wellness retreats risks turning genuine experiences into commodified products for profit. The lack of standardized regulations for wellness practices, accreditation of service providers, and monitoring of quality often lead to inconsistencies in tourist satisfaction. From a sustainability perspective, destinations like Rishikesh face environmental stress due to high tourist inflows, which threaten the ecological and spiritual sanctity of the area. The challenge lies in balancing the demand for wellness experiences with the need to protect natural and cultural resources. Secondary research also highlights the emerging debate on "wellness washing," where destinations and businesses market wellness experiences without delivering true health or spiritual benefits. This trend could erode traveler confidence in the long run (Al-Ansi et al., 2025).

5. Discussion

5.1. Redefining the Purpose of Travel

The findings of this study suggest that wellness tourism is redefining the very purpose of travel. Traditionally, tourism was associated with leisure, entertainment, and sightseeing. However, wellness tourism emphasizes health, rejuvenation, and personal transformation as primary objectives. This reorientation indicates a paradigm shift in how individuals perceive travel – not as a break from routine but as an investment in holistic well-being. This redefinition aligns with global trends in preventive health care, where individuals take proactive steps to maintain physical and mental health rather than waiting for illness to occur. Case studies of Kerala, Rishikesh, and Goa show how destinations are increasingly branding themselves not just as holiday spots but as sanctuaries for healing and mindfulness. Kerala emphasizes Ayurveda, Rishikesh promotes yoga and spirituality, while Goa merges wellness with leisure. From a broader perspective, this shift also challenges traditional tourism providers to rethink their offerings. Hotels, resorts, and destinations are now required to embed wellness components into their services, such as organic food, meditation spaces, or fitness programs. The discussion raises questions about whether wellness tourism is becoming a necessity rather than a luxury in modern life, particularly in the context of urban stress and rising health concerns (Pereira et al., 2023).

5.2. The Role of Culture and Authenticity in Wellness Tourism

An important discussion point is the role of culture and authenticity in shaping wellness tourism experiences. The findings reveal that travelers are motivated not only by the desire for relaxation or health improvement but also by the search for authentic, culturally rooted practices. This makes destinations like India uniquely positioned, as they offer wellness traditions deeply embedded in cultural heritage, such as Ayurveda, yoga, and meditation. The case studies demonstrate this clearly. Rishikesh draws global attention for its association with ancient yogic practices and spiritual retreats. Kerala markets Ayurveda not as a commercial spa therapy but as a 5,000-year-old healing science. These examples highlight how cultural authenticity differentiates wellness tourism from generic leisure activities and provides travelers with a sense of deeper purpose and self-discovery. However, the discussion must also acknowledge the challenge of maintaining authenticity amidst commercialization. The proliferation of unlicensed Ayurvedic centers in

Kerala or overly commercialized retreats in Goa risks eroding the very cultural uniqueness that wellness tourists seek (Chen et al., 2023).

5.3. Wellness Tourism and Mental Health

The study highlights that stress relief and mental well-being are central motivations for wellness tourism, sparking a wider discussion on its role in addressing the global mental health crisis. Increasing levels of anxiety, burnout, and depression caused by modern lifestyles and digital overload have created an urgent need for accessible wellness solutions. Wellness tourism, with its emphasis on meditation, mindfulness, yoga, and nature immersion, provides one such avenue. Destinations like Rishikesh illustrate this dynamic, as tourists flock there not only for physical health but for mental clarity and spiritual balance. Similarly, Goa's retreats often combine yoga and mindfulness with leisure to attract travelers seeking emotional renewal. These practices allow individuals to temporarily disconnect from stressful environments and recalibrate their psychological well-being. The discussion, however, extends beyond temporary relief. Wellness tourism is increasingly viewed as contributing to long-term lifestyle changes, equipping participants with tools such as yoga techniques, mindfulness practices, or dietary adjustments that they can adopt in their daily lives. This positions wellness travel as more than just escapism – it becomes a pathway to sustained mental health improvement (Polat & Koseoglu, 2023).

5.4. Economic Potential and Sustainable Development

Another important discussion point is the economic significance of wellness tourism and its potential to contribute to sustainable development. Findings show that wellness travelers are "high-value" tourists who spend significantly more than leisure tourists. This spending extends beyond accommodations to include therapies, organic food, wellness activities, and local crafts, creating wide-ranging economic benefits. Case studies highlight this impact. Kerala has seen Ayurveda tourism create employment for therapists, farmers growing medicinal herbs, and hospitality workers. Rishikesh benefits economically through yoga schools, retreats, and the annual International Yoga Festival, which brings in global participants. Goa's wellness retreats have diversified its economy, reducing reliance on mass beach tourism and encouraging eco-friendly initiatives such as organic farming. The economic potential of wellness tourism also aligns with sustainable development goals (SDGs) by promoting environmentally responsible practices, preserving cultural traditions, and empowering local communities. For example, eco-retreats in Goa and nature-based therapies in the Himalayas attract wellness tourists while emphasizing conservation (Kim et al., 2024).

5.5. Challenges of Standardization and Credibility in Wellness Tourism

The final discussion point concerns the challenges of standardization and credibility within wellness tourism. As the sector expands rapidly, maintaining authenticity and quality becomes a pressing issue. Wellness practices such as Ayurveda, yoga, and meditation require trained practitioners and adherence to traditional methods. However, the proliferation of unlicensed centers and commercialized retreats raises concerns about inconsistent quality and visitor dissatisfaction. In Kerala, the Ayurvedic tourism sector illustrates this dilemma. While many resorts offer authentic treatments supervised by licensed practitioners, others market "Ayurvedic massages" without scientific grounding, risking the credibility of the entire sector. Similarly, in Goa, some wellness retreats prioritize profit over authenticity, blending alternative therapies without proper regulation. Such practices contribute to what researchers term "wellness washing," where experiences are branded as wellness but lack genuine benefits. Destinations like India, with globally recognized wellness traditions, have an additional responsibility to protect their heritage from dilution. Moreover, credibility also influences repeat visitation and word-of-mouth marketing. Wellness tourists, often seeking transformational experiences, are highly sensitive to authenticity (Sthapit et al., 2023).

6. Conclusion

The study highlights how wellness tourism has emerged as one of the fastest-growing segments of global travel, transforming leisure trips into purposeful journeys focused on health, balance, and well-being. No longer confined to spas and retreats, wellness tourism now encompasses preventive health care, stress management, spiritual growth, and lifestyle enhancement. This shift underscores the rising demand for travel experiences that not only rejuvenate but also contribute to long-term personal wellness. The case studies of Kerala, Rishikesh, and Goa illustrate how India has positioned itself as a leading wellness destination. Kerala's Ayurveda-driven healing emphasizes preventive care, Rishikesh represents spiritual wellness through yoga and meditation, while Goa combines leisure with alternative therapies for holistic rejuvenation. Together, these examples show the adaptability of wellness tourism in meeting diverse traveler motivations and highlight India's unique advantage rooted in its cultural heritage. The findings also confirm that wellness tourism contributes significantly to economic development by creating employment, promoting eco-friendly initiatives, and attracting high-value visitors who spend more than conventional tourists. At the same time, the study identifies challenges such as maintaining authenticity, ensuring quality standards, and balancing growth with environmental sustainability (Lee & Kim, 2023).

References

Al-Ansi, A., Kim, S., Xu, Y., Chen, C., Chua, B. L., & Han, H. (2025). Wellness tourism attributes and tourist outcomes: An analysis of configurational effects. *Journal of Travel Research*, *64*(5), 1244–1261.

Aswathy, V. K., & Kumar, S. (2025). Traditional healing practices for international tourists: Ethnographic account of ayurvedic tourism in Kerala, South India. In A. E. J. Ruiz, V. Rudkouskaya, N. L. Bejarano, & S. Bhartiya (Eds.), *Promoting sustainability in psychosocial travel techniques* (pp. 189–204). IGI Global.

Backman, S. J., Huang, Y. C., Chen, C. C., Lee, H. Y., & Cheng, J. S. (2023). Engaging with restorative environments in wellness tourism. *Current Issues in Tourism*, *26*(5), 789–806.

Bo⊠kus, D., Vento, E., Tammi, T., Komppula, R., & Kolesnikova, N. (2023). Comparing the motivations behind wellness tourism in three source markets. *European Journal of Tourism Research*, *33*, 3303–3303.

Chen, K. H., Huang, L., & Ye, Y. (2023). Research on the relationship between wellness tourism experiencescape and revisit intention: A chain mediation model. *International Journal of Contemporary Hospitality Management*, *35*(3), 893–918.

Clerici, A. P., Murphy, C., & Almeida, N. M. C. (2023). The future of wellness tourism after COVID-19. *European Spatial Research and Policy*, *30*(1), 103–122.

Dini, M., & Pencarelli, T. (2022). Wellness tourism and the components of its offer system: A holistic perspective. *Tourism Review*, *77*(2), 394–412.

Gulyas, G., & Molnar, E. I. (2023). Wellness tourism management research a bibliometric analysis. *Management & Marketing*, *18*(2), 172–191.

He, M., Liu, B., & Li, Y. (2023). Tourist inspiration: How the wellness tourism experience inspires tourist engagement. *Journal of Hospitality & Tourism Research*, *47*(7), 1115–1135.

Kim, S. I., Al-Ansi, A., Lee, J. S., Chua, B. L., Phucharoen, C., & Han, H. (2024). Wellness tourism experience and destination brand love. *Journal of Travel & Tourism Marketing*, *41*(7), 988–1004.

Lee, J., & Kim, J. J. (2023). A study on market segmentation according to wellness tourism motivation and differences in behavior between the groups—Focusing on satisfaction, behavioral intention, and flow. *International Journal of Environmental Research and Public Health*, *20*(2), 1063.

Li, Y., Deng, Q., Peng, F., & He, M. (2025). Development and verification of the wellness tourism experience scale. *Journal of Travel Research*, *64*(1), 158–171.

Liao, C., Zuo, Y., Xu, S., Law, R., & Zhang, M. (2023). Dimensions of the health benefits of wellness tourism: A review. *Frontiers in Psychology*, *13*, 1071578.

Liu, B., Li, Y., Kralj, A., Moyle, B., & He, M. (2022). Inspiration and wellness tourism: The role of cognitive appraisal. *Journal of Travel & Tourism Marketing*, *39*(2), 173–187.

Liu, L., Zhou, Y., & Sun, X. (2023). The impact of the wellness tourism experience on tourist well-being: The mediating role of tourist satisfaction. *Sustainability*, *15*(3), 1872.

Majeed, S., & Gon Kim, W. (2023). Emerging trends in wellness tourism: A scoping review. *Journal of Hospitality and Tourism Insights*, *6*(2), 853–873.

Matsuoka, S. (2025). The changing landscape of Ayurveda in Kerala, India: Vaidyas' practices, livelihoods, and their interactions with Institutional Medicine. https://www.researchsquare.com/article/rs-6527697/v1

Nair, V. T., Saranya Mol, S. T., & Suja, S. R. (2024). Case studies-Part IX: Healing art of tribal communities of Kerala, India. *Journal of Traditional and Folk Practices*, *12*(1), 64–68.

Pan, H., Mi, H., Chen, Y., Chen, Z., & Zhou, W. (2024). Measurement and evaluation of the development level of health and wellness tourism from the perspective of high-quality development. *Sustainability*, *16*(18), 8082.

Pereira, R., Costa, V., & Gomes, H. (2023). Health and wellness tourism: An overview of thermal tourism in Portugal. *Journal of Tourism, Sustainability and Well-being*, *11*(3), 136–147.

Polat, E., & Koseoglu, M. A. (2023). Wellness tourism scholarship: A research agenda. *Journal of Hospitality and Tourism Insights*, *6*(5), 1860–1889.

Shivanand, B. S., Tushara, M., Unnikrishnan, P. M., & Krishnamurthy, J. (2022). Do integrative approaches to health contribute to self-reliance in primary healthcare? reflections from a community case study in Kerala, India. *Health Psychology and Behavioral Medicine*, *10*(1), 1124–1135.

Sthapit, E., Björk, P., & Coudounaris, D. N. (2023). Towards a better understanding of memorable wellness tourism experience. *International Journal of Spa and Wellness*, *6*(1), 1–27.

Suban, S. A. (2022). Wellness tourism: A bibliometric analysis during 1998–2021. *International Journal of Spa and Wellness*, *5*(3), 250–270.

Xia, L., Lee, T. J., & Kim, D. K. (2024). Relationships between motivation, service quality, tourist satisfaction, quality of life, and spa and wellness tourism. *International Journal of Tourism Research*, *26*(1), e2624.

Xie, L., Guan, X., He, Y., & Huan, T. C. (2022). Wellness tourism: Customer-perceived value on customer engagement. *Tourism Review*, *77*(3), 859–876.

Chapter 19

The Prospect of Wellness Tourism in India

Moushumi Banerjee

Faculty of Hotel Management & Applied Sciences, MS Ramaiah University of Applied Sciences, Bangalore, India

Abstract

This chapter looks into the growing popularity of a special kind of tourism called yoga tourism and spiritual tourism, which are both big parts of wellness tourism. Spiritual tourism has become a big hit in the global market, and people plan special trips for personal growth and transformation. When yoga tourism is combined with spiritual tourism, it becomes a strong tool for marketing to bring in more tourists. Yoga therapy is widely accepted by international travelers as a way to gain spiritual peace and improve health. The chapter explores the reasons why western yoga fans travel to India for spiritual and wellness purposes. India is a beautiful place that offers the perfect setting for health and wellness seekers. The chapter also looks at the types of people who visit and the reasons behind their choices, which is key for developing a strong wellness tourism business in India. The results of this study are expected to help yoga-focused wellness service providers. Moreover, future research will focus more on quality marketing strategies and what motivates tourists.

Keywords: Yoga; wellness; rejuvenation; spiritual tourism; tourist motivation

1. Introduction

This research explores the marketing strategies India has used to position itself as a top destination for yoga tourism. The growing popularity of yoga has led many people around the world to travel to practice it (Connell, 2007). This has turned into a trend known as yoga tourism (Lehto et al., 2006), which is now a

Advancement in Medical and Wellness Tourism, Part A: Entrepreneurship and Technology, 253–262

doi:10.1108/978-1-80592-983-320261019

major and profitable part of the wellness tourism industry (SRI International, 2017). India is the birthplace of yoga and remains the most popular place for yoga practice (Aggarwal et al., 2006; Maddox, 2014). It became a leading spiritual destination after the Beatles visited for a yoga experience (Saltzman, 2000; Sharply & Sundaram, 2005), and it is known for hosting yoga retreats (Philp, 2008). Most of India's marketing efforts are focused on the British market, as recent data (CBI, 2015; CCI, 2016) shows that the UK has always been a major part of India's travel industry. In recent years, India has become one of the most attractive non-European destinations for British travelers (Skyscanner, 2011) and one of the emerging global markets with huge potential (Enderwick, 2010; Sakarya et al., 2007). The yoga tourism market in India is still in its early stages, and there is very little research on this market. A study by Aggarwal et al. (2008, p. 463) suggested that India needs to shift from its traditional marketing approach to a more competitive and modern one. Marketing strategies for yoga tourism in India are not strong enough to fully tap into the potential market. This study aims to discover the marketing strategies India has used to become a competitive yoga destination in the global market. This research can help create new concepts and ideas for promoting yoga tourism. The findings will offer useful methods for the Indian tourism market to compete internationally. Additionally, it will help destination marketing organizations (DMOs) in India to analyze the importance of yoga tourism and create suitable strategies. This can support both practitioners and policy-makers in developing campaigns to attract yoga-focused tourists, leading to more wellness-focused trips in India and boosting the country's economy. The study's results will help improve India's marketing strategies and increase the effectiveness of its yoga tourism industry. Lastly, this research can help understand the factors that drive tourists and explore the potential of yoga tourism, offering opportunities to explore other aspects of yoga therapy and knowledge for profitable tourism.

2. Objectives of the Study

- To identify the factors to create an image of India as a yoga destination.
- To analyze the marketing policies being applied for yoga tourism in India.
- To develop methods to preserve the originality in yoga tourism marketing strategies for India.

3. Review of Literature

Marketing India as a yoga destination, India was one of the first yoga destinations, and it is still the most popular, presumably because it is the origin of yoga practices.

- Maddox (2014) argues that, as the cradle of yoga, India is positioned advantageously in promoting this type of tourism. In the process of finding India's efforts to reinforce itself as a top yoga destination, four different approaches can be identified. Three of these correspond to the positioning of yoga tourism;

these are based on interpretations of yoga as a wellness, sport, or spiritual activity. India markets itself as a giver of an "authentic" yoga experience, highlighting that it is the origin of this practice.

- The promotion of yoga as a symbiosis of spirituality and wellness, in order to tap into these motivations, appears to have gained great popularity in India's yoga market (Chen et al., 2013). Given that the spirituality logic of yoga was initially influenced by gurus of Indian descent but also by their later disciples of American descent (Ertimur & Coskuner-Balli, 2015), the USA constitutes a potential competitor market in the yoga tourism sector.
- The country's marketing activities are focused on portraying the destination as a place where achieving holistic well-being is more possible than anywhere else in the world (Day, 1999; Toyne & Walters, 1989).
- The broadly understood concept of wellness is ingrained in the branding of the so-called "India experience," with yoga as the main constituent component (Chen et al., 2013).
- Yoga is being projected as a process of stress-relief, health, and mind rejuvenation, in association with what they describe as an emotion-focused or palliative strategy to soften the symptoms of stress. These effectively target international visitors who, on the one hand, are seeking a "divine" experience but, on the other, are expecting relaxation in a luxury environment.
- Destination selects combinations of brand components for attracting customers and facilitating loyalty. Although it presents yoga as a practice that is exceptionally beneficial to both physical health and mental well-being (Mohsin & Lockyer, 2010).
- This marketing approach is intended as a part of the wellness-related package holidays that usually include spa activities and gourmet food, accompanied by the promise of "royal" treatment provided with modern comforts (Heo & Hyun, 2015).

4. Purpose

The chapter looks into the marketing strategies that India is currently using to become a competitive place for yoga.

4.1. Research Methodology

The research followed a well-organized approach that included a qualitative method and data collection through interviews. The data were gathered from semi-structured interviews with yoga practitioners from different backgrounds and skill levels who had traveled to India for yoga tourism.

4.2. Qualitative Data Collection

This study used a qualitative approach based on the constructivism philosophy, which views reality as something created by individuals. This means that getting the target audience to share their personal views is important for achieving the study's goals. Qualitative research can provide a lot of detailed information even from a small group of participants.

4.3. Sampling Procedure

For qualitative research, the sampling method needs to help understand the topic deeply. This study used two types of non-probability samples. First, a purposive sample was selected, meaning participants were chosen because they were most suitable to answer the study's three research questions. These participants were non-Indian yoga practitioners who had traveled to India for yoga tourism. The authors used their personal connections in the yoga industry to invite people who had been on yoga trips to India. The second method used was a snowball technique, which helped find more interviewees.

4.4. Interview Design

A semi-structured interview format was used because it is considered the best way for this type of research. This method allowed participants to express their opinions freely in their own words.

4.5. Data Collection

The chapter aimed to explore India's marketing strategies that attract yoga practitioners to visit the country. During the interviews, some personal questions were asked to build a profile of all the respondents. The data from these interviews are shown in Table 19.1.

Four of the first six people who were approached agreed to take part in the study. Another 6 participants were selected using the snowball method described earlier, making a total of 10 yoga practitioners who took part in the interviews. Most of the participants had different jobs, and the group included a variety of people in terms of their marital status, the type of yoga they practiced, and how experienced they were with yoga. All 10 interviews were conducted in India and were face-to-face. Each interview lasted between 32 and 53 minutes, and all were recorded digitally. Some of the questions asked during the interviews were: "How do you see India as a yoga destination? Does this country have any advantages over other yoga destinations?" and "Have you seen any marketing efforts promoting India as a competitive yoga destination? If so, do you think they are effective?" All the interview recordings were transcribed exactly as they were spoken, in preparation for the analysis of the data that follows.

5. Results and Discussion

The analysis software NVivo 11 was used to categorize the interview data, as it is widely recognized as the standard tool for qualitative data analysis. The analysis of the interview data revealed a wide range of opinions and insights related to the main topics of the study. This section will now present the key findings, including direct quotes from the interviewees.

Table 19.1. Profile of Interviewees.

	Age/ Gender	Marital Status	Occupation	Type of Yoga Practiced	Level of Advancement
Interviewee 1	52/F	Widow	Art teacher	Iyengar Yoga	Advanced
Interviewee 2	26/F	Single	Shop assistant	Hatcha Yoga	Beginner
Interviewee 3	28/F	Single	Nursery assistant	Hatcha Yoga	Intermediate
Interviewee 4	37/F	Married	Bank assistant	Hatcha Yoga	Beginner
Interviewee 5	32/M	Divorced	IT Professional	Iyengar Yoga	Intermediate
Interviewee 6	21/F	Student	Waitress	Hatcha Yoga	Intermediate
Interviewee 7	30/F	Married	Flight attendant	Hatcha Yoga	Advanced
Interviewee 8	24/F	Single	Shop assistant	Hatcha Yoga	Beginner
Interviewee 9	27/M	Single	Personal trainer	Hot Yoga	Intermediate
Interviewee 10	42/F	Divorced	Nutritionist	Iyengar Yoga	Advanced

5.1. Spiritual Aspects of Yoga Tourism in India

The data confirmed that traveling for yoga can be classified into categories such as sport and spiritual tourism, with elements of wellness included in both. In the cases discussed, well-being was understood in different ways: for some, it was connected with activities that were "still mainly physical," while others viewed it as a "highly spiritual practice." These differences came from each person's own understanding of the world, which is consistent with a constructivist perspective. When analyzing the data, a pattern emerged: long-term yoga practitioners were more likely to see their practice as spiritual rather than for beginners. This observation could be useful when promoting a yoga destination. The findings also showed that some yoga practitioners viewed traveling for yoga as a "personalized spiritual journey." India is actively promoting itself as a spiritual destination, and this aligns with the motivations of these individuals.

5.2. Sport and Wellness Aspects of Yoga Tourism in India

The image of India as a yoga destination was shaped by the three categories of tourism: sport, wellness, and spiritual. It was established that yoga falls under all these categories. According to the interviewees, apart from spirituality, sport tourism also relates to wellness because physical activity is often seen as part of well-being.

Interviewee 8 said, "I would like to have lots of walking – spending time outdoors in an active way would be a great extra to my yoga retreat." It seems that the perception of a yoga vacation as a wellness-related holiday was the most common, with many participants expressing a strong preference for combining yoga practice with outdoor activities such as walking and nature-based experiences. This highlights the growing demand for holistic travel experiences that integrate physical activity, mental relaxation, and connection with nature.

Interviewee 6 stating, "Thanks to yoga, I can look deep into my inner self and get to know myself better." Therefore, promoting yoga as part of wellness holidays or equating it with gym exercise doesn't accurately reflect what yoga practitioners think about the activity. None of the respondents saw yoga as belonging to just one of these categories. As a result, the findings suggest that the category of wellness tourism should be broadened to include the leisure aspect of yoga.

5.3. Educational Aspects of Yoga Tourism in India

None of the marketing strategies used by India directly targeted people who want to learn more about yoga. This was surprising, given that:

Interviewee 9 said, "I really want to learn more about yoga, find out about 18 different styles and try them out." The strategy that comes closest to this educational pursuit is the promotion of the authenticity of the yoga experience, as this implies that yoga practiced in India is deeply rooted in Indian culture. It was also considered to be of "better quality," which might attract those interested in yoga education. However, the educational aspects of yoga travel seem to be overlooked by India's tourism market.

5.4. Social Aspects of Yoga Tourism in India

Social interaction is part of the approach that promotes yoga as a recreational activity. This strategy is often supported by images of yoga classes attended by smiling and attractive people. By linking yoga with fitness classes, this kind of promotion can be argued to meet the needs of people who are looking for "good company" during their yoga holidays. For example, *Interviewee 2 said*, "If I go on such a vacation, I need to be sure there are great people to spend time with because I'm a very social person." However, when promoting yoga as a spiritual activity, it is often advertised as something done in solitude, probably to emphasize its reflective nature. Thus, the marketing activities do not clearly recognize the connection between the desire for spiritual enlightenment and the need for social interaction, as revealed by the interviewees' responses.

5.5. Cuisine

Our data show that yoga practitioners consider the link between yoga and nutrition and the availability of healthy food to be one of the most important features of a yoga destination. As our findings suggest, India has significant potential to address this area, and this aspect is worth considering in future marketing efforts to make India an attractive yoga destination. The findings also identified the need to apply this innovative perception to India's marketing approach in order to more accurately respond to the needs of target markets.

6. Conclusions

6.1. Key Conclusions

This chapter aimed to examine the marketing strategies that India is using to position itself as a competitive yoga destination in the global tourism market. To achieve this, we looked at existing theories, formed three key research questions, and conducted an in-depth study with yoga practitioners who have traveled to India for yoga tourism. By analyzing the interview data, we have now drawn our conclusions based on the three research questions. The research asked how India is currently marketed as a yoga destination, what marketing strategies are being used for yoga tourism in India, and what role authenticity plays in these strategies. The findings suggest that yoga tourism in India is being re-positioned with a unique approach that combines a broader concept of wellness with a lack of religious references, similar to the US market. This study concludes that incorporating wellness-related concepts into all marketing efforts can be a key goal to attract a wider range of yoga tourists.

The term "well being" should be understood more broadly than it currently is by Indian DMOs. The study also found that marketing efforts often overlook the fluid boundaries between different types of tourism that yoga is connected to. We offer several recommendations based on these findings that Indian DMOs may find helpful in promoting yoga tourism. First, it is believed that more holistic marketing strategies will better align with the trend for healthy lifestyles that is common among yoga practitioners in Western markets like the USA. So, focusing on just one aspect of yoga tourism might not be enough to attract visitors. Therefore, we recommend that a greater emphasis be placed on all dimensions of yoga, with the concept of wellness included in all of them.

The study also shows that presenting yoga as an integral part of the overall India experience has great potential to boost not only the promotion of India as a yoga destination, but also as a general holiday destination. We suggest that this can be achieved by including more yoga-related information in marketing campaigns by the Indian tourism industry, such as "Incredible India!," or by creating yoga-focused advertising that highlights various aspects of the activity alongside other attractions in the country. Portraying India as a culturally diverse and heritage-rich destination can attract potential visitors, but this should still be a true picture of India without any excessive glamorization. In this way, Indian DMOs can promote the authenticity of the entire "India experience," not just yoga. This would make marketing efforts more holistic and trustworthy, and more likely to appeal to consumers.

7. Limitations and Future Research

7.1. Practical Applications

It was suggested that Indian tourism leaders should develop strategies that offer a genuine yoga experience to attract Western visitors seeking wellness and spiritual growth. Indian DMOs should target those looking for traditional and authentic yoga therapies to achieve spiritual and mental health. Marketing policies should reflect the realistic experience of those seeking yoga.

7.2. Originality/Value

The findings of this study have led to a repositioning of yoga tourism in India using a unique approach that weaves wellness with spiritual growth. It was also found that the motivations of yoga tourists were not properly addressed by tourism marketers, which limited the market's potential.

7.2.1. Marketing Strategies for Yoga Tourism in India

Yoga is increasingly being marketed as a pathway to achieving a healthier self. In India, promotional strategies often emphasize the physical and therapeutic benefits of yoga, positioning it as a tool for improving overall health and well-being. This approach is closely linked to the expansion of medical and wellness tourism, as highlighted by a Hannam and Diekmann (2010) and Remya (2015). By foregrounding its curative properties, yoga is frequently "medicalized" and presented as a form of therapeutic exercise.

At the same time, yoga tourism can be associated with elements of sport tourism, as it involves physical activity and active participation. Another prominent strategy involves promoting India as a spiritual destination, targeting tourists seeking personal enlightenment and self-discovery. Marketing campaigns often depict India as an unmodernised and exotic land, a representation that, while appealing, is both outdated and overly simplistic. Such portrayals rely on imagery of India as a relic of the past, emphasizing tranquillity, authenticity, and a slower pace of life in contrast to the stressful routines of modern societies.

Authenticity plays a crucial role in yoga tourism marketing. As noted by, As noted by Beverland et al. (2010), India's identity as the birthplace of yoga is a powerful symbolic asset that cannot be overlooked. Yoga, deeply embedded in Indian culture and tradition, enhances the country's image as a premier destination for authentic yoga experiences. Practicing yoga in India is therefore often perceived as more genuine and meaningful than practicing it elsewhere.

Overall, the four dominant approaches to marketing yoga as a tourism product in India – health and wellness, medical benefits, sport-related activity, and spiritual authenticity – not only target diverse segments of tourists but also reflect different interpretations of yoga holidays.

7.3. Approaches Toward Marketing India as a Yoga Destination

India can be promoted as a yoga destination by presenting yoga not just as an activity, but as a way of life deeply rooted in the country's culture and traditions. By linking yoga with wellness tourism, India offers visitors a chance to relax, heal, and rejuvenate through a blend of yoga, Ayurveda, spa therapies, and holistic healing. Spiritual tourism adds depth by allowing travelers to experience the true essence of yoga through meditation, mindfulness, and learning in ashrams and sacred places. At the same time, sport tourism highlights yoga as a practical path to physical fitness, mental balance, and stress management through retreats, workshops, and wellness events. Most importantly, emphasizing authentic experiences by showcasing India as the birthplace of yoga, guided by traditional gurus and ancient wisdom, creates trust and emotional connection. Together, these approaches make India an inviting, meaningful, and genuine destination for yoga seekers from around the world and were developed by the author (2023).

The discussion above shows that types of tourism and how they are promoted are connected in some way. It also seems that India's efforts to promote itself as a yoga destination cover a wide range of ideas about yoga and the reasons people travel to practice it. The role of India as a yoga tourism spot has been covered, along with the ways it has been marketed. However, there's always a chance that the people interviewed might not have given their true opinions due to personal bias. Because of this, building trust between the researchers and the participants was important. If there had been more time and resources, the project could have been more complete. More interviews with different groups could have been done to look at more cases like the one studied. Even though our sample size was small, the process of analyzing interviews from different sources helped us reach a point where no new information was coming in – this is called saturation. For future research, it would be useful to look at a bigger and more varied group of yoga practitioners from different countries and backgrounds. Maybe by comparing different groups, we could find more insights. The methods and number of participants used here were enough for the goals of the study, but expanding the research to include more contexts or destinations could improve it. This study has contributed to academic knowledge about yoga tourism and could also help Indian DMOs in practical ways. If similar studies are done with people from different nationalities, it could lead to more detailed findings and allow for comparisons between different groups of yoga tourists.

References

Aggarwal, R., Guglani, R., & Goel, R. K. (2008). Changing paradigms in Indian tourism marketing. *South Asian Journal of Tourism and Heritage*, *1*(2), 459–468.

Aggarwal, R., Guglani, R., & Goel, R. K. (2006). *Wellness tourism and holistic health management*. (pp. 85–102). Sage Publications.

Beverland, M. B., Lindgreen, A., & Vink, M. W. (2010). Projecting authenticity through advertising: Consumer judgments of advertisers' claims. *Journal of Advertising*, *39*(1), 1–12.

CBI. (2015). *Tourism trends in the United Kingdom market*. Ministry of Foreign Affairs, Netherlands.

CCI. (2016). *Indian tourism industry report*. Chambers of Commerce and Industry India.

Chen, J. S., Prebensen, N. K., & Huan, T. C. (2013). Determining the motivation of wellness travelers. *Tourism Analysis*, *18*(2), 153–165.

Connell, J. (2007). Medical tourism: Sea, sun, sand and … surgery. *Tourism Management*, *28*(4), 1093–1100.

Day, G. S. (1999). Creating a market-driven organization. *MIT Sloan Management Review*, *41*(1), 11–22.
Enderwick, P. (2010). Emerging economies and the global tourism industry. *Tourism Recreation Research*, *35*(1), 5–14.
Ertimur, B., & Coskuner-Balli, G. (2015). Navigating the institutional logics of markets: Implications for strategic brand management. *Journal of Marketing*, *79*(2), 40–61.
Hannam, K., & Diekmann, A. (2010). *Beyond medical tourism: Mobilities, globalisation and health*. Routledge.
Heo, C. Y., & Hyun, S. S. (2015). Do luxury spa experiences influence customer satisfaction and loyalty? *International Journal of Hospitality Management*, *46*, 155–164.
Lehto, X. Y., Brown, S., Chen, Y., & Morrison, A. M. (2006). Yoga tourism as a niche within the wellness tourism market. *Tourism Recreation Research*, *31*(1), 25–35.
Maddox, A. (2014). Tourism and spirituality: A global perspective. (pp. 120–138). Routledge.
Mohsin, A., & Lockyer, T. (2010). Customer perceptions of service quality in luxury hotels. *International Journal of Contemporary Hospitality Management*, *22*(2), 256–269.
Philp, T. (2008). *Spiritual tourism: Travel and transformation*. Channel View Publications.
Remya, V. (2015). Wellness tourism in India: Opportunities and challenges. *International Journal of Multidisciplinary Research and Development*, *2*(2), 73–78.
Sakarya, S., Eckman, M., & Hyllegard, K. H. (2007). Market selection for international expansion. *International Marketing Review*, *24*(2), 208–238.
Saltzman, M. (2000). *The Beatles in India*. Penguin Books.
Sharpley, R., & Sundaram, P. (2005). Tourism: A sacred journey? The case of ashram tourism, India. *International Journal of Tourism Research*, *7*(3), 161–171.
Skyscanner. (2011). *Travel trends report: Emerging destinations for UK travellers*. Skyscanner Ltd.
SRI International. (2017). *Global wellness tourism economy report*. Global Wellness Institute.
Toyne, B., & Walters, P. G. P. (1989). *Global marketing management*. Allyn & Bacon.

Chapter 20

Wellness Tourism: Prospects and Challenges

Piali Haldar and Dev Kumar Mandal

Department of Management, Brainware University, Kolkata, India

Abstract

Wellness tourism refers to travel aimed at maintaining a healthy body and mind to improve quality of life, including destressing, emotional and physical rejuvenation, mental relaxation, and spiritual growth. Unlike medical tourism, it focuses on preventive health care. Wellness tourism with personalized healing experiences is in demand following the COVID-19 pandemic, where travelers are seeking locations rich in wellness retreats, yoga ashrams, or eco-resorts for preventive health care. This chapter will unveil the prospects and challenges the hospitality industry is facing in meeting the increasing demand for wellness tourism. The demand for wellness tourism will not only help countries attract foreign tourists for Ayurvedic, panchakarma, or yogic therapy, but it will also enable these countries to earn foreign exchange and generate employment opportunities. In addition to this, this chapter will elaborate on the opportunities for destination, local communities, and individuals, as well as the challenges in the wellness tourism sector, like standardization and quality control, risk of over-commercialization, unchecked expansion can lead to environmental degradation, commodification of healing treatment, falsification, and misrepresentation of origin practices may harm the wellness tourism sector. Furthermore, this study discussed the prospects of wellness tourism, its practical implications, conclusions, and future research directions.

Keywords: Wellness tourism; dimensions; opportunities; challenges; prospects

Advancement in Medical and Wellness Tourism, Part A: Entrepreneurship and Technology, 263–277

doi:10.1108/978-1-80592-983-320261020

1. Introduction to Wellness Tourism

The world is growing increasingly fast-paced, stressful, and hyper-connected. This is driving people to seek out wellness tourism as a means to regain mental, physical, and spiritual balance (Mujtaba, 2025). Wellness tourism, in its broadest sense, refers to trips taken for the purpose of improving one's state of health and overall well-being, be it physical, psychological, or spiritual (Grénman & Räikkönen, 2015; Haldar, 2023). This type of tourism goes beyond the conventional idea of traveling for recreation and rest, incorporating a distinct health-enhancing experience into its very essence. In contrast to medical tourism, which focuses on treatment and curative health services, wellness tourism centers on prevention, lifestyle improvement, and holistic well-being (Global Wellness Institute (GWI), 2021).

The wellness tourism market experienced impressive growth over the last 10 years (Majeed & Gon Kim, 2023). The GWI (2021) stated that wellness tourism earned revenues of $720 billion in 2019, which made up over 17% of all tourism expenditures. Even though the COVID-19 pandemic brought about a period of decline, the wellness tourism segment has shown a strong bounce-back since the pandemic. Its recovery seems in keeping with the general travel recovery. The interest of these pandemic-weary travelers in self-care seems, if anything, heightened. These travelers are not just seeking your garden-variety vacation. They are after something that impacts their health, well-being, or both (United Nations World Tourism Organization (UNWTO), 2022).

The idea of wellness has developed from its ancient beginnings in systems such as Ayurveda, Traditional Chinese Medicine (TCM), and ancient Greek medicine, all of which viewed health as a balanced state of mind, body, and spirit (Ray, 2025). This current surge in the concept of wellness has occurred because of the appearance in the last decade of an ever-rising tide of non-communicable diseases and mental health conundrums that are affecting people all around the world. As more people seek remedies to these conditions and are driven by the desire to live longer and healthier, they are looking for experiences that go way beyond just seeing the local doctor, and this has resulted in an upswing in wellness tourism (Smith & Puczkó, 2014). These offerings are often located in serene and eco-sensitive environments, thereby also aligning with principles of sustainable tourism.

One of the unique features of wellness tourism is its multidimensional nature. It is not merely about traveling to relax or rejuvenate (Cohen et al., 2017); it is about experiencing a transformative journey that incorporates physical activities (like hiking or fitness camps), mental practices (such as meditation and cognitive behavioral workshops), and cultural exchanges (like participation in indigenous healing rituals) (Dini & Pencarelli, 2022; Huang & Xu, 2014; Norman & Pokorny, 2017). This holistic configuration appeals to a wide demographic, from millennials seeking mindfulness retreats to retirees opting for Ayurvedic rejuvenation therapies. The wellness travelers are typically more affluent, spend more than the average tourist, and often demonstrate strong environmental and ethical consciousness (Voigt & Pforr, 2013).

The drivers of wellness tourism are manifold. Socioeconomic factors such as rising disposable incomes, urbanization, and aging populations have played a significant role in expanding the wellness tourism market (Marak et al., 2014). At the same time, growing awareness around mental health, body positivity, and integrative medicine has influenced travel motivations (Dar & Kashyap, 2022; Haldar, 2021; Smith & Puczkó, 2014). Digital detoxification has emerged as a major trend, with people deliberately seeking destinations where they can disconnect from screens and reconnect with nature, themselves, or a spiritual path (Yeung & Johnston, 2020). These wellness-motivated journeys often include lifestyle counseling, nutritional guidance, and eco-therapy, promoting long-term behavioral change.

Asia has long served as a wellness tourism destination, thanks to its longstanding traditions in wellness practices such as Ayurveda, yoga, and meditation. For example, India draws thousands of visitors each year to the state of Kerala for Ayurvedic therapies and spiritual retreats, as well as to the towns of Rishikesh and Dharamshala for yoga teacher training and Buddhist retreats (Annavarapu, 2018; Babu et al., 2014; Lahariya, 2020). Meanwhile, Thailand is another destination that has incorporated ancient healing traditions into luxury wellness resorts (Chundasutathanakul & Chirapanda, 2021; Han et al., 2018; Kongtaveesawas et al., 2022). Simultaneously, the United States, Australia, and Germany have turned the concept of wellness into a profitable niche in the hospitality industry (Clift & Hancox, 2010; Csirmaz & Pető, 2015), with organic farm stays, spa resorts, fitness cruises, and other creative vacation ideas (GWI, 2021). This globalization of wellness has created a rich tapestry of offerings that blend indigenous knowledge systems with modern science.

Nevertheless, wellness tourism is not without its obstacles. Opponents say that the wellness tourism industry may be expanding too quickly, and thus is not necessarily a good thing. Some fear that it is converting places that were once serene into too commercialized spaces, in short, that it's doing to such destinations what it has done to yoga in recent years. Critics also worry about the high price of some wellness retreats, which seem accessible only to the upper classes. And there's a more pressing concern, like poor regulation, which impacts the tourists who partake in them or the local communities whose practices remain largely unknown (Kelly, 2012). Sustainability is another pressing concern; as wellness destinations grow in popularity, they may face pressures on local ecosystems, water resources, and cultural heritage.

In response to these concerns, several frameworks have been developed that promote responsible and sustainable wellness tourism. Certifications such as Leadership in Energy and Environmental Design (LEED), Green Rating for Integrated Habitat Assessment (GRIHA), and the Green Spa Network ensure that wellness tourism destinations uphold environmental standards. Additionally, organizations such as the GWI promote sound practices in ethics, cultural sensitivity, and ecological responsibility. Governments have also begun stepping in; for example, the Indian Ministry of AYUSH (Ayurveda, Yoga, and Naturopathy; Unani; Siddha; and Homeopathy) promotes authentic wellness services that ensure quality (among other objectives) (Ministry of AYUSH, 2020).

Moreover, an ever-increasing role is being played by technology in molding the future of tourism focused on wellness. Programs centered on wellness are increasingly finding a place in artificial intelligence (AI), virtual reality (VR), and mobile app technology. The future, AI, VR, and a proliferation of other mobile app technologies set to potentially become the new geeky wellness tools of tomorrow, will add more high-tech to the world of wellness via real-world waypoints (Johnston et al., 2018).

The global tourism industry has a blossoming subset called wellness tourism. It has the potential to deliver not only health benefits to its consumers but also to address significant global health challenges. Wellness tourism is sophisticated and complex, and it picks up ancient traditions as much as modern health practices to ensure inclusivity, cultural integrity, and ecological sustainability.

This chapter aims to discuss the following:

- To investigate the prevailing trends and growth drivers of wellness tourism in Asia, with a particular concentration on India's status in the international wellness market.
- To evaluate the contribution of economic growth, tourism development, and job creation to the emerging wellness tourism sector.
- To pinpoint the main issues that wellness tourism must deal with, like quality assurance, authenticity, over-commercialization, and sustainability.
- To propose strategic recommendations for establishing a wellness tourism ecosystem that can compete on a global scale, yet is rooted in local culture and is environmentally sustainable.

2. Literature Review

2.1. Definition of Wellness Tourism

Wellness tourism is a form of travel with the exact motivation of pursuing well-being. According to the GWI (2021), "wellness tourism is travel associated with the pursuit of maintaining or enhancing one's well-being." Like all forms of tourism, wellness tourism contains grains of place and space. The types of experiences sought by those traveling for wellness reasons are as varied as the destinations they choose. Unlike traditional tourism, which may prioritize leisure, adventure, or cultural exploration, wellness tourism centers on health-enhancing experiences (Smith & Puczkó, 2014).

2.2. Different Dimensions of Wellness Tourism

Wellness tourism is built upon a range of core components that contribute to the traveler's holistic well-being, including:

2.2.1. Wellness Activities of a Physical Nature

The wellness tourism activities directly affect the body's health, fitness, and vitality. They are best performed in a spacious, naturally lit, and well-ventilated area, though they can also be accomplished outdoors in any weather. Activities like yoga, hiking, nature walks, detoxing, and nutritional therapy can be performed in ways that promote physical wellness. And together, they enhance energy, flexibility, and a stamina that literally makes the heart grow fonder (Voigt & Pforr, 2013).

2.2.2. Mental and Emotional Wellness

Emotional well-being activities include programs in meditation, mindfulness, stress reduction, and mental coaching. These help travelers achieve emotional balance and psychological resilience (Kelly, 2012).

2.2.3. Spiritual and Philosophical Exploration

Numerous wellness tourists pursue spiritual development through means such as meditation, chanting, spiritual counseling, or trips to holy places. These practices are meant to take self-awareness to the next level and to help people figure out the kind of life they really want to lead (Johnston et al., 2018).

2.2.4. Environmental and Natural Connection

Wellness tourism places a strong emphasis on immersing oneself in nature. Eco-sensitive environments enable travelers to experience serenity, whether the chosen destination is a mountain, a forest, or a beach. Such places allow for relaxation and even rejuvenation. Somehow, the natural world is perceived to have therapeutic value (Yeung & Johnston, 2020).

2.2.5. Lifestyle and Preventive Health Services

Tourism-focused on wellness often provides beneficial workshops addressing nutrition, sleep hygiene, time management, and holistic living. Such workshops promote healthy, sustainable lifestyle choices that are likely to continue long after the travel experience ends (GWI, 2021).

Cultural and indigenous healing practices: Numerous wellness tourism packages derive from ancient traditions like Ayurveda (India), TCM, Thai massage, or Native American healing rituals. Such offerings not only provide a form of cultural immersion but also promise various therapeutic benefits (Smith & Puczkó, 2014).

2.3. Benefits of Wellness Tourism

The wellness tourism industry is capable of providing a wide range of benefits at the social, health, and environmental levels. It also creates an incredibly large set of chances and opportunities in innumerable ways, for destinations, local communities, and individuals, both tourists and residents.

2.3.1. Social Benefits

Cultural exchange and preservation are advanced by wellness tourism (Huang & Xu, 2014; Shyngysbaeva et al., 2023). Though it is a relatively new segment of the overall tourism industry, it is growing rapidly. It improves health and well-being through blending traditional healing systems with modern wellness practices. It emphasizes prevention, relaxation, and holistic living.

2.3.2. Health Benefits

Wellness tourism serves to boost both individual and collective health. On the individual front, the World Health Organization defines wellness tourism as travel under the motivation or intention to achieve or maintain a state of mental and physical well-being (Gkinton et al., 2023). This can occur during and after the trip, as the experiences tend to be immersive and transformative, leading to some long-lasting changes in health. Typical activities that make up the wellness tourism experience include the following:

- Engaging in yoga and/or meditation.
- Enjoying spa treatments and relaxing in a variety of settings, from the traditional to the more inventive.
- Participating in nutritional programs that are toning, detoxifying, or palate-opening.
- Experiencing something equivalent to or an actual eco-therapy (healing with nature).

These components are mostly about the upkeep, and in some cases, the restoration of both kinds of health.

2.3.3. Environmental Benefits

Sustainable and regenerative practices often converge within wellness tourism, which favors settings that are natural, serene, and, usually, ecologically preserved (Huang & Xu, 2018). That encourages investments in green infrastructure, biodiversity conservation, and responsible land use. Those considerations are important for most of the spa and wellness centers. However, the sector is nudging destinations to adopt environmental practices more than in the past. Clean energy, water conservation, and effective waste management systems are now more often part of the conversations that spa and wellness center staff have with prospective clients.

To sum up, well-being tourism brings about an all-encompassing development strategy that combines individual change with societal and environmental improvement, which gives a lift to all three in development parlance. It focuses on well-being at all levels, and in development terms, that makes it a potential powerhouse to transform destinations into places of sustainable prosperity, benefiting both hosts and guests. Well-being at all levels makes this a potentially transformative strategy.

3. Discussion

3.1. Comparison Across Related Tourism Experiences

Comparison across related tourism experiences involves analyzing the distinct purposes, target audiences, and activities associated with different forms of tourism. Although wellness tourism and medical tourism may appear to be on opposite ends of the healthcare spectrum, many travelers seeking healing intend to achieve a state that associates them with yoga, meditation, or spa therapies, and choose wellness tourism in comparison to health care in medical tourism. However, mass tourism and leisure recreation often see these groups in popular destinations and in large numbers. Their enjoyment is typically gained from viewing less-traveled spots or just being at a very popular destination. At the same time, tourism focused on adventure attracts those who seek the kind of excitement that comes from engaging in physically demanding and sometimes risky activities, such as trekking, climbing, mountaineering, paragliding, caving, white-water rafting, and scuba diving. Grasping these distinctions allows the tour operators to meet the requirements of all types of travelers. They can also create very specialized tourism programming for the varied segments of the market, as discussed in Table 20.1.

Wellness tourism is not your run-of-the-mill vacation, but it combines health, spirituality, and environmental awareness in a way that transcends basic leisure. People go on wellness vacations to rejuvenate, to get in better shape, to become reoriented toward a more balanced state of being.

The quickly expanding branch of global tourism called wellness tourism emphasizes holistic health and preventive health care. Its main ingredients, from yoga and fitness to spiritual retreats and lifestyle coaching, serve an audience that yearns for travel that resonates on more than just the surface. Unlike medical, adventure, or mass tourism, wellness tourism focuses on long-term transformation and personal growth.

3.2. Opportunities

Tourism centered on wellness represents a significant opportunity for destinations, local communities, and individuals to diversify their economies, enjoy sustainable development, and experience personal metamorphosis.

3.2.1. Opportunities for Destinations

Economic diversification: Wellness tourism aids destinations in moving beyond the traditional mass tourism economy to attract health-seeking, high-spending travelers who desire to engage with the destination in a deeper, longer-term way.

Brand positioning: Places can position themselves as convergence points for wellness (e.g., there are places such as Kerala that operate in the business of branding themselves as wellness tourism destinations).

All-season wellness: In many parts of the world, wellness tourism can occur in all four seasons, unlike niche segments such as beach or adventure tourism that operate only part of the year.

Infrastructure development: Investing in wellness infrastructure like spas, yoga centers, nature parks, and clean public spaces heightens a destination's overall visual appeal.

Table 20.1. Comparative Chart.

	Wellness Tourism	**Medical Tourism**	**Mass/Leisure Tourism**	**Adventure Tourism**
Definition	Wellness tourism involves traveling with the primary purpose of enhancing one's well-being – physically, mentally, emotionally, or spiritually – through activities that promote health, relaxation, and self-care	Medical tourism involves traveling to another country or region to receive medical treatment or surgery, often combining it with recovery in a vacation setting	Mass or leisure tourism refers to large-scale travel focused on recreation, relaxation, and entertainment, often in popular tourist destinations	Adventure tourism involves travel that includes physically challenging, risk-oriented, and exploratory activities in natural or remote environments
Key features	Focus on preventive care and holistic well-being	Focus on curative health care (e.g., surgeries, dental care, fertility treatment, cosmetic procedures)	Typically includes beach holidays, city tours, cruises, and theme parks	Activities include trekking, rock climbing, white-water rafting, scuba diving, and paragliding, which appeal to thrill-seekers and nature enthusiasts
Purpose	Preventive health, relaxation	Curative health treatment	Recreation and relaxation	Exploration and thrill-seeking
Focus	Holistic well-being	Healthcare services	Entertainment and sightseeing	Physical challenge, nature
Activities	Yoga, meditation, detox, spa, Ayurveda	Surgery, dental care, diagnostics	Beach, shopping, cultural tours	Trekking, rafting, climbing, diving
Experience	Holistic, inward-focused, calm	Clinical, hospital-based, often invasive	Social, fun, outward-focused	High-adrenaline, risk-involved

Source: Authors' own work.

3.2.2. Opportunities for Local Communities

Inclusive employment: Wellness tourism generates work opportunities for therapists, local yoga teachers, organic farmers, cooks, artisans, and hospitality workers. These are predominantly jobs for women and youth, making the sector a bastion of inclusive employment.

Cultural preservation: It offers a means to display and profit from age-old medicinal practices, rites, craftsmanship, and culinary arts, spurring the conservation of long-standing cultural traditions.

Community-based tourism: Community-based wellness lodges, eco-villages, and healing centers hardly resemble the multibillion-dollar corporations. Instead, they are small businesses owned by local citizens and staffed by locals. They promote community participation, generate local tax revenues, and help keep the profits from tourism in the community.

Social cohesion: Wellness tourism can strengthen social community ties; cohabitants can undertake this form of travel together, thus achieving shared experience and potentially fostering stronger relationships.

3.2.3. Opportunities for Individuals

Personal well-being: Visitors gain from enhanced bodily, cognitive, and emotional wellness via direct participation in detox programs, mindfulness retreats, forest therapy, spa treatments, and the like.

Self-discovery and growth: Being well is good, but that might mean different things to different people. Some people might need to exist in a particular space to feel well and might need to travel multiple times to that space to achieve optimal wellness. For a person whose only pathway to the wellness side of the road is to sit in a particular kind of temple, then that space is, indeed, a space of worship.

Education and awareness: Traveling exposes individuals to differing health ideologies and sustainable practices, potentially leading to lifetime behavior changes and better overall health.

Accessibility of traditional knowledge: People are initiated into age-old systems such as Ayurveda, naturopathy, TCM, and medicinal energy healing, thereby widening the spectrum of personal healthcare options.

Wellness tourism is much more than just a travel segment. It nurtures a triple-bottom-line impact, promoting economic, social, and environmental good. For places and communities, it enhances sustainable livelihoods and brings cultural vibrancy to the fore. For individuals, it unfurls opportunities for deep healing, self-discovery, and reconnection with the larger world.

3.3. Challenges of Wellness Tourism

Despite its promising outlook, wellness tourism faces several challenges that need to be addressed for sustained growth.

3.3.1. Lack of Standardized Quality Assurance

A significant obstacle is the lack of uniform standards for wellness services and therapies. This can result in inconsistent quality and even types of services offered to the consumer, a particular worry for international travelers who still expect the high-quality, globally accepted health standards they are used to.

3.3.2. Infrastructure and Accessibility Issues

Numerous attractive health resorts are situated in far-flung, picturesque locales. Although these locations augment the ambiance, they are afflicted with bad road systems, scarce public transportation, and a dearth of nearby airports or hospitals. The facilities sometimes can't deliver the "five-star" experience they promise because they are poorly built, have unreliable infrastructure, and can't provide sufficient internet or power to satisfy even half a dozen power-users.

3.3.3. Shortage of Skilled Manpower

To provide first-rate wellness experiences, a different kind of economy must emerge, one powered by a diverse range of qualified professionals. These include not just therapists and yoga instructors but also wellness chefs and holistic lifestyle coaches, and a range of common skills.

3.3.4. Marketing and Positioning Challenges

Some places that have a strong wellness tradition don't have the branding or the ability to tell their stories to stand comfortably alongside the premium wellness destinations in the worldwide marketplace. They don't have the digital marketing expertise or the multilingual content. Thus, a shortcoming of place branding is that it is not the kind of branding that's necessary to attract the kind of travelers who spend large sums of money on wellness.

3.3.5. Risk of Over-commercialization and "Wellness Washing"

With growth in the industry comes the risk that some providers will put profit before purpose, serving up something that looks like wellness but isn't. The offerings of wellness experiences that aren't genuine or effective. This is sometimes called "wellness washing," and it's just as bad for the sector's reputation as what might be called "health washing" by some fitness companies.

3.3.6. Environmental Concerns

Although sustainable practices are becoming more common, the overall growth of tourism, including wellness tourism, still presents an increasing environmental footprint. Making sure the providers of that niche adopt eco-conscious practices, don't let their impact on natural resources spiral out of control, and do everything possible to keep the local environment healthy for the next wave of residents and tourists is a persistent challenge.

3.3.7. Maintaining Authenticity

There is a high demand for true cultural and traditional wellness treatments. Nonetheless, when these treatments are commercialized, the practices associated with them are sometimes diluted or misrepresented, which does not benefit the very cultures that are being imitated.

3.3.8. Cost and Affordability

Even though certain places provide low-cost wellness alternatives, a large segment of the luxurious wellness sector is very pricey, often prohibitively so, resulting in a kind of wellness that many can't afford.

Although wellness tourism offers enormous possibilities for growth and economic development. It stems from a worldwide shift toward health-oriented lifestyles, and it derives fantastic opportunities from technological innovation. But, if this new industry is to reach its full potential, it must somehow tackle the seemingly straightforward but really quite complex issues of standardization, infrastructure, an adequate supply of well-trained, skilled labor, marketing, and ensuring viable, sustainable, and, above all, authentic practices that live up to the Wellness Tourism brand.

4. Future Prospects of Wellness Tourism

The future of wellness tourism appears exceptionally bright, driven by several key factors.

4.1. Growing Global Awareness of Health and Well-being

Society is moving toward a model of health management that emphasizes pro-activity, just as it has in other areas of life, like personal finance. Individuals are taking health directives to heart and work to fulfill them with their travel choices. The young and the affluent seem particularly intent on this shift, but it's hard to see how it won't trickle down to the rest of society.

4.2. High-yield Tourism

Travelers focused on health and wellness typically shell out way more than the average tourist when they hit the road. That makes these folks a pretty desirable target for the kinds of places and businesses that want to rake in more cash.

4.3. Diversification of Offerings

Wellness communities built around holistic health are one aspect of the wider array of experiences that the market is now offering, moving beyond traditional spas and yoga retreats. Detox programs, organic meals, immersion in nature, and "adventure wellness" are some of the other experiences on offer.

4.5. Integration with Hospitality

An increased number of hotels and resorts are incorporating wellness practices into their services. Although many hotels have long offered on-site fitness facilities, such as a gym, they have now taken the idea much further by providing luxury fitness experiences in conjunction with what can only be described as health resorts.

4.6. Technological Advancements

Technology is emerging as a vital part in ensuring that wellness encounters are both reachable and tailored for the individual. This encompasses:

Wearable technology: Fitness trackers and smartwatches allow travelers to monitor their health carefully. These devices give real-time feedback and enable decision-making of an informed nature.

AI and machine learning: These technologies create personalized wellness programs by analyzing each individual's unique data and using it to power their recommendations for the individual in question around activities, nutrition, and stress management.

VR and augmented reality (AR): VR/AR can form immersive experiences that serve for relaxation, mindfulness, and stress reduction, ranging from virtual meditation in tranquil landscapes to simulated nature retreats.

Remote health monitoring and telemedicine: These technologies bridge geographical barriers, allowing medical advice and consultations to be accessed by travelers, ensuring continuity of care.

Digital platforms: Websites, mobile apps, and social media are used to get information, make reservations, and promote wellness travel. These platforms help travelers select suitable wellness travel destinations.

Focus on sustainability and eco-friendly practices: An increasing number of wellness travelers desire experiences that not only refresh them but also help conserve the environment and benefit local communities. This has given rise to what could be called eco-wellness tourism, a burgeoning niche that places an even greater emphasis on organic food, natural healing therapies, energy-efficient lodgings, and immersive experiences in nature.

Government initiatives and investment: Several nations are actively pushing wellness tourism through targeted campaigns and focused infrastructure development because they recognize its potential for driving both social and economic dividends. For example, India is seeking to become a global leader in wellness tourism, and it's doing so by promoting both its ancient healing traditions (Ayurveda and yoga) and more modern governmental initiatives, like "Heal in India."

5. Practical Implications and Recommendations

This study on wellness tourism has carried out some findings that now have several practical implications for policymakers, tourism stakeholders, wellness practitioners, and local communities.

5.1. For Policymakers and Governments

To boost the wellness tourism sector, it is vital to pay attention to quality, authenticity, and accessibility. Clear quality standards and certification systems can build international credibility, ensuring that the practices imparted to travelers are authentic and reliable. Meanwhile, targeted branding initiatives from various levels of government can position wellness traditions such as Ayurveda, yoga, and naturopathy as unique societal assets ripe for wellness tourism. Infrastructure investment, be it in improved road networks, digital connectivity, or eco-friendly structures, can make even the most remote wellness destinations accessible while maintaining a satisfactory environmental balance. Public–private partnerships can boost accessibility, scale up wellness offerings, and do all of the above in a way that upholds the practices' cultural and ecological integrity. These are the measures that will enhance the global standing of the wellness tourism sector.

5.2. For Tourism and Hospitality Businesses

Tourism and hospitality businesses need to integrate wellness into mainstream services to meet the changing expectations of travelers. Hotels and resorts can position themselves as holistic wellness destinations by offering a rich array of services that comprise much more than the traditional spa. This offers an invigorating chance to develop a new kind of customer relationship before, during, and after travel.

5.3. For Local Communities

Local communities can generate truly inclusive and sustainable livelihoods from wellness tourism, all while preserving the cultural heritage that defines them. Nevertheless, the wellness tourism market is a competitive one, and any destination aiming to attract those traveling for health and wellness must be prepared to meet a certain standard. The wellness destinations must equip themselves with trained personnel who not only can serve as yoga instructors, but also are capable of leading an early-morning sun salutation atop a dune in the right way, so that the mallet strikes sound with a timbre all its own. As always, the best practices in this field align with principles of sustainability, not just in preserving the natural resources that wellness travelers seek to experience, but also in making good use of the cultural resources that wellness communities can provide.

6. Conclusion

Wellness tourism is emerging as a transformative force within the global travel industry by blending health, culture, and sustainability into meaningful experiences. Unlike conventional tourism, which has a much broader focus, wellness tourism zeroes in on preventive care, holistic well-being, and enhancement of the lifestyle. That focus makes it especially germane in today's health-obsessed world. For destinations, wellness tourism is a pathway to something that all tourism officials dream of: economic diversification, off-season visitation, and, hopefully, at least, enhanced global positioning if not a larger market share of the travel industry.

7. Future Research Directions

Although the academicians and industry worlds have devoted considerable attention to wellness tourism, certain areas remain undertheorized and offer rich possibilities for future investigation. There is an urgent need for more studies to develop theoretical frameworks that enable the global certification and benchmarking of wellness services, ensuring that such services are authentic, safe, and trustworthy. Further, it is required to examine the extent to which eco-friendly practices can be implemented on a large scale throughout wellness tourism. Further, researchers need to ask what role digital innovations, that is, AI, wearable devices, tele-wellness, and VR/AR play in personalizing the wellness travel experience, in making it more accessible, and in enhancing post-travel engagement. Finally, researchers need to look at some cross-national studies to see what best practices, competitive positioning, and collaborative efforts can boost wellness tourism across the world.

References

Annavarapu, S. (2018). Consuming wellness, producing difference: The case of a wellness center in India. *Journal of Consumer Culture*, *18*(3), 414–432.

Babu, A. S., Madan, K., Veluswamy, S. K., Mehra, R., & Maiya, A. G. (2014). Worksite health and wellness programs in India. *Progress in Cardiovascular Diseases*, *56*(5), 501–507.

Chundasutathanakul, S., & Chirapanda, S. (2021). Thailand 4.0: A new value-based economy and its implication on wellness business. *Content Page*, 113–131.

Clift, S., & Hancox, G. (2010). The significance of choral singing for sustaining psychological wellbeing: Findings from a survey of choristers in England, Australia and Germany. *Music Performance Research*, *3*, 79–96.

Cohen, M. M., Elliott, F., Oates, L., Schembri, A., & Mantri, N. (2017). Do wellness tourists get well? An observational study of multiple dimensions of health and wellbeing after a week-long retreat. *The Journal of Alternative and Complementary Medicine*, *23*(2), 140–148.

Csirmaz, É., & Pető, K. (2015). International trends in recreational and wellness tourism. *Procedia Economics and Finance*, *32*, 755–762.

Dar, H., & Kashyap, K. (2022). Wellness travel motivations in the wake of COVID-19. *International Journal of Tourism Policy*, *12*(1), 24–43.

Dini, M., & Pencarelli, T. (2022). Wellness tourism and the components of its offer system: A holistic perspective. *Tourism Review*, *77*(2), 394–412.

Gkinton, E., Telonis, G., Halkiopoulos, C., & Boutsinas, B. (2023). Quality of life and health tourism: A conceptual roadmap of enhancing cognition and well-being. In V. Katsoni, (Ed.), *Tourism, travel, and hospitality in a smart and sustainable world. IACuDiT 2022. Springer Proceedings in Business and Economics* (pp. 651–666). Springer International Publishing. https://doi.org/10.1007/978-3-031-26829-8_41

Global Wellness Institute (GWI). (2021). *Wellness tourism: Global market report*. https://globalwellnessinstitute.org

Grénman, M., & Räikkönen, J. (2015). Well-being and wellness tourism – Same, same but different? Conceptual discussions and empirical evidence. *Matkailututkimus*, *11*(1), 7–25.

GWI. (2021). *The global wellness economy: Looking beyond COVID*. The Global Wellness Institute. https://globalwellnessinstitute.org/wp-content/uploads/2022/02/GWI-WE Monitor-2021_Wellness-Tourism.pdf

Haldar, P. (2021). Wellness tourism: A niche that India can offer. *Food, Tourism and Hospitality Perspectives*, 198–216.

Haldar, P. (2023). Wellness tourism: An empirical study on tourists motivation. *OPJU Business Review*, *2*, 58–69.

Han, H., Kiatkawsin, K., Jung, H., & Kim, W. (2018). The role of wellness spa tourism performance in building destination loyalty: The case of Thailand. *Journal of Travel & Tourism Marketing*, *35*(5), 595–610.

Huang, L., & Xu, H. (2014). A cultural perspective of health and wellness tourism in China. *Journal of China Tourism Research*, *10*(4), 493–510.

Huang, L., & Xu, H. (2018). Therapeutic landscapes and longevity: Wellness tourism in Bama. *Social Science & Medicine*, *197*, 24–32.

Johnston, C., Smith, M., & Puczkó, L. (2018). *Wellness and tourism: Mind, body, spirit, place*. Routledge.

Kelly, C. (2012). Wellness tourism: Retreats, sanctuaries, and spas. *Tourism Recreation Research*, *37*(2), 205–206.

Kongtaveesawas, N., Prasarnphanich, P., Sinthupinyo, S., & Ashton, A. S. (2022). Attribute framework validation for wellness tourism within the context of Thailand. *Sustainability*, *14*(10), 5953.

Lahariya, C. (2020). Health & wellness centers to strengthen primary health care in India: Concept, progress and ways forward. *The Indian Journal of Pediatrics*, *87*(11), 916–929.

Majeed, S., & Gon Kim, W. (2023). Emerging trends in wellness tourism: A scoping review. *Journal of Hospitality and Tourism Insights*, *6*(2), 853–873.

Marak, J., Oparka, S., & Wyrzykowski, J. (2014). Factors conditioning the creation of the combined product "Health Resort, Spa and Wellness Tourism" in a region. *Tourism Role in the Regional Economy*, *7*, 39–75.

Ministry of AYUSH. (2020). *AYUSH and wellness tourism guidelines*. Government of India. https://ayush.gov.in

Mujtaba, B. G. (2025). Workplace well-being and health in a fast-paced era: How education, experience, and mindfulness shape stress management. *Health Economics and Management Review*, *6*(2), 108–119.

Norman, A., & Pokorny, J. J. (2017). Meditation retreats: Spiritual tourism well-being interventions. *Tourism Management Perspectives*, *24*, 201–207.

Ray, A. (2025). Five elements of TCM vs Ayurveda for health, healing & wellness. *Yoga and Ayurveda Research*, *1*(1), 24–26.

Shyngysbaeva, S., Saipov, A., Aldasheva, A., Ataeva, G., Makhanova, N., & Cantürk, E. R. İ. M. (2023). Current issues of health and wellness tourism based on population health preservation in Eastern Kazakhstan. *GeoJournal of Tourism and Geosites*, *49*(3), 1144–1151.

Smith, M., & Puczkó, L. (2014). *Health, tourism and hospitality: Spas, wellness and medical travel*. Routledge.

United Nations World Tourism Organization (UNWTO). (2022). *Tourism and COVID-19: Rebuilding for health and sustainability*. https://unwto.org

Voigt, C., & Pforr, C. (2013). *Wellness tourism: A destination perspective*. Routledge.

Yeung, R., & Johnston, C. (2020). The digital detox holiday: An exploratory study of motivations and experiences. *Tourism Management Perspectives*, *33*, 100606.

Printed and bound by CPI Group (UK) Ltd, Croydon, CR0 4YY

21/09/2026

14966034-0003